GOD IS LOVE

American Academy of Religion
Academy Series
Edited by
Carl A. Raschke

Number 50

GOD IS LOVE:
A STUDY IN THE THEOLOGY
OF KARL RAHNER
by
Mark Lloyd Taylor

Mark Lloyd Taylor

GOD IS LOVE:
A Study in the Theology
of Karl Rahner

Scholars Press
Atlanta, Georgia

BT
102
.R272
T39
1986

GOD IS LOVE

by
Mark Lloyd Taylor

© 1986
American Academy of Religion

Library of Congress Cataloging in Publication Data

Taylor, Mark, 1953–
  God is love.

  (American Academy of Religion dissertation series
; no. 50)
    Thesis (Ph.D.)—Southern Methodist University, 1982,
    Bibliography: p.
    1. God—History of doctrines—20th century. 2. Love—
Religious aspects—Catholic Church—History of doctrines—
20th century. 3. Catholic Church—Doctrines—History—
20th century. 4. Rahner, Karl, 1904–   I. Title
II. Series.
BT102.R272T39 1986   231   85-19611
ISBN 0-89130-925-X (alk paper)
ISBN 0-89130-926-8 (pbk. : alk. paper)

CONTENTS

PREFACE

My chief aim in the following study is to contribute to a solution to the problem of the concept of God as this problem is raised for Christian systematic theology by the claim that God is love. I have chosen to address this systematic issue by way of a critical appraisal of one particular theologian's concept of God, namely, that of Karl Rahner. Rahner has been selected as the chief discussion partner for this study for three basic reasons: (1) As I try to show more fully in Chapter I, Rahner's analysis of the nature of theological reflection and the situation of contemporary theology seems to me to be one of the most lucid and powerful accounts of such matters available in contemporary theology. I find Rahner's approach to theology as a whole to be most helpful. (2) Rahner has made the theme of the divine love central to his concept of God, indeed to his theology as a whole. He seems to have raised, in a way that few, if any, other theologians have done, virtually all of the pertinent issues relative to the meaning and truth of the claim that God is love. (3) Although Rahner's account of the meaning and truth of the assertion "God is love" provides very rich resources for the construction of a contemporary understanding of the divine reality, it seems to me that Rahner's concept of God is plagued by a certain internal inconsistency. Indeed, at a number of crucial points, Rahner's thought leads to an impasse, in that he seems to hold certain things to be the case relative to the divine reality that contradict the fundamental thrust of his thought. Hence, it seems to me that some alternative understanding of the divine reality, and the divine love in particular, is called for, precisely to resolve certain fundamental tensions in Rahner's own theology. I will attempt to sketch the outlines of just such an alternative concept of God in Part III of this study.

Although the primary reason for devoting my time and effort to a study of Rahner's concept of God has been to enable me to contribute to a solution to the contemporary systematic

problem of how the divine reality is most adequately to be
conceived within Christian theology, nevertheless, a secondary
goal of this study is to contribute to a better understanding and a
deeper appreciation of the theology of Karl Rahner. I think
there are two specific contributions this study makes to the
scholarly discussion of Rahner's theology. (1) As far as I have
been able to determine, this is the first full length analysis, in
English or German, of Rahner's concept of God. There are a
number of studies that touch upon Rahner's concept of God in
relation to the problems of theological method, anthropology,
revelation, christology, and the relation between nature and
grace. But there are no studies that deal specifically and primarily with Rahner's concept of God. And further, many interpreters of Rahner, both critics and proponents, seem to view
Rahner's concept of God as being merely another formulation of
the view of God of classical scholastic thought. While I will argue
in Part II of this study that Rahner himself, in the final analysis,
has not provided a coherent alternative to scholasticism, nevertheless, Rahner shows clearly that some alternative to the scholastic concept of God must be provided, precisely if theology is to
proclaim, with the New Testament, that God is love in a way that
is credible to contemporary persons. (2) I feel my study provides
a more balanced understanding of Rahner's theological anthropology, which is at the heart of his thought as a whole, than
is available in many of the other studies of his theology. In
particular, I have tried to show that Rahner's anthropology neither is simply a metaphysics of knowledge that ignores the
phenomena of human freedom and love, nor offers only an
analysis of personal experience without any consideration of the
interpersonal aspect of human being. As a result of my study of
his thought, I would argue that it is an analysis of the transcendental conditions of freedom and love, and not of knowledge,
that has come to dominate Rahner's attention over the past two
decades. I would argue that, for Rahner, relatedness to other
persons is a third necessary element (along with self-relatedness
and God-relatedness) of our most fundamental experience as
human persons.

There are a number of problems involved in writing in
English such a critical study of the thought of a German the-
ologian. First, almost none of the secondary literature on
Rahner written in German has been translated into English.

Thus, I have had to provide the translations of all citations taken from this literature. Rahner's own works have been widely translated into English. If, however, there are good reasons, in general, for not relying upon translations in critical studies, these reasons are even more compelling in Rahner's case. For while there are some reliable English translations of Rahner's works (notably William Dych's translation of *Grundkurs des Glaubens*, which is entitled *Foundations of Christian Faith*), many are not reliable, and some are positively misleading. Further, so many persons have had a hand in translating Rahner's collected essays, *Schriften zur Theologie*, that there is a remarkable lack of consistent renderings of key Rahnerian terms in the volumes of *Theological Investigations*.

For these reasons, I have not made use of any of the English translations of Rahner's works in this study. All citations from Rahner represent my own translations of the original texts. In footnote references to Rahner's works I have given not only page references to the various volumes of *Schriften zur Theologie*, but have also supplied the titles of the essays that are cited. Following the references to the original texts, however, I have provided, in parentheses, references to the corresponding passages in the available English translations.

There is one exception to this practice that deserves comment. A special problem exists in relation to two early books of Rahner's, namely, *Geist in Welt* and *Hörer des Wortes*, beyond that of the relative merits of the English translations of these works. In both cases, there are two German editions: Rahner's original editions, and revised, second editions prepared by Rahner's student Johann Baptist Metz. The revisions Metz makes in *Geist in Welt* are relatively insignificant. But there are wholesale changes made in the original text of *Hörer des Wortes*. Passages are shifted from one chapter to the next, an entire chapter is removed, and many new terms are introduced into the text, some of which derive from Rahner's later works, some of which are Metz's own, reflecting the special concerns of his own theological enterprise. Although Rahner states that Metz's revision of his work has been done with his approval, it simply is not possible to read the second edition of *Hörer des Wortes* as if it were a work by Karl Rahner, although many interpreters of Rahner, both in this country and in Germany, have done precisely that. Therefore, my work has been based exclusively on the first

editions of these two books. But the available English translations of *Geist in Welt* and *Hörer des Wortes* are translations of the
second editions. (To date, no complete English translation of the
first edition of either book has been published, although a partial translation by Joseph Donceel of the first edition of *Hörer des
Wortes* has been published in *A Rahner Reader,* ed. by Gerald
McCool, New York: Seabury Press, 1975, pp. 1-65.) It seemed to
me that it would only confuse matters to provide references to
the English translations of the second editions of these two books
alongside of my citations from the first German editions. Hence,
all references to *Geist in Welt* and *Hörer des Wortes* are to the first
editions of these works alone.

I have chosen to leave a few technical Rahnerian terms
untranslated: *"beisich," "das Beisichsein," "der Vorgriff," "das Woraufhin,"* although the first time each term is introduced I have
tried to indicate some English equivalents. My translations of
terms used by Rahner that derive from the thought of Martin
Heidegger deserve special note, for, at this point, the published
English translations are often wholly inadequate (see "The Theology of the Symbol," in vol. 4 of *Theological Investigations*). I have
translated *"das Sein"* as "being," *"das Seiende,"* as "that which is,"
and *"ein Seiendes"* as "a particular being" or "an entity." I have also
followed the practice of several other translators and have left
the two key German words "existentiell" and "existential" untranslated, although I have not italicized them. "Existentiell" is
used here in the same sense in which it is used in the works of
Heidegger and Rudolf Bultmann. It refers to that which has to
do with a human person's concrete situation, with her or his free
decisions, with her or his understanding and appropriation of
her- or himself. "Existential," then, refers to that which has to do
with a particular type of philosophical reflection, one that is
concerned to illuminate the existentiell character of our most
fundamental experience.

I am indebted to a number of persons and organizations,
who, each in their own way, have helped to make this study
possible. First of all, I wish to express my heartfelt gratitude to
my advisor, Schubert Ogden, for his guidance, example, friend-
ship, and personal concern throughout the course of my doc-
toral studies. I would like to thank the other two members of my
dissertation committee, William Babcock and Charles Wood, for
their careful and critical reading of my work. I am convinced

that this study has been strengthened by the very different insights each of these three persons has offered. I would like to express a special word of gratitude to Prof. Dr. Karl Rahner for his ungrudging willingness to meet with me over the course of my year of study in München and discuss his theology.

I wish to thank Prof. Dr. Hansgerd Schulte and the Deutscher Akademischer Austauschdienst for the study grant that made the year in Germany possible for me and my family. I am also grateful to the Danforth Foundation and the Graduate Program in Religious Studies of Southern Methodist University for their part in helping to finance the year of study abroad. I want to express my love for the small group of Christian sisters and brothers in Dallas, who, over the past several years, have lived out the gospel of God's love in my presence, challenging me to hear and proclaim the good news in the struggle for social justice.

Finally, and above all, I want to thank Deborah, my wife, for all of her support. Her love has made all of the difference in my life and serves as a tangible symbol of the divine love that I have attempted to illuminate somewhat in this study.

LIST OF ABBREVIATIONS

ET: English translation
FCF: Foundations of Christian Faith
GG: Grundkurs des Glaubens
GW: Geist in Welt
HW: Hörer des Wortes
KtW: Kleines theologisches Wörterbuch
LTK: Lexikon für Theologie und Kirche
SM: Sacramentum Mundi
SM(eng): Sacramentum Mundi, English translation
ST: Schriften zur Theologie
TI: Theological Investigations

The ground then for this book is the conviction that a magnificent intellectual content—far surpassing that of such systems as Thomism, Spinozism, German idealism, positivism (old or new)—is implicit in the religious faith most briefly expressly in the three words, God is love, which words I sincerely believe are contradicted as truly as they are embodied in the best known of the older theologies, as they certainly have been misunderstood by atheists and skeptics.

Charles Hartshorne, in *Man's Vision of God*, p. ix.

INTRODUCTION
THE PROBLEM OF THE CONCEPT OF GOD
IN CONTEMPORARY THEOLOGY

CHAPTER I
THE SITUATION OF CONTEMPORARY THEOLOGY

The primary goal of this study is to contribute to the contemporary theological discussion of the concept of God through an analysis of the meaning and truth of a central Christian assertion concerning God, namely, the assertion that God is love. This primary goal is accomplished by way of a critical appraisal of Karl Rahner's concept of God, and, in particular, his understanding of the meaning and truth of "God is love." In this first chapter of the study, using the thought of Rahner, in addition to that of other theologians, I will seek to make explicit the understanding of the nature and task of theology in general, as well as the view of the particular situation of contemporary theology, that will provide the background for this inquiry into the concept of God. Then, in the next chapter, I hope to show why the concept of God is problematic in the contemporary theological situation. The primary resource in this account of the problematic nature of the concept of God again will be Rahner's thought.

Perhaps the most obvious characteristic of the situation of contemporary Christian theology is the genuine pluralism of available theological options. In recent years, this pluralistic situation itself has become the object of theological reflection.[1] Rahner has spoken of the current situation in theology as one of "gnoseological concupiscence."[2] He holds that this theological pluralism is a symptom of a new and deeper spiritual pluralism that characterizes the contemporary human situation as a whole.[3] He says that the sum of human experiences has become so vast that no one individual could even hope to survey, let alone systematize, it. The diverse sources of human experience are incapable of integration. No single social authority can hold sway over this totality of human experience. And yet the totality of human experience is relevant to the church's life, its mission, and its theology. With respect to this irreducible pluralism,

Rahner remarks: "Each theology and philosophy knows too much to be merely itself, and knows too little to become *the* philosophy and *the* theology."[4]

Without denying this genuine theological pluralism, I contend that in order adequately to portray the contemporary theological situation two points of general consensus, shared by most contemporary theologians, must be recognized. Admittedly, these points of consensus are so general and vague that they can easily be overlooked. And yet it is the general agreement on these two points that allows theological discussion to be possible at all, even if this discussion is characterized by sharp disagreement on other matters.

Both of these points of general consensus, which have to do with the understanding of the nature and basic task of theology, are aspects of the heritage of the liberal theology of the nineteenth century.[5] This is to say that part of the reason discussion is possible between representatives of very different theological positions is because most of these theologies remain within the broad tradition of liberal theology, at least at these two points.

It goes without saying that I cannot provide a detailed defense of the claim that there is a basic consensus in contemporary theology concerning the nature and task of theological reflection. The most that I can do in the following few pages is refer to other attempts to demonstrate the existence of a general consensus in contemporary theology and to the work of a few representative twentieth century theologians.

The winter 1980 issue of the *Journal of Ecumenical Studies* is devoted to the topic: "consensus in theology."[6] The issue includes seminal essays by Hans Küng and Edward Schillebeeckx and responses to these essays from a number of perspectives. Küng's essay, which is a comparison of the theological methodologies and understandings of hermeneutics in Schillebeeckx's *Jesus* and Küng's own book, *On Being A Christian*, is a demonstration of the existence, within contemporary Catholic thought, of precisely the consensus concerning the nature and task of theology I propose here.[7] Arthur Crabtree, in an essay entitled "Methodological Consensus? A Protestant Perspective," shows that Küng's and Schillebeeckx's understanding of theological method is shared by a large number of twentieth century Protestant theologians, such as Barth, Brunner,

Bultmann, Tillich, Gordon Kaufman, and Wolfhart Pannenberg.[8]

My view of the general consensus in contemporry theology is also supported by David Tracy's analysis of what he calls the five basic models of contemporary theology (the orthodox, liberal, neo-orthodox, radical, and revisionist models).[9] Tracy argues that in all but "orthodox" theology some attempt is made to respond to the basic problematic of liberal theology, namely, the problem of reconciling a commitment "to the cognitive claims and fundamental values of the Christian vision" with a commitment "to the basic cognitive claims and ethical values of the modern secular period."[10] For Tracy, neo-orthodox, radical, and revisionist theologies are all attempts to provide a more adequate solution to this problem than is available in liberal theology itself. Tracy shows that neo-orthodox theology (represented, of course, by Barth, Bultmann, the Niebuhrs, Tillich, and Brunner, but also by Moltmann and the theology of liberation) is best understood to be a self-critical phase of liberal theology, committed to the same values as liberal theology, only with a more adequate understanding of the meaning of the biblical message.[11] For radical theology, a reconciliation of Christian faith and secular values can be accomplished only if the traditional Christian cognitive claims concerning the reality of God are abandoned.[12] And, of course, the revisionist theological model that Tracy himself adopts, along with such thinkers as Schubert Ogden, John Cobb, Leslie Dewart, and Gordon Kaufman, is described as:

> Being committed to . . . the dramatic confrontation, the mutual illuminations and corrections, the possible basic reconciliation between the principal values, cognitive claims, and existential faiths of both a reinterpreted post-modern consciousness and a reinterpreted Christianity.[13]

The Turn to the Subject

But now to a characterization of this general consensus within contemporary theology itself. The first point of agreement is that theology cannot be undertaken in abstraction from the actual experience of human persons. In some sense, the

existing human subject and her or his experience must form the
starting point and basis for theological reflection. This means
that theology, in its own way, must take the "turn to the subject"
characteristic of modern philosophy. The origin of this turn to
the subject is to be found in Descartes's epochal discovery that
"nothing is more easily or manifestly perceptible to me than my
own mind."[14] Kant, the German idealists, the phe-
nomenologists, and the philosophers of *Existenz* all contribute to
a better understanding and a more critical grounding of the
turn to the subject.

To illustrate what I mean by the turn to the subject, I want to
appeal to the work of two twentieth century philosophers who
have paid particular attention to the methodological implications
of such a turn for philosophical reflection: Martin Heidegger
and Alfred North Whitehead. One of Heidegger's chief contributions to twentieth century philosophy is his insight that the
question of being is inseparably linked with the question of
human existence, for human being is that entity whose existence
is always a question and a task, not simply something given.
"Therefore," Heidegger argues, "fundamental ontology, from
which all others alone can arise, must be sought in the existential
analysis of *Dasein* [i.e., the mode of being that characterizes
human being]."[15] The starting point for philosophical reflection
must be the being of the human subject itself, for human being
is the site of the disclosure of being.

Similarly, Whitehead formulates what he calls the reformed
subjectivist principle: "The whole universe consists of elements
disclosed in the analysis of the experiences of subjects."[16] In the
case of both Heidegger and Whitehead, the adoption of such an
anthropological starting point leads to a philosophical revolution. It demands a dismantling *(Destruktion)* of classical metaphysics, which is not oriented to the experiences of subjects as
the prime philosophical data, but rather to impersonal, objective
substances.

A distinctively modern anthropological orientation in theology is evident in the work of Friedrich Schleiermacher. Proposition 15 of Schleiermacher's *Der christliche Glaube* asserts that
"Christian doctrines are apprehensions of the Christian affec-
tions of piety set forth in speech."[17] Thus, for Schleiermacher,
the immediate object of theological reflection is no longer the
objective, God-given propositions of revelation, but rather the

self-consciousness of the believer. Christian dogmatics is a theoretical portrayal of the modifications of the human "feeling of absolute dependence," that is, a portrayal of the experience the believer has of self, world, and God in the various modes of religious consciousness, in which everything is related to the redemption brought by Jesus of Nazareth.

This anthropological starting point is maintained by liberal theology and by the dialectical theology, represented by the early Barth, Bultmann, Brunner, Gogarten, and others, that reacts against liberal theology. The turn to the subject is given classic expression in Bultmann's call for a demythologization or existential interpretation of the New Testament kerygma.[18] Bultmann writes that, although the kerygma of the New Testament is expressed in a mythological fashion, one in which assertions are made concerning various realities, such as miraculous healings, a bodily parousia of Christ, the resuscitation of a dead person, angels, demons, and so forth, the real point of this message is to present to its hearers or readers the possibility of a new self-understanding, one in which the human person is released from the past of her or his sins by the grace of God and opened up to a future of obedience and love. In a passage that illustrates this turn to the subject, Bultmann says:

> To believe in the cross of Christ does not mean to consider a mythical event that has been accomplished outside of us and our world, an objectively observable occurrence that God has judged to have occurred for our benefit. Rather, to believe in the cross means to take over the cross of Christ as our own, to be crucified with Christ. As the event of salvation, the cross is not an isolated event that has befallen Christ as a mythical personage. Rather, this event has, in its significance, a "cosmic" dimension. And its decisive meaning, which alters history, is brought to expression by saying that it is *the eschatological event;* i.e., it is not an event of the past that one looks back to; rather, it is the eschatological event in time and beyond time in that understood in its significance, that is, for faith, it is always present.[19]

Since 1960 or so, the position of Bultmann, as well as the positions of other neo-orthodox theologians, have come under attack for being too individualistic. Such charges, on the part of Moltmann, Pannenberg, Metz, and the theology of liberation do not, it seems to me, constitute a denial of the anthropological starting point of theological reflection, but simply represent a greater awareness of the social and political situation of the existing human subject with which theological reflection begins. There is a greater realization in recent theology that it is the experience of the poor, oppressed "non-person" that raises the really pressing theological question today, and not the experience of the educated Westerner with her or his crisis of belief.

This first point of consensus within contemporary theology, namely, that the experience of the human subject must form, in some way, the basis for theological reflection, is admittedly vague. Up to this point I have shown *that* such a turn to the subject is taken by representatives of a number of contemporary theological movements, but have not shown, in any systematic fashion, what this turn to the subject entails for theology. I wish to refer to the thought of Karl Rahner in order to present a fuller understanding of the necessary anthropological orientation of contemporary theology, an understanding that will prove to be foundational for the inquiry that is carried out in this study. Rahner argues that:

> No one can deny that, in the last two centuries, changes in the history of culture have occurred that, in scope and depth and the power to shape man, correspond, at the very least, to those that took place between the time of an Augustine and the time of high scholasticism.[20]

He states that these basic cultural changes have resulted from the turn to the subject or Copernican revolution in modern philosophy that begins with Descartes and is continued by Kant, idealism, and the philosophy of *Existenz*.[21] This turn to the subject is characterized by the conviction that any truly philosophical investigation (one that asks after an object within the horizon of the totality of reality), necessarily implies the question concerning the knowing or questioning human subject her- or himself.[22] Rahner goes on to express his belief that theology too must take such an anthropological turn.

> Today, dogmatic theology must be theological anthropology. . . . The question concerning man and the answer to it, therefore, should not be considered as an area that is materially and regionally distinct from other areas of theological discourse, but rather as the whole of dogmatic theology.[23]

Rahner shows that this turn to the subject must not only be broadly existential, in the sense just indicated, but must also involve an explicitly transcendental or metaphysical analysis of the existing human subject. This is to say that not just any human experience can provide the starting point for theological and philosophical reflection. The only critically justified starting point for theology and philosophy is a universal human experience, one that is a necessary condition of the possibility of all other types of human experience, one "that, in its unavoidability and in its final structures, is once again implicitly affirmed in the act of its being denied or doubted."[24] The fundamental human experience that provides the starting point for theology and philosophy must be an experience that is implied by all human activity and experience whatsoever.

Because this must be the case, this most fundamental human experience can only be disclosed through metaphysical or transcendental reflection, for this experience is not simply one aspect of the totality of reality, but is in a real sense the disclosure of the totality of reality itself.[25] For Rahner, "a transcendental inquiry . . . is given when and insofar as the conditions of the possibility of the knowledge of a specific object in the knowing subject itself are asked after."[26] What transcendental reflection discloses is that every act of human experience always includes an implicit experience of the experiencing subject her- or himself. It is this internal, implicit experience of our own selves as experiencing subjects, and not any external experience of other subjects, that is the most fundamental human experience. This experience of self must be the starting point and paradigm for theological and philosophical reflection. Thus, for Rahner, the modern turn to the subject is carried out fully only by way of a critical, transcendental reduction of the whole of human experience to the necessary conditions of its possibility. The turn to the subject does not mean the arbitrary selection of some human experience as the starting point for theological and philosophical reflection. Rather, the anthropological orientation of theology and philosophy is justified critically only on the basis of a transcendental or metaphysical analysis of human experience that discloses this most fundamental human experience that is necessarily implied by all other modes of human experience.[27]

The main purpose of Chapter III of this study is to explicate, in detail, Rahner's transcendental or metaphysical anthropology. I do not wish to anticipate the results of that analysis
here, except to give a very general picture of the nature of his
understanding of this most basic human experience disclosed by
transcendental reflection. According to Rahner, the fundamental human experience, which is a condition of the possibility of
all other human experience, is an experience of the self as a
person, a free subject who must constitute her- or himself
through her or his own acts and decisions. This self-experience
and self-constitution, however, can only occur through the mediation of other persons and God. Thus, in short, the basic
human experience that provides the starting point and paradigm for all theological and philosophical reflection is the implicit experience we have of ourselves as free persons who
constitute ourselves through our relationships to other persons
and to God.[28]

The Dual Task of Theology

The second point of general consensus in contemporary
theology involves the understanding of the nature of theology
itself and would seem to be a consequence of the turn to the
subject in theology. Most contemporary theologians understand
theology to be the secondary (or second order) activity of reflection upon the more primary phenomenon of Christian faith
itself. The task of theology as such a secondary, reflective activity,
is to clarify and express the meaning of Christian faith in such a
way as to be credible to contemporary persons. Now, it has
always been clear that Christian theology, if it is to remain
Christian at all, must be faithful to the essential message of
Christian faith as normatively expressed in scripture. What is
distinctive of the approach of liberal theology is the explicit
realization that an adequate theology cannot simply repeat the
traditional expressions of the Christian faith, but must rein-
terpret this faith in terms of the particular self-understanding of
the persons addressed by the Christian proclamation. The major
problem with the liberal theology of the nineteenth century is
that too often it surrendered essential aspects of the Christian
proclamation in the face of the particular world view of that
century. The great contribution of neo-orthodox theology is

precisely the recovery of facets of the Christian message that did not appeal to, or even scandalized, liberal theologians.

All of this is to say that there is general consensus among contemporary theologians that the adequacy of theological statements is to be evaluated both in terms of the faithfulness of such statements to the normative expression of the Christian faith in scripture and in terms of the understanding such statements show of the situation and experience of contemporary persons. Both of these demands must be met if theology is to serve the proclamation of the gospel. Theology must be faithful to the gospel as it is normatively presented in scripture, and yet it must express the gospel in such a way as to be understood by the persons to whom it is addressed.

Such an understanding of the nature of theology is evident in the thought of Paul Tillich, who adopts a "method of correlation." According to Tillich, Christian theology must correlate the existentiell questions of modern persons with the answers provided by Christian revelation. He argues that:

> The method of correlation explains the contents of the Christian faith through existential questions and theological answers in mutual interdependence. . . . Theology formulates the questions implied in human existence, and theology formulates the answers implied in divine self-manifestation under the guidance of the questions implied in human existence. . . . The answers implied in the event of revelation are meaningful only in so far as they are in correlation with questions concerning the whole of our existence, with existential questions.[29]

Thus, for Tillich, theology has a dual task. It must make "an analysis of the human situation out of which the existential questions arise," and it must demonstrate "that the symbols used in the Christian message are the answers to these questions."[30]

A similar view of theology is operative in Bultmann's call for a demythologization of the kerygma of the New Testament. Consider, for instance, the following programmatic question of Bultmann's: "can there be a demythologizing interpretation that discloses the truth of the kerygma for the man who does not think mythologically?"[31] Here, the dual task of theology with respect to the scriptural message, on the one hand, and the self-understanding of modern persons, on the other, is clearly evident. The demythologization of the New Testament is required

for two reasons: because the mythological world view of the New
Testament authors is incredible to contemporary persons, and,
even more importantly, because only through demythologization or existential interpretation can the New Testament kerygma be properly understood in and of itself. Bultmann writes
that:

> If the task of demythologization was demanded first of
> all by the conflict between the mythological world pic-
> ture *[das Weltbild]* of the Bible and the world picture that
> is formed by scientific thinking, it soon became apparent
> that *demythologization is a demand of faith itself.* For faith
> demands *liberation from its ties to every world picture that is
> sketched by objectifying thinking,* whether it be mythological
> or scientific thinking. The conflict between mythological
> and scientific thinking indicates that faith has not found
> its proper form of expression. . . . The criticism of the
> mythological world picture of the Bible and of the
> church's traditional proclamation that arises from the
> modern world picture performs the great service for
> faith of calling it back to a radical consideration of its
> own essence. Demythologization wants to follow pre-
> cisely this call.[32]

Only a few contemporary examples of this understanding
of the dual task of theology can be offered. David Tracy argues
that theology has a dual task corresponding to its two sources.
Theology must provide a phenomenological analysis of the religious dimension present in everyday and scientific language and
experience, and a historical or hermeneutical investigation of
classical Christian texts.[33] Schubert Ogden writes that theological understanding is subject to assessment by dual criteria of
adequacy:

> One such criterion requires that no theological statement
> be deemed adequate unless it is appropriate, in the sense
> that it represents the same understanding of faith as is
> expressed in the "datum discourse" of the Christian wit-
> ness. . . . As for the other criterion it requires that no
> theological statement be assessed as adequate which is
> not also understandable in that it meets the relevant
> conditions of meaning and truth universally established
> with human existence.[34]

Gustavo Gutierrez speaks of theology as "critical reflection on
Christian praxis in the light of the Word."[35] He argues that
theological reflection "is a criticism of society and the Church

insofar as they are called and addressed by the Word of God."[36] Gordon Kaufman writes that:

> Theology has a two-pronged task. On the one hand, it must see all human existence in the light of God's act. . . . On the other hand, it is necessary to appropriate God's act(s) from our situation. . . . These two prongs or aspects of the theological task give us two fundamental norms for theological work. On the one hand, there is a *historical* norm: what we take to be God's decisive act should correspond for our time to what the Christian community of other generations has known it to be. We must be able to make sense of Bible and Christian tradition and we may not seriously distort either. . . . On the other hand, there is the *experiential* norm: our theology must make sense of our own experience, of the world we live in. . . . Theology is the continuous attempt to understand our present in terms of the revelatory event in the past, and to appropriate this past from our present situation.[37]

Similar understandings of the nature and task of theology are shared by twentieth century theologians such as Küng, Schillebeeckx, Brunner, and Pannenberg.[38]

Of course, to say that there is general agreement that theology is a secondary activity of reflection upon Christian faith that must be evaluated in terms of the adequacy of its interpretation of the normative expressions of the Christian faith and the adequacy of its interpretation of the self-understanding of contemporary persons, is to make only a most general and noncommittal claim. Important differences between the understandings of the nature of theology held by Tillich, Ogden, and Gutierrez, for example, are ignored in this portrayal of the basic contemporary view of the nature and task of theology. Once again, I want to turn to the thought of Rahner in order to obtain a more detailed and adequate account of the nature of theology and the criteria in terms of which theological statements are to be evaluated.

Theology, for Rahner, is understood to be a secondary activity of critical reflection, the object of which is the act and content of Christian faith (i.e., both the *fides qua* and the *fides quae*).[39] Theology is the science of faith. There are two important consequences of this definition, for Rahner, as he indicates in the following passage:

Theology as science certainly may not be confused with
kerygma, with *parenesis*, with the immediate spiritual
word. But theology also may not forget, as it only too
often does, that it arises from this spiritual word and
must serve it, because this spiritual word and the theology that is derived from it are related to the primordial
experience of the Spirit or else they lose their subject
matter altogether.[40]

On the one hand, as the *science* of faith, theology is distinct
from faith. It is not faith itself, but critical reflection upon faith.
In this sense theology is secondary to faith. For Rahner, "philosophy, in the strict sense, can be nothing other than the meth-
odologically exact, reflective, and optimally controlled representation and articulation of [our] primordial self-understanding."[41] Similarly, theology is "the reflective and methodically
supervised illumination and explication of the revelation of God
that is grasped and accepted in faith."[42] Rahner is careful to
distinguish experience and subsequent reflection upon experience. The two cannot be identified. Our basic experience of
ourselves is immediate and given unthematically. Reflection represents a thematization of the original experience through the
mediation of language and concepts, a thematization that never
fully succeeds in capturing and reproducing the original experience.[43] Thus, with reference to 1 Peter 3:15, Rahner writes that
theology is an explicit, thematic account of the Christian hope,
but not that hope itself.[44]

As such a secondary enterprise of critical reflection, on the
other hand, theology is not unimportant to, or an alien imposition upon, "simple faith," precisely because theology is the science of *faith*. For Rahner, as for Heidegger, although immediate
self-possession and reflection can and must be distinguished,
nevertheless, our immediate possession or experience of ourselves always entails reflection. "Experience as such and conceptual, objectifying reflection on this experience are not absolutely separate from one another. Experience always brings at
least a certain initial reflection with it."[45] Indeed, reflection is not
merely accidental to human experince, but is necessary to it. "In
the instant in which this moment of reflection were no longer
given, this original self-possession itself would cease to be."[46]
Precisely as reflection upon faith, theology is a moment of faith.

Theology is not only a scientific, methodical reflection on
the consciousness of faith *[das Glaubensbewusstsein]* of the

church, but is also an inner moment of the consciousness
of faith itself, such that this consciousness of faith, with
the help of this reflection (called theology) unfolds itself
and comes to itself more reflectively.[47]

For Rahner,

There is a most essential distinction between proclamation and theology, although, concretely, proclamation
always already includes within itself a moment of theological reflection, and, on the other hand, theology never
adequately transposes proclamation into theological reflection.[48]

But, while theology is not itself kerygma, it has a kerygmatic
function. Without theology there could be no proclamation, no
kerygma.[49] Theology is not, for Rahner, idle speculation that
has nothing to do with faith, but is rather faith's own reflective
explication and account of itself.

Because theology is reflection that provides a critical
justification for faith and is essentially oriented to witness and proclamation, all theology is necessarily "kerygmatic" theology. In those instances where theology does
not wish to be kerygmatic or is no longer kerygmatic, it
would be simply speculative philosophy of religion. In
spite of its essential kerygmatic character (i.e., its relatedness to proclamation), theology is critical, reflective science, not directly meditation (as prayer) or exhortation.
It is precisely *as* critical reflection that it serves proclamation.[50]

As the science of faith, theology has as its basis, norm, and
goal, the Christian faith itself.[51] This is to say that no theology
could be judged to be adequate that is not faithful to the classic
expressions of the historic Christian faith. And, for Rahner, it is
scripture that is the *norma non normata* of Christian theology. It is
important to notice why this is the case. According to him,
scripture is finally normative for theology because scripture is
the "objectification of the faith of the primordial church *[die
Urkirche].*"[52] Or, even more precisely, scripture is "the pure and,
therefore, the one absolutely normative objectification that
forms the *norma non normata* of the eschatological beginning of
the end that is the primordial church."[53] Scripture is the
thematization of the original experience of the event of Jesus
Christ had by the apostles.[54] The normativity and "inerrancy" of
scripture are constituted by the fact that it objectifies the experi-

ence of the apostles, and have nothing to do with divine inspira-
tion, if this is understood to mean that God is the literary author
of scripture.[55]
    Rahner argues that theology must seek to refer persons
back to this original, apostolic experience of Jesus Christ.

> The task of theology must be to appeal to this primordial
> experience of grace in all of its conceptually differenti-
> ated objectifications; to show man, ever anew, that this
> whole, immensely differentiated sum of Christian state-
> ments of faith, although unfolded in all dimensions of
> man, basically expresses nothing but the one immense
> truth that the absolute mystery, which is, which holds
> sway over and supports everything, and which always
> remains, has communicated itself as itself to man in
> forgiving love.[56]

Theology cannot fulfill this task simply by repeating scripture or
tradition. It must interpret the normative faith of the apostles to
contemporary persons in a way that is credible to such persons.

> Theology is a genuinely kerygmatic theology only to the
> extent that it succeeds in finding a point of contact with
> the total profane self-understanding that man has in a
> particular epoch, and succeeds in entering into con-
> versation with this self-understanding, in taking it up
> and letting its language, and even more, its subject mat-
> ter itself be enriched by this self-understanding.[57]

This means that theology must also be evaluated in terms of its
ability to interpret the specific historical situation and self-understanding of contemporary persons.

> Theology is reflection upon the message of the gospel in
> a particular cultural and historical situation, in con-
> versation with the spirit of a particular age. It arises
> from, and is directed toward, the horizons of under-
> standing that are provided by a particular age.[58]

Theology, if it is to be adequate as the reflection of Christian
faith upon itself, must adopt an "appropriate epochal shape" in
each new historical situation.[59] Theology must re-express the
Christian faith in such a way that "man can recognize how that
which is expressed in [theological assertions] is connected with
his self-understanding that is attested in his experience."[60]
    Thus, for Rahner, theology must reflect upon both the
meaning of the Christian faith and the basic self-understanding

of contemporary persons, if theology is to aid the proclamation of the Christian faith to these persons. This means that theology must be fully critical reflection, including a moment of metaphysical or transcendental reflection upon human experience. Theology is a rigorous and scientific enterprise, one that excludes nothing from the scope of its critical questioning.[61] Theology is not, for Rahner, simply a "positive science" in Heidegger's sense of the term.[62] This is to say that theology is not simply a regional science, one that investigates some particular region of that which is, in this case, the Christian faith or self-understanding. Rather, theology, like metaphysics, is a universal science, one that in asking the question of human being, which is *quodammodo omnia,* also asks the question of the totality of reality.[63] Further, theology claims that the Christian proclamation of faith expresses a universal truth, that it is a thematization of what all persons implicitly experience even if they deny the explicit formulations of Christianity. Thus, theology cannot simply appeal, in a fideistic fashion, to its own special criteria of meaning and truth.[64] Since Christianity claims to thematize a universal aspect of human experience, the final criteria of the credibility of the Christian proclamation must be derived from human experience itself as illuminated by the secular arts and sciences, including metaphysics. According to Rahner, if theology does not reflect upon common human experience, including a moment of transcendental reflection on the a priori conditions of the possibility of human experience, then theology cannot make good its claim to be an expression of something that is true for human existence as such. And in failing to do this, theology would have also failed to remain faithful to the apostolic kerygma, which indeed makes the universalistic claim that the faith in God that it proclaims is a possibility for all persons.

Theology, then, is critical reflection on the particular Christian understanding of human being in the world in relation to others and to God. It must provide an interpretation of the normative Christian understanding of existence found in the apostolic witness of scripture, and must provide an interpretation of common human experience that is adequate when judged by the standards of meaning and truth that are presupposed in contemporary human existence. Its task is to show that the apostolic message, as interpreted in the contemporary situation, is the most appropriate thematization of the original, un-

thematic experience of self, other persons, and God, that all
persons share by virtue of existing as human beings.

Rahner's thought has been chosen to play a crucial role in
this inquiry because his approach to the situation, nature, and
task of theology, it seems to me, provides a fully explicit formulation of what is assumed implicitly in most other contemporary
theological views. But I also believe that Rahner's approach to
theology, however similar to other recent theologies, has important advantages over several alternative views. In the first place,
his account of the turn to the subject in contemporary theology
would seem to respond more adequately to the demand, presupposed in our existence as contemporary persons, that all theological (and philosophical) claims ultimately must be evaluated in
terms of common human experience. He shows that a fully
critical, and thus fully adequate, turn to the subject in contemporary philosophical thought must involve an explicitly transcendental or metaphysical analysis of the necessary conditions of
human experience. Further, Rahner shows, as neo-orthodox
theologians such as Barth do not, that the claims of theology,
including its claims concerning the reality of God, must be
justified not solely on the basis of the Christian witness of faith,
but, finally, on the basis of human existence and experience
itself. Theology must show that human existence as such is
necessarily oriented to the reality of God, prior to the proclamation of the special revelatory events of the Christian faith. Otherwise, talk of grace, divinization, the indwelling of God, and so
forth, appears to contemporary persons to be nothing more
than "conceptual poetry" and "indemonstrable mythology."[65]
Rahner's interpretation of our common human experience takes
more seriously the demands of critical thinking than do some
other theological approaches.

But, at the same time, the thoroughgoing, critical anthropo-
centricity of Rahner's thought does not represent any diminu-
tion of the essentially theocentric character of the Christian
faith. A real problem in radical theology is that secular intellectual and existentiell values are maintained only at the cost of an
explicit denial that Christian faith makes or implies any cognitive
claims concerning the divine reality. A similar problem arises
when one evaluates the adequacy of Bultmann's theology.
Bultmann claims, for instance, that talk of God, in Christian
faith, must always at the same time be talk about human being,

and vice versa. As such, this is a statement of the turn to the subject that I have argued is characteristic of the situation of contemporary theology. The problem is that, despite this formulation, which states that theological language must imply anthropological language *and* that anthropological language must imply theological language, in fact, Bultmann has very little to say about God and is concerned, rather onesidedly, only to transpose talk about God into talk about ourselves. Because Bultmann does not allow natural theology as a necessary aspect of an adequate Christian theology, his thought effects an implicit reduction of theology to anthropology.[66] Rahner's approach to theology seems to be particularly promising precisely because it is both anthropologically oriented (affirming that the final truth of theological claims is to be verified either in human experience or not at all), and yet explicitly theocentric (affirming that the human experience that provides the final criterion for the evaluation of the claims of Christian faith includes necessarily an immediate, a priori awareness of the divine reality). In short, Rahner seems to respond to the contemporary task of theology more adequately than do other alternative contemporary theologies, that is, the task of showing that the Christian faith, normatively expressed in the apostolic witness to Jesus Christ found in the New Testament, is the most appropriate thematization of the basic experience of self in relation to others and to God that all persons share implicitly.

NOTES

[1] The work of David Tracy is a good example of this. See *Blessed Rage for Order: The New Pluralism in Theology* (New York: Seabury Press, 1975).

[2] "Philosophie und Philosophieren in der Theologie," *ST*, 8:73 (ET: *TI*, 9:52). For Rahner's reflections on the pluralism of contemporary society in general, as well as of theology, see "Kleine Frage zum heutigen Pluralismus in der geistigen Situation der Katholiken und der Kirche," *ST*, 6:34–45 (ET: *TI*, 6:21–30); "Über den Dialog in der pluralistischen Gesellschaft," *ST*, 6:46–58 (ET: *TI*, 6:31–42); "Vom Dialog in der Kirche," *ST*, 8:426–444 (ET: *TI*, 10:103–121); "Theologische Reflexionen zur Säkularisation," *ST*, 8:637–666 (ET: *TI*, 10:318–348); "Der Pluralismus in der Theologie und die Einheit des Bekenntnisses in der

Kirche," *ST*, 9:11–33 (ET: *TI*, 11:3–23); "Überlegungen zur Methode der Theologie," *ST*, 9:70–126 (ET: *TI*, 11:68–114); "Häresien in der Kirche heute?" *ST*, 9:453–478 (ET: *TI*, 12:116–141).

[3] "Vom Dialog in der Kirche," *ST*, 8:429–430 (ET: *TI*, 10:106–107).

[4] "Philosophie und Philosophieren in der Theologie," *ST*, 8:79 (ET: *TI*, 9:57).

[5] I mean to include both Protestant "liberalism" and Roman Catholic "modernism" within what I call "liberal theology."

[6] This issue has been published separately as *Consensus in Theology? A Dialogue with Hans Küng and Edward Schillebeeckx*, ed. Leonard Swidler (Philadelphia: The Westminster Press, 1980).

[7] *Journal of Ecumenical Studies*, 17 (1980):1–17.

[8] Ibid., pp. 75–80.

[9] *Blessed Rage for Order*, pp. 22–42.

[10] Ibid., pp. 25–26.

[11] Ibid., pp. 27–31. It seems to me that some of the Latin American theologians of liberation, notably Gutierrez and Segundo, might more correctly be classified as revisionist theologians, to use Tracy's scheme. What is important for my purposes here, however, is simply the realization that liberation theology too is heir to the legacy of nineteenth century liberal theology. For a discussion of the liberal heritage of liberation theology, see Schubert Ogden, *Faith and Freedom: Toward a Theology of Liberation* (Nashville: Abingdon, 1979), pp. 17–39, 115–124.

[12] *Blessed Rage for Order*, pp. 31–32. Tracy includes within "radical theology" not only Altizer and Hamilton, but also Van Buren. I would argue that other thinkers influenced primarily by linguistic analysis, such as R. B. Braithwaite, R. M. Hare, and D. Z. Phillips, might be included within radical theology. See, for example, R. B. Braithwaite, *An Empiricist's View of the Nature of Religious Belief* (Cambridge: Cambridge University Press, 1955) and R. M. Hare, "Theology and Falsification," in *New Essays in Philosophical Theology*, ed. Antony Flew and Alasdair MacIntyre (New York: Schocken, 1971). Again, the important point is that, however radical or reductive the position of such thinkers is with respect to classical Christian theology, radical theology is nonetheless a response to the liberal problem of the reconciliation of Christian faith and secular understanding.

[13] *Blessed Rage for Order*, p. 32.

[14] *Meditations on First Philosophy*, in *Descartes's Philosophical Writings*, trans. and ed. E. Anscombe and P. T. Geach (Indianapolis: Bobbs-Merrill, 1971), p. 75. This is not to deny that Augustine, for example, held a similar position long before Descartes. What is significant about Descartes's thought is the way in which he made the human subject's experience of itself the methodological starting point for philosophical reflection.

[15] *Sein und Zeit,* 15th ed. (Tübingen: Max Niemeyer Verlag, 1979), p. 13.

[16] *Process and Reality: An Essay in Cosmology,* corrected ed. by David Griffin and Donald Sherburne (New York: Macmillan, 1978), p. 166.

[17] Berlin: Walter de Gruyter & Co., 1960, p. 105.

[18] See "Neues Testament and Mythologie: Das Problem der Entmythologisierung der neutestamentlichen Verkündigung," in *Kerygma und Mythos: Ein theologisches Gespräch,* vol. I, 2nd ed., ed. Hans Werner Bartsch (Hamburg: Herbert Reich-Evangelischer Verlag, 1951), pp. 15–48 (ET: *Kerygma and Myth,* vol. I, trans. and ed. Reginald Fuller (New York: Harper & Row, 1961), pp. 1–44).

[19] Ibid., p. 42 (ET: ibid., p. 36).

[20] "Über den Versuch eines Aufrisses einer Dogmatik," *ST,* 1:10 (ET: *TI,* 1:2).

[21] "Theologie und Anthropologie," *ST,* 8:56 (ET: *TI,* 9:38).

[22] Ibid., p. 50 (ET: ibid., p. 34).

[23] Ibid., p. 43 (ET: ibid., p. 28).

[24] "Selbsterfahrung und Gotteserfahrung," *ST,* 10:134 (ET: *TI,* 8:123).

[25] "Theologie und Anthropologie," *ST,* 8:50 (ET: *TI,* 9:34).

[26] "Überlegungen zur Methode der Theologie," *ST,* 9:98 (ET: *TI,* 11:87).

[27] Rahner attempts to provide a critical justification for transcendental metaphysics in *Geist in Welt: Zur Metaphysik der endlichen Erkenntnis bei Thomas von Aquin* (Innsbruck: Verlag Felizian Rauch, 1939) and *Hörer des Wortes: Zur Grundlegung einer Religionsphilosophie* (München: Verlag Kösel-Pustet, 1941). In this regard, see Emerich Coreth, *Metaphysik: Eine methodische systematische Grundlegung,* 2nd ed. (Innsbruck: Tyrolia Verlag, 1964).

[28] Rahner is aware that to make this human experience of self fundamental to theological reflection entails a radical revision of much of traditional theology. If the most fundamental theological categories are to be derived from this experience of self in relation to others and to God, then many of the categories of traditional theology, which are derived from the human experience of impersonal objects, suddenly become inappropriate. Much of Rahner's theological reflection is devoted to the attempt to allow the personal categories derived from our most fundamental experience of ourselves to inform the Christian understanding of God, grace, Jesus Christ, last things, and so forth.

[29] *Systematic Theology,* 3 vols. (Chicago: University of Chicago Press, 1967), 1:60–61.

[30] Ibid., p. 62.

[31] "Neues Testament und Mythologie," p. 26 (ET: *Kerygma and Myth,* vol. I, p. 15).

[32] Ibid., p. 207 (ET: ibid., p. 210).

[33] *Blessed Rage for Order*, pp. 47, 49.

[34] "What is Theology?" *Journal of Religion* 52 (1972):25.

[35] *A Theology of Liberation: History, Politics and Salvation*, trans. Caridad Inga and John Eagelson (Maryknoll, N.Y.: Orbis Books, 1973), p. 11.

[36] Ibid., p. 13.

[37] *Systematic Theology: A Historicist Perspective* (New York: Charles Scribner's Sons, 1968), pp. 75–76.

[38] See *Journal of Ecumenical Studies* 17 (1980):1–17, 33–48, 75–80, 86–93.

[39] "Theologie," *SM*, vol. 4, col. 863 (ET: *SM(eng)*, vol. 6, pp. 234–235).

[40] "Überlegungen zur Methode der Theologie," *ST*, 9:123 (ET: *TI*, 11:111).

[41] "Philosophie und Theologie," *ST*, 6:94 (ET: *TI*, 6:74).

[42] "Theologie," *SM*, vol. 4, cols. 861–862 (ET: *SM(eng)*, vol. 6, p. 234).

[43] For Rahner's view of the relationship between reflection and experience or self-possession, see *GG*, pp. 26–27 (ET: *FCF*, pp. 15–16), and "Gotteserfahrung heute," *ST*, 9:163–164 (ET: *TI*, 11:151–152).

[44] "Theologie," *SM*, vol. 4, col. 863 (ET: *SM(eng)*, vol. 6, p. 235).

[45] "Gotteserfahrung heute," *ST*, 9:163 (ET: *TI*, 11:151–152).

[46] *GG*, p. 27 (ET: *FCF*, p. 16).

[47] "Heilige Schrift und Theologie," *ST*, 6:112 (ET: *TI*, 6:90–91).

[48] "Theologie und Anthropologie," *ST*, 8:55 (ET: *TI*, 9:37–38).

[49] "Philosophie und Theologie," *ST*, 6:101 (ET: *TI*, 6:80).

[50] "Theologie," *SM*, vol. 4, cols. 863–864 (ET: *SM(eng)*, vol. 6, p. 235).

[51] Ibid., col. 863 (ET: ibid.).

[52] "Heilige Schrift und Theologie," *ST*, 6:111 (ET: *TI*, 6:90).

[53] Ibid. (ET: ibid., p. 89).

[54] "Überlegungen zur Methode der Theologie," *ST*, 9:122–123 (ET: *TI*, 9:110).

[55] Cf. *GG*, pp. 358–364 (ET: *FCF*, pp. 369–377). Although Rahner does acknowledge that all scriptural texts are not of equal material and existentiell weight, and that, therefore, there is a hierarchy of truths within scripture itself, he does not give much consideration to the problem of the canon within the canon as this relates to the authority and normativity of scripture for theology. However, it seems to me that his basic understanding that the authority of scripture lies in its being the objectification of the faith or experience of the apostles is open to the suggestion made by Willi Marxsen and Schubert Ogden (cf. Marxsen, *Das Neue Testament als Buch der Kirche* (Gütersloh: Gütersloher

Verlagshaus-Gerd Mohn, 1968); and Ogden, "The Authority of Scripture for Theology," *Interpretation* 30 (1976):242–261) that it is not scripture as a whole, or even the New Testament that is the *norma non normata* of theology, but rather the original apostolic witness to Jesus that is contained in the New Testament, i.e., the Jesus-kerygma of the synoptic gospels, to use Marxsen's phrase. The Old Testament is authoritative in that it provides the necessary presuppositions for this apostolic witness of faith, and, likewise, the remainder of the New Testament in that it is composed of various interpretations of this original apostolic witness. Just as Rahner argues for the normativity of the objectification of the experience or faith of the apostles (by which he means all of the New Testament writers) in relation to subsequent theology or tradition, so one might argue that it is the experience or faith of the original witnesses to the event of Jesus Christ that is normative with respect to the New Testament as a whole. In any case, in this study, I will speak of the apostolic witness that is contained in scripture as being normative for theology, rather than scripture or the New Testament in an unqualified sense.

56 "Überlegungen zur Methode der Theologie," *ST*, 9:123 (ET: *TI*, 11:110).

57 *GG*, p. 19 (ET: *FCF*, pp. 7–8).

58 "Ökumenische Theologie der Zukunft," *ST*, 10:505 (ET: *TI*, 14:256).

59 "Die Zukunft der Theologie," *ST*, 9:153–154 (ET: *TI*, 11:143).

60 "Theologie und Anthropologie," *ST*, 8:60 (ET: *TI*, 9:41). Rahner is willing to call this re-expression of the Christian faith "demythologization," provided that this term is "understood to refer to nothing more than the ever new, necessary encounter of faith, which unavoidably expresses itself in historically conditioned concepts, and the ever developing secular understanding of existence" ("Heilsauftrag der Kirche und Humanisierung der Welt," *ST*, 10:551 (ET: *TI*, 14:299).

61 "Theologie," *SM*, vol. 4, col. 826 (ET: *SM(eng)*, vol. 6, p. 234).

62 Cf. *Phänomenologie und Theologie* (Frankfurt am Main: Vittorio Klostermann, 1970), pp. 17–21.

63 "Selbsterfahrung und Gotteserfahrung," *ST*, 10:133–134 (ET: *TI*, 13:122–123).

64 "Theologie und Anthropologie," *ST*, 8:51 (ET: *TI*, 9:34).

65 Ibid., p. 54 (ET: ibid., p. 37).

66 For a detailed justification of this charge, see Schubert Ogden, "Bultmann's Demythologizing and Hartshorne's Dipolar Theism," in *Process and Divinity: The Hartshorne Festschrift*, ed. William Reese and Eugene Freeman (LaSalle, Ill.: Open Court, 1964), pp. 493–513.

CHAPTER II
FREEDOM, LOVE, AND THE CONCEPT OF GOD

I have said that the primary goal of this study is to contribute to a solution to the problem of the concept of God. Of course, the task of expressing faithfully and credibly the meaning of faith in God, which is the very heart of the Christian proclamation, has been a perennial challenge for Christian theology. But in any historical period, the problem of the concept of God is given its own unique form by the particular self-understanding of the persons of that period. Central to this study is the conviction that one of the most fruitful approaches to the contemporary problem of the concept of God is provided by critical reflection on the meaning and truth of the assertion "God is love." In this chapter I will seek to show, again using the theology of Karl Rahner as my primary resource, why the assertion "God is love" raises the basic issues of the contemporary problem of the concept of God, and why the assertion "God is love" is problematic in the contemporary theological situation given the understanding of the nature and task of theology that is adopted here.

The meaning and truth of the assertion "God is love" must always be an issue for Christian theology because the Christian witness of faith, upon which theology reflects, clearly claims that God is love. It could be argued, in fact, that the claim that God is love is one of the most fundamental elements of the Christian witness of faith concerning God, if not *the* most fundamental element of this witness. Rahner writes that "the decisive experience that man has in the history of salvation is that God the Father in his Son has graciously called us into his innermost communion. This experience is expressed in the proposition: God is love (I Jn 4:16)."[1] The claim that God is love is made or implied throughout scripture.[2] Theology, therefore, if it is to fulfill its task adequately, must provide some account of the scriptural assertion that God is love. And, in particular, theology must provide this critical account of the assertion "God is love" in relation to the experience and self-understanding of contemporary human persons. Thus, in the most general terms, one could say that a central aspect of the contemporary problem of the concept of God is expressed in the following question: What does it mean to assert, in our contemporary spiritual, intellectual, cultural, and social situation, that God is love, and under what conditions could this assertion be judged to be a true assertion? This is the question that will occupy our attention in this study. But, first, this very general formulation of the question of the meaning and truth of the assertion "God is love" must be focused in terms of the specific form this question takes in the contemporary theological situation.

The Turn to the Subject and the Concept of God

As I have shown, Rahner understands the contemporary theological situation to be decisively shaped by the turn to the subject characteristic of modern philosophy. This turn to the subject demands that the starting point and prime datum of philosophical and theological reflection must be the human person's most fundamental experience of her- or himself. The question is immediately raised whether this methodological stricture also applies to theological reflection on the reality of God. That is, does our most fundamental experience of ourselves as human persons also provide the basic concepts for an understanding of the divine reality, or is reflection on the reality of God somehow an exception to the rule that theological reflection must be anthropologically oriented?

It is abundantly clear, in Rahner's thought, that the question of God itself must be posed and answered in terms of the basic characteristic of the contemporary theological situation, namely, the turn to the subject. The turn to the subject must inform reflection on the reality of God. Rahner gives a number of reasons why this must be the case.

First of all, he makes the obvious point that if human concepts were not to apply to God at all, no knowledge of God would be possible. We can only conceive God using human concepts. Since there is an awareness of God given universally and unfailingly in human experience, and since human experience always includes a reflective moment, it is clear that some human concepts can apply appropriately to God. Rahner argues:

> That which supports and grounds every reality [God] . . . makes itself known in that which is supported and grounded, and can be named from the latter. Otherwise, no relationship between ground and that which is grounded can be conceived.[3]

Because God is the ground of all that is, there must be some commonality between infinite and finite being that makes reflection on and speech about the reality of God possible.[4]

> It is immediately self-evident that the ground of a reality that exists must beforehand possess in itself in absolute fullness and purity this reality that it grounds. For, otherwise, this ground could not be the ground of that which is grounded at all; for, otherwise, it would finally be the empty nothingness that—if one takes the term seriously—would express nothing and could ground nothing.[5]

Rahner concludes from this principle that God must be capable of being conceived using personal categories derived from our own experience, if the divine ground of our own personal being is to be fully illuminated. He states that the assertion that God is personal is as metaphysically self-evident as the assertions that God is absolute being, absolute mystery, absolute good, and so forth.[6]

Second, Rahner argues that personal concepts derived from our own experience of ourselves as subjects can and must also apply to God because subjectivity is an ontological category. Reality, including God (at least in an analogical sense), is only disclosed through our own experience of ourselves. According to Rahner, the first proposition of general metaphysics is: "The essence of being is knowing and being known in a primordial unity that we want to call the being with itself [*das Beisichsein*], or the luminosity, of being."[7] Everything that exists has a certain amount of self-presence, or subjectivity.

Being, for Rahner, is an analogical concept. Therefore, beings vary widely according to the degree of subjectivity each possesses. The degree of being of an entity corresponds to its degree of subjectivity or self-possession.[8] "The degree of the intensity of being manifests itself in the degree to which the particular being in question is able to turn back to itself, to reflect upon itself, to be luminous for itself."[9] Although being and subjectivity are analogical or variable concepts, nevertheless, it remains true, for Rahner, that:

> Everything strives to return to itself, intends to come to itself, intends to take possession of itself, because it is being to the extent . . . that it takes possession of itself. All doing and all acting, from that which is purely material up to the inner life of the triune God, are only variations upon this one metaphysical theme, this one meaning of being: self-possession.[10]

Thus, because God is, God is characterized by subjectivity or self-possession. Indeed, as absolute being, God possesses the highest degree of subjectivity. For this reason, personal categories derived from our own experience of ourselves as spiritual subjects are most appropriate for use in conceptualizing the divine reality.

The third reason why reflection on the divine reality is not exempted from the modern turn to the subject in theology, for Rahner, has to do with the peculiar nature of the problem or question of God. According to him, the question concerning God is not an empirical question but rather a metaphysical or transcendental one.

> The question about God, if, indeed, God is not to be missed from the outset, cannot be posed as a question concerning an individual, particular being *within* the horizon of our transcendence and our historical experience, rather, it must be posed as the question concerning the supporting ground, the origin, and the future of the question that we ourselves are. Therefore, necessarily, it already has in itself the answer to the questions of whether [God exists] and what [God is], all in one.[11]

The reality of God is the ground and goal of the question that the human person is. So, when human beings reflect on the reality of God, they are reflecting upon the ultimate ground, origin, and future of their own existence. In such reflection, indeed in the very posing of the question of God as the question of the final horizon of human being, a turn to the subject has already decisively been made.

Finally, Rahner argues that in the modern world there has been and still is a real crisis of belief in God, if God is conceived in impersonal terms. He says that God can no longer be conceived as part of the world order, even if the highest and most perfect part of the world. The physical universe has been radically (and justifiably) de-divinized.[12] The world is no longer understood to be open to the causal influence of God at any particular point. In our present situation, the transcendental experience persons have of God is no longer mediated by the world of nature.

> In the first place, over against earlier times, this mediation has been displaced from the world to human existence. Earlier, the external world in its order and harmony was that by which man's experience of transcendence was kindled; today it is his existence with its abysmal depths.[13]

Rahner says that the world from which God can be recognized is not the world of things, but rather "the world to which man as one who experiences himself belongs. In himself and in his intercommunication [with other persons] he recognizes God."[14] Thus, the only God who can credibly be proclaimed in the contemporary world is a God who is portrayed in terms of our own experience of ourselves as persons in relation to other persons, and not one who is portrayed in terms of our experience of an external world of things.

It is important to make clear why I have been careful, when describing the problem this study addresses, to speak of the problem of the *concept* of God, not simply of the problem of God. Since, for Rahner, all human beings necessarily have an unthematic experience of God, which experience is a condition of the possibility of human existence as such, there is a sense in which, at the transcendental level, there is no question of God. That is to say, in all human acts, even in an act of radical, moral denial of God (an ultimately self-contradictory act), God is once again affirmed as the transcendental horizon within which all human spiritual activity occurs. The question of God, assuming that the human person has not denied her or his transcendental orientation to God through a self-contradictory act of radical, culpable unfaithfulness to her or his own conscience, is a question of the proper objectification or thematization of the transcendental experience of God.[15] Rahner holds that advances in the doctrine of God do not represent discovery of a new God, or a new experience of God, but are rather the destruction of false concepts of God and the formulation of more adequate concepts of God.[16] The problem of God to which theology as a reflective activity must respond is the problem of a proper concept of God, the problem of most adequately thematizing the universal, immediate, necessary human experience of the divine reality.[17]

For the four reasons just given, Rahner holds that the turn to the subject must also be taken with respect to reflection upon the reality of God. He argues that:

> The image that the absolute ground of all reality is something like a reclusive cosmic law that has the qualities of a thing, an impersonal structure of things that is not given in itself, a fountain that empties itself without possessing itself, that gives rise to spirit and freedom without being spirit and freedom itself, the image, as it were, of a blind, primordial ground of the world that cannot look at us, even if it wanted to, is an image whose paradigm is derived from the context of the impersonal things of the world. It does not arise from the genuine locus of a primordial transcendental experience, namely, from the finite spirit's free, subjective experience of itself. In this its constitutive essence, finite spirit as such always experiences itself as having its origin in another and as being given to itself by another that cannot be misunderstood as an impersonal thinglike principle.[18]

This means that, stated most generally, the contemporary problem of the concept of God is the problem of how concepts that are derived from our most basic experience of ourselves as persons are to be applied to the divine reality. As Rahner shows, it is not a question of whether such concepts are to be applied to God. If contemporary persons are to reflect on God in an adequate philosophical or theological fashion, the basic concepts for such reflection on God must be derived not from our experience of things but from our basic, existentiell experience of ourselves. The only question is how this is most properly to be done.

Several propositions taken from Heinrich Ott's extended discussion of the contemporary problem of a personal concept of God will help to deepen our understanding of some of the basic categories derived from our experience of ourselves as persons that are to be used in conceiving the reality of God most adequately. First, Ott sheds some light on the distinction between personal and impersonal forms of thought.

Whether we talk of things, natural objects or artifacts, and thinglike situations, or whether we talk of persons and relationships between persons makes a difference. In each case different forms of thought (categories) are called for. The forms of thought that are finally confirmed in metaphysics, that are influential even in our everyday thinking, in which we are accustomed to think, are derived from the model of natural and artificial things. Their apparent limit is to be found in the fact that the specific historicity of responsible personal experience cannot be conceived using these impersonal forms of thought.[19]

Ott then refers to the philosophy of Martin Buber and argues that a central presupposition of such a personal form of thought is that persons are constituted by their relations to other persons.

Among models of personal relationship, forms of thought are to be promoted that facilitate an appropriate conception of personal reality, in distinction from thinglike or impersonal reality. Reciprocity, the "between," proves to be the phenomenological point of departure for the attainment of a concept of personal being and the pervasive characteristic of the various personal phenomena: that which has most essentially to do with persons does not merely occur within persons, but rather between them. Thus, a person cannot exist and be conceived "in himself," but only as open with respect to other persons in the between. This fundamental structure can be verified in everyday human experience. . . . Because personal being is a being in the between, persons are not sharply marked off from one another. Rather, the spheres of their personal reality overlap and interpenetrate. A man is not merely external to the other (as one who is opposite), but, insofar as he has something to do with the other, is also internal to the other. Human being, as personal being, consists of such relationships. In abstraction from them, no concept of the personal self is possible. If one were to distinguish the responsible self from these its relationships, one would fall back into the impersonal substance ontology. . . . Personal existence is characterized by a "mineness" [eine Jemeinigkeit] that can neither be fully grasped nor surrendered. Nevertheless, the primordial being of the individual is not that of isolation or detachment. The human person not only enters into community with other persons in the being-with-the-crowd

of others of everyday life, but rather, more primordially,
also and precisely by decisively taking over his own-most
being, man exists in a form of solidarity with the neighbor that, as such, qualifies his "mineness."[20]

As I will demonstrate in Chapter III, Rahner also believes
that human being is essentially constituted by relations to other
persons (a relatedness that conditions and is conditioned by an
essential relatedness to self and to God). He says, "the personal
Thou [is] the mediation of the being with self [das Beisichsein] of
the subject."[21] Likewise:

Man only comes to himself in the encounter with the
other man who is presented historically to one's experience in knowledge and love, who is not a thing but a
man. . . . In knowledge and freedom, which are the
concrete realization of life, the I is always related to a
Thou, is primordially as much with the Thou as with the
I, always only experiences itself as differentiated from
and identified with the other in the encounter with the
other person.[22]

It is precisely this fundamental experience of the self as related
to other selves, as determined by others, as including others
within one's own personal reality, that is to provide the basic
categories for an adequate, contemporary concept of God.

Rahner argues, however, that the doctrine of God in twentieth century Roman Catholic theology has not really been affected by "the turn from Greek thought that is oriented
primarily to things to the legitimate anthropocentrism of modern times."[23] He says that theology, contrary to the essential
message of the Christian faith itself, too often has understood
God and God's relationship to the creatures in static and impersonal, rather than in dynamic, personal terms.[24] What is needed
in contemporary theology, according to him, is a theological
counterpart to Heidegger's treatment of the concept of being,
that is, reflection on the reality of God that is grounded in the
existentiell experience human subjects have of themselves.[25]
The doctrine of God should be formulated using personal categories such as intimacy, freedom, and love, rather than abstract
categories such as quality, accident, and attribute that derive
from our experience of the external world.[26]

At this stage, the contemporary problem of the concept of
God can be formulated as follows: How is God to be conceived

on the basis of the human subject's most fundamental experience of her- or himself as a person constituted essentially by relations to other persons?

The Contemporary Experience of Freedom and Love

But this formulation of the problem of the concept of God is still too general and does not take into account a distinctive characteristic of contemporary experience and self-understanding. According to Rahner, an essential characteristic of the contemporary self-understanding of human persons is a radically new sense of the freedom and autonomy of the human subject. For the first time in history human beings can view their world and themselves as being the product of human activity and creativity. Rahner says:

> Today, in his historical development, man has clearly and definitively entered into the phase of a characteristic creativity and has become the active and powerful master who rationally plans himself and his environment.[27]

Because of scientific and technological developments, human beings no longer live in nature, but alter it. Human beings no longer experience themselves to be distinct from sub-human nature simply because of their rational and spiritual capacities. Rather, sub-human nature itself has become a human tool.

> Nature, for contemporary man, is no longer the exalted representative of God that lies beyond man's disposal, but is the material he requires in order to practice his *own free creativity* and to build for himself his world according to his own laws.[28]

Today, human beings have been delivered into their own hands in a physical, and not just in a spiritual, sense. Human beings have become subjects in a radical way. The world as a whole has been dedivinized and hominized, not just theoretically but practically. According to Rahner:

> The man of today and tomorrow is the man who has genuinely become a subject. He is not just theoretically, but practically responsible for himself. He has carried through, not just intellectually and religiously, but practically, the Copernican turn from "cosmocentrism" to "anthropocentrism." He plans; he is in direct contact

> with that science that does not simply view the world with
> aesthetic-philosophical contemplation, but rather (even
> in the theoretical branches of science) reflects upon how
> man can master and overpower nature, wrest from
> nature the law of its activity and make it his own. He
> establishes new goals and tasks; he invents new needs,
> which he himself creates and promises to satisfy. . . . In
> his experience, he really stands in the realm of nature as
> in a quarry or a construction site upon which the world
> man wishes to live in as his own world must first be built,
> the world in which he once again encounters himself—
> *almost* as if he were his own creator and God.[29]

Rahner holds that this new and radical sense of being a
subject is evident not just in contemporary persons' understanding of their relationship to the physical world (including our own
bodies, even our genetic structure), but also in our understanding of our relationships to the social structures in which we
live.[30] We experience ourselves no longer to be merely the objects of history, but to be in a real sense the subjects, the creators,
of history. Human being is radically free and responsible for
itself, not just in the sense that we create our final validity before
God, but also in the sense that we create our own history and the
social arrangements that shape our historical existence.[31] We
must make of ourselves whatever we are to be, and, conversely,
whatever historical realities or social structures exist have been
created by human persons and are to be evaluated and criticized
as such. Human beings, today, are aware, in a radical sense, of
their own responsibility for other persons, indeed for all persons.[32] The social and political future of this one world is seen as
being in the hands of human beings. We are free to make of this
world either a humane and just, or an inhumane and unjust,
place in which human beings are to live.[33]

The socio-political implications of this "hominization" of the
world of which Rahner speaks are formulated well by Gustavo
Gutierrez:

> The social praxis of contemporary man has begun to
> reach maturity. It is the behavior of man ever more
> conscious of being an active subject of history; he is ever
> more articulate in the face of social injustice and of all
> the repressive social forces which stand in the way of his
> fulfillment; he is ever more determined to participate in
> the transformation of social structures and in effective
> political action. It was above all the great social revolu-

tions—the French and the Russian, for example, to mention only two important milestones—together with the whole process of revolutionary ferment that they initiated which wrested—or at least began to—political decisions from the hands of an elite who were "destined" to rule. Up to that time the great majority of people did not participate in political decisions or did so only sporadically and formally. Although it is true that the majority of people are far from this level of awareness, it is also certain that they have had confused glimpses of it and are oriented in this direction. The phenomenon that we designated with the term "politicization"—which is increasing in breadth and depth in Latin America—is one of the manifestations of this complex process. And in the struggle for the liberation of the oppressed classes on this continent—which is implicit in the effective and human responsibility of all—people are searching out new paths.[34]

As this passage indicates, the maturation of contemporary social praxis, or the practical turn to the subject in contemporary human existence, to use Rahner's terminology, also raises new problems for human beings. Rahner writes that human freedom itself has become a crucial existentiell and theoretical problem in the contemporary situation. It is no longer the forces of nature, but our own freedom that appears to be dark, uncontrollable, and threatening.[35] Persons are anxious in the face of their own freedom and before the mysterious, even foreboding, future of society that human beings are now creating. He states that this "Promethean undertaking," in which human beings create themselves and the structures of society, may indeed lead to catastrophe.

As we already notice today, this development [i.e., the active alteration of human being and society] does not unambiguously indicate an unhindered triumphal procession into a glorious future of freedom and carefree happiness; this development can just as easily become a path that leads to new tyranny, to absurdities, and to destruction.[36]

The injustice, oppression, and inhumanity that characterize much of contemporary society is a crucial problem for our understanding of ourselves as free subjects who are constituted by our relations to others. In the contemporary situation, being responsible for ourselves and society, being the subjects, and not

just the objects, of history, means to take responsibility for the
evolutionary or revolutionary alteration of unjust and oppressive social structures.[37] Rahner writes that the liberation of
oppressed persons and the construction of a more humane
world often appear to be the only task to which a person, in good
conscience, can devote her- or himself.[38]

The contemporary world, according to Rahner, is in a
global revolutionary situation. A revolutionary situation is present when:

> First, there exists a sufficiently large group within a
> society that is, nevertheless, not integrated into the so-
> ciety; second, there is a revolutionary potential; third,
> this group has become sufficiently aware of its situation;
> and fourth, this group has a sufficient social organiza-
> tion.[39]

That there exists, in contemporary societies, large, uninte-
grated groups is clear.

> Today there are poor who should not be poor. There are
> underdeveloped peoples whose poor number in the mil-
> lions. And because—first of all, at least in principle—
> something *can* be changed in this situation, something
> *must* be changed in it. Today, above all, the under-
> developed peoples are the Lazarus before the door of
> the rich reveller. The boundary line between Lazarus
> and the reveller is the north-south line that runs around
> the entire world. Of course, there are also poor people
> enough even in the highly industrialized, privileged na-
> tions. There are people who just simply do not have
> enough to eat, who are forced out of the labor force
> against their will after forty years, who are discriminated
> against racially, who are victims of unjust political per-
> secution, who are kept from a reasonable and possible
> advancement, who eke out a meager existence on fixed
> incomes, sick people who could be helped if someone
> were willing to help, people who cannot help themselves
> in life because, from the outset, they have not been given
> a human or an economic chance, and so forth: people
> who are conspicuously poor.[40]

As Rahner's reflections on the hominization of the world and
Gutierrez' remarks about the maturation of social practice and
the politicization of the poor of the Third World indicate, the
poor in the contemporary world have become aware of the
injustice of their situation, are becoming socially organized, and

therefore represent a revolutionary potential in society. This revolutionary situation is global. It affects North America and Europe not just because our world has become closely united by modern means of communication, but, more importantly, because the poverty and oppression that have spawned the potential for social revolution are a function of the gap between the developed and the undeveloped nations, between the northern hemisphere and the southern hemisphere.[41] The development and wealth of the industrialized nations have been accomplished at the expense of the Third World. Rahner says of Europeans and North Americans:

> We, the ones who cannot count ourselves among the poor, are rich (to some extent, however varied) *precisely because* (notice the words "precisely" and "because") the poor people are poor. We do not give or do not give in sufficient quantity, biblical "alms," which today must consist of an evolutionary or revolutionary alteration of social structures in order to create greater justice.[42]

A revolutionary process, according to Rahner, has both a negative and a positive aspect: "the criticism or the attempt to remove unjust or repressive social relationships," and "the creation of social conditions and relationships within which men can live out their social relations in the greatest possible freedom."[43] There are three dimensions that characterize any revolution:

> The dimension of the original motivation: the revolution arises against the injustice that is inflicted upon the oppressed, whose frustration incites the revolution. The dimension of the normative understanding: the original motivation becomes the occasion for the understanding that the social conditions within a particular society can be changed. A new structure of a better society is conceived, and, retrospectively, from this point of view, the original motivation becomes clearer and more concrete. The dimension of general and particular revolutionary strategy: different methods are conceived through which the new society can be realized. These different methods are tested as to their actual effectiveness, the chosen methods are made operable, and, finally, by way of the genuine revolutionary procedures the new structures of society are concretely realized.[44]

This, then, is the situation in which human persons, as free subjects constituted essentially by relations to other persons, find themselves. It is a revolutionary situation, one in which the pressing problem both for thought and action is the problem of the alleviation of the structural injustice of contemporary society. To be essentially related to others as a free, self-determining subject means, today, that one must recognize the intolerable oppression of a majority of the persons to whom one is related and must seek to liberate those persons from their oppression by creating more just social relations. Rahner writes that the basic themes of philosophical reflection now and in the future will be hope, that is, hope for a more just society in the future, the nature of society, the criticism of ideology, and "the new shape of freedom in a new social order."[45] He says that the key concepts within the contemporary spiritual situation are: universal justice, emancipation, and hope.[46]

It is the self-understanding of persons in this revolutionary situation that the Christian faith must address. Rahner argues that:

> The church certainly should have, and does have, the task of preaching, to itself, to its members, and to the world, justice for the poor, and of recognizing and seeking the poor wherever social relationships and structures of ownership and power allow the poor to be wronged and burdened, and the rich to be unjustly privileged, whether this wronging of the poor consists in the immediate deprivation of economic goods or in other forms of disenfranchisement.[47]

In a situation of global injustice, theology is called to give a credible account of the Christian faith. This holds true, above all, for reflection on the very foundation of Christian faith, namely, the reality of God. As Gustavo Gutierrez puts it, the question today "is not therefore how to speak of God in an adult world, but how to proclaim him as Father in a world that is not human."[48] In other words, the contemporary problem of the concept of God arises out of the concrete problems of human freedom and liberation. While God still is to be conceived in terms of the basic human experience of self as a free, responsible subject essentially related to other subjects, today, this experience of self is decisively qualified by the realization that a large number of human persons are oppressed and denied their most basic rights. A theological concept of God can be judged to be adequate, in the contemporary situation, only if it reflects a sensitive understanding of oppression of our fellow human beings.

A final specification of the contemporary problem of the concept of God must now be made, one that will, at last, show the connection between the discussions of the turn to the subject in theological reflection, our contemporary experience of radical freedom and radical oppression, injustice, and bondage, the problem of the concept of God, and the question concerning the meaning and truth of the assertion "God is love" with which the argument of this chapter began.

As I will show in more detail in the next chapter, the human person, as a free subject related to other subjects, is most authentically realized in love, that is, in the act in which an autonomous person freely opens and abandons her- or himself to another person or persons. The capacity to love, according to Rahner, is the single, final structure that adequately expresses the authentic nature of the human person.[49] "The act of personal love for the human Thou is the encompassing fundamental act of man that provides the meaning, directionality, and standard for every other act."[50] Love is not just a particular event in human being, but is the totality of that which the human person is. Love is the sole act in which a human person possesses her- or himself fully and authentically. In love, the mystery of human being is gathered together and actualized. Indeed, Rahner claims, "all anthropological statements must be read as statements concerning this love."[51]

But Rahner does not understand love for the human Thou, the love of neighbor spoken of in the New Testament, solely in the individualistic sense of the love of a single individual for another. He says that:

> The love of a neighbor cannot be merely inclination of the heart or private intercommunication, which can be the most sublime form of egoism precisely because it can be so intimate and make one so happy. Rather, the love of neighbor must also be the sober service of "political" love, which is directed toward the whole of humanity and makes the most distant person one's neighbor.[52]

Today, the New Testament demand that we love our neighbor should be understood to refer to an active, socially oriented and socially engaged love of all other persons.

Even if one rejects "collectivism" in the perjorative sense, one cannot and may not overlook the fact that today humanity must necessarily realize (and in fact, has already begun to realize) higher levels and forms of sociality, if each person, in act and truth, is to affirm the existence of every other person. Humanity is beginning to enter a post-individualistic phase of history, which brings into new danger the genuine and unique personality and worth of the individual. This genuine and unique personality and worth of the individual must be altered; not eliminated, but actually provided with a wider scope of genuine freedom. This means, however, that the loving intercommunication [constitutive of personal being] itself receives a new form; now it can and must become the servant of this new form of the sociality of man. Indeed it can and must become the servant of humanity, because humanity is beginning to exist as a concrete reality, and not just as an "idea," or an ideology. If "society" is reality in a new sense, if it is slowly and inevitably constructing itself anew, then it can become, in a new way, the partner of the love of neighbor. . . . Understood in this fashion, however, the love of neighbor must will and help to realize these higher actualizations of society and humanity, as they are and must be in their epochal form: as shaping themselves in view of a future through self-manipulation.[53]

Rahner identifies love of neighbor with responsibility for the world. This includes the responsibility to take revolutionary action to alter unjust and oppressive social structures, which was shown above to be a key aspect of the self-understanding of contemporary persons.[54] A similar view of the relationship between the reconstruction of society and love is expressed by M.-D. Chenu:

Man has always had [a] social dimension, since he is social by his very nature. Today, however, not accidentally but structurally, the advent of the collective extends and intensifies this dimension. The collective, as such, has human value and is, therefore, the medium and the object of love. Human love walks along these "tedious" paths, these systems of distributive justice, and these administrative structures.[55]

Rahner states that "active love," that is, the love of one's fellow human beings that is expressed in the struggle to eliminate oppressive social and political structures, is "the locus of the illumination of the existence of modern man."[56] This has important consequences for his understanding of the problem of the concept of God. Recall that, for him, the question of God "must be posed as the question concerning the supporting ground, the origin, and the future of the question that we ourselves are."[57] If the whole meaning of contemporary human existence is given in the socially active love of neighbor, then the question of God, as the question of the ground, origin, and future of human existence, is raised precisely in the love of neighbor.

> In this love of neighbor, in its claim for eternal validity and finality, in which man's moving away from himself in knowledge and freedom is more radically realized, it becomes clear for contemporary man for the first time what is meant by God and the existence of God in a way that was not required in earlier times.[58]

The contemporary problem of the concept of God, for Rahner, is the problem of how God is to be conceived as the ground, origin, and future of the full realization of the freedom of the human subject in love, a love that is active on behalf of the liberation of the oppressed. But if God is to be the ground of human being, then God must possess in absolute fullness and purity that which God grounds. If God is the ground, origin, and future of human freedom and love, then God must Godself, in an absolutely full and pure sense, be free and loving.

> When we reflect here upon transcendence as will and freedom, we must take into consideration a loving *terminus* or horizon *[das Woraufhin]* and source of this transcendence. It is this *Woraufhin* that is absolute freedom, that is active in loving freedom as that which is not at our disposal, that which is nameless, and that which disposes absolutely. It is the opening of my own transcendence as freedom and love. . . . If free, loving transcendence is oriented toward a *Woraufhin* that itself opens up this transcendence, then we can say that the one that disposes absolutely, the one that is nameless, the one that is not at our disposal, itself acts in loving freedom.[59]

Thus, the most precise formulation of the problem of the concept of God, as this problem is raised in the particular situation of contemporary persons, is given, for Rahner, in the question concerning the meaning and truth of the assertion "God is love." That is to say, a most pressing theological question is the question of what it means to affirm, in the contemporary situation (a

situation in which the basic experience persons have of themselves as free subjects is always also an experience of the demand
that one struggle to liberate the oppressed if one is to actualize
authentically, that is, lovingly, one's essential relatedness to other
persons), that God, as the ground, origin, and future of human
freedom and love, is Godself a free person who opens and
abandons Godself to others in love.

An Overview of the Present Study

What I have tried to show in this chapter, using Rahner's
theology as my guide, is that the question concerning the meaning and truth of the assertion "God is love" is a crucial question
for contemporary Christian theology. It is a question that is
raised by both aspects of the dual task of theology. That is to say,
the meaning and truth of "God is love" are problematic both
with respect to the normative expressions of the Christian faith
found in scripture, upon which theology reflects, and with respect to the experience and self-understanding of contemporary
persons, upon which theology also must reflect. I have tried to
demonstrate that the question is not *whether* God is love, for both
the apostolic witness of faith and our experience of ourselves as
free subjects fulfilled in love for other persons demands that
God be conceived as love. The question is *how* this is to be done
most appropriately. A whole host of specific questions are raised
by the question of how God is to be conceived as love: To what
extent is divine love like human love? What limits, if any, are
placed on the use of concepts derived from our human experience of love when these concepts are applied to the divine
reality? For instance, does "God is love" imply a relatedness of
God to the creatures? If so, how is such a view to be reconciled
with the traditional Western philosophical and theological belief
that God is radically *a se* and not really related to the world? In
what sense is the divine love a free act of God? What relationship
is there between divine love and divine activity as a whole? How
do we know that "God is love" is true, granted that Christian
theology seemingly must affirm this to be the case?

I believe that Rahner's theology provides a rich and important resource for an adequate solution to these specific questions, all of which are raised by the more general question
concerning the meaning and truth of the assertion "God is love."

The initial step in this study will be to develop an understanding of Rahner's account of the meaning and truth of the assertion "God is love" (Part I). First, the meaning of the subject and predicate of this assertion in Rahner's thought must be established through an explication of the fundamental elements of his theological anthropology (Chapter III). Then, I will discuss what it means, according to him, to apply the predicate "love" to the subject "God," and on what grounds God can truthfully be said to be love. Rahner's view is that the ecstatic act in which God bestows Godself in love upon the nondivine realm is the fundamental act of God, which encompassses all divine activity (Chapter IV). And yet he holds that the divine love for others is a wholly free and gratuitous act on God's part, one that is demanded neither by the divine essence, nor by human nature (Chapter V). Next I will discuss the nature of the God-world relationship that Rahner holds is necessarily implied by the assertion "God is love" (Chapter VI).

The second step in this study will be to analyze critically Rahner's account of the meaning and truth of "God is love," using the very criteria for the adequacy of theological statements that Rahner himself proposes, namely, that theology must faithfully interpret the normative expressions of the Christian faith found in scripture, and that theology must credibly interpret the experience and self-understanding of contemporary persons (Part II). I will argue that Rahner's understanding of "God is love" is finally inadequate, when judged by these two criteria, because, although he clearly points in the direction of an adequate solution to the problem of the meaning and truth of the assertion "God is love," his thought finally leads to a threefold impasse. I will try to show that Rahner's chief claim concerning the God-world relationship, namely, that this relationship is a dialectic of identity and difference in which God, in God's other (the human nature of Jesus Christ), is relative to the world, while remaining strictly nonrelative in Godself, is either merely a verbal solution to the problem of the divine relativity that is raised by the divine love, or, in fact, entails a real relatedness of God in Godself, something Rahner clearly denies (Chapter VII). Next, I will argue that Rahner is able to defend the strict gratuity or freedom of the divine love only at the cost of denying that God is essentially love of others, a view that provides neither an adequate interpretation of the normative expression of the Christian witness of faith given in scripture, nor an adequate interpretation of our common human experience (Chapter VIII). Then, I will try to show, on the basis of several recent studies of the concept of love, that Rahner's view that divine love is to be understood as ecstatic self-communication necessarily presupposes something that Rahner explicitly denies: the real relatedness of God to other individuals (Chapter IX). Finally, I will suggest that these inconsistencies in Rahner's account of the divine love can be traced to the fact that, contrary to his own most fundamental intentions, Rahner has not carried through fully the modern turn to the subject in his reflections on the reality of God (Chapter X).

The final step will be to sketch the outlines of an alternative concept of God, one that will lead beyond the impasse created by Rahner's understanding of the divine love, while remaining true to his basic insights into the meaning and truth of the assertion "God is love" (Part III). The central affirmation of this alternative concept of God is that "God is love" is to be understood, on the basis of our own most fundamental experience of ourselves, to mean that God, too, is to be conceived as a free self-creating subject constituted by an essential relatedness to other free self-creating subjects. I will then try to illustrate how this understanding of God as essentially love of others avoids the impasse created by Rahner's thought and yet does not entail an ignoring or slighting of the concerns that led to the impasse, concerns such as: the existential independence of God, the sovereign activity of God in relation to the world, the freedom of God, the grace of God, the self-communication of God, and the essentially mysterious character of God (Chapter XI). Finally, I will show how this alternative view of God responds more adequately, than does Rahner's understanding of God, to the demand that contemporary theology must proclaim Christian faith in God in a way that is supportive of the struggle for the liberation of oppressed persons (Chapter XII).

NOTES

[1] *"Theos* im Neuen Testament," *ST,* 1:134 (ET: *TI,* 1:117). The German text reads "Gott der Väter in seinem Sohn," but I take this to be a

typographical error and assume, from the context, that Rahner means to say "Gott der Vater in seinem Sohn," that is, "God the Father in his Son," and not "God of the fathers in his Son."

2 I will have occasion to discuss the biblical, and particularly the New Testament, understandings of the claim "God is love," in some detail in Chapter VIII.

3 *GG,* p. 79 (ET: *FCF,* p. 71).

4 Ibid., pp. 79–83 (ET: ibid., pp. 71–75). "It is impossible for a Christian concept of creation to deny the assertion that that which is created, because it is caused by God, is *similar* to the cause. Therefore, that which is created 'participates' in the perfection of God according to the degree of its own ontological intensity of being. Otherwise, all positive statements concerning God would be absolutely impossible from the outset. The consequence of this would be a *theologia negativa,* which would be identical to atheism" ("Zum theologischen Begriff der Konkupiszenz," *ST,* 1:386, n. 1 (ET: *TI,* 1:356, n. 1)).

5 *GG,* pp. 81–82 (ET: *FCF,* pp. 73–74).

6 Ibid., p. 81 (ET: ibid., p. 73).

7 *HW,* p. 50.

8 Ibid., pp. 60–62.

9 Ibid., p. 61.

10 Ibid., pp. 63–64.

11 "Bemerkungen zur Gotteslehre in der katholischen Dogmatik," *ST,* 8:179–180 (ET: *TI,* 9:139).

12 "Gotteserfahrung heute," *ST,* 9:172–173 (ET: *TI,* 11:161–162).

13 Ibid., p. 173 (ET: ibid., p. 162).

14 "Der eine Mittler und die Vielfalt der Vermittlungen," *ST,* 8:228 (ET: *TI,* 9:178).

15 Rahner writes that there are four possible ways in which a person can be related to God: (1) a free, moral acceptance of one's transcendental relationship to God along with a proper thematization of that relationship; (2) a free, moral acceptance of one's transcendental relationship to God together with an inadequate or even explicitly atheistic thematization of one's transcendental experience; (3) a proper concept of God coupled with a free, sinful denial of one's transcendental relationship to God; (4) an improper or false concept of God and a sinful denial of one's transcendental relationship to God. See "Atheismus und implizites Christentum," *ST,* 8:200–202 (ET: *TI,* 9:155–157).

16 "Bemerkungen zur Gotteslehre in der katholischen Dogmatik," *ST,* 8:165–166 (ET: *TI,* 9:127–128).

17 This is not to deny that theology, as critical reflection upon faith, must make clear that the prior question of God is precisely the existentiell question of whether I will open myself in faith to God, others, and my own truest self or whether I will contradict myself ultimately by

denying in my acts my essential relatedness to God and others. While theology as reflection can show this to be the key question of human existence, it cannot answer this existentiell question. We answer this fundamental question with our whole personal being, not just with our minds.

18 *GG*, p. 83 (ET: *FCF*, p,. 75).

19 *Wirklichkeit und Glaube*, vol. 2: *Der persönliche Gott* (Göttingen: Vandenhoeck & Ruprecht, 1969), p. 68. Of course, as Rahner argues, along with Heidegger and Whitehead, the only metaphysical "forms of thought" that are critically justified are those that are derived from the implicit experience we have of ourselves as persons.

20 Ibid., pp. 74, 82, 96–97.

21 "Über die Einheit von Nächsten- und Gottesliebe," *ST*, 6:288 (ET: *TI*, 6:241).

22 "Selbsterfahrung und Gotteserfahrung," *ST*, 10:138 (ET: *TI*, 13:127).

23 "Bemerkungen zur Gotteslehre in der katholischen Dogmatik," *ST*, 8:171–172 (ET: *TI*, 9:132–133). The same thing could be said, it seems to me, of much of contemporary Protestant theology.

24 "Christologie im Rahmen des modernen Selbst- und Weltverständnisses," *ST*, 9:233–237 (ET: *TI*, 11:221–225).

25 "Bemerkungen zur Gotteslehre in der katholischen Dogmatik," *ST*, 8:175–177 (ET: *TI*, 9:136–137).

26 See "Über das Verhältnis von Natur und Gnade," *ST*, 1:343 (ET: *TI*, 1:316) and "*Theos* im Neuen Testament," *ST*, 1:119–143 (ET: *TI*, 1:104–125).

27 Cf. "Der Mensch von heute und die Religion," *ST*, 6:15 (ET: *TI*, 6:5).

28 Ibid., p. 19 (ET: ibid., p. 8).

29 Ibid., p. 20 (ET: ibid., pp. 8–9).

30 See "Experiment Mensch," *ST*, 8:260–285 (ET: *TI*, 9:205–224).

31 Ibid., pp. 270–272 (ET: ibid., pp. 213–214).

32 "Der Mensch von heute und die Religion," *ST*, 6:26–27 (ET: *TI*, 6:14–15).

33 "Heilsauftrag der Kirche und Humanisierung der Welt," *ST*, 10:554–555 (ET: *TI*, 14:301–303).

34 *A Theology of Liberation*, pp. 46–47.

35 "Der Mensch von heute und die Religion," *ST*, 6:25–26 (ET: *TI*, 6:13–14).

36 "Heilsauftrag der Kirche und Humanisierung der Welt," *ST*, 10:555 (ET: *TI*, 14:302).

37 "Die Unfähigkeit zur Armut in der Kirche," *ST*, 10:521–522 (ET: *TI*, 14:271–272).

38 "Heilsauftrag der Kirche und Humanisierung der Welt," *ST*, 10:555 (ET: *TI*, 14:302).

39 "Zur Theologie der Revolution," *ST*, 10:577 (ET: *TI*, 14:322).

40 "Die Unfähigkeit zur Armut in der Kirche," *ST*, 10:521 (ET: *TI*, 14:271).

41 "Zur Theologie der Revolution," *ST*, 10:578–579 (ET: *TI*, 14:323–324).

42 "Die Unfähigkeit zur Armut in der Kirche," *ST*, 10:521–522 (ET: *TI*, 14:271–272).

43 "Zur Theologie der Revolution," *ST*, 10:573 (ET: *TI*, 14:318–319).

44 Ibid., p. 574 (ET: ibid., pp. 319–320).

45 "Theologie und Anthropologie," *ST*, 8:57–58 (ET: *TI*, 9:39–40). In this same passage, Rahner argues that such a re-orientation in philosophy does not represent the end of transcendental anthropology, for the main concern of this left-wing Hegelian and Neo-Marxian thought is still "man and his being, which he himself has submitted to planning and thus also to that which is beyond his control." In a similar fashion, I would argue that the current awareness of the concrete oppression of persons does not contradict the affirmation that human beings have an immediate awareness of themselves as free, responsible subjects. In fact, it is precisely the transcendental awareness of the essential dignity and freedom of human persons that makes all forms of bondage so intolerable.

46 "Glaube als Mut," *ST*, 13:255.

47 "Die Unfähigkeit zur Armut in der Kirche," *ST*, 10:522 (ET: *TI*, 14:272).

48 "Liberation, Theology and Proclamation," trans. J. P. Donnelly, in *The Mystical and Political Dimension of the Christian Faith*, ed. Claude Geffré and Gustavo Gutierrez (New York: Herder & Herder, 1974), p. 69.

49 "Theologie der Freiheit," *ST*, 6:227 (ET: *TI*, 6:188).

50 "Über die Einheit von Nächsten- und Gottesliebe," *ST*, 6:288 (ET: *TI*, 6:241).

51 Ibid., p. 289 (ET: ibid., p. 242). Rahner does not intend, in statements such as this, to deny the reality of hate. Hate is a real possibility for human persons; although it is an inauthentic possibility. Hate represents the radical nonfulfillment of the human person.

52 "Christlicher Humanismus," *ST*, 8:240–241 (ET: *TI*, 9:188).

53 "Experiment Mensch," *ST*, 8:280–281 (ET: *TI*, 9:221).

54 "Zur Theologie der Revolution," *ST*, 10:570–571 (ET: *TI*, 14:316–317).

55 "Les masses pauvres," in *Eglise et pauvreté*, ed. G. Cottier, et. al., Unam Sanctam, no. 57 (Paris: Editions du Cerf, 1965), p. 174.

[56] "Über die Einheit von Nächsten- und Gottesliebe," *ST*, 6:278 (ET: *TI*, 6:232).

[57] "Bemerkungen zur Gotteslehre in der katholischen Dogmatik," *ST*, 8:179–180 (ET: *TI*, 9:139).

[58] "Heilsauftrag der Kirche und Humanisierung der Welt," *ST*, 10:562 (ET: *TI*, 14:308–309).

[59] *GG*, p. 74 (ET: *FCF*, pp. 65–66).

PART I
RAHNER'S CONCEPT OF GOD

CHAPTER III
TRANSCENDENTAL ANTHROPOLOGY AND THEOLOGY

The first step in this investigation of Rahner's understanding of the meaning and truth of the assertion "God is love" must be to establish the meaning of the subject and predicate terms of this assertion in his thought. This involves an exposition of his theological anthropology. But if, for Rahner, theological anthropology is in some sense coextensive with the whole of Christian theology, and not simply one particular theme within theology, then a fully adequate exposition of Rahner's theological anthropology would require a full length study in its own right.[1] It should be obvious, therefore, that I cannot offer an adequate treatment of Rahner's theological anthropology in this chapter. I hope to accomplish just three modest goals in the following discussion: to outline briefly the key elements in Rahner's understanding of the human person, demonstrating the centrality of the concepts of freedom and love in his theological anthropology; to show that God, according to Rahner, is unthematically, but necessarily, affirmed to be the transcendental horizon and goal of human freedom and love; and to indicate the basic view of the divine reality that Rahner derives from his analysis of human transcendence.[2]

Human Being as Spiritual

A helpful point of entrance into Rahner's transcendental anthropology is suggested by the title of his first major work: *Geist in Welt (Spirit in World)*. In the Preface to the book, he indicates that the term "world" in the title refers to the "reality that is accessible to the immediate experience of man."[3] That is to say, "world" refers to the material world. Therefore, the title of the book calls our attention to two concepts, "spirit" and

"matter." Rahner holds that spirit and matter can only be understood properly "as moments of the one man, moments in which
the primordially unitary essence of man necessarily displays and
unfolds itself."[4] If this essential unity of spirit and matter is kept
in mind, then there should be no confusion when, in what
follows, the two moments of the one essence of human being are
discussed separately.

> *Spirit* is the one man is so far as he comes to himself in an
> absolute   having-been-given   to   self   [ein
> Sichselbstgegebensein]; precisely such that he is always
> already referred to the absoluteness of reality as such
> and to its one ground, called God; and such that this
> return to himself and being referred to the absolute
> totality of possible reality, and to its ground, mutually
> condition one another.[5]

According to this definition, the spiritual moment of human
being has two mutually conditioning aspects. First, the human
being is characterized as a subject or a person.[6] In all acts of
human experience, the human person not only knows or wills
the object of its experience, but is also aware of and affirms itself
precisely as the subject of this experience. This awareness and
affirmation of self is a necessary element in human experience.
But this self-experience, although always present, is different
from the experience of objects. An object is directly or explicitly
experienced, while the subject co-experiences itself indirectly or
implicitly along with the experience of an object. Such self-
experience often is not brought to conscious awareness. It can
easily be passed over, for the co-experience of the self does not
present the self as an object of experience. The self or subject is
present, rather, as the illuminated space within which objects
appear as known or willed. The subject's implicit experience of
itself is a condition of the possibility of the explicit experience of
objects.

Rahner asserts, therefore, that the essence of the act of
knowledge is not "a coming into contact with something," or "an
intentional stretching outwards" of the knower, but is rather "the
Beisichsein [being with self] of being."[7] Knowing is the self-lumi-
nosity, or being reflected into itself, of being. Likewise, the act of
freedom (will), primordially, is not the choice or taking possession of a particular object, but is a taking possession of self on
the part of the willing or free subject.[8] Willing is the coming to

itself (*das Zuschselberkommen*) of the subject. In all genuinely human activity (and knowing and willing represent two basic modes of human activity for Rahner) there is a return of the subject to itself, a *reditio in seipsum* . It is this return of the subject to itself that allows objects of experience to be experienced in their differentiation from the subject itself.[9]

The other aspect of the spiritual moment of human being, which conditions and is conditioned by the return of the subject to itself, is the human subject's being always already referred to, or oriented toward, the whole of reality, including the divine ground of reality.[10] Rahner characterizes human being as essentially dynamic and restless. He states that human being "remains fundamentally always on the way."[11] Human being is open and unfinished. This is apparent in the human ability to ask questions. Persons can bring everything into question. Each individual assertion can be questioned on the basis of other assertions. Each answer is the occasion for new questions. Likewise, in human action, each accomplished goal is "always already relativized as something provisional, as a stage."[12]

This characteristic human ability to call everything into question provides the starting point for Rahner's metaphysical anthropology in *Hörer des Wortes*. To call everything into question, to be unsatisfied with all particular answers, is to ask the question of being.

> [Man] wants to know what everything is, particularly in its unity, in which everything always already encounters him. He asks after the final backgrounds; he asks after the one ground of all things; and, in so far as he knows every individual thing as existent [*seiend*], he asks after the being of all that is [*nach dem Sein alles Seienden*].[13]

This question about being is implied in all other questions persons ask. Therefore, Rahner says, the human person in her or his every act is always already doing metaphysics.

That the question of being is so unfailingly asked by persons presupposes that that which is (*das Seiende*) is knowable.[14] Because of the fundamental unity of knowing and being, everything that is, to the degree that it is, is with itself (*beisich*), luminous, and thus knowable. The ability to ask the question of the being of this particular being also presupposees that human beings are open to all reality and have some prior awareness of being, such that a particular being can be distinguished from being as such. In the act of knowing any particular being, the human subject is already "beyond" this immediate object and has an awareness of the whole range of possible objects, or being as such.[15] In this sense human being is *quodammodo omnia* (in a certain sense everything).[16]

But just as the human subject's knowledge of itself was seen to be an implicit, nonobjective co-knowing accompanying the act of knowing an object, so this necessary knowledge of being is of a different type than the knowledge of particular beings. Rahner holds that "what being is, is indeed always already manifest and acknowledged, but not known thematically."[17] In *Geist in Welt*, in interpreting the *excessus ad esse* of Thomas, Rahner introduces the term *"Vorgriff"* (pregrasp) to characterize the particular type of knowledge persons have of being.[18] Human beings have a *Vorgriff*, a pregrasp of being that accompanies the objective grasp of particular beings. "The *Vorgriff* is the . . . opening of the horizon within which the individual object of human knowledge is known."[19] The horizon of human knowledge (being as such) is not itself an *object* of knowledge. It is rather the space within which objects of knowledge appear. This horizon, that toward which the *Vorgriff* is directed, is necessarily co-known in each act of objective knowing.

Further, according to Rahner, without this *Vorgriff* of being, the human knowledge of particular beings would not be possible. Individual objects or beings could not be judged to be individual or particular unless human knowers had some awareness of the horizon of the whole of being against which the particular could be contrasted. Without a prior awareness of the universal (being), the individual (a particular being) would not be recognizable as such.

> The *Vorgriff* is the condition of the possibility of the universal concept, of the abstraction which, in return, is the making possible of the objectification of that which is sensibly given, and so, the making possible of the knowing self-subsistence [of the human person].[20]

Rahner's long chapter on abstraction in *Geist in Welt* might be summarized by saying that, without the *Vorgriff* of being, the human person would simply be given over to the world in sense experience (*praesentia mundi*), but could not, in thought, recognize the object of sense experience as an object set over against the subject *(oppositio mundi)*. Only if such an objectification of the object of experience is accomplished can the subject return fully to itself as an autonomous subject set over against *its* world of experience.

With this background, we can now discuss Rahner's understanding of transcendental experience. Because it is so central to his thought, a rather lengthy citation, in which transcendental experience is defined, is called for.

> We call the subjective, unthematic co-consciousness [*das Mitbewusstsein*] of the knowing subject, which is necessarily and unfailingly co-given in every spiritual act of knowledge, and the subject's openness to the unlimited breadth of all possible reality *transcendental experience*. It is an experience because this knowing of an unthematic, but inescapable, sort is a moment in and condition of the possibility of every concrete experience of any object whatsoever. This experience is called *transcendental* experience because it belongs to the necessary structures of the knowing subject itself (which cannot be abrogated) and because it consists precisely in the surpassing [*der Übersteig*] of a specific group of possible objects and categories. Transcendental experience is the experience of transcendence *(die Transzendenz)*, in which experience the structure of the subject and with it the final structure of all conceivable objects of knowledge are given together and in identity. Of course, this transcendental experience is not merely an experience of pure knowledge, but also of will and freedom, to which belong the same character of transcendentality, so that, fundamentally, the goal and source of the subject as one who knows and as one who is free can always be asked after together.[21]

On the basis of this definition and the previous discussion of spirit, it can be said that, for Rahner, human being is characterized as spiritual because persons unfailingly have such transcendental experience. Further, this definition makes clear that the unthematic experience of self and the unthematic experience of being (the openness to all of reality), which together constitute transcendental experience, are not simply coordinate with other forms of human experience, but are in fact necessary conditions of the possibility of other forms of human experience. Finally, Rahner indicates in this passage his belief that both human knowledge and freedom reveal the transcendentality of the human person.

Before we look at Rahner's account of transcendental experience in detail, it should be noted that some critics have detected
a certain equivocation in his use of the term "transcendental."
Bert van der Heijden asserts: "Transcendental means, according
to Rahner: (1) the quality of a particular mode of knowledge and
(2) the quality of a particular mode of being that is connected
with the transcendental mode of knowing."[22] In its first meaning, according to van der Heijden, "transcendental" is synonymous with "nonobjectively co-known," and refers to the way
in which persons know themselves, being, and God. Here, "objective," "conceptual," "thematic," and "categorial" are antonyms
of "transcendental." In its second meaning, "transcendental"
refers to *some* of the realities that correspond to our transcendental (first meaning) way of knowing. Here, "transcendental"
refers not to our "knowing in a nonobjective [*ungegenständlich*]
fashion," but rather to "that which *is* transobjective [*übergegen-
ständlich*]." "Categorial" is also an antonym of "transcendental" in
this second meaning of the term, but here, "categorial" refers to
"that which is comprehensible in categories." Those realities,
according to van der Heijden, which are "categorial" in this
second sense "do not coincide with the entire extent of the
horizon [of knowledge] and thus can be gathered into basic
groups within the horizon."

Up to this point, it seems to me, van der Heijden indicates a
genuine ambiguity in Rahner: the transcendental/categorial contrast is ambiguous in that it is used, on the one hand, as equivalent to the thematic/unthematic contrast, while, on the other
hand, it is used to refer to two sets of concepts, of which one set
applies universally to all of reality, while the other does not. But
van der Heijden also holds that the transcendental/categorial
distinction ("transcendental" in its second meaning), in Rahner,
is equivalent to the distinction between the fullness of being: the
perfect subjectivity of absolute being, or God, and that which is
not the fullness of being: finite being, being that is deficient in
subjectivity.[23] Alexander Gerken agrees that Rahner identifies
the transcendental with the infinite and the categorial with the
finite.[24] This, I think, is a misrepresentation. While Rahner
certainly uses the adjective "transcendent" to refer to the absolute or infinite being of God, in such cases, he seems consistently
to avoid the use of "categorial" as a contrasting term to "transcendent." Unfortunately, neither van der Heijden nor Gerken

give any citations from Rahner to support their claims at this point. This is particularly striking in van der Heijden's case, for elsewhere in his book, his criticisms of Rahner are extensively documented. While it is possible that there are passages where Rahner does use the transcendental/categorial contrast in this way, van der Heijden and Gerken have not indicated such passages. Furthermore, it seems clear that in Rahner's most definitive statements such a usage is avoided.

Many interpreters of Rahner focus their attention exclusively on his account of the transcendentality of human knowledge. This seems to me to be a one-sided approach. There are good reasons for orienting an analysis of Rahner's view of the transcendentality of the human person around the phenomenon of free human acting, as I do in the following pages, rather than around the phenomenon of human knowing. First of all, since Rahner holds love to be the full, authentic realization of the transcendental freedom of the human person, this orientation of our discussion toward freedom, rather than toward knowledge, is of more immediate use in accomplishing the primary task of this chapter, namely, an identification of the meaning of the terms "love" and "God" in Rahner's thought. Secondly, Rahner himself has always acknowledged a certain priority of freedom and love in relation to knowledge in an adequate understanding of human being. He says that the final fulfillment of the human person is to be found in love not in knowledge. He even argues that "knowledge is fulfilled in its *own* essence and meaning only when and in so far as the subject is more than knowledge, that is, precisely free love."[25] The third reason why I wish to emphasize Rahner's understanding of the trascendentality of freedom is to contribute to an overcoming of the one-sidedly intellectualistic approach to his theological anthropology.[26] While only the chapter as a whole can fully justify the soundness and the helpfulness of my approach to Rahner's thought, an initial justification of it, in dialogue with other interpreters of Rahner, is called for.

Peter Eicher orients his detailed explication of Rahner's anthropology around the question of being as Rahner develops this question in his metaphysics of knowledge.[27] In the first three parts of the book, which are entitled, respectively: "Introduction to the transcendental-philosophical anthropology," "The anthropological turn," and, most significantly, "The on-

tological constitution of man," the human person is considered
solely as a knower. Only in the brief fourth part of the book,
entitled "The unfolding of anthropology," is Rahner's view of
the human person as a free actor considered. Bert van der
Heijden writes that Rahner's treatment of the self-realization *(der
Selbstvollzug)* of the human person is:

> Often restricted in the sense that only the conditions of
> the possibility of knowing, and particularly those of the
> objectifying knowledge of being, are considered. . . .
> Later [i.e., in the development of Rahner's thought] fur-
> ther dimensions of man are also explicitly thematized in
> a transcendental fashion. But the essence of [Rahner's]
> total view remains always the transcendental considera-
> tion of the realization [*der Vollzug*] of knowledge from
> the standpoint of the objectification of the question of
> being.[28]

There is no question that Rahner, in *Geist in Welt,* restricts
his attention to the conditions of the possibility of knowing.
After all, the subtitle of the book is "On the metaphysics of finite
knowledge according to Thomas Aquinas." There is no attempt
in *Geist in Welt* to display the transcendental structures of the
human person as a whole. But in *Hörer des Wortes,* Rahner is
concerned to portray the human subject as the one who necessarily listens for a possible word from God in history. Here the
emphasis is still on the conditions of knowledge, but there is
nevertheless an extended discussion which seeks to uncover the
transcendental conditions of human freedom.[29] In this discussion, the central proposition of Rahner's full understanding of
the transcendentality of freedom is already anticipated: a free
act is the decision of the human subject for or against her- or
himself.[30] In the first volume of *Schriften zur Theologie,* Rahner
makes clear that this free self-disposition of the human subject is
always also a disposition of the human subject over against
God.[31] He writes:

> Such a human decision of freedom can be more closely
> qualified in two ways: it is first of all, an act through
> which man is explicitly or implicitly placed before God,
> the absolute good, and decides before God, in so far as
> God is at least implicitly comprehended in every free
> decision. . . . The free decision of man is, second, an act
> through which man disposes of himself as a whole.[32]

In the subsequent volumes of *Schriften zur Theologie* there are a number of essays which are either entirely or in large part devoted to a transcendental consideration of human freedom and its fulfillment in love.[33] In these essays, Rahner's mature position on the transcendentality of freedom is stated over and over again. Indeed, in Rahner's essays dating from the 1960s and 1970s, contrary to van der Heijden's claim, it is the question of freedom and not the question of knowledge which is at the heart of Rahner's work. Finally, in *Grundkurs des Glaubens*, Rahner is careful to refer simultaneously to the transcendentality of knowledge and of freedom.[34]

Human freedom, according to Rahner, reveals the same structure of transcendentality as does human knowledge, namely, the free human person has a necessary orientation to her- or himself and a concomitant orientation to God. Within the horizon of these mutually conditioning moments (the return to self and the openness to God) all concrete human activity takes place. Rahner characterizes human being as "the radically open, unfinished [*unfertig*], entity."[35] In language that is taken directly from Heidegger, Rahner says

> . . . man is that particular being for whom, in his being, his being itself is an issue, who always already has a relationship to himself, who is subjectivity not simply nature, always already a person, never simply neutrally there [*vorfindlich*], but always already personally situated [*befindlich*].[36]

Human beings, in distinction to things, have no final, finished nature determined for them from the outset. Rather, whatever fulfillment or finality the person achieves, is chosen freely by her- or himself.[37] Freedom in this sense is a freedom of being (*eine Seinsfreiheit*) and is a transcendental or essential determination of the human person.[38] Freedom is the human person's taking responsibility for her- or himself that is an element in all human activity.[39] Thus, for Rahner,

> . . . freedom is primordially not the ability to choose an object nor the ability to choose a particular way of relating oneself to this or that, but is the freedom of self-understanding, the possibility of saying yes or no to oneself, the possibility of decision for or against oneself.[40]

Just as in human knowing, so in an act of human freedom, there is a necessary return of the human subject to itself. A free act is, for Rahner,

> . . . not so much the positing of another, something that is alien, a work that stands over against the act itself in otherness, but is the fulfilling of [the subject's] own essence, a taking possession of itself, a taking possession of the reality of its own creative power over itself.[41]

In freedom the human subject disposes of itself as a whole.[42] The free person, primordially, does not choose something, but chooses itself; the free person does not first of all do something, but does itself. Freedom is the self-realization of the human person:

> Freedom in itself cannot be understood . . . as a neutral ability to do this or that in some sort of serial order and in a temporality that would be broken up only from outside. Rather, freedom is the ability to do oneself once for all. It is the ability that is directed essentially toward the freely accomplished final validity of the subject as such.[43]

But at the same time, this ability of the human subject to create itself is conditioned by (and conditions) a necessary orientation of the human person toward the absolute good, which is God. "[O]nly in the dynamism toward the absolute good can the finite good be freely affirmed or rejected."[44] Just as individual, concrete objects of knowledge can only be known as the human person grasps the unlimited horizon of all possible objects of knowledge, so the immediate object of valuation and choice can be grasped only because the free human actor transcends these particular objects. "Genuine personal freedom is only possible where the particular good and the particular value is surpassed, in transcendentality, through a *Vorgriff* toward the absolute good as such, even if unthematically."[45] There is, therefore, a necessary, if unthematic, affirmation or *Vorgriff* of God as the absolute value that makes concrete, particular acts of free choice possible.

Human Being as Material

Thus far in this discussion of Rahner's anthropology human being has been considered solely as spirit. But, for him, human being is not pure spirit. Persons do not return fully to themselves. The human knower is not fully with her- or himself (*beisich*). The free human actor, notwithstanding what was said above, does not fully succeed in constituting her- or himself in accordance with her or his existentiell plans. "There remains always and essentially a gap between what man is simply as an existent entity (as 'nature') and what he, in his free decision (as 'person'), wishes to accomplish; between what he is passively and the self that he actively posits."[46] Likewise, the dynamic human orientation toward the whole of reality is not complete. There is an orientation toward being as such in human transcendence, but not a possession of being. Persons have a *Vor-griff*, an anticipatory grasp of being, including the absolute being of God, but not a full and perfect comprehension *(Be-griff)* of being. This is the case because human being is finite spirit, spirit essentially related to the world, material spirit.

It is important to note that matter, in Rahner's thought, is not disparaged even though it is the principle of human finitude. He criticizes, as erroneous and heretical, the view of matter "as that which is dark, opposed to God, ominous, chaotic, . . . which stands in contradiction to, and in bitter struggle with, spirit, the true likeness and representative of God."[47] Rather, he holds that the goodness of matter is a consequence of the Christian dogma of creation. Matter is a means by which human spirit comes to its own fulfillment. Matter is not in and of itself a hindrance to the fulfillment of human spirit, even if the materiality of human being does clearly differentiate this fulfillment from the perfection of absolute or divine spirit.

In the same passage from which the definition of spirit cited above was taken, Rahner offers his definition of matter.

> As matter, man comprehends himself and the environment that belongs necessarily to him such that the act of returning to himself in the experience of being referred to the mystery that must be accepted in love [i.e., God], always and primarily occurs only in an encounter with that which is individual, with that which manifests itself, with that which is concrete and cannot be disposed of, and with that which is finite, even though it is unfailingly given. . . . Matter is the condition of the possibility of that which is objectively other; the condition of that which we experience immediately as space and time (precisely when we cannot objectify it conceptually); the con-

dition of the otherness that alienates man from himself
and in so doing brings him to himself; and the condition
of the possibility of an immediate intercommunication
with other spiritual subjects in space and time which
constitutes history. Matter is the ground of the prior
givenness of the other as the material of freedom.[48]

According to this definition, the return of the human subject to itself and its orientation toward God (i.e., the spiritual
moment of human being) is given only through an encounter
with other finite realities. Rahner holds that "all creaturely spirituality has an essential relation to matter, because, finally, even if
in different ways, creaturely spirituality is receptive and intercommunicative spirituality (even in the case of 'angels')."[49] For
him, the meaning of the material moment of human being is to
be sought in the receptive and intercommunicative character of
human being.

In *Geist in Welt* and *Hörer des Wortes*, Rahner argues that the
being with self *(das Beisichsein)* of the human knower is primordially or essentially a being with another in knowledge.[50] "Man
has [knowledge] only in that an object from itself, shows itself to
him. . . . He is only with himself [*bei sich*] in that he grasps
another object that is distinct from him, an object that must
encounter him."[51] How this can be the case is not immediately
clear, for, in both books, knowledge has already been defined as
the being with self of being and not as an intentional stretching
out of the knower to the known. Is it not a contradiction to say
that knowing is being with self and at the same time assert that
knowing is a receptive being with another? With respect to this
apparent contradiction, Rahner points out that "being with self"
(das Beisichsein), like "being" *(das Sein)*, is an analogical concept.
Human being is not absolute being, and so human being cannot
be characterized by absolute *Beisichsein*. Only in the case of the
divine being is there complete, perfect *Beisichsein*.[52]

Rahner goes on to fill out the content of this formal affirmation that human knowing is *Beisichsein* and, at the same time,
Beim-anderen-sein (being with another). Rahner holds that for
human knowing to be *Beisichsein* precisely by way of *Beim-anderen-sein*

> . . . the knower itself must be the being of the other as
> such. The being of the entity that intuits receptively
> must be the being of another. . . . Only if a being is

> ontologically divorced from itself in such a way that it is not being of its own being but being of the "other," can it have the possibility of possessing an alien actuality as its own, such that everything that is its own is simply something alien, because the being of the knower in question is not being for itself but being for and in another.[53]

This means that precisely as with itself *(beisich)*, the human knower bears within her- or himself the principle of otherness that makes receptive knowing possible. In other words, in one aspect of its being, the human subject *is* that other.[54] The human subject is not absolutely with self, not fully actual. Rather, the human subject stands "permanently in potentiality, is undetermined and therefore determinable."[55] For a being to be given over to another, to be potential and not fully actual, to be receptive and not fully self-subsistent, is, to use Thomistic terminology, to be material. Matter is, in the most primordial sense of the word, nothing but this principle of otherness, possibility, and receptivity.

On the basis of this Thomistic understanding of matter, Rahner argues that the material human person is spatial and temporal.[56] His understanding of space and time is not derived from human sense experience, but rather from the existentiell experience the human person has of her- or himself. Therefore, spatiality is presented not in terms of extension, but in terms of plurality. Matter is the condition of the possibility of a repetition of that which is essentially the same. The material is composed of a number of genuinely discrete entities, which are, nevertheless, all alike in being material. This plurality, this quantitative nature of the material is nothing other than spatiality.[57] Rahner understands temporality not as "the external measure of the duration of the presence on hand [*die Vorhandenheit*] of a thing," but as "the inner stretching of a thing itself into the realized wholeness of its possibilities."[58] This stretching of an entity toward its own fulfillment is a dynamic process. Each individual possibility is oriented toward another, futural possibility which lifts the original possibility to a higher level by partially preserving and partially cancelling it. Temporality is the process by which a human person realizes her- or himself. Indeed, human beings alone are temporal in a primordial sense. "Man possesses himself, disposes of himself, understands himself in that he retains his past in *anamnesis* [*anamnetisch seine Vergangenheit behält*] and already allows the outstanding future to be present in *prognosis* [*prognostisch die ausständige Zukunft schon anwesend lässt*]."[59]

Because human being is not characterized by an absolute *Beisichsein*, human being is spatial. The human subject is not internally simple but possesses thought only through the mediation of the senses (a *conversio ad phantasma*).[60] Nor is human being simple when taken racially. There is a plurality of individual human persons. This means that the self-realization of the human person, the subject's return to itself, occurs only through the mediation of objects of sensibility and, more importantly, through the mediation of other persons. Likewise, because human being is not characterized by an absolute *Beisichsein*, human being is temporal. The human subject does not fully possess itself in a single moment. There is a sequential nature to human being. This means that the self-realization of the human person, the subject's return to itself, occurs only through a continuous process of retaining past moments of self-realization (*anamnesis*) and projecting future possibilities (*prognosis*).

Human Being as Interpersonal

Although more could be said about Rahner's understanding of the receptive character of human knowledge, I wish to focus my discussion of the material aspect of human being around the interpersonal character of human freedom, for the same reasons that I emphasized the transcendental character of human freedom, rather than of knowledge, above.

A number of critics have questioned the adequacy of Rahner's treatment of the interpersonal nature of human being. Metz, in his foreword to the second edition of *Hörer des Wortes*, speaks of the need to supplement Rahner's argument in the first edition by transposing "the (Thomistic) concept of the world of objects into the more primordial concept of a (personal) shared world [*eine Mitwelt*]."[61] Two of Rahner's strongest critics at this point are Eberhard Simons and Alexander Gerken.[62] Simons argues that Rahner's metaphysical anthropology developed in *Hörer des Wortes* illuminates only the conditions of the possibility of the knowledge of sense objects, and does not account for the knowledge of another human person, who is a Thou and not a thing.[63] According to Simons, Rahner ignores the fact that "man essentially stands over against an 'object,' which, in its own right, is also a subject."[64] Gerken asserts that his own book can be viewed as a theological criticism of Rahner that parallels Simons' philosophical criticism.[65] Gerken charges, with respect to Rahner's theology, that

> . . . the significance of the personal for the act of faith is too lightly assessed because it is viewed solely as the "categorialization" of that which is nonobjective and transcendent. Despite the effort not to conceive faith as a mere holding-to-be-true of propositions, Rahner does not achieve a genuinely personal concept of faith."[66]

While the arguments of Simons and Gerken are both flawed rather seriously, the key question concerning the role of the interpersonal aspect of human being in Rahner's anthropology remains.[67]

A number of interpreters of Rahner reject Simons' and Gerken's criticisms as one-sided and maintain that Rahner does indeed seek to integrate an understanding of the importance of the interpersonal aspect of human being into his anthropology. These interpreters, however, hold that this integration is not fully successful. Bert van der Heijden writes: "Many of Simons' critical remarks can, with a more exacting attentiveness to what Rahner really wants to say, be construed as an appropriate explication of *Hörer des Wortes*."[68] Van der Heijden argues that Rahner gives more explicit consideration to the interpersonal nature of human being in his later works. But he judges that Rahner's treatment of the interpersonal nature of human being remains finally "limited to statements that are merely asserted after the fact and to incidental, partial reflections."[69] Klaus Fischer holds that although Rahner begins to express himself in terms of the dialogical principle of Martin Buber and others in his later works, he, nevertheless, "does not advance to a systematic, transcendental grounding of the 'dialogical principle.'"[70] Anselm Grün argues that in Rahner's most recent works the anthropological starting point is precisely the human encounter with other persons.[71] Earlier, according to Grün, Rahner began with the human knowledge of things and extended his reflections first to the personal and finally to the interpersonal realms. But, adds Grün, "when Rahner speaks of a transcendental grounding of intersubjectivity, he indicates more of a desire than a fully executed achievement."[72]

My own assessment of this issue is as follows. There is no

doubt that the interpersonal nature of human being is hardly considered at all in *Geist in Welt*. There, the problem is how a human knower bound to a world of sensible objects can also have a knowledge of being. But, in *Geist in Welt*, it is crucial that matter is portrayed at the necessary condition for human receptivity, spatiality, and temporality.[73] In *Hörer des Wortes*, where Rahner raises the question of how it is possible for human being to attend to a free revelation of God, this characterization of matter given in *Geist in Welt* becomes the basis upon which Rahner's understanding of the historical character of human being is built. Here the foundations of a view of interpersonal human existence are laid: as spatial and temporal, the human person exists in essential relatedness to other persons in history.[74] Nevertheless, the discussions of *Geist in Welt* and *Hörer des Wortes* remain oriented toward the human knowledge of material objects.

Although in the first four volumes of the *Schriften zur Theologie* Rahner's emphasis is on the personal nature of human being, that is, the self-realization of the individual human subject in knowledge and freedom, still, there are passages where relations to other persons are viewed as essential to the self-realization of the individual.[75] In an essay entitled "Theologisches zum Monogenismus," which first appeared in 1954, one finds the following unequivocal statement:

> Personal spirit is spirit that is directed toward the other. Absolutely solitary spirit is a contradiction in itself and is—insofar as there can be such—hell. If [man is to be conceived as spirit] then this means that the embodied spirit that man is, exists necessarily in relation to a Thou. . . . Whoever posits man, posits necessarily, not only factually, human community, that is bodily, personal, and spatio-temporal human community.[76]

Then, throughout Rahner's later essays, beginning with "Die Christologie innerhalb einer evolutiven Weltanschauung," there are numerous statements that reflect an explicit, well-developed position on the interpersonal nature of human being. It seems to me that to charge that Rahner only envisions, but does not fully achieve, a consistent position on human intersubjectivity (Anselm Grün), is to require of Rahner something that he need not provide. Certainly, Rahner has never written a study designed to provide a philosophical account of human intersubjectivity. Rahner's discussions of the interpersonal nature of human being are always carried out in connection with or in preparation for discussions of christology, the doctrine of grace, the doctrine of God, or some other theological topic. But the fact that Rahner has not provided "a systematic transcendental grounding of the dialogical principle" (Klaus Fischer), does not mean that his appropriation of such a principle for his own theological purposes is inadequate. And, finally, Rahner's reflections on human intersubjectivity are "incidental" (Bert van der Heijden) in precisely the same sense in which his discussions of christology or nature and grace are incidental or occasional. If Rahner's view of human intersubjectivity is inadequate because of the occasional style of the essays in which it is elucidated, then Rahner's theology as a whole must be judged to be inadequate for the same reason. In the remainder of this section I will seek to explicate Rahner's mature view of human intersubjectivity, that is, the essential relatedness of the human person.

For Rahner, human being, because it is material spirit, is not fully *beisich*, but only comes to itself, only realizes itself, through the mediation of an "other." Whereas earlier this "other" was not specified (beyond saying that it, like the knowing or willing subject, is material), it must now be shown that this "other" is precisely another human subject. According to Rahner, "the personal Thou [is] the mediation of the being with self [*das Beisichsein*] of the subject."[77] Or, likewise: "Man only comes to himself in the encounter with the other man, who is presented historically to one's experience in knowledge and love, who is not a thing but a man."[78] The other person, the human Thou is neither a projection of the I, nor simply an aspect of the self-realization of the I. The Thou stands over against the I in her or his own reality. The Thou is equiprimordial with the I and makes possible the experience of the I as a subject. "In knowledge and freedom, which are the concrete realization of life, the I is always related to a Thou, is primordially as much with the Thou, as with the I, always only experiences itself as differentiated from, and identified with, the other in the encounter with the other person."[79]

It cannot be stressed strongly enough that, for Rahner, this intersubjectivity or relatedness to others is essential to human being.

> The intercommunication [i.e., intersubjectivity] in its in-
> exorability, in which the other is always there necessarily,
> making demands of me and sustaining me, would be
> merely apparent if I could withdraw myself into a region
> where I was absolutely alone, and where no other, who
> would be necessary for me or for whom I would be
> partly responsible, could follow.[80]

The other person does not exist alongside, but is a necessary
moment in, my self-realization as an individual.

This discussion reveals that the transcendentality of the
human person, which is implicitly affirmed in all human activity,
does not consist of two aspects: a return of the subject to itself
and an openness to or orientation toward being as such and
therefore God (as will be shown in the next section), but three.
The necessary orientation toward or relatedness to other human
persons is also a transcendental aspect of human being. Rahner
states that

> . . . these three relations of the subject: to itself, to God,
> to the other [person] do not simply stand side by side
> and separate from one another like the relationships the
> individual subject has to different contingent states of
> affairs or to objects of a posteriori experience, but are
> necessarily given together as mutually conditioning in
> every act of the spiritual and free subject (whatever this
> act may be), even if unthematically and unreflectively.[81]

Therefore, for Rahner, human freedom understood in the primordial sense of the taking possession of self on the part of the
human subject occurs only along with, and because of, a necessary relatedness of the human subject to other persons and God.

This orientation toward or relatedness to other persons may
take different forms (such as love or hate), but in any case the
Thou is there with the I necessarily.

> The one basic moral (or immoral) act in which man
> comes to himself and disposes of himself, is therefore
> the (loving or hating) communication with the concrete
> Thou, at which point he experiences and accepts or
> rejects his basic a priori orientation to the Thou in gen-
> eral. Everything else is a moment within, a consequence
> of or preparation for this basic act.[82]

Love for another person, in Rahner's view, represents the
authentic realization of the freedom of the human person. Love

is freedom in its deepest, most authentic form. Freedom itself
has been seen to be the self-possession or self-disposal of the
human subject as a whole. Therefore, "the act of personal love
for the human Thou is. . . the encompassing fundamental act
[*der Grundakt*] of man that provides the meaning, directionality,
and standard for every other act."[83] The spiritual reality of the
human person can be reduced to love for another human person. Indeed, all anthropological assertions must also be read as
assertions concerning love. Human corporeality, temporality,
and historicity, the inability fully to capture oneself in reflection,
the unfathomable and risk-taking character of human being, the
anticipation of the future in hope or despair, human disillusion-
ment, the continual confrontation with the nameless, silent, absolute mystery that encompasses human being, the readiness for
death, are all essential characteristics of love for another person.

> In the act of love for the other, and in this act alone and
> before all else, the primordial unity of what man is and
> what the totality of his experience is, is gathered together
> and fully realized. The love for the other concrete Thou
> is not something that exists in man alongside many other
> things, but is man himself in his total realization.[84]

I have shown that love, for Rahner, is the one experience in
which the human subject as spirit and matter can be seen as a
whole and as authentically realized. But this discussion has not
shed much light on how Rahner understands the nature of love
itself. His concept of love must now be investigated.

Love, Rahner writes:

> It not a natural flowing out of the self [*ein naturhaftes
> Sichverströmen*], but is the free self-bestowal of a person
> who possesses himself, who therefore can refuse himself,
> whose giving away of self, therefore, is always an event
> of wonder and grace. And love, in the full, personal
> sense, is not merely any sort of relation between two
> persons who meet one another in some third thing,
> whether this third thing is a work, a truth or anything
> else. Rather, love is the abandoning [*das Überlassen*] and
> opening [*das Eröffnen*] of one's innermost self to and for
> the other, who is loved.[85]

This abandoning and opening of the self to the other involves
the moving away from oneself into the uncontrollability and
mystery of the other person.[86] Love involves risk, for it is an

acceptance of what cannot be seen and anticipated in the other person. Personal love is a "trusting giving away of oneself [*eine vertrauende Weggabe*] to the other person without any guarantee [of reciprocation] precisely because the other person is and remains free and incalculable."[87] Because love involves such a stepping away from oneself into the other, the beloved, Rahner often speaks of love as *ecstasis*.[88] And even when Rahner does not use the term *ecstasis*, it is clear that he understands love essentially as being beyond oneself in the beloved through a free act of self-giving, even self-abandonment.[89] Just as human knowledge is made possible by a *Vorgriff* or *excessus*, so, likewise, the human person as a free, intersubjective agent is characterized by a reaching beyond itself in the *ecstasis* of love.[90]

God as the Woraufhin of Human Transcendentality

Human being, for Rahner, has been characterized as consisting of a return of the subject to itself or a free constituting of the self, which is mediated by the subject's relations to other human subjects. Further, this self-constitution of the human subject through interpersonal relationships was shown to be conditioned by an a priori orientation toward the totality of all possible objects of experience. Rahner argues that human beings have a *Vorgriff* of being as such that makes possible all particular acts of knowing and willing. While it has been indicated that this *Vorgriff* has as its goal or *terminus (das Woraufhin)* the absolute being of God, up until now, Rahner's justification for this view has not been discussed. In both *Geist in Welt* and *Hörer des Wortes*, he takes some pains to make clear that the *Woraufhin* of the *Vorgriff* is God.[91]

Rahner states that there have been three basic solutions to the problem of the nature of the *Woraufhin* of human transcendence in the western philosophical tradition:

> [The solution] of the philosophia perennis, which in this case reaches from Plato to Hegel, that of Kant, and that of Heidegger. The first answers: the breadth of the *Vorgriff* is directed toward being as such, which has in itself no inner limit and so includes also the absolute being of God. Kant answers: the horizon within which our objects are conceptually given to us is the horizon of sensible intuition which, fundamentally, does not reach beyond space and time. Heidegger says; the transcen-

dence that grounds the *Dasein* of man is directed toward nothingness [*das Nichts*].⁹²

He then proceeds to evaluate the adequacy of each of these three solutions, namely, the views that human transcendence is oriented toward either absolute being, finite being, or nothingness.

First, Rahner argues against Heidegger's position in *Was ist Metaphysik?* that the *Woraufhin* of the *Vorgriff* cannot be nothingness.⁹³ *Prima facie*, human knowledge appears to be related to that which is, to something existent rather than to the nonexistent. The immediately given object of human knowledge is affirmed as being not as nonbeing. Thus, it would seem to follow that the *Vorgriff*, which makes this knowledge of particular objects possible, should also be oriented toward being and not nothingness. On a higher level of reflection, Rahner argues that the *Vorgriff* cannot be directed toward nothingness because, if it were, the necessary conditions of the possibility of the knowledge of particular objects would not be provided.⁹⁴ In the act of knowing a particular object to be a finite, particular entity, there is an implicit negation or denial that this particular entity is coextensive with the totality of all possible objects of knowledge. In knowing particular objects, says Rahner, human beings grasp the immediately given object of knowledge as distinct from the horizon of all possible objects of knowledge (being). The human knower, in an act of negation, is able to distinguish the horizon of knowledge from that which appears within that horizon. But since nothingness, literally, is nothing and does not exist, it cannot provide this horizon against which particular objects of knowledge can be seen to be finite and particular.⁹⁵ That is to say, nothingness is not a horizon at all.

> Non-being [*non-ens*] is known, not insofar as that which is [*ens*] is contrasted with nothingness [*das Nichts*], but rather insofar as being as such is co-known. Otherwise, there would have to be a grasp of nothingness as such. Because this "nothingness" has "nothing" to do with that which is, this grasp could not be given in our knowledge of particular beings. . . . If every negation is grounded in an affirmation, then this must be true also of the most radical negation: non-being. It is grounded in the transcendental affirmation of being as such that is necessarily co-posited in every affirmation whatsoever.⁹⁶

Nothingness "is" nothing that could be contrasted with particular beings. Only a positively infinite horizon, Rahner argues, can make possible the negation that a particular entity is the totality of all possible objects of knowledge that is given implicitly in every act of human knowledge. Only through an affirmation of a horizon that *is* can a particular object be distinguished from the horizon within which it appears. It is an unthematic orientation toward being, and not toward nothingness, that makes this distinction possible.

> Being [*esse*] is always already co-known in the apprehension of a particular being [*ens*]; that which is, itself, is always already surpassed by the *Vorgriff* of being as such. Insofar as a particular being, in order to be known as an object, is grasped in this *Vorgriff*, it is always already known as limited, as "negated." It is negated not . . . through a glance at "nothingness" [*das Nichts*] that limits the particular being and whose empty space it [the particular being] cannot fill, but rather through the knowledge of being as such. . . . The negation of that which is given sensibly belongs to the a priori conditions of the possibility of objective knowledge. The negation . . . is nothing but the thematization of the *Vorgriff* that transcends all particular beings and is directed toward being.[97]

In an obvious reference to Heidegger's *Was ist Metaphysik?* Rahner writes: "Therefore, it is not nothingness that negates, but rather the infinity of being, toward which the *Vorgriff* is directed, that reveals the finitude of everything that is immediately given."[98]

If the *Vorgriff* cannot be directed toward nothingness, but must have something positive or existent as its *Woraufhin*, then the only question is whether this *Woraufhin* of human transcendence is the absolutely unlimited being of God or the relatively unlimited spatiotemporal horizon of sensible intuition as Kant affirms. Rahner argues that the very act of positing a relatively unlimited *Woraufhin* of the *Vorgriff* contradicts the content of that which is posited. A human knower, according to Rahner, could only affirm the totality of all objects of knowledge to be finite if that finite totality were already transcended in a *Vorgriff* toward infinite or absolute being. Only within an infinite horizon can the finite be known as finite. Now, on Kant's presuppositions, such an infinite horizon could not be absolute being in itself since the in itself (*an sich*) is unknowable. The only possible infinite horizon for Kant would be nothingness. Heidegger's understanding of the *Woraufhin* of human transcendence is, therefore, the consistent logical conclusion of Kant's reflections.[99]

Rahner began with three possible solutions to the problem of the nature of the *Woraufhin* of human transcendence: Heidegger's solution (the *Woraufhin* of the *Vorgriff* is nothingness), Kant's solution (the *Waraufhin* of the *Vorgriff* is finite being), and the solution of the philosophia perennis (the *Woraufhin* of the *Vorgriff* is absolute being). Since Heidegger's solution has been shown to be untenable, and since Kant's solution has been shown to be finally reducible to Heidegger's, Rahner concludes that the solution of the philosophia perennis is the correct one, that is, the *Woraufhin* of human transcendence must be infinite or absolute being.

> The affirmation of the real finitude of a particular being requires as the condition of its possibility the affirmation of the existence of an absolute being [*esse absolutum*]. Such an affirmation has already implicitly been made in the *Vorgriff* toward being as such, through which the limitation of the finite, particular being is known, precisely as such, for the first time.[100]

In a "meditation" on the word "God," Rahner states that "God" functions to indicate the objective pole of that unique experience in which the whole of reality and our own being is brought before us.[101] The absolute, infinite horizon that is affirmed in every particular act of human knowledge or will is none other than the absolute being of God. For Rahner the *Vorgriff* is directed toward God, which is to say, God is the *Woraufhin* of human transcendence.

This means that the transcendental experience of the return to self of the human person through the mediation of finite objects of knowledge and, above all, relationships to other persons, is at the same time a transcendental experience of God. The experience of God is not the possession of a few mystics, Rahner says, but belongs to every human person.

> The experience of God may not be thought of as if it were a particular experience alongside others. . . . The experience of God is rather the final depth and radicality of every spiritual, personal experience and therefore is

the one primordial wholeness of experience in which the
spiritual person has itself and is responsible for itself.[102]

Rahner holds that the experience of transcendence and the
experience of God (as the *Woraufhin* of that transcendence) are
intimately linked. Indeed, the transcendental experience of self
and the experience of God are most properly understood as the
subjective and objective poles of the one, original experience of
transcendence that characterizes human being. "The act and the
goal of the act in this primordial, transcendental act are only
available and can only be understood as a unity."[103] For this
reason, Rahner remarks that it is a secondary issue whether one
speaks of the experience of God (focusing on the objective pole)
or the experience of the transcendental human orientation toward God (focusing on the subjective pole).[104] Rahner himself
uses both formulations interchangeably.

This experience of human transcendence is the sole, original source of human knowledge of God.

> The most primordial, nondeducible knowledge of God
> [*das Wissen von Gott*], which grounds all other knowledge
> about God [*das Wissen um Gott*], is given in transcendental
> experience. This is so, in that the *Woraufhin* of transcen-
> dence, which we call God, is given precisely there; always
> nonobjectively and inexpressly, but also inescapably and
> unfailingly.[105]

Rahner characterizes this primordial knowledge of God
given in transcendental experience as transcendental a posteriori knowledge. Some care must be taken here to ensure that his
exact meaning is grasped.

The primordial human knowledge of God is properly called
transcendental, according to Rahner, because this knowledge or
experience of God is not coordinate with other types of human
knowledge and experience, but is a condition of the possibility of
all other human knowledge and experience. It belongs to the
essence of human being that persons know and will particular
objects only within the infinite horizon of the divine being. Put
differently, a transcendental knowledge or experience of God is
co-given in all human activity. The transcendental experience of
God is not given sporadically in human existence. Rather, the
experience or knowledge of God as the *Woraufhin* of human
transcendence "is a condition of the possibility of that which man
is and must be, even in the lostness of everyday life."[106] This

transcendental knowledge of God is a permanent moment of the human person, as a spiritual subject. It may be ignored or suppressed, but the transcendental knowledge of God remains and is active in all moments of human spirituality. "He alone is man, in that he is always already on the way to God whether he knows it expressly or not, whether he wishes it or not, for man is always the infinite openness of the finite for God."[107]

Although he affirms that this knowledge of God is transcendental knowledge since it is given necessarily in human experience, Rahner seeks to distinguish his position from ontologism, which would hold that "all human spiritual knowledge has its necessary ground of possibility in an immediate (although unthematic) *intuition* of the divine being *in itself*."[108] He asserts, over against ontologism, that "there is only an a posteriori knowledge of God from and through the encounter with the world to which we belong naturally."[109] For him, God is indirectly co-known as the horizon of all objective knowledge. This horizon or *Woraufhin* itself is not an immediate object of human knowledge. In this sense, the transcendental knowledge of God deserves to be called a posteriori knowledge, for it is given unthematically in the categorial knowledge of particular objects.

> The *Vorgriff* is directed toward God. Not as if it were immediately directed toward God so that it immediately represented the absolute being in its own self objectively, or so that the absolute being in itself were brought to immediate givenness. The *Vorgriff* is directed toward absolute being in the sense that the *esse absolutum* is always and fundamentally co-affirmed through the unlimited breadth of the *Vorgriff*.[110]

While the transcendental knowledge of God, according to Rahner, must be understood as a posteriori knowledge, in the sense just indicated, this knowledge of God is very different from our ordinary, a posteriori knowledge of objects. He argues that

> this a posteriori character of the knowledge of God would be falsified if the transcendental element in it were overlooked and if this knowledge of God were conceived according to the model of just any kind of a posteriori knowledge whose object comes purely from outside [the subject] and impinges upon a neutral faculty of knowledge.[111]

It seems to me that Rahner's account of the human transcendental awareness of God provides a significant contribution to two of the classic twentieth century discussions of the question of God. A central tenet of the dialectical theology represented by Karl Barth is that human being is given an awareness or knowledge of God only through revelation, indeed, through the explicit Christian revelation. The possibility of a "natural" knowledge of God thematized by metaphysics is denied. Against this position of Barth, Rahner argues:

> If theology comes to stand on its own in the false sense that it no longer has any relationship at all to metaphysics, and thus to the essence of man that is uncovered in metaphysics, then the danger is close at hand that theology, at least consequentially, can be nothing more than a no to man. For all its utterances, which indeed must make use of human words, can really be only the mere no to man and can refer in an exclusively negative fashion to the divine that in itself remains wholly unknown. Thus, there could be no more talk of a real self-disclosure of God for men.[112]

For Rahner, the special, categorial revelation brought by Christianity can only be received by persons if they already have a relationship to God established by general, transcendental revelation.

This affirmation of the metaphysical status of language about God also provides a way out of the dilemma posed by Antony Flew in the so-called theology and falsification debate.[113] Flew, presupposing that all meaningful assertions are factual assertions, argues that utterances about God can count as assertions only if it is possible for such utterances to be factually falsified. John Hick has responded to this challenge by arguing that utterances about God are indeed factual assertions, which will be finally verified only in an afterlife. Others, notably R. M. Hare and Paul van Buren, have denied that theological utterances are assertions at all, arguing that such utterances function noncognitively to express the believer's own view of reality. But both options accept Flew's premise that all genuine assertions are factual assertions. Although Rahner himself does not think in terms of the question of God as raised in Anglo-Saxon philosophy of religion, his position is a genuine alternative to the challenge raised by Flew. For Rahner, language about God is indeed cognitive. Such language functions to assert the existence

of God. However, such theological assertions are by definition
incapable of empirical falsification, for they are metaphysical
rather than factual assertions. The question of God is a strictly
metaphysical question, a question concerning the possibility of
our empirical experience as a whole, rather than a question
about God as a particular object of our empirical experience.

> The question about God, if, indeed, God is not to be
> missed from the outset, cannot be posed as a question
> concerning an individual being *within* the horizon of our
> transcendence and our historical experience. Rather, it
> must be posed as the question concerning the support-
> ing ground, the origin, and the future of the question
> that we ourselves are. Therefore, necessarily, it already
> has in itself the answer to the questions of whether [God
> exists] and what [God is] all in one.[114]

It is possible that an improper understanding of Rahner's
claim that the transcendental knowledge of God is also a posteriori knowledge might obscure his real contribution to a clarification of the logic of the question of God. The a posteriori
character of the knowledge of God does not deny the strictly
metaphysical nature of assertions about God.

> The classical scholastic thesis (against ontologism and the
> innate idea of God) that God can be known only a pos-
> teriori from the creation does not mean to say, when it is
> rightly understood, that man comes upon God as if God
> were just any accidentally given object (a flower, Aus-
> tralia) with which man, viewed from the perspective of
> the a priori structure of his knowledge, could just as well
> have nothing to do.[115]

It does mean that human knowledge of God is co-given in
particular human acts of knowledge as the horizon within which
such a posteriori knowledge is possible.

> For this *Woraufhin* is not experienced in itself, but is
> known only nonobjectively in the experience of subjec-
> tive transcendence. The givenness of the *Woraufhin* of
> transcendence is the giveness of such a transcendence,
> which is always only given as the condition of the pos-
> sibility of categorial knowledge and not for itself
> alone.[116]

Although, according to Rahner, all persons necessarily and
unfailingly have such a transcendental experience of God, not all

persons conceptually grasp this experience as an experience of God.[117] Indeed, Rahner holds that conceptual atheists probably constitute an ever growing majority within humanity. The experience of God, like the primordial experience of self, is an experience in which the human person possesses her- or himself as a whole. Such experience precedes reflection. It is a nonobjective or preconceptual experience. Subsequent reflection on this primal experience never fully succeeds in capturing the depth and richness of the experience. Each act of reflection upon transcendental experience is itself made possible by the very same transcendence that is to be reflected upon. Thus, transcendental experience always already outstrips reflection.

It follows that the transcendental experience of God, while always given at the primordial level of the human subject's own self-possession, may be distorted, ignored or even denied on the level of conceptual reflection.[118] In fact, says Rahner, the experience of God is particularly easy to cover up or ignore, since it is an experience that is only given along with the experience of categorial objects. Persons can simply immerse themselves in the world of objects immediately given to them and pay no attention to the horizon within which those objects appear. It may be that only a very intense experience (loneliness, love, the anticipation of death) can call some persons back from their lostness in everyday life to an awareness of God.[119]

With this understanding of the distinction between the transcendental experience of God and the subsequent reflection upon that experience, Rahner's position on the classical proofs of God's existence can be approached. He is always careful to emphasize that the proofs of God's existence are conceptual or reflective proofs. This is to say that the proofs are more or less successful thematizations of the original, transcendental experience of God. The proofs are not to be viewed as instruments of indoctrination. They do not provide a previously lacking knowledge of God in the same way that a knowledge of subatomic particles might be conveyed by a physicist to her or his students.[120]

> A reflective proof of God is not intended to mediate a knowledge in which a previously completely unknown and, therefore, indifferent object is brought before a man from outside, the meaning and importance of which object for the man are only revealed subsequently

through further determinations that are given to the object.[121]

Such a "proof" would tell us nothing about God. In Rahner's view, "a theoretical proof of God is intended solely to mediate a reflective consciousness of the fact that man, in his spiritual existence, always and unavoidably has to do with God whether he reflects upon this fact or not, whether he accepts this fact freely or not."[122] Using language reminiscent of Romans 1:18–21, Rahner remarks that the knowledge that comes to expression in the proofs of God's existence is "a moment of the one finally indissoluble experience of God in faith that even remains with the true unbeliever, although rejected and suppressed, precisely so that his unbelief brings him to judgment and damnation."[123]

Rahner's treatment of the proofs of God's existence is distinct from that of more traditional Roman Catholic dogmatics in at least two ways. First, there is, for him, strictly speaking, just one proof of the existence of God, Thomas' five ways notwithstanding.[124] The various proofs of traditional dogmatics are to be viewed as different categorial points of departure into the one original, transcendental experience of human being, which, upon reflection, is seen to require God as its source and *Woraufhin*.[125] The one proof of God's existence arises from bringing concrete human being radically into question. Second, Rahner indicates that his own proof of God as the *Woraufhin* of human transcendence is not "an a priori proof of God derived from the eternal truths in the sense of an Augustine or an Anselm or a Leibnitz."[126] Rahner does not argue, as he understands traditional expositors of the ontological proof of God's existence to have done, that "the particular finite being that is affirmed factually to be present on hand [*vorhanden*] demands as its prior condition the existence of an infinite being."[127] Rather, he formulates his proof of God's existence as follows:

> The affirmation of the real finitude of a particular being demands as the condition of its possibility the affirmation of the existence of an absolute being. This affirmation is already implicitly made in the *Vorgriff* toward being as such, through which the limitation of the particular finite being is known as such for the first time.[128]

Paul Wess offers an extended criticism of this Rahnerian formulation of the proof of God's existence.[129] Wess summarizes

Rahner's position as follows: "As soon as a man were to assert
that his horizon is finite, he would already have reached beyond
that horizon."[130] Making use of Nicolai Hartmann's distinction,
Wess speaks of possibilities of thought *(Denkmöglichkeiten)* and
real possibilities *(Realmöglichkeiten)*. Wess holds that God, as the
infinite horizon of human existence, can only be a possibility of
thought or a projection of thought for human beings. God in
Godself (God as a real possibility) remains fundamentally unknown and unknowable. Wess argues that Rahner, like Anselm
before him, moves illicitly from idea to reality, from the legitimate projection of God as a possibility of thought to the illegitimate assertion of the divine reality as a real possibility. This
criticism seems to ignore Rahner's own differentiation of his
understanding of the proof of God's existence from that of
Anselm, i.e., that he does not move from the idea of God to an
assertion that God exists, but rather shows that the act of human
knowledge of finite objects already includes a transcendental
knowledge of God as the *Woraufhin* of the act of knowledge.[131]

Wess' own constructive position is another example of the
fideism to which Rahner is so fundamentally opposed. Wess
argues as follows: God is unknown and unknowable, nevertheless, because of the life, death, and resurrection of Jesus Christ,
we can come to love God as a Thou. When asked why we have
the confidence that Jesus is indeed related to God as the Messiah,
i.e., as God's definitive self-revelation, Wess answers: "to this
question we have no answer to offer. An answer cannot be
possible for man, because self-communication is ultimately a
divine act and, in the case of Christ as well, its way of working is
encompassed by the mystery of his person."[132] Rahner's charge
that God's self-disclosure becomes a pure "no" to human being if
human beings as such do not unfailingly have a prior awareness
of God is as applicable to Wess as it is to Karl Barth.

God as Holy Mystery

There are, according to Rahner, a number of ways of speaking about the *Woraufhin* of human transcendence.[133] It can be
characterized as being itself, the primordial ground, the abyss,
the first cause, Or, using more theological terms, one can call this
Woraufhin God, the illuminating Logos, or, simply, Father.
Rahner argues that the use of such traditional philosophical and

theological terminology to speak of the *Woraufhin* of human transcendence is problematic today. Many persons understand classical Western philosophical terms such as being, ground, or first cause to be nothing more than empty abstractions unrelated to their actual experience. On the other hand, theological terms like Logos, Father, or even God, are too specific because they are so highly conceptual. Such terms are so laden with images and representations that have nothing to do with their referent that many persons can no longer grasp what is genuinely meant by "God." Although Rahner has no hesitancy in affirming that the *Woraufhin* of human transcendence is nothing other than the God testified to in the Christian tradition, he is concerned to avoid speaking of this *Woraufhin* using terms that are so heavily laden with conceptual baggage as to be misleading. Rahner seeks to find a way of speaking of the *Woraufhin* of transcendence that will direct the attention of his readers to their own experience of transcendence and not to any traditional concept of God. The term Rahner chooses for this purpose is "holy mystery." "We want to call the *Woraufhin* and source [*das Wovonher*] of our transcendence 'holy mystery'—although this word must be understood, broadened, and then eventually presented in its identity with the word 'God.' "[134] An analysis of what Rahner means by "holy mystery" will shed further light on Rahner's basic concept of God.

Rahner is careful to distinguish his understanding of mystery from that of traditional scholastic theology.[135] For him, strictly speaking, mystery applies only to God. It does not refer to something that is provisionally unclear because of the limitations of human knowledge. Rather, mystery is that which is primordial and permanent. The mysterious character of God is precisely God's ownmost essence. Rahner holds that even in the *visio beatifica* the mystery of God will not be done away with, but rather will be fully and immediately present to the souls of the blessed.

Rahner lists three chief characteristics of God as mystery that are disclosed in transcendental experience. First, God as mystery is nameless. Names distinguish that which is named from other entities and thus limit that which is named. But the horizon, the *Woraufhin* of human transcendence cannot be distinguished as one entity among others. It cannot be given a name. "The condition of the naming that makes distinctions [between entities] can itself, essentially, have no name."[136] The *Woraufhin* of transcendence, the condition of all categorial naming, can only be designated as that which is different from all finite beings. To call the *Woraufhin* infinite, in this sense, is not to give it a name, but is to indicate that it is the nameless as such. All concepts or names of God *(Begriffe)* are derived solely through reflection upon the *Vorgriff* of God as the infinite, nameless horizon of human transcendence.

Second, God as mystery is unlimited. The *Woraufhin* of transcendence is distinguished from the particular objects of human knowledge. The *Woraufhin* is the horizon within which such objects appear. This distinction between the horizon and the objects that appear within the horizon is the condition of the possibility of all further distinctions among the various objects of human knowledge. But the transcendental condition of all categorial distinctions cannot itself be limited by the act of categorial distinguishing. "The horizon itself cannot be given within the horizon; . . . the final measuring stick cannot be measured; the limit that circumscribes everything cannot be determined in return by a limit that lies still further removed."[137] The mystery toward which the human *Vorgriff* is directed is totally unlimited.

Third, God as mystery is that which is not at our disposal *(das Unverfügbare)*. It might appear, Rahner says, that logic and ontology "catch" the *Woraufhin* of transcendence in a conceptual net. But, "this catching [*das Einfangen*] itself occurs again through the *Vorgriff* toward that which was supposed to be determined."[138] Every spiritual act of the human person is made possible by the *Vorgriff* toward this mysterious, nameless unlimited *Woraufhin*. It is the human person who is disposed of by mystery, not the other way around. The *Woraufhin* of transcendence "is always only there as it disposes [of something]. It avoids, not only physically, but logically, every disposition on the part of the finite subject."[139]

The mysterious *Woraufhin* of human transcendence is given to the human subject "in the mode of self-refusal, silence, distance, permanent retention of itself in inexpressibility."[140] The *Woraufhin* or horizon recedes from view precisely by making possible the presence of categorial objects to the human person. Rahner remarks that "the rationality whose essence it is to define things [i.e., human rationality] derives its life from the undefinable; the brightness of spirit that makes things transparent derives its life from its openness to the divine darkness (which in itself is hyper-bright)."[141] Human being, in its spiritual essence, is possible only because of its orientation toward mystery. It is the unthematic co-experience of the *Woraufhin*, the experience of the *Woraufhin* as nameless, unlimited, and beyond our control that makes possible the naming, limiting, and controlling of finite things that is characteristic of human being. Categorial knowledge is possible only because of the transcendental orientation of the human person toward the mystery of God. Human existence has its final source in that which is mysterious, or, as Rahner sometimes says, the essence of human being is mystery.[142]

Rahner designates the divine *Woraufhin* of human transcendence as *holy* mystery in order to emphasize that God is the *Woraufhin* not only of human knowing, but also of the transcendence of human freedom, will, and love. The *Woraufhin* of the transcendence of human freedom and love must itself in some sense be lovingly free. "It is the *Woraufhin* of an absolute freedom, which, as that which cannot be disposed over, which is nameless, and which disposes over everything absolutely, holds sway in loving freedom. It is the opening up of my own transcendence as freedom and love."[143] As the ground and horizon of human freedom and love, according to Rahner, the mysterious *Woraufhin* of human transcendence is eminently worthy of being called holy.

If the essence of human being is constituted by an orientation toward holy mystery, then the fulfillment of human being can be found only in the fulfillment of this orientation toward holy mystery. According to Rahner, the transcendental openness of human being is fulfilled or perfected in a loving *ecstasis* or giving away of oneself to the holy mystery that encompasses us. "Love, in the final analysis, is precisely the acceptance of the incomprehensibility (which we call God in his essence and freedom) as sheltering us, as affirming us as of value forever, as accepting us."[144] Rahner writes that the final existentiell question facing every human person is whether we love more the tiny island of our knowledge and that which is at our disposal, or the ocean of the infinite, encompassing holy mystery, which we do not know and which we cannot control.[145]

Love of God and Love of Neighbor

Thus far in this chapter I have discussed the key elements of Rahner's theological anthropology. The concepts of freedom and love of others have been central in this discussion. I have also shown that, for Rahner, God is the *Woraufhin* of the transcendentality of human freedom and love. In this final section, I want to present Rahner's understanding of the relation between the love we have for our fellow human beings and the love we have for God.

Freedom, for Rahner, was shown to be

> . . . the subject's taking responsibility for itself, so that freedom, in its basic essence, is directed toward the subject as such and as a whole. In true freedom the subject always intends itself, understands and posits itself, finally does not do *something*, but rather does itself.[146]

It was also shown earlier that the human subject's return to itself in knowledge is accomplished only through a *Vorgriff* of God. Likewise, the self-possession of the human person in freedom involves a necessary orientation of the person toward God. Rahner asserts that human freedom, as such, has a theological character, even when the human subject is not performing categorial acts of religious devotion. Nor is the theological character of human freedom to be explained simply by affirming that God, as the primal source of all reality, is also the ground of human freedom. For Rahner, in the human person's own constitution of her- or himself, she or he decides freely over against God.[147] The human person is free to create, once for all, her- or himself in final validity before God. Human freedom not only comes from God as its ground *(die Freiheit von Gott her)*, but is also oriented toward God as its final goal *(die Freiheit auf Gott hin)*. Just as human knowing is possible because of the *Vorgriff* of God,

> . . . to the same degree and for the same reason, freedom has to do primordially and unavoidably with God himself. . . . Freedom, in its original nature, is the freedom of the yes or no to God and, therein, the freedom of the subject with respect to itself.[148]

To say that freedom is oriented toward God, or is the freedom of the yes or no to God, does not mean that God is willed or chosen as one among other categorial objects of human freedom. God is willed precisely as the transcendent *Woraufhin* or horizon of all particular acts of human freedom. Rahner distinguishes between "the explicit, categorial, conceptually represented object" of the human person as a free actor, and "the a priori formal object, the transcendental horizon, the 'space' within which a particular individual object is encountered."[149] It is this unthematic, implicit willing of God as the horizon of freedom that makes possible the explicit willing of particular objects. While God is not willed as a particular object of human freedom, but is only *co*-willed as the horizon of human freedom, nevertheless God is genuinely co-*willed*. All acts of human freedom include implicitly a certain posture of the human agent over against God.

According to Rahner, the radical nature of human freedom is revealed most clearly in the fact that human beings can deny or reject the very horizon of their own freedom, namely, God.

> This freedom, however, is freedom over against its supporting ground itself. That freedom can deny the condition of its own possibility in an act that once again necessarily affirms this condition, is the extreme expression of the essence of creaturely freedom.[150]

Such a free denial of God is of course an act of ultimate self-contradiction: an act that affirms God implicitly while at the same time explicitly denying God.

For Rahner, as has been seen, the full realization or authentic employment of human freedom occurs in an act of ecstatic, self-giving love for God or, in the mode of radical non-fulfillment, in an act of hate, in which the human person is wholly self-oriented, closed off from the holy mystery that surrounds her or him. But, the self-constitution and self-possession that is human freedom was also seen, in another context, to involve the mediation of other human persons. There, the final fulfillment of human freedom was asserted to be love for another human person. This raises the question whether, for Rahner, the love of God or the love of another human person, the neighbor, finally fulfills the human person. Rahner's answer is that the love of God and the love of neighbor are to be identified. "The primordial relation [of the human person] to God is love of neighbor."[151]

The neighbor, according to Rahner, is not loved for God's sake, nor is the love of neighbor a moral consequence of the person's more primary love for God. Rather, the neighbor is

loved precisely for her or his own sake, and it is this concrete act
of love that Rahner affirms to be the love of God. This is the case
because the categorial act of love of a particular human person
or neighbor occurs within the horizon of the transcendental love
of God. "The explicit, categorial love of neighbor is the primary
act of the love of God, which, in the love of neighbor as such,
intends God . . . unthematically, but genuinely and without
fail."[152] Echoing the language of I John 4:20–21, Rahner writes:

> . . . it is radically true, i.e., with an ontological and not
> merely a "moralistic" or psychological necessity, that the
> one who has not loved the brother whom one sees, also
> cannot love God whom one has not seen, and that one
> can only love the God one does not see by loving the
> visible brother.[153]

As was shown earlier, Rahner does not restrict this love of
neighbor to the love a person has for those individuals closest to
her or him. The love of neighbor must be "the sober service of
political love, . . . which is directed toward the whole of humanity and makes the most distant person one's neighbor."[154]

The importance of this identification of the love of God and
the love of neighbor in Rahner's thought cannot be overesti-
mated. In this identification of love of God and love of neighbor
one has reached the highpoint, the one final summation of
Rahner's theological anthropology. Only in the act of loving a
fellow human being does a person attain "the whole of categorially given reality and possess, therein, the transcendental
and gracious, yet immediately given, experience of God."[155]
Love is, for Rahner, the primordial human experience that
illuminates most perfectly human existence as a whole. In a rich
passage, which deserves to be cited in full, he claims that:

> A descriptive phenomenology of love and of the respon-
> sibility, faithfulness, risk, openendedness, and eternity
> that are hidden in love, must show: what heights and
> abysmal depths the love of the Thou implies; how in love
> man really experiences what he is; how the no to love
> closes the whole man up in the deadly, lonely damnation
> of self-created absurdity; how the totality of reality only
> discloses itself as self-bestowing, as accepting, as blessed
> incomprehensibility (which alone is self-evident) when
> man radically opens his own self in the act of love and
> submits himself to the whole.[156]

Now that we have discussed the meaning of the terms "God" and "love" in Rahner's thought, we can move on to a consideration of the meaning and truth of the assertion "God is love."

NOTES

[1] A number of such studies are available, for example: Peter Eicher, *Die anthropologische Wende: Karl Rahners philosophischer Weg vom Wesen des Menschen zur personalen Existenz* (Freiburg: Universitätsverlag Freiburg Schweiz, 1970); Joseph Speck, *Karl Rahners theologische Anthropologie: Eine Einführung* (München: Kösel Verlag, 1967); Klaus Fischer, *Der Mensch als Geheimnis: Die Anthropologie Karl Rahners* (Freiburg: Verlag Herder, 1974). Fischer's study is especially noteworthy in that it is an attempt to explicate Rahner's entire theology from the perspective of his theological anthropology.

[2] It would seem helpful, at the outset, to distinguish my own approach to Rahner's thought and his theological anthropology in particular, from another common but less helpful approach. A number of interpreters of Rahner speak, without qualification, of his "philosophy," and analyze his thought as such. Gerald McCool expresses the common judgment that Rahner's "approach to theology has been determined by the nature of the philosophical instrument he fashioned for himself in *Geist in Welt* and *Hörer des Wortes*. . . . His system is, in other words, a philosophical anthropology" ("The Philosophy of the Human Person in Karl Rahner's Theology," *Theological Studies* 22 (1961):560). Perhaps the most striking example of this approach to Rahner as a philosopher is Eicher's book *Die anthropologische Wende*, which bears the significant subtitle "Karl Rahner's philosophical way from the essence of man to personal existence." Rahner, in his preface to Eicher's book, says that it is remarkable that anyone should write a philosophical book on his work since he is not a philosopher and since his work is too prescientific [*vorwissenschaftlich*] to be considered philosophical (pp. ix–xiv). Of course, Rahner holds that there must be philosophizing within theology (cf. "Philosophie und Philosophieren in der Theologie," *ST*, 8:66–87 (ET: *TI*, 9:46–63)). Theology "of itself, allows for philosophy, as an independent fundamental discipline, as the condition of the possibility of theology" ("Philosophie und Theologie," *ST*, 6:91 (ET: *TI*, 6:71)). Thus there is some justification for viewing Rahner's thought, and especially his first major works, *Geist in Welt* and *Hörer des Wortes*, as such philosophizing. However, it seems to me that it must be emphasized more strongly that Rahner's philosophizing occurs within a theological

system. He does philosophy in order to develop an adequate Christian theology.

3 P. xiv.

4 "Die Christologie innerhalb einer evolutiven Weltanschauung," *ST*, 5:188 (ET: *TI*, 5:162).

5 Ibid., p. 189 (ET: ibid., pp. 162–163).

6 For this entire paragraph, see *GG*, pp. 28–30, 37–42 (ET: *FCF*, pp. 17–19, 26–31).

7 *HW*, pp. 52, 55. Walter Hoeres, in *Kritik der transzendentalphilosophischen Erkenntnistheorie* (Stuttgart: W. Kohlhammer Verlag, 1969), argues: "the objection must be made against the theoreticians of *Beisichsein*, especially Maréchal and Rahner, that they, in their theory, do not orient themselves to the *phenomenon* of knowing at all. They no longer take seriously, let alone make explicit, the self-experience of knowing. Rather, they begin a priori from a particular speculative theory about knowing. Otherwise they could not have simply overlooked the fact that knowledge always shows itself as the reception of something that manifests itself [*als Hinnahme eines Offenbaren*], which is already to say that the primordial experience is precisely not that of *Beisichsein*, but rather the consciousness of another to which I am receptively related" (p. 66). Hoeres is right, it seems to be, that the phenomenon of knowing is better characterized as being with the other that I encounter receptively, than as *Beisichsein*. However, Hoeres does not emphasize adequately enough that human knowing, for Rahner, is precisely always receptive being with another. More importantly, Hoeres' further claim to have shown the invalidity of the transcendental method as such, through his demonstration of the irreducibility of the phenomenon of knowledge (as receptive being with another) is not convincing. To have shown that Rahner himself may not attend sufficiently to the phenomenon of receptive knowing is not, without further argument, to have shown that one could not ask after the transcendental conditions in the subject of such *receptive* knowing. Hoeres does not provide such a further argument. Johannes Heinrichs' essay "Sinn und Intersubjektivität: Zur Vermittlung von transzendentalphilosophischem und dialogischem Denken in einer 'transzendentalen Dialogik,' " *Theologie und Philosophie*, 2 (1970):161–191, provides just such a transcendental reflection on human knowing, conceived not as *Beisichsein* but as receptive and interpersonal being with another.

8 *HW*, p. 123.

9 See Rahner's extended discussion of how the return of the subject to itself is a condition of the possibility of judgment in the chapter on abstraction in *Geist in Welt*, pp. 79–168. It is beyond the scope of this study to investigate the philosophical background that lies behind Rahner's key anthropological concepts. The chief influences on his

thought at this point are Thomas, Kant, Heidegger, and Maréchal. Many studies of the philosophical background of his thought have been undertaken. Of particular merit are: Peter Eicher, *Die anthropologische Wende*, and Anne Carr, *The Theological Method of Karl Rahner*, AAR Dissertation Series, no. 19 (Missoula, Montana: Scholars Press, 1977), especially pp. 7–57.

[10] For the moment I wish to focus solely on the subjective pole of this experience of being oriented toward being as such and God. That is to say, at this point I will consider only the essential openness of human spirit, without investigating the nature of that to which the human person is open.

[11] *GG*, p. 43 (ET: *FCF*, p. 32).

[12] Ibid. (ET: ibid.).

[13] *HW*, p. 44.

[14] Ibid., pp. 50–51.

[15] Ibid., pp. 75–77.

[16] *GW*, p. 131.

[17] *HW*, p. 49. Note that although Rahner carefully and consistently distinguishes the knowledge of being from the knowledge of particular beings, the former characterized as unthematic and implicit, the latter as thematic and explicit, nevertheless he does use the terms knowledge *(die Erkenntnis)* and knowing *(das Erkennen, das Wissen)* to refer to both.

[18] *GW*, p. 98.

[19] *HW*, p. 77.

[20] Ibid.

[21] *GG*, pp. 31–32 (ET: *FCF*, pp. 20–21).

[22] See *Karl Rahner: Darstellung und Kritik seiner Grundpositionen* (Einsiedeln: Johannes Verlag, 1973), pp. 102–103.

[23] Ibid., pp. 91, 103.

[24] *Offenbarung und Transzendenzerfahrung: Kritische Thesen zu einer künftigen dialogischen Theologie* (Dusseldorf: Patmos Verlag, 1969), pp. 19–22.

[25] "Über den Begriff des Geheimnisses in der katholischen Dogmatik," *ST*, 4:60 (ET: *TI*, 4:44).

[26] Most of the representatives of this intellectualistic approach to Rahner's theological anthropology base their arguments almost exclusively on his earliest works: *Geist in Welt*, *Hörer des Wortes*, and the first volume of *Schriften zur Theologie*.

[27] *Die anthropologische Wende*.

[28] *Karl Rahner*, pp. 79–80.

[29] See chapter 8, "Der freie Hörende," pp. 116–137.

[30] Ibid., p. 132.

[31] "Zum theologischen Begriff der Konkupiszenz," *ST*, 1:377–414 (ET: *TI*, 1:347–382).

32 Ibid., pp. 391–392 (ET: ibid., pp. 360–361).

33 "Würde und Freiheit des Menschen," *ST*, 2:247–277 (ET: *TI*, 2:235–263); "Schuld und Schuldvergebung als Grenzgebiet zwischen Theologie und Psychologie," *ST*, 2:279–297 (ET: *TI*, 2:265–281); "Das Leben der Toten," *ST*, 4:429–437 (ET: *TI*, 4:347–354); "Das Christentum und der 'neue Mensch,'" *ST*, 5:159–179 (ET: *TI*, 5:135–153); "Die Christologie innerhalb einer evolutiven Weltanschauung," *ST*, 5:183–221 (ET: *TI*, 5:157–192); "Das 'Gebot' der Liebe unter den anderen Geboten," *ST*, 5:494–517 (ET: *TI*, 5:439–459); "Der Mensch von heute und die Religion," *ST*, 6:13–33 (ET: *TI*, 6:3–20); "Die Einheit von Geist und Materie im christlichen Glaubensverständnis," *ST*, 6:185–214 (ET:*TI*, 6:153–177); "Theologie der Freiheit," *ST*, 6:215–237 (ET: *TI*, 6:178–196); "Schuld-Verantwortung-Strafe in der Sicht der katholischen Theologie," *ST*, 6:238–261 (ET: *TI*, 6:197–217); "Über die Einheit von Nächsten- und Gottesliebe," *ST*, 6:277–298 (ET: *TI*, 6:231–249); "Der eine Mittler und die Vielfalt der Vermittlung," *ST*, 8:218–235 (ET: *TI*, 9:169–184); "Experiment Mensch," *ST*, 8:260–285 (ET: *TI*, 9:205–224); "Zur Theologie der Hoffnung," *ST*, 8:561–579 (ET: *TI*, 10:242–259); "Immanente und transzendente Vollendung der Welt," *ST*, 8:593–609 (ET: *TI*, 10:273–289), "Gotteserfahrung heute," *ST*, 9:161–176 (ET: *TI*, 11:149–165); "Christologie im Rahmen des modernen Selbst- und Weltverständnisses," *ST*, 9:227–241 (ET: *TI*, 11:215–229); "Selbsterfahrung und Gotteserfahrung," *ST*, 10:133–144 (ET: *TI*, 13:122–132); "Erfahrung des Geistes und existentielle Entscheidung," *ST*, 12:41–53 (ET: *TI*, 16:24–34); "Die Freiheit des Kranken in theologischer Sicht," *ST*, 12:439–454 (ET: *TI*, 17:100–113); "Erfahrung des heiligen Geistes," *ST*, 13:226–251.

34 See, for example, pp. 44–45.

35 "Experiment Mensch," *ST*, 8:270 (ET: *TI*, 9:213).

36 "Schuld-Verantwortung-Strafe in der Sicht der katholischen Theologie," *ST*, 6:244 (ET: *TI*, 6:202). Cf. Heidegger, *Sein und Zeit*, p. 12.

37 This, of course, within limits imposed by the presence of other free persons.

38 "Theologie der Freiheit," *ST*, 6:222 (ET: *TI*, 6:184).

39 *GG*, pp. 46–47 (ET: *FCF*, pp. 35–36).

40 "Theologie der Freiheit," *ST*, 6:223 (ET: *TI*, 6:185).

41 *HW*, p. 123.

42 "Zum theologischen Begriff der Konkupiszenz," *ST*, 1:392 (ET: *TI*, 1:361).

43 "Theologie der Freiheit," *ST*, 6:221 (ET: *TI*, 6:183).

44 "Zum theologischen Begriff der Konkupiszenz," *ST*, 1:391 (ET: *TI*, 1:361).

45 "Die Freiheit des Kranken in theologischer Sicht," *ST*, 12:440 (ET: *TI*, 17:101).

46 "Zum theologischen Begriff der Konkupiszenz," *ST*, 1:393 (ET: *TI*, 1:362).

47 "Die Einheit von Geist und Materie im christlichen Glaubensverständnis," *ST*, 6:188 (ET: *TI*, 6:155).

48 "Die Christologie innerhalb einer evolutiven Weltanschauung," *ST*, 5:189-190 (ET: *TI*, 5:163).

49 "Christologie im Rahmen des modernen Selbst- und Weltverständnisses," *ST*, 9:230 (ET: *TI*, 11:218).

50 *GW*, pp. 35–78; *HW*, pp. 150–175.

51 *HW*, pp. 47–48.

52 Ibid., pp. 150–151.

53 *GW*, p. 49.

54 *HW*, p. 152.

55 Eicher, *Die anthropologische Wende*, p. 218.

56 *GW*, pp. 63–78; *HW*, pp. 162–166.

57 *HW*, p. 163.

58 Ibid., p. 164.

59 "Theologische Prinzipien der Hermeneutik eschatologischer Aussagen," *ST*, 4:410 (ET: *TI*, 4:331). I think Rahner's discussion of spatiality and temporality becomes clearer when it is read against the background provided by Heidegger's similar attempt to move behind the traditional views of spatiality as extension and temporality as duration toward the more primordial nature of space and time given implicitly in the human experience of care. Heidegger's discussion of spatiality can be found in Section 22–24 of *Sein und Zeit*. The entire second half of the book (entitled "Dasein und Zeitlichkeit") is devoted to uncovering the primordial temporality of human being. Rahner's statement about the *anamnesis* and *prognosis* of human being is very reminiscent of the following key Heideggerian formulation: "Only that particular being [human being], which, in its being, is essentially *futural*, such that, free for its death, it can allow itself to be thrown back on its factual there by shattering against its death; that is, only that particular being, which, as futural, equiprimordially is *past*, can take over its own thrownness by handing down to itself its inherited possibility, and can be *present in the moment* for its time" (*Sein und Zeit*, p. 385).

60 See *GW*, pp. 169–280.

61 München: Kösel Verlag, 1963.

62 See Simons, *Philosophie der Offenbarung: Auseinandersetzung mit Karl Rahner* (Stuttgart: W. Kohlhammer Verlag, 1966), and the book by Gerken, *Offenbarung und Transzendenzerfahrung*, to which I have already made reference.

63 *Philosophie der Offenbarung*, pp. 37–40.

64 Ibid., p. 127.

65 *Offenbarung und Transzendenzerfahrung*, p. 72.

66 Ibid., p. 73.

67 Simons' argument is based solely on an examination of *Hörer des Wortes*. Gerken's central, but very dubious, claim that Rahner equates the transcendental with the infinite and the categorial with the finite has been discussed above.

68 *Karl Rahner*, p. 136.

69 Ibid., pp. 136–137.

70 *Der Mensch als Geheimnis*, p. 199.

71 *Erlösung durch das Kreuz: Karl Rahners Beitrag zu einem heutigen Erlösungsverständnis* (Münsterschwarzach: Vier-Türme-Verlag, 1975), p. 15.

72 Ibid., p. 16.

73 See pp. 35–78.

74 See pp. 165–166.

75 See "Würde und Freiheit des Menschen," *ST*, 2:251–252 (ET: *TI*, 2:239) and "Theologie der Macht," *ST*, 4:492 (ET: *TI*, 4:396).

76 *ST*, 1:313 (ET: *TI*, 1:287).

77 "Über die Einheit von Nächsten- und Gottesliebe," *ST*, 6:288 (ET: *TI*, 6:241).

78 "Selbsterfahrung und Gotteserfahrung," *ST*, 10:138 (ET: *TI*, 13:127.

79 Ibid. (ET: ibid.)

80 "Der eine Mittler und die Vielfalt der Vermittlungen," *ST*, 8:226 (ET: *TI*, 9:176).

81 "Selbsterfahrung und Gotteserfahrung," *ST*, 10:139–140 (ET: *TI*, 13:128).

82 "Über die Einheit von Nächsten- und Gottesliebe," *ST*, 6:288 (ET: *TI*, 6:241).

83 Ibid. (ET: ibid.)

84 Ibid. (ET: ibid., p. 243) Hate, as a passage cited earlier indicated, does not represent a denial of the essential relatedness of the human person for Rahner. Rather, hate is an inauthentic, even self-contradictory, realization of this essential relatedness. For in hate a person implicitly affirms her or his essential relatedness to others, and yet, at the same time, explicitly denies that this particular person (the one who is hated) is related to one in such a way as to cause her or him to open and abandon her- or himself to the other.

85 "*Theos* im Neuen Testament," *ST*, 1:141 (ET: *TI*, 1:123).

86 "Zur Theologie der Hoffnung," *ST*, 8:568–570 (ET: *TI*, 10:249–251).

87 "Die menschliche Sinnfrage vor dem absoluten Geheimnis Gottes," *ST*, 13:125.

88 See "Kirchliche Christologie zwischen Exegese und Dogmatik," *ST*, 9:213 (ET: *TI*, 11:200), "Die Frage nach der Zukunft," *ST*, 9:526 (ET: *TI*, 12;189).

89 Klaus Fischer, in *Der Mensch als Geheimnis*, stresses the impor-

tance of the influence of Ignatian spirituality on Rahner's theology (cf. pp. 19–87, 106–112, 187–189). In particular, Fischer claims that Rahner's view that love is essentially *ecstasis* is derived from Ignatian mysticism.

[90] In an essay entitled, "On the Mystery of Life" ("Vom Geheimnis des Lebens," *ST*, 6:171–184 (ET: *TI*, 6:141–152)), Rahner suggests that the concept of life can be used to thematize the essence of reality as such. (This, of course, in an analogical sense, with gradations of "life" stretching from bare matter to the divine being itself.) Life, employed as such a universal concept, is to be understood to refer to an active self-transcendence or self-construction on the part of that which is living. This self-construction requires at least some measure of interiority (or subjectivity) and some measure of relatedness to others (or intersubjectivity). Within such a scheme, matter represents the zero point of subjectivity and intersubjectivity, while human being is characterized by a relatively complete subjectivity, as well as a relatively unlimited openness or relatedness to others. "Beginning with the concept of life, 'spirit' and 'person' can indeed be understood as a radicalization and a self-surpassing of life. From environment [*die Umwelt*] comes world [*die Welt*] in an absolute sense; from interiority comes being a subject; from the assimilation of the environment through the taking of food comes the appropriation of the environment through culture and the machine, through the hominization of the environment beyond its own properly biological sphere; from interiority as consciousness comes self-consciousness; from limited openness to an environment comes unlimited transcendence toward being as such" (p. 182 (ET: pp. 150–151)). Thus all that was said about the essential structures of the transcendentality of the human person (her or his necessary affirmation of and relatedness to self, others, and being as such) can be seen as anticipated analogically in nonhuman reality.

[91] See *GW*, pp. 98–132 and *HW*, pp. 77–87.

[92] *HW*, p. 79.

[93] Cf. Martin Heidegger, *Was ist Metaphysik?* (Frankfurt a.M.: Vittorio Klostermann, 1970).

[94] *GW*, pp. 215–217.

[95] For a discussion of Heidegger and Rahner's views concerning being, nothingness, and the terminus of the transcendentality of the human person, cf. Robert Masson, "Rahner and Heidegger: Being, Hearing, and God," *The Thomist* 37 (1973):455–468. Masson's chief claim in this essay might be represented as follows: "[Heidegger] argues that *Dasein* transcends to Being as nothing. Heidegger claims that a metaphysical analysis such as Rahner's leaves unasked the question about the meaning of Being as different from beings" (p. 482). It would seem to me, however, that Rahner is in fact cognizant of what Heidegger would call the ontological difference (between *das Sein* and *das Seiende*). Surely, for Rahner, as much as for Heidegger, being as such is

"no-thing," to use Masson's locution. That is to say, being as such, for Rahner, cannot be confused with any particular being, or even with all that has being. Yet, at the same time, it would seem that Rahner does not completely understand what Heidegger means by nothingness in *Was ist Metaphysik?* For, as Masson rightly indicates, human being, in Heidegger's scheme in this essay, transcends toward being precisely as that which is not a particular being, that is, nothing.

96 *GW*, pp. 216–217.

97 Ibid., p. 216.

98 *HW*, p. 80. Heidegger's original claim in *Was ist Metaphysik?* runs as follows: "Nothingness [*das Nichts*] is more primordial than the not [*das Nicht*] and negation [*die Verneinung*]. . . . Nothingness itself negates [*das Nichts selbst nichtet*] (pp. 29, 34).

99 *HW*, pp. 80–81.

100 Ibid., p. 83.

101 *GG*, pp. 54–61 (ET: *FCF*, pp. 44–51).

102 "Gotteserfahrung heute," *ST*, 9:166 (ET: *TI*, 11:154).

103 "Über den Begriff des Geheimnisses in der katholischen Theologie," *ST*, 4:68–69 (ET: *TI*, 4:49–50).

104 "Gotteserfahrung heute," *ST*, 9:168 (ET: *TI*, 11:156).

105 "Über den Begriff des Geheimnisses in der katholischen Theologie," *ST*, 4:69 (ET: *TI*, 4:49–50).

106 *HW*, p. 85.

107 Ibid.

108 "Ontologismus," in *KtW*, p. 270, my emphasis. For a more thorough introduction to ontologism, see "Ontologismus," in *LTK*, vol. 7, cols. 1161–1164. Much of the material in this article is available in English in *SM(eng)*. vol. 4, pp. 290–292.

109 *GG*, p. 61 (ET: *FCF:* pp. 51–52).

110 *HW*, p. 82.

111 *GG*, p. 62 (ET: *FCF*, p. 53).

112 *HW*, pp. 39–40.

113 *New Essays in Philosophical Theology*, ed. Antony Flew and Alasdair MacIntyre (New York: The Macmillan Company, 1955), pp. 96–130. See also John Hick, "Theology and Verification," *Theology Today* 17 (1960):12–31 and Paul van Buren, *The Secular Meaning of the Gospel* (New York: The Macmillan Company, 1963).

114 "Bemerkungen zur Gotteslehre in der katholischen Theologie," *ST*, 8:179–180 (ET: *TI*, 9:139).

115 "Über die Einheit von Nächsten- und Gottesliebe," *ST* 6:293 (ET: *TI*, 6:245).

116 *GG*, p. 73 (ET: *FCF*, p. 64).

117 Ibid., pp. 26–30 (ET: ibid., pp. 14–19).

118 "Theologische Überlegungen zu Säkularisation und Athe-

ismus," *ST*, 9:177–196 (ET: *TI*, 11:166–184).

[119] "Gotteserfahrung heute," *ST*, 9:168–170 (ET: *TI*, 11:157–159).

[120] Ibid., p. 161 (ET: ibid., p. 149).

[121] *GG*, p. 77 (ET: *FCF*, p. 68).

[122] Ibid. (ET: ibid., p. 69).

[123] "Bemerkungen zur Gotteslehre in der katholischen Dogmatik," *ST*, 8:180 (ET: *TI*, 9:140).

[124] Ibid., p. 181 (ET: ibid.).

[125] *GG*, pp. 78–79 (ET: FCF, pp. 70–71).

[126] *HW*, p. 85.

[127] Ibid., p. 83.

[128] Ibid.

[129] *Wie von Gott sprechen? Eine Auseinandersetzung mit Karl Rahner* (Graz: Verlag Styria, 1970).

[130] Ibid., p. 51.

[131] Of course Charles Hartshorne has long argued that Anselm's true discovery does not involve an illicit move from idea to reality at all. See *Anselm's Discovery: A Re-examination of the Ontological Proof for God's Existence* (LaSalle, Ill.: Open Court, 1965).

[132] *Wie von Gott sprechen?*, p. 157.

[133] See *GG*, p. 69 (ET: *FCF*, p. 60).

[134] Ibid., p. 70 (ET: ibid., pp. 60–61).

[135] For Rahner's most extended discussion of the concept of mystery see "Über den Begriff des Geheimnisses in der katholischen Dogmatik," *ST*, 4:51–99 (ET: *TI*, 4:36–73).

[136] Ibid., p. 70 (ET: ibid., p. 51).

[137] Ibid., p. 71 (ET: ibid.).

[138] Ibid., p. 72 (ET: ibid., p. 52).

[139] *GG*, p. 72 (ET: *FCF*, p. 64).

[140] Ibid., p. 73 (ET: ibid.).

[141] "Über den Begriff des Geheimnisses in der katholischen Dogmatik," *ST*, 4:59 (ET: *TI*, 4:42).

[142] Ibid., p. 68 (ET: ibid., p. 49).

[143] *GG*, p. 74 (ET: *FCF*, p. 65).

[144] "Die menschliche Sinnfrage vor dem absoluten Geheimnis Gottes," *ST*, 13:124.

[145] "Über den Begriff des Geheimnisses in der katholischen Theologie," *ST*, 4:79 (ET: *TI*, 4:59–60).

[146] *GG*, p. 101 (ET: *FCF*, p. 94).

[147] "Theologie der Freiheit," *ST*, 6:216–221 (ET: *TI*, 6:179–182).

[148] Ibid., p. 220 (ET: ibid., p. 182).

[149] "Über die Einheit von Nächsten- und Gottesliebe," *ST*, 6:284 (ET: *TI*, 6:237).

[150] "Theologie der Freiheit," *ST*, 6:218 (ET: *TI*, 6:181).

151 Ibid., p. 229 (ET: ibid., p. 189).

152 "Über die Einheit von Nächsten- und Gottesliebe," *ST,* 6:295 (ET: *TI,* 6:247).

153 Ibid. (ET: ibid.)

154 "Christlicher Humanismus," *ST,* 8:240–241 (ET: *TI,* 9:188).

155 "Theologie der Freiheit," *ST,* 6:229 (ET: *TI,* 6:189).

156 "Über die Einheit von Nächsten- und Gottesliebe," *ST,* 6:290 (ET: *TI,* 6:242).

CHAPTER IV
DIVINE LOVE AND DIVINE SELF-COMMUNICATION

The preceding chapter has shown that human existence, for Rahner, is most authentically realized in the act of ecstatic love for another human person. Such an act is always implicitly a giving away of the self to God as holy mystery. God is affirmed as the *Woraufhin* of human transcendence in all free, loving acts. But God, as the *Woraufhin* of human love, is only obliquely pre-grasped by persons, not directly grasped in Godself, for God is nameless, unlimited, and not at our disposal.

This view of God as the mysterious *Woraufhin* of human transcendence is derived by Rahner from a transcendental analysis of human existence. Such a view of God expresses nothing particularly Christian. Philosophical reflection, Rahner holds, can show that God is the asymptotic goal of the dynamism that characterizes human being. But philosophical reflection cannot answer the question of whether human beings actually attain this goal.

> That this holy mystery can be given not merely as the unattainable *Woraufhin* of transcendence within a categorial experience of that which is finite, that is, always mediated by the finite, but can communicate itself as itself . . . immediately to creaturely spirit, remains completely questionable from the standpoint of the creature and from the philosophical concept of mystery, and can be known only through revelation.[1]

The central proclamation of the Christian faith, which comes to expression in the dogmas of the incarnation and grace, is, for Rahner, that God is not just distant and unapproachable, but communicates Godself to human beings as the fulfillment of their existence. Christian faith affirms that "God is given in the mode of nearness and not only in the mode of distant presence . . . as the distant, incomprehensible, asymptotic *Woraufhin* of our transcendence."[2]

Putting the same point differently, one can say that the central Christian proclamation is that God not only is the *Woraufhin* or transcendental horizon of human freedom and love, but is Godself free, self-giving love. Rahner remarks that the most decisive discovery human beings have made in the entirety of salvation history is that God has called persons into the most intimate communication with God. This discovery is expressed quite simply in I John 4:16: God is love. That this is the case, Rahner says, is not immediately apparent.

> That God loves us, that he is "dear God" [*der liebe Gott*], is not a self-evident truth of metaphysics, but is rather the incomprehensible wonder that the New Testament must continually proclaim and that requires the highest effort of man's power of faith to be believed.[3]

The term Rahner uses to speak about this divine love or grace is "the self-communication of God" *(die Selbstmitteilung Gottes)*. To say that God is love is to say that God communicates Godself to human beings.[4] Or, conversely, God communicates Godself because God is an ecstatic, overflowing fullness of love that pours itself out to those who are empty.[5] For Rahner, therefore, the innermost core of the Christian understanding of existence is that the divine mystery that encompasses us does not finally refuse itself and remain aloof, but communicates itself in love to us.[6]

It is not an overstatement to say that the self-communication of God is the central concept in Rahner's theology. In his system, the self-communication of God presupposes the creation of the world and human being, includes within itself all talk of the incarnation, grace, and the triune nature of God, and implies an ecclesiology and a doctrine of the Christian life. Bert van der Heijden concurs with this judgment that the self-communication of God is the most fundamental concept in Rahner's theology.[7] He writes that, if properly understood, the shortest and best creedal formula for Christianity would be, in Rahner's mind, "the self-communication of God."[8] Therefore, any adequate treatment of Rahner's thought must attend with care to the concept of the self-communication of God.

But the self-communication of God is an especially crucial concept for this study, because it is the means by which Rahner

explicates the meaning of the assertion "God is love." Through
the use of the concept of divine self-communication Rahner
shows clearly that he does attribute to God qualities that derive
from the most fundamental human experience, love. Rahner
states explicitly that he uses the concept self-communication (and
other concepts such as love, personal nearness, and intimacy) in
his doctrine of grace, rather than more traditional concepts such
as quality, accident, and *habitus,* in order to overcome the one-
sided use in theology of concepts deriving not from our inner
experience of ourselves as persons, but from our external experience of things.[9] Because of its particular relevance to this
study, the concept of the self-communication of God will be the
object of discussion throughout the next three chapters. In this
chapter I want to establish what Rahner means by divine self-
communication; show that divine self-communication is an existential in human existence; discuss the model of quasi-formal
causality that he uses to elucidate divine self-communication;
talk briefly about his doctrine of the trinity, which has divine self-
communication as its starting point; and demonstrate that love
of others, or self-communication, is, for Rahner, the fundamental act of God.

The Meaning of Divine Self-Communication

   I have already said that Rahner uses the concept of the self-
communication of God to talk about the love or grace of God.
"Divine love" and "divine self-communication" are synonymous
for him. It should be noted that he employs the same basic
understanding of love in his discussions of divine love as he does
in his portrayal of human love. Human love, for Rahner, is
characterized as *ecstasis,* a being outside of oneself, a giving away
of oneself to another person. Likewise, the love or self-communication of God is understood as *ecstasis.* "God himself goes
out from himself as the fullness that lavishes itself."[10] God is "the
enduring, infinite fullness, . . . he is love, i.e., the will that wishes
to fill up that which is empty."[11] The term self-communication
itself suggests this image of the ecstatic being outside of oneself
of love. But Rahner also uses a number of other terms as synonyms for self-communication that reveal even more clearly that
he views the divine love as *ecstasis:* e.g., the self-expression of
God *(die Selbstaussage Gottes),* the self-manifestation of God *(die*

Selbstäusserung Gottes), the self-alienation of God *(die Selbstent-
äusserung Gottes).*[12]

It must be understood, first and foremost, that divine self-
communication does not mean, for Rahner, the communication
of something about God.[13] Divine self-communication is not
mere speech about God, even if such speech were to be autho-
rized or directed by God. Rather, "at issue is an *ontological* self-
communication of God."[14] In divine self-communication it is the
being of God itself that is communicated to the human person.
"It is decisive for the understanding of the self-communication
of God to man to grasp that the giver is himself the gift, that the
giver in himself and through himself gives himself to the creature as its very own fulfillment."[15]

Rahner makes use of the scholastic concept of uncreated
grace to stress the point that in divine self-communication the
giver is the gift itself.[16] He argues that scholastic theology de-
parts from the dominant view of the New Testament and the
Fathers by understanding created grace to be a pre-condition of
uncreated grace. That is to say, scholastic theology holds that an
ontic change in the human person must precede the indwelling
of the divine spirit. The formal ground of participation in God
(uncreated grace) is the existence of the theological virtues that
are imparted to the believer by God (created grace). Rahner, on
the other hand, suggests that the fundamental meaning of grace
is in fact uncreated grace, while created grace is a consequence
of uncreated grace, its material disposition. Viewed in this light,
grace is the indwelling of the Holy Spirit of God in the human
person and not the impartation of a created quality or virtue to
persons by God.

> Grace is God himself, his communication, in which he
> sends himself to man as the divinizing boon that he
> himself is. Here God's work is God himself (as the one
> who is communicated). Such grace, from the outset, can-
> not be thought of as separable from the personal love of
> God.[17]

Rahner states that such an understanding of the primacy of
uncreated grace, which is God Godself imparted to the spiritual
creature, better expresses the mystery and wonder of God's love
as it is proclaimed by Christianity than does the usual scholastic
view.

Bert van der Heijden charges that Rahner's concept of self-communication is ambiguous. He asks: "Is it a matter of the communication of the being of God or of the person (the self) of God? Are both the same? If not, what can the immanent difference between divine being and divine 'self' be?"[18] Van der Heijden specifies two possible meanings of "the self-communication of God":

> First of all, it can mean that God does not communicate something nondivine about himself, but communicates himself, i.e., as the reality (absolutely self-subsistent being) that is distinct from every creature. Second, it can also mean that God communicates himself formally as a subject, as a person, that he establishes a personal relationship with us.[19]

Van der Heijden's chief criticism of Rahner's theology is that his understanding of revelation is inadequate in that it is so one-sidedly oriented toward the first of these two understandings of divine self-communication that God, finally, is portrayed as the ungraspable *ipsum esse,* not as a personal reality having existentiell significance for human persons.

It seems to be that van der Heijden, at this point, sees ambiguity where there is none. Rahner would not distinguish the communication of the divine being from the communication of the divine self in the way that van der Heijden does. In fact, Rahner explicitly identifies them, arguing that "if God is really God, absolute reality in personal spirituality, then communication of divine being and divine self-communication [*Seinsmitteilung und Selbstmitteilung Gottes*] must be the same."[20] The self-communication of God is the communication of the divine being, for it is uncreated grace, the indwelling of the Holy Spirit. But Rahner cautions against understanding this genuine communication of God's being in an impersonal manner, as if God were communicated to human beings as a thing. He says that this "ontological" self-communication of God ought not to be understood in a merely objectivistic and reifying sense. Both the giver and the recipient of divine self-communication are persons, spiritual beings, not things. Therefore, the self-communication of God is a personal encounter between God and the human person.[21]

In self-communication, God is disclosed to persons as love.

> The man who has anything at all to do with his transcen-
> dental experience of holy mystery makes the discovery
> that this mystery is not only the distant horizon, the
> repelling, distancing and condemning judgment of his
> consciousness and environment and co-world, that
> which is uncanny, which frightens him back into the
> confining home of everyday life, but that this holy mys-
> tery is also the sheltering nearness, the forgiving inti-
> macy, home itself, the love that communicates itself, that
> which is familiar, which one can approach and to which
> one can flee from the uncanniness of the empty and
> threatened character of his own life.[22]

Because of the self-communication of God, the holy mystery that
surrounds human being is not experienced simply as the distant,
aloof horizon that makes the experience of categorial objects
possible and that is only known obliquely through the mediation
of such categorial objects. In the self-communication of God,
God is given directly, as Godself, to the human person.[23]

Yet, at the same time, Rahner maintains that the mystery of
God is not abolished by divine self-communication. As was
shown earlier, the mystery or incomprehensibility of God is not
a function of the finitude of human *ratio*, but is the very essence
of the divine being. The self-communication of God is the radical nearness of God to the human person precisely as holy
mystery.[24]

> Divine self-communication means, therefore, that God
> can communicate himself as himself to the nondivine
> without ceasing to be infinite reality and absolute mys-
> tery. . . . Nothing of what was said earlier about the
> presence of God as absolute mystery or essential in-
> comprehensibility has been negated or denied through
> this self-communication. Even in grace and the immedi-
> ate vision of God, God remains God, i.e., the first and last
> measure that cannot be measured. . . . God remains the
> absolutely nameless and inexpressible God who never,
> even in his self-communication in grace and immediate
> vision, can be conceived, . . . who never can be arranged
> within a human system of coordinates in knowledge or
> freedom.[25]

God remains absolute mystery in divine self-communication, but
self-communication or grace makes it impossible to overlook the
mysterious character of God. Mystery is made immediately present to human being.

Rahner also holds that while God is immediately present in divine self-communication and no longer merely given as the *Woraufhin* of human transcendence through the mediation of categorial objects, nevertheless, God is not presented to human beings as an individual categorial object. The reality of God is given in itself and yet does not lose its infinite nature.[26]

In love, God calls human beings to an intimate fellowship with God.[27] Divine self-communication is thus the invitation from God to human persons to enter into communion with God as person.[28] Rahner says that "God establishes an absolute inter-communication between himself and man, i.e., in absolute self-communication—called 'grace'—God gives himself in immediate partnership and nearness and does not, as radical, self-refusing distance, merely set the creature apart from himself as something other."[29] As a result of divine self-communication, persons genuinely participate in the divine being and therein attain salvation, that is, the final, permanent validity of their existence.[30]

The sense in which the self-communication of God provides the ultimate fulfillment or salvation of the human person merits further consideration. It was shown that human being, for Rahner, is characterized by a dynamic transcendence of particular, categorial objects toward God. Human beings are open to God and strive for God, at least implicitly, in all their acts. It was also seen that the most authentic human response to the holy mystery of God is that of love for the incomprehensible goal of human transcendence, which, of course, is mediated by the love for fellow human beings. What is expressed in Rahner's concept of the self-communication of God is the wonder and grace that this *Woraufhin* of the human drive toward self-possession and self-realization in knowledge and freedom does not remain merely a neutral, asymptotically approached goal, but bestows itself immediately upon human beings. Without the self-communication of God, he asserts, human persons could only hope that their striving for God, which is the very essence of human being, would be successful and result in fulfillment rather than in final disappointment. In the self-communication of God, the final goal of human striving becomes immanent within the striving person her- or himself. The striving of the human person for fulfillment is satisfied by the self-communication to human persons of that which is striven for. The goal that persons cannot attain in their own power, itself provides the possibility of the attainment of the goal.[31]

This means, for Rahner, that God

> . . . does not stand over against the world and its history merely as its transcendent first cause that remains unaffected by the world, but, in the ecstasy of his love, has established himself within the world as its innermost entelechy and directs this whole world and its history toward that point at which God, face to face, will be the innermost and most immediate fulfilling of our existence in eternal blessedness.[32]

In grace, God is "not just the fulfillment or the goal of the spiritual creature, but, at the same time, the most proper, necessary and only true co-natural principle of the movement toward the fulfillment of this goal."[33] Thus, for Rahner, the final transcendent goal of the human person (God) becomes the most immanent principle of the human dynamism toward that goal. Likewise, the most immanent fulfillment of the human person is precisely its divine, transcendent *Woraufhin*.[34]

In his essays of the 1960s and 1970s, Rahner introduces the term "absolute future" to speak of God as self-communicating love.[35] This new terminology represents Rahner's appropriation of the shift of emphasis in theology from the individual's decision of faith over against God to the social and political dimensions of Christian faith in God that is evident in the thought of Jürgen Moltmann, Wolfhart Pannenberg, Johann Baptist Metz, and others. Rahner holds that Christianity is a religion of the future. Christian faith, he says, understands human being as constituted essentially by hope.[36] Hope is the courageous act of acceptance of the basic human orientation toward God as the mystery that cannot be controlled or manipulated. In this act of acceptance, God, precisely in God's mysterious character, is seen to be that which saves and blesses human beings. Hope is the courage to let oneself be drawn away from oneself in love toward the incomprehensibility of God. For Christianity, further, the human person projects possibilities of existence for her- or himself prognostically. The world as a whole is open to the future. The meaning of the past and present are fully realized only in the future.

But Rahner goes on to say that Christianity is not an ideology, that is, Christianity neither is committed to nor expresses any particular view of the inner-worldly future. Christianity is the religion of the absolute future, which is God.[37] As was shown earlier in this section, the final fulfillment or consummation of human existence is not a categorial state, but the absolute, transcendent being of God. The free human agent attains a genuine, final validity over against God in her or his free self-constitution. Thus, the final horizon or future of human existence is not endless, temporal succession, which would render all human acts indifferent and meaningless, but rather the divine being which makes possible the lasting significance of personal decision and activity.[38] Rahner argues this same point elsewhere and says:

> Christianity understands itself in terms of salvation *history*. That means, however, that Christianity is not, finally and fundamentally, a doctrine of a static nature of the world and man which, always remaining the same, repeats itself in an empty time-space without really progressing further. Rather, Christianity is the proclamation of an absolute becoming, one that does not continue into emptiness, but really attains the absolute future, indeed already moves *in* the absolute future. . . . The infinite reality of this future is active as an inner, if independent, constituent of this becoming, which supports this becoming.[39]

The "absolute future" is another name for God. Rahner transposes his discussions of the relationship between God as the transcendental *Woraufhin* of human knowledge and love and the categorial objects, the experience of which the *Vorgriff* of God makes possible, into language concerning the relationship between the absolute future and the inner-worldly futural projects of human beings. For instance, he writes that the absolute future is not known as a particular individual object within the scope of human knowledge and planning of the future, but rather is the ground of the futurity of human being as such. The absolute future cannot be exactly characterized, it is essentially mysterious. An implicit knowledge of the absolute future is given along with all human acts of existentiell decision, which are always acts of self-projection.[40]

More importantly, Rahner also uses terms derived from his discussions of the self-communication of God to speak of the absolute future. As the long passage cited above already indicated, the absolute future is not simply the ever receding goal of the human person's projection of her- or himself into the future. Rather, the absolute future is an inner principle of the dynamism of this self-projection itself.

> Christianity is the religion of the absolute future inasmuch as God is not only "above us" as the ground and horizon of history, but is "before us" as our ownmost future, as that which we must overtake, as that which supports history as its future. For Christianity confesses the absolute, infinite, transcendent God, who exists as radical and infinite mystery to be the one who in free grace communicates himself, in his absolute mystery, to the world as its inner principle and final future, who drives history as that which is most properly his own and does not simply set it apart from himself in creation.[41]

Divine Self-Communication as the Supernatural Existential

Thus far in this chapter, I have attempted to characterize the basic meaning of the concept of divine self-communication in Rahner's theology. Now, in this section, I want to discuss the anthropological ramifications of the self-communication of God, that is, the difference that is made in human existence by the love of God for human persons. This discussion will reveal that grace is an intrinsic moment, or existential, of concrete human being.

Although the self-communication of God, according to Rahner, is always experienced as a wondrous, unanticipated gift of love, this does not mean that he understands the self-communication of God to occur only sporadically within a person's life. Nor does Rahner conclude from the fact that the self-communication of God cannot be deduced as an a priori constituent of the essence of human being that the love of God is a merely accidental or unimportant aspect of concrete human existence. Likewise, to say that it is Christianity, in particular, that proclaims that God is love, does not mean that this love of God is bestowed on some human beings (i.e., Christians) and not on others. For Rahner, the understanding of the love or self-communication of God as something that is present within human existence in a hit or miss fashion and that is fundamentally irrelevant to human existence is a consequence of an extrinsicist view of grace, one that he holds to be theologically inadequate.

In the following passage Rahner gives a description of what he takes to be the extrinsicist view of grace.

> Grace appears as a mere superstructure, very fine indeed in itself, which is imposed upon nature by God's free command such that the relationship between the two [grace and nature] is not much more intense than an absence of contradiction between them (a purely negatively understood *potentia oboedientialis*). Nature does indeed acknowledge the goal and means of the supernatural order (grace and glory) as the highest goods, but it is not clear why nature has time for these highest goods.[42]

According to him, the error of extrinsicism lies in viewing grace as an external imposition upon a human nature that functions perfectly well without grace. The religious consequences of extrinsicism are disastrous. Persons come to understand themselves as such a self-sufficient nature and view grace and the whole supernatural realm either as irrelevant or as an undesirable intrusion.[43] Over against this extrinsicist view, Rahner seeks to show that grace is an inner constitutive element of concrete human existence.[44]

This understanding of grace as intrinsic to concrete human nature is brought succinctly to expression when Rahner says that "man is the event of the absolute self-communication of God."[45] He holds that this proposition applies to all persons, the gratuity of the self-communication of God notwithstanding. The supernatural character of grace does not mean grace is not offered to all human persons, nor does the love of God become any less of a wonder because of its universality within human existence.[46] Rahner introduces his famous concept of the supernatural existential (*das übernatürliche Existential*) to explicate this universal presence of the self-communication of God within human existence.[47] While much could be said about Rahner's understanding of the supernatural existential, and indeed much has been written about it, I wish to make just five basic points relative to this concept.

First, although there has been some development in the meaning of the supernatural existential in Rahner's thought, it ought to be understood as synonymous with the offer of the self-communication of God. It is, to use Klaus Fischer's words, "nothing less than God himself insofar as he bestows himself upon man."[48] Rahner, at one point, speaks of the supernatural existential as "the existential of man's absolute immediacy to God through divine self-communication.[49] The supernatural existential is simply a way of indicating that God is given immediately to all human person in their transcendental experience.[50]

Second, Rahner speaks of the supernatural existential as the *offer* of the self-communication of God in order to emphasize that the self-communication of God is addressed to human persons precisely in their freedom. The self-communication of God, to reiterate a point made earlier, is not to be understood in an impersonal fashion. It is neither the communication of some *thing,* nor is it a pantheistic diffusion of the divine being.[51] Divine self-communicaton is the most free act of God's love offered to free human beings who, in freedom, must either accept or reject the self-communication of God. But the acceptance or rejection of the offer of the self-communication of God or the supernatural existential is very different from the acceptance or rejection of any categorial offer.

> Just as the essence of man, his spiritual personhood, despite its permanence and inescapable giveness for each free subject, is posed for this freedom in such a way that the free subject can possess itself in the mode of yes or no, in the mode of patient and obedient acceptance or in the mode of protest against this essential freedom with which it is entrusted, so, too, the existential of absolute immediacy to God permanently offered to human freedom through the self-communication of God can exist in the mode of mere indifferent givenness, in the mode of acceptance, and in the mode of rejection.[52]

For Rahner, the self-communication of God provides the condition of the possibility of its own acceptance in the human person, but it does not and cannot ensure that grace will be accepted by all persons. One can only say that grace is unfailingly offered to all persons. While we cannot know how many persons finally reject divine self-communication and, thereby, their own selves, if any at all, the possibility of such a rejection must be affirmed because of the radical nature of human freedom. However, for Rahner,

> . . . this way in which the self-communication of God is given in relation to human freedom [i.e., as rejected, accepted or indifferently there] does not cancel the real givenness of this self-communication as offered, for, of

course, a freely rejected offer or one that is merely given, must not be thought of as a communication that could exist, but does not. Rather it must be thought of as a communication that has really taken place and by which our transcendental freedom is and remains really and inescapably confronted.[53]

The supernatural existential is the permanent offer of the love or self-communication of God, which must be freely appropriated by persons.

Third, the supernatural existential is "a transcendental divinization of the basic situation, of the final horizon of the knowledge and freedom of man."[54] It is not something alien that is imposed upon human being. The supernatural existential is the supernatural elevation of human transcendentality. Rahner argues that the self-communication of God

> . . . grasps man in his most primordial ground, in the center of his spiritual essence and orients this essence toward the immediacy of God. It grants to the human essence a gracious, supernatural dynamism and finality toward God himself and elevates the unlimited transcendentality of the spiritual person such that this transcendentality becomes not just the condition of spiritual, personal, free, human being, but transcendentality toward God himself.[55]

The supernatural existential is a gracious, but permanent moment within human existence, one that is always a co-determinant of the self-realization of the human person, whether in the mode of acceptance or rejection. However, just as persons need not have a conscious awareness of their "natural" transcendentality (the orientation toward self, others, and God as *Woraufhin*), so, too, they need not be consciously aware of the supernatural existential. It is active, nevertheless, as a transcendental moment of the human person.[56]

It was said above that the self-communication of God establishes a personal communion or relationship between God and human beings. This relationship is made possible by the supernatural existential, that is, the supernatural elevation of human transcendentality provides an orientation of the human person toward God precisely as a personal reality with whom one could have communion. Whereas human persons, when considered without reference to the supernatural existential, are oriented toward God as the distant, self-refusing *Woraufhin* of transcendence, through the supernatural existential they are oriented toward God as the one who is immediately given as love.[57] It can now be seen that the sketch of Rahner's theological anthropology given in the previous chapter did not fully present his understanding of actual, concrete human existence. For, in fact, human beings are always already oriented toward the God of loving immediacy, not just the God of distant mystery. All human activity occurs within the horizon of God's love. Indeed, through the self-communication of God, God's love is a constituent, an existential within human existence as such. The supernatural existential is the offer of the self-communication of God to human beings, which leads and directs persons to God, not from without, but from within human existence itself.

> Therefore, this self-communication of God to the spiritual creature can and must be characterized as supernatural and unexacted even prior to sin, without thereby introducing a two-storied dualism into the unitary reality of man. The self-communication of God is that which is innermost to man in the one, real concrete order of human existence. At least as offered, it is antecedent to the freedom of man as the condition of his highest, obligatory realization.[58]

Fourth, this elevation of human transcendentality is what Rahner calls transcendental revelation or the transcendental aspect of revelation.

> The communication of a supernatural formal object (otherwise expressed: the supernatural horizon within which, unreflectively but really, the material objectivity of the ethical is grasped; the opening of the spiritual transcendentality of man to the immediate presence of God) is in a true sense already "revelation." . . . Gracious supernatural elevation already implies revelation and the possibility of faith.[59]

It is precisely the character of God as the mysterious one who communicates Godself in absolute nearness that is "revealed" in this transcendental aspect of revelation. Because transcendental revelation is given with the supernatural existential, Rahner asserts that the history of revelation is not restricted to the history of faith recorded in the Old and New Testaments, but is co-extensive with human history itself.[60] Where there is human being there is given unfailingly the self-communication of God and thus transcendental revelation.

Fifth, for Rahner, the free acceptance of the supernaturally elevated transcendentality of the human person (the supernatural existential) is salvation. God's salvific will is universal, for all persons are offered the self-communication of God which is the final fulfillment of human being. Anyone who accepts her or his own personhood, which includes a supernatural orientation toward God, attains salvation, whether or not that person has any relationship to Christianity as a categorial thematization of transcendental revelation.[61] This view is developed by Rahner in his famous concept of "anonymous Christianity."[62] He argues:

> If there is a man who possesses, as the innermost center of his existence, the self-communication of God, called grace, who has accepted this self-communication in unconditioned faithfulness to his conscience, who, therefore, is, in a true, but not a verbally objectified sense, a believer, in other words, if there is a man who even as a "heathen" already possesses the blessing of salvation, which in the final analysis is the only thing that matters to Christianity, its gospel, all its institutions, for which everything else is only a means, a historical objectification, a sacramental sign, or social manifestation, then I do not see why such a man, whose possibility and actuality Catholic theology may not doubt, should not be called an anonymous Christian, if he indeed possesses, unbeknownst to himself and others, that which constitutes the essence of Christianity: the grace of God that is grasped in faith.[63]

The view that the self-communication of God is a supernatural existential within human being is the key to Rahner's position on the relationship between nature and grace. In opposition to an extrinsicist understanding of this relationship, he argues that grace is an inner constituent of concrete human existence. "Grace is nothing other than the radicalization of the essence of man, and not a new additional upper story that is imposed upon a foundation (called nature), which is essentially self-contained."[64] The self-communication of God is offered to all persons and is present and active in the lives of all persons, even those who choose to deny their orientation toward the God of self-communicating love.[65] Wherever actual human being exists, grace is also present. In Rahner's view all human persons, precisely as such, are addressees of divine self-communication and, therefore, always exist within the order of grace.

The Model of Quasi-Formal Causality

According to Rahner the self-communication of God establishes a "new" relationship between God and the human person.[66] He remarks that this new relationship between God and human being cannot be constituted by an essential change in either God (since God is immutable) or human being (since a change in the creature would not alter the basic relationship of this creature to God as its transcendent creative ground). This raises the question of how this new relationship is to be understood.

Rahner states that the model of efficient causality is not sufficient to explicate the self-communication of God and the God-creature relationship it inaugurates.[67] By efficient causality God creates *ex nihilo* an other, a creature, that is distinct from Godself. In efficient causality the effect is different from the cause. But this is not the case in divine self-communication. It was shown that divine self-communication is not the communication of a created quality by God to human being, but is uncreated grace, the bestowing of God's own self upon the spiritual creature. In the self-communication of God the giver is itself the gift, the cause is the effect. Grace involves the giving of Godself to the creature, not the communication of something distinct from God.

Rahner writes that there is another model of causality within the scholastic tradition that better explicates the self-communication of God, namely, the model of formal causality. In formal causality "a particular being, a principle of being is a constitutive moment in another subject, such that it communicates itself to this subject and does not simply effect something different from itself."[68]

Rahner holds that the model of formal causality must be modified slightly in order to be applied to the divine being. For in becoming an inner constitutive principle of human being in grace, God remains transcendent and unaffected. There is no essential relativity of God to the creature in divine self-communication, nor does God lose Godself in the communication of the divine being to human being. Therefore, Rahner speaks of the quasi-formal causality of God. This "quasi" is not intended to qualify the claim that God is really given as an inner constituent of the creature in divine self-communication. It simply points out the analogical nature of all our concepts of God.[69]

So, Rahner proposes that the self-communication of God can best be understood using a model of quasi-formal causality. In the self-communication of God, God relates God's absolute being to creaturely being in quasi-formal causality, that is, God does not effect the production of something distinct from God, but makes the divine reality a constitutive aspect of concrete human being.

> The one God communicates himself as absolute self-expression and absolute gift of love. His communication . . . is true *self*-communication, i.e., God gives his creature not merely a (mediated) share in himself in that he creates and bestows created, finite realities through his omnipotent *efficient* causality, rather, in a quasi-formal causality, he gives himself genuinely and in the strongest sense of the word.[70]

The novelty of the event of grace consists in the immediate presence of God to the spiritual creature.

In grace there occurs "a self-communication of God to the created spirit . . . that is not the creation through efficient causality of a creaturely quality or effect that is different from God. It is rather the communication (through quasi-formal causality) of God's self to man."[71] Here, God is God's own work or effect. According to Rahner, all strictly supernatural events (grace and incarnation) occur by way of such a quasi-formal causality. Indeed, the presence of the quasi-formal causality, thus, divine self-communication, distinguishes the supernatural from the natural. "The essential and radical distinction between nature and the supernatural is unambiguously grounded in this distinction between the efficient and the quasi-formal causality of God."[72]

The Triune Nature of Divine Self-Communication

For Rahner, the Christian faith testifies to a threefold character of the human experience of the self-communication of God.

> It is the self-communication in which that which is com-
> municated remains sovereign and incomprehensible,
> and abides, even upon being received, in its unoriginate
> nature, beyond our grasp and not at our disposal. It is
> self-communication in which the God who discloses him-
> self "is there" as self-expressive truth and free, disposing
> power, which is active in history. And it is self-communi-
> cation in which the self-communicating God effects the
> acceptance of his communication in the one who receives
> it, precisely such that the acceptance does not reduce the
> communication to a merely created level.[73]

If, as has been shown in this chapter, the self-communication of
God means precisely a real communication of the being of God,
then, in self-communication, God is given to human spirit as
God really is. Therefore, the threefold character of the experience of divine self-communication implies a threefold character
of the divine being itself. Rahner develops his doctrine of the
trinity on the basis of this view that the experience of God as self-
communicating love is already an experience of God as in Godself triune.[74] Expressed in more traditional theological terms,
the basic axiom of Rahner's position regarding the trinity is: "the
economic trinity is the immanent trinity and vice versa."[75]

Rahner is aware of the difficulties involved in formulating
an adequate, credible doctrine of the trinity in the contemporary
setting. He remarks that most Christians, despite the orthodoxy
of their confession of the trinity, are almost sheer "monotheists"
in their actual religious self-realization. Most religious literature
would remain unchanged if the doctrine of the trinity were
suddenly to disappear. The tract "De trinitate," furthermore,
remains isolated within the system of dogmatics. Once the tract
itself has been finished, there is no further mention of the
doctrine of the trinity throughout the rest of the theological
system. There is no distinction of the three divine persons made
in the doctrines of creation or of grace. Even in christology, it is
said, simply, that God, and not specifically the Logos, became
flesh. The usual scholastic procedure, since the time of the
emergence of Thomas' *Summa* as the key dogmatic textbook, has
been to treat the tract "De deo uno" first, as dealing with the
heart of the doctrine of God, namely, the one divine essence that
is prior to the distinctions between Father, Son, and Spirit. The
tract "De deo trino" follows and plays a very subservient role. As
a result of all these factors, the trinity, according to Rahner, has

come to be understood as a mystery that was revealed simply for its own sake because God so willed, but that has no existentiell relevance to persons.

Rahner argues that this understanding must be false for the trinity is in fact a mystery of salvation. Wherever the topic of the salvation of the human person is raised (and, at least indirectly, this topic must figure in every aspect of the theological system), the doctrine of the trinity must be encountered. Rahner's own view is that the mystery of the trinity is, in essence, identical to the mystery of God's self-communication. If human being is essentially the event of the free self-communication of God, then the triune nature of God must already be given, to some extent, in human existence. "If man has comprehended himself only when he has understood himself as the addressee of this divine self-communication, then it can be said that the mystery of the trinity is the final mystery of our own reality and, in fact, is experienced in that reality."[76] The mystery of the trinity already resonates with the transcendentality of human being, although, of course, at an unthematic level. For this reason, Rahner asserts that:

> The doctrine of the trinity is not a subtle conceptual game within theology, but is an assertion that cannot be avoided. Only through it can the following straightforward proposition (replete with inconceivability and self-evidence at the same time) be taken with radical seriousness and upheld without qualification: God himself, the permanent, holy mystery, the incomprehensible ground of the transcending mode of being of man [das transzendierende Dasein des Menschen], is not only the God of infinite distance, but intends to be the God of absolute closeness in true self-communication and so is given in the spiritual depths of our existence as well as in the concreteness of our bodily history.[77]

The basic axiom in Rahner's understanding of the trinity was stated to be that the economic trinity is the immanent trinity and vice versa. If this is the case, then, for there to be a genuine self-*communication* of God, the divine communication must respect the capacities of the human addressee of the communication. There is a real sense in which the self-communication of God must correspond to the essential nature of the addressee.[78] Now, for Rahner, the human experience of reality has two aspects. In all human experience of reality there is an experience of individual objects within an unlimited horizon. Neither the object that is given explicity, nor the horizon that is given implicitly, is experienced apart from the other. They are mutually conditioning moments within the *one* human experience of the real. Rahner characterizes these two moments of experience in terms of four pairs of contrasting concepts: origin/future, history/transcendence, offer/acceptance, knowledge or truth/love.[79]

Corresponding to this human essence, the experience of the self-communication of God has a threefold character. First, it is an experience of the one God as the final, permanent, unoriginate mystery that encompasses human existence as self-communicating closeness. This *one* experience of God, however, has two modalities, which, along with the one experience of God as such, constitute the threefold character of our experience of God. There is an objective, a posteriori, historical modality of the experience of God, and an unthematic, a priori, transcendental modality. Because the human person is radically free, the self-communication of God is present as an *offer*. The offer of the self-communication of God is the *origin* or source of reality as such.[80] For this offer of divine self-communication, which is the origin of human being, to be fully available to human persons, it must be given not just as a transcendental (thus transhistorical) horizon, but also as a particular reality within *history*. These three concepts: offer, origin, and history are identified with truth, for Rahner, because *truth* is the manifestation of a free person that must be waited upon and encountered by those who are party to such a self-manifestation. Thus the self-communication of God "as the manifestation of the essence of God," in relation to the a posteriori, objective moment within human experience "is, for us, *truth*. This manifestation occurs as a faithful *offer,* thus establishes an *origin* and makes itself conclusively present in the concreteness of *history*."[81]

At the same time, the self-communication of God is experienced as the absolute *future,* the final fulfillment of human existence that makes possible the dynamism of human *transcendence*. The self-communication of God is not just the asymptotic goal of human transcendence, but becomes the innermost principle of that transcendence and makes possible the *acceptance* of the supernatural goal. Such a self-communication that wills itself absolutely and establishes the conditions of its own acceptance can be described as nothing less than genuine, personal *love*.[82]

Rahner's axiom must again be recalled: the economic trinity is the immanent trinity and vice versa. This means that the self-communication of God must be a real self-communication of God. Therefore, these three distinct moments within the human experience of the self-communication of God must be grounded in real distinctions in the divine being.

> If the difference given in something that is communicated by God is *only* on the side of the creature, then there can be no question at all of a self-communication of God in the strict sense. However, if it really is a matter of a *self*-communication, in which there is a real difference given in that which is communicated as such, thus "for us," then God, without prejudice to his unity, must in himself be differentiated.[83]

The threefold character of God's relation to human beings in self-communication or grace is already an indication of the threefold nature of God in Godself. If God were not experienced, in grace, as being triune, then persons would have no knowledge of God as being in Godself triune. But, at the same time, if God were not already in Godself triune, then, of course, the human experience of grace would not have a threefold nature.

As was indicated in the passage cited at the very beginning of this section, a distinction can be made between God as absolute mystery that communicates Godself, God as the true self-manifestation of God that is communicated, and God as the loving acceptance within the human person of the self-communication of God. Rahner calls the three modalities of divine self-communication the three distinct ways in which God subsists (*die drei distinkten Subsistenzweisen*).[84] In traditional terms, of course, these distinct ways of subsistence are the three persons of the trinity. God the Father is God experienced as the one, unoriginate, holy mystery that communicates itself to human persons. Rahner, affirming a pre-Augustinian tradition, speaks of the one God of the creed not as an impersonal divine essence prior to the distinction between Father, Son, and Spirit, but rather precisely as the Father. God the Father is *ho theos* as such, to use New Testament language, the one center of divine activity, the one God to whom all human persons are related.[85] The Logos, or Son, then, is the true self-manifestation of the Father that is communicated in human history in Jesus Christ. The Holy Spirit is the loving acceptance of the self-manifestation of the Father through the Son present within the transcendentality of every human person. In Rahner's own words:

> . . . the absolute self-communication of God to the world as the mystery that draws near is called, in its absolutely primordial and nondeducible character, Father; as the principle that itself acts and that, because it is necessary to this free self-communication, must act within history, Son; and as lavished upon us and accepted by us, Holy Spirit.[86]

Rahner chooses to speak of "three distinct ways in which God subsists," in order to avoid the traditional term "persons," which he holds to be fundamentally misleading.[87] Whereas "person" originally meant *"hypostasis"* in trinitarian terminology, the term has taken on a very different meaning outside of this context. "Person" now is understood to mean an individual center of consciousness and activity. Rahner holds it to be antithetical to the Christian confession of the trinity to assert that there are three persons in God, in the modern sense of "person." There is just one single center of consciousness and activity in God.

While the distinctions between God as unoriginate source, as Logos, and as Holy Spirit are real distinctions, they are nevertheless relative, not absolute, distinctions. Rahner argues:

> Because it is really a matter of the self-communication of God in himself, this threefold character is one within God himself, it indicates a differentiation in God himself. Because, in each of these two cases [the Logos and the Holy Spirit], it is a matter of the self-communication of God himself and not of two created realities brought forward by efficient causality, it is thus always a matter of one and the same God. God as the unoriginate source of supernatural self-communication, God himself as the principle that acts and expresses itself in the world, and God as the God who has come to us, who has been communicated to and accepted by us, possess one and the same essence.[88]

To deny that these distinctions within the divine being are relative, is, for Rahner, to slip into tritheism.

Precisely to avoid a tritheistic misunderstanding of the traditional language about the three persons in God, Rahner urges that all such concepts must constantly be referred back to the primordial experience of God in grace. The Holy Spirit is experienced *as* God, the Logos is experienced *as* God, and the unoriginate source of this twofold divine self-communication is experienced *as* God. The affirmation that there are three persons in God is a subsequent generalization from this original experience. In the following formulation, the grounding of the trinitarian distinctions in the experience of salvation history is made clear.

> To the extent that [God] has come into the innermost core of the existence of each individual man as the salvation that divinizes us, we call him in truth, "holy pneuma," "Holy Spirit." To the extent that precisely this God, one and the same, strictly as himself, is there for us in the concrete historicity of our existence in Jesus Christ—he himself and not a representative—we call him "Logos" or Son in an absolute sense. To the extent that precisely this God who comes to us as Spirit and Logos is always the ineffable one, the holy mystery, the incomprehensible ground and source of his arrival in Son and Spirit and maintains himself as such, we call him the one God, the Father. To the extent that, in the strictest sense, it is a matter of God giving himself and not something else that is different from him in Spirit, Logos-Son, and Father, it is to be said that, in the strictest sense, Spirit, Logos-Son, and Father are, in the same sense, one and the same God in the unlimited fullness of divinity and are in possession of one and the same divine essence. To the extent that the way in which God is given for us as Spirit, Son, and Father does not indicate the same manner of givenness, inasmuch as true and genuine differences are present for us in this way in which God is given, these three modes of givenness are for us to be radically distinguished. . . . And yet inasmuch as these modes of givenness of one and the same God may not cancel for us the true self-communication of the one, solitary God, these three modes of givenness of one and the same God must belong to him, in himself and for himself, he who is one and the same.[89]

For Rahner, the internal distinction of God as Father, Son, and Spirit is a condition of the possibility of the communication *ad extra* of God in these three distinct ways in which God subsists.

> In God in himself exists the real difference between one
> and the same God as necessarily and in one the unorigi-
> nate one who communicates himself to himself (Father),
> the one who in truth is expressed for himself (Son), and
> the one who in love is received and accepted for himself
> (Spirit). As a result, God is the one who in freedom can
> communicate himself externally.[90]

The communication of Godself to others, to nondivine creatures, is a *free*, gratuitous act that has as a condition of its
possibility the *necessary* intradivine communication of Godself.
Because God is Father, Son, and Spirit, God can communicate
Godself in this threefold manner to persons in salvation history.

This view of the trinity may bear some similarity to the
traditional "psychological" doctrine of the triune God, especially
since Rahner, like Augustine, uses human knowledge and
human love to explicate the divine triunity. Heinrich Ott says, in
relation to Rahner's understanding of the trinity, that "truth and
love are not only structures of human existence and not only
structures of revelation to human existence, but, before that, are
already structures of the divine self that communicates itself to
man in this way."[91] But despite this similarity, Rahner warns
against the dangers of a psychological doctrine of the trinity. He
argues that such a view, finally, does not explain what it sets out
to explain, namely, why the Father expresses himself in the
Logos and, with the Logos, breathes the Spirit. A psychological
doctrine of the trinity, according to him, must presuppose "the
Father as already knowing and loving himself and cannot allow
him to be constituted as knowing and loving for the first time
through the expression of the Logos and the breathing of the
Pneuma."[92]

But even more decisive for Rahner is the fact that, in his
view, a psychological doctrine of the trinity violates the basic
axiom of all trinitarian thought, namely, that the economic trinity is the immanent trinity, by failing to remain true to the
salvation-historical starting point of all our talk about God. He
argues:

> The psychological doctrine of the trinity leaps over the
> experience of the trinity in the economy of salvation in
> favor of what seems to be an almost gnostic speculation
> concerning how things go on in the interior of God. In
> so doing, it really forgets that the countenance of God, as
> it is turned toward us in the self-communication meant

here, is, in the threefold character of this orientation, precisely the in itself of God himself, if indeed the divine self-communication in grace and glory is really the communication to us of God in himself.[93]

Rahner does indeed speak of a divine self-love, as will be seen shortly. But he avoids speaking of this love in terms of the love of the Father for the Son, which love is the Holy Spirit.[94]

Love as the Fundamental Divine Act

While Rahner may not speak of the intertrinitarian love of God for Godself after the manner of a psychological doctrine of the trinity, the concept of the free love of God for, or self-communication of God to, nondivine persons plays a central role in his theology. It was shown in the previous chapter that, for him, the act of love for a fellow human being is the all-encompassing, fundamental act *(der Grundakt)* of human being. All other human acts are to be viewed from the perspective of the act of love. What I want to show in this section is that Rahner holds, likewise, that the fundamental act of God is the act of love for others. It is in the light of God's love for the creatures, he says, that all other divine activity is to be understood.

In Rahner's view, "God desires to communicate himself, desires to lavish his love, the love that he himself is. This is the first and the last consideration of his actual plans and, therefore, also of his actual world."[95] This love, which is the self-communication of God, is the fundamental act *(der Grundakt)* of God that grounds and encompasses all other divine activity.[96] Rahner uses a number of other terms as synonyms for *"der Grundakt"* of God, such as: the primordial act *(der Urtat)*, the primordial phenomenon *(das Urphänomenon)*, and the primordial possibility *(die Urmöglichkeit)* of God.[97] All these terms express the same idea: the fundamental act of God, which is the purpose behind, and unifying goal of, all other divine acts, is God's ecstatic act of love for the creatures in divine self-communication. "The primordial phenomenon is precisely the self-alienation, the becoming, the *kenosis* and *genesis* of God."[98] As was seen in the previous section, this fundamental act of love of the one God, as the unoriginate source of all, has a twofold character, in that it is enacted in grace and in the incarnation.

According to Rahner, all other divine activity is to be understood in relation to the act of divine love. He contrasts divine creation and divine self-communication in the following way.

> The entire creation, within the factual order, is from the outset established as the condition of the possibility, or the addressee, of the self-communication of God *ad extra*. The entire supernatural reality in grace and incarnation (both understood as mutually conditioning moments of the one self-communication of God) no longer appears as a subsequent addition to a world conceived as the creation of God. Creation, as the constitution of the nondivine "out of nothing," appears as the presupposition and condition of the realization of the highest possibility "*ad extra*": God's self-communication, in which he does not constitute an other distinct from himself, but communicates himself and thereby reveals himself truly to be self-bestowing agape.[99]

The self-communication of God is the primordial act of God. But an act of self-communication requires an addressee. God's creation *ex nihilo* provides the addressee of divine self-communication, and thus can be said to occur for the sake of the self-communication of God.

> God is not only the creator of a world that is distinct from him. He has made himself the inner principle of this world, through the spiritual creature that belongs to this one world, in genuine, immediate self-communication, called grace. This grace can be conceived such that the divine possibility of creating out of nothing is a moment of the higher and more encompassing possibility of God as the one who can communicate himself in free love. God has factually willed the creation . . . because he wished to alienate himself and abandon himself, to step away from himself in free love.[100]

Creation is not an end in itself. It is a deficient mode of self-communication. This is the case, for Rahner, precisely because creation does not involve a radical act of self-giving love on the part of God. Just as human being is realized in its fullness only in an act of ecstatic love for another person, so, for him, God is fully revealed only in the act of loving self-communication. The creation of another distinct being over against God cannot provide such a final disclosure of the divine reality. This disclosure occurs where God gives Godself away to the spiritual creature, and does not merely produce or give some created entity or

quality. In self-communication alone the true personhood of
God is revealed and God is shown to be love.[101]

Rahner argues that the ability of God to establish a loving
personal relationship with human persons (here, in the mode of
the incarnation) is more basic than the ability to create the
nondivine world, and thus human beings, *ex nihilo*.

> God goes out of himself, he himself, he as the fullness
> that lavishes itself. Because he can do this, because the
> ability to become historical [*das Selbst-Geschichte-werden-
> Können*] is his free, primordial possibility (not primordial
> necessity) for which reason he is defined as love in scrip-
> ture, . . . God's ability to be the creator, the ability to
> posit the merely other in itself, to allow it to spring forth
> from its own nothingness, without releasing himself to
> the other, is only the derived, limited, secondary pos-
> sibility that is grounded in this primordial possibility.[102]

God's final, all-embracing desire is to communicate Godself
in love to the spiritual creature. The goal of divine activity is the
establishment of an intimate communion between the divine
person and human persons. This communion is not brought
about by efficient causality but rather by quasi-formal causality in
which the transcendent God becomes an immanent principle
within human being.[103] Divine creation, which establishes the
creature in its difference from God, in its otherness, is not the
final word, according to Rahner, concerning the relationship of
God to the world. Rather, the creation of that which is other than
God is merely a condition of the possibility of the communion
between God and the creature established in divine self-communication.

Therefore, in Rahner's mind, the supernatural order, the
communion between God and the nondivine brought about by
self-communication, is not a superfluous addition to nature.
Grace is, instead, "the true essence of that which constitutes the
ontological relationship between God and the creature."[104] The
natural order (which, to reiterate what was said above, never
actually exists apart from grace) is a condition of the possibility
of the bestowal of the supernatural communion between God
and creature. Nature is required, according to Rahner, so that
there will be an addressee for the free, self-giving act of divine
love.

When one focuses on the historical or a posteriori modality

of the self-communication of God, the incarnation appears as "the unambiguous ontological goal of the movement of creation."[105] The possibility of divine creation rests upon the possibility of the incarnation of God within history. This view is stated quite sharply when Rahner says:

> Creation itself occurs in Christ. It is not difficult to see that the first, primordial, encompassing, eternal intention of God is his own self-expression in which the Logos of God comes to ex-ist [*eksistieren*] in the emptiness of that which is outside of God [*das Aussergöttliche*], and that in *this* intention God desires the humanity of Christ and thus the whole creation as its environment. There is no fundamental difficulty in understanding factual creation (as the production of the "natural") as occurring as the presupposition that God posits because he, the eternal one, himself desires to have a history of self-abandoning love.[106]

It has been shown in this chapter and in the previous one that human being in its very essence strives for God as the *Woraufhin* of its transcendence. Because of the self-communication of God, which divinizes human being by providing it with a supernatural existential, this striving is not just a dynamism toward God as an aloof, ungraspable horizon, but is a striving for God as the radically proximate and attainable fulfillment of human existence. Since the whole of the material cosmos is fulfilled in the spiritual creature, one can say, for Rahner, that the dynamism of all of creation itself is a movement toward immediate communion with God. At the same time, God's most fundamental purpose and act is the establishment of intimate, loving communion with the creatures. Therefore, the divine-creaturely communion is the final goal and fulfillment of the actual being of both parties, God and the nondivine. Grace represents the transcendental mode of this communion between God and the creatures. The transcendental offer of grace is always mediated in some fashion by historical realities. The absolute historical meeting point of the human (and thus creaturely) dynamism toward God and God's self-communicating movement toward the creatures is found in the incarnation of the Logos in Jesus Christ.[107] Here, the self-communication of God is given in history as absolute, irreversible, and finally victorious. There is a real sense in which the creation of the world is not complete until the event of the incarnation, until that point at which the world is immediately present to God in history, not just in transcendentality, and God's self-giving love for the creatures actually adopts the reality of the creature as its own. Using the language of Colossians 1:15, Rahner writes that Jesus Christ is that point at which God becomes the all in all.[108] Or, in the terms of the discussion of the first two chapters of this part of the study, the incarnation is the historical point at which the fundamental act of human being and the fundamental act of God, both of which are nothing other than the act of ecstatic, self-giving love, coincide.

NOTES

[1] "Über den Begriff des Geheimnisses in der katholischen Theologie," *ST*, 4:84 (ET: *TI*, 4:61).

[2] *GG*, p. 125 (ET: *FCF*, p. 119).

[3] "*Theos* im Neuen Testament," *ST*, 1:131 (ET: *TI*, 1:115).

[4] "Die Forderung nach einer 'Kurzformel' des christlichen Glaubens," *ST*, 8:160 (ET: *TI*, 9:122–123).

[5] "Zur Theologie der Menschwerdung," *ST*, 4:148 (ET: *TI*, 4:114–115).

[6] *GG*, p. 122 (ET: *FCF*, p. 116).

[7] *Karl Rahner*, pp. vi, 3–4, 17–18, 55–56.

[8] Ibid., p. 57.

[9] "Über das Verhältnis von Natur und Gnade," *ST*, 1:343 (ET: *TI*, 1:316).

[10] "Zur Theologie der Menschwerdung," *ST*, 4:148 (ET: *TI*, 4:115).

[11] Ibid. (ET: ibid.).

[12] Ibid., pp. 148–152 (ET: ibid., pp. 114–118).

[13] *GG*, pp. 122–123 (ET: *FCF*, p. 116).

[14] Ibid., p. 122 (ET: ibid.).

[15] Ibid., p. 126 (ET: ibid., p. 120).

[16] See "Zur scholastischen Begrifflichkeit der ungeschaffenen Gnade," *ST*, 1:347–375 (ET: *TI*, 1:319–346), "Natur und Gnade," *ST*, 4:220–224 (ET: *TI*, 4:174–178).

[17] "Natur und Gnade," *ST*, 4:223 (ET: *TI*, 4:177).

[18] *Karl Rahner*, p. 12.

[19] Ibid., p. 107.

[20] "Um das Geheimnis der Dreifaltigkeit," *ST*, 12:323 (ET: *TI*, 16:258).

[21] *GG*, pp. 122–123 (ET: *FCF*, p. 116).

22 Ibid., p. 137 (ET: ibid., p. 131).

23 "Über den Begriff des Geheimnisses in der katholischen Theologie," *ST*, 4:77, 83–84 (ET: *TI*, 4:55–56, 61).

24 Ibid., p. 77 (ET: ibid., p. 56).

25 *GG*, p. 126 (ET: *FCF*, pp. 119–120).

26 Ibid., p. 125 (ET: ibid., p. 119). I am not convinced that Rahner
gives sufficient justification for this assertion. It seems to me that his
view of God vacillates ambiguously between the position that God is
absolutely distinct from categorial reality and the position that God, in
the incarnation, takes upon Godself categorial reality as God's own. I
will return to this point in Part II.

27 "*Theos* im Neuen Testament," *ST*, 1:134 (ET: *TI*, 1:117).

28 "Über den Begriff des Geheimnisses in der katholischen Theologie," *ST*, 4:92 (ET: *TI*, 4:67).

29 "Der eine Mittler und die Vielfalt der Vermittlungen," *ST*, 8:228
(ET: *TI*, 9:178).

30 *GG*, p. 126 (ET: *FCF*, 120).

31 Ibid. (ET: ibid.).

32 "Kirchliche Christologie zwischen Exegese und Dogmatik," *ST*,
9:212–213 (ET: *TI*, 11:200).

33 "Immanente und transzendente Vollendung der Welt," *ST*, 8:602
(ET: *TI*, 10:282).

34 Ibid., pp. 601–603 (ET: ibid., pp. 282–283). It should be noted
that just as the nonhuman realm comes to itself in human existence, so,
for Rahner, the self-communication of God to the spiritual creature
provides the final fulfillment of the material world as a whole. See ibid.,
pp. 604–607 (ET: ibid., pp. 284–287).

35 See "Das Christentum und der 'neue Mensch,'" ST, 5:159–179
(ET: *TI*, 5:135–153); "Marxistische Utopie und christliche Zukunft des
Menschen," *ST*, 6:77–88 (ET: *TI*, 6:59–68); "Christlicher Humanismus," *ST*, 8:234–259 (ET: *TI*, 9:187–204); "Experiment Mensch," *ST*,
8:260–285 (ET: *TI*, 9:205–224); "Fragment aus einer theologischen
Besinnung auf den Begriff der Zukunft," *ST*, 8:555–560 (ET: *TI*,
10:235–241); "Zur Theologie der Hoffnung," *ST*, 8:561–579 (ET: *TI*,
10:242–259); "Immanente und transzendente Vollendung der Welt,"
ST, 8:593–609 (ET: *TI*, 10:273–289); "Die Frage nach der Zukunft," *ST*,
9:519–540 (ET: *TI*, 12:181–201).

36 See "Zur Theologie der Hoffnung," *ST*, 8:561–579 (ET: *TI*,
10:242–259).

37 "Marxistische Utopie und christliche Zukunft des Menschen,"
ST, 6:79–84 (ET: *TI*, 6:61–65).

38 "Das Christentum und der 'neue Mensch,'" *ST*, 5:170 (ET: *TI*,
5:144–145).

39 "Marxistische Utopie und christliche Zukunft des Menschen,"
ST, 6:78 (ET: *TI*, 6:60).

[40] Ibid., pp. 80–81 (ET: ibid., pp. 62–63).

[41] "Experiment Mensch," *ST,* 8:278–279 (ET: *TI,* 9:219).

[42] "Über das Verhältnis von Natur und Gnade," *ST,* 1:324 (ET: *TI,* 1:298). For a first-rate discussion of the various extrinsicist views of nature and grace, as well as the place of Rahner's own thought within the twentieth century discussion of the issue, see William Shepherd, *Man's Condition: God and the World Process* (New York: Herder & Herder, 1969).

[43] "Über das Verhältnis von Natur und Gnade," *ST,* 1:326 (ET: *TI,* 1:300).

[44] As will be seen in the next chapter, one must say concrete human nature because, for Rahner, it is possible that God could have created human beings without bestowing grace upon them.

[45] *GG,* p. 132 (ET: *FCF,* p. 126).

[46] Ibid., p. 133 (ET: ibid., p. 127).

[47] In this chapter the focus of attention will be on the universality of grace (supernatural *existential*) while, in the following chapter, I will discuss the sheer gratuity of grace (*supernatural* existential).

[48] *Der Mensch als Geheimnis,* p. 249.

[49] *GG,* p. 134 (ET: *FCF,* p. 128).

[50] It should be noted that Rahner displays a slightly different understanding of the supernatural existential in the early article in which the concept is first extensively discussed ("Über das Verhältnis von Natur und Gnade," *ST,* 1:323–345 (ET: *TI,* 1:297–317)). There, he holds that the supernatural existential is the human potency for, or disposition toward, grace. He says, "the capacity for the God of personal love, who lavishes himself, is the central and permanent existential of man as he actually is" (p. 339 (ET: p. 312)). However, Rahner soon drops this mention of the supernatural existential as a predisposition toward grace and speaks of the supernatural existential as the offer of grace, or the self-communication of God, as such. For a discussion of the development of the meaning of the concept of the supernatural existential in Rahner, see Bert van der Heijden, *Karl Rahner,* pp. 21–41. Van der Heijden rightly points out that, within the context of Rahner's original discussion of the concept, his proposal of a supernatural existential does not solve the problem it was intended to solve (the problem of how grace can be both intrinsic to human being and yet unmerited), but merely poses the same problem on a different level. Rahner could be asked, in relation to his original formulation of the concept, how the supernatural act whereby God imparts a disposition toward grace (the supernatural existential) is both intrinsic to human being and yet unmerited. The result of such questioning, according to van der Heijden, would be the assertion of an infinite number of such predispositions toward the supernatural activity of God. But when the supernatural existential is understood as the offer of grace itself, then this problem of

infinite regress is removed. I will argue, in Part II of this study, that the real problem of Rahner's notion of the supernatural existential, even when understood as the self-communication of God itself, lies in his view of the gratuity of the divine love.

51 See *GG*, pp. 122–123, 129–130 (ET: *FCF*, pp. 116, 123–124).

52 Ibid., pp. 133–134 (ET: ibid., p. 128).

53 Ibid., p. 134 (ET: ibid., p. 128).

54 "Bemerkungen zum Begriff der Offenbarung," in *Offenbarung und Überlieferung*, by Karl Rahner and Joseph Ratzinger, Quaestiones Disputatae 25 (Freiburg: Verlag Herder, 1965), p. 17 (ET: *Revelation and Tradition* (New York: Herder and Herder, 1966), p. 16).

55 "Kirche, Kirchen und Religionen," *ST*, 8:359 (ET: *TI*, 10:34).

56 Ibid., pp. 359–360 (ET: ibid., pp. 34–35).

57 *GG*, p. 135 (ET: *FCF*, p. 129).

58 Ibid., p. 130 (ET: ibid., p. 124).

59 "Atheismus und implizites Christentum," *ST*, 8:209 (ET: *TI*, 9:162).

60 See "Bemerkungen zum Begriff der Offenbarung," pp. 16–19 (ET: *Revelation and Tradition*, pp. 16–18); *GG*, pp. 147–157 (ET: *FCF*, pp. 142–152).

61 "Natur und Gnade," *ST*, 4:226–229 (ET: *TI*, 4:179–181).

62 See "Die anonymen Christen," *ST*, 6:545–554 (ET: *TI*, 6:390–398); "Atheismus und implizites Christentum," *ST*, 8:187–212 (ET: *TI*, 9:145–164); "Kirche, Kirchen und Religionen," *ST*, 8:355–373 (ET: *TI*, 10:30–49); "Anonymes Christentum und Missionsauftrag der Kirche," *ST*, 9:498–515 (ET: *TI*, 12:161–178); "Bemerkungen zum Problem des 'anonymen Christen,'" *ST*, 10:531–546 (ET: *TI*, 14:280–294).

63 "Bemerkungen zum Problem des 'anonymen Christen,'" *ST*, 10:543–544 (ET: *TI*, 14:292).

64 "Die theologische Dimension der Frage nach dem Menschen," *ST*, 12:401–402 (ET: *TI*, 17:66).

65 *GG*, p. 134 (ET: *FCF*, p. 128).

66 "Über das Verhältnis von Natur und Gnade," *ST*, 1:356–359 (ET: *TI*, 1:328–331). As will be shown in more detail later, there is a tension in Rahner's thought as to whether the novelty of the relationship between God and human beings established by the divine self-communication is to be understood in a temporal, or only in a logical, sense.

67 See "Über den Begriff des Geheimnisses in der katholischen Theologie," *ST*, 4:90 (ET: *TI*, 4:65–66) and *GG*, p. 127 (ET: *FCF*, p. 121).

68 *GG*, p. 127 (ET: *FCF*, p. 121).

69 "Über das Verhältnis von Natur und Gnade," *ST*, 1:358–359 (ET: *TI*, 1:330–331). Kenneth Ebehard's claim, in "Karl Rahner and the Supernatural Existential," *Thought* 46 (1971):537–561, that Rahner qualifies the formal causality that is operative in divine self-communica-

tion as "quasi"-formal causality because "this formal causality does not annihilate the distinct individuality of the person it effects" (pp. 548–549) is mistaken. Indeed, for Rahner, grace does not violate the autonomy of the human person. But it is not for this reason that he speaks of a quasi-formal causality.

[70] "Bemerkungen zum dogmatischen Traktat *De Trinitate*," *ST*, 4:125–126 (ET: *TI*, 4:96).

[71] "Natur und Gnade," *ST*, 4:220 (ET: *TI*, 4:175). In the essay in which Rahner first speaks of the model of quasi-formal causality in relation to the self-communication of God, there is a somewhat different distinction drawn between efficient and formal causality ("Zur scholastischen Begrifflichkeit der ungeschaffenen Gnade," *ST*, 1:347–375 (ET: *TI*, 1:319–346)). There, Rahner states that efficient causality is "a producing out of the cause" *(ein Aus-der-Ursache-Heraus-stellen)*; while formal causality is "a taking up into the ground (form)" *(ein In-den-Grund (forma)-Hinein-nehmen)*, see p. 358 (ET: p. 329). This description of formal causality is curious in that, based on what has been said above, one would expect formal causality to be characterized as a placing of the ground or form (God) within that which is grounded (human being), rather than as a taking up of that which is grounded into the ground or form. It seems to me that in this description of quasi-formal causality as an *In-den-Grund (forma)-Hinein-nehmen*, Rahner is attempting to emphasize the fact that the self-communication of God brings about a genuine participation of the human person *in* the divine being (cf. William Shepherd, *Man's Condition: God and the World Process*, p. 194). This is how Klaus Fischer understands this *In-den-Grund (forma)-Hinein-nehmen:* "In that God approaches man, he [God] grasps him [man] and takes or draws him into the ground that he [God] himself is." *(Der Mensch als Geheimnis*, pp. 360–361. The original text reads, "Indem er auf den Menschen zukommt, ergreift er ihn und nimmt oder zieht ihn in den Grund hinein, der er selber ist.") While I think Fischer's interpretation of this somewhat curious definition of quasi-formal causality is correct, it is significant that this definition is found in a very early work of Rahner's; one originally published in 1939. This formulation, as far as I know, does not recur in Rahner's works. In all of his other explanations of the model of quasi-formal causality, it is the presence of God as a constitutive moment of the spiritual creature that is emphasized, rather than the elevation or participation of the spiritual creature in God.

[72] "Über den Begriff des Geheimnisses in der katholischen Theologie," *ST*, 4:91 (ET: *TI*, 4:66).

[73] "Bemerkungen zum dogmatischen Traktat *De Trinitate*," *ST*, 4:126 (ET: *TI*, 4:97).

[74] For Rahner's doctrine of the trinity, see "Der dreifaltige Gott als transzendenter Urgrund der Heilsgeschichte," in *Mysterium Salutis*, ed.

Johannes Feiner und Magnus Löhrer, vol. 2 (Einsiedeln: Benziger Verlag, 1967), p. 317–401 (ET: Karl Rahner, *The Trinity* (New York: Seabury Press, 1974)). Unless otherwise indicated, all material in this section is derived from this essay.

75 "Der dreifaltige Gott als transzendenter Urgrund der Heilsgeschichte," p. 328 (ET: *The Trinity*, p. 22).

76 Ibid., pp. 345–346 (ET: ibid., p. 47).

77 *GG*, p. 142 (ET: *FCF*, p. 137).

78 Rahner argues this point in Part IV ("The Place of the Free Message") of *Hörer des Wortes*, pp. 138–211. There he says, simply: "God can only reveal what man can hear" (p. 142).

79 "Der dreifaltige Gott als transzendenter Urgrund der Heilsgeschichte," pp. 376–378 (ET: *The Trinity*, pp. 91–94).

80 It will be shown in the next section that, for Rahner, divine creation occurs for the sake of divine self-communication, that is, creation is a condition of the possibility of self-communication.

81 "Der dreifaltige Gott als transzendenter Urgrund der Heilsgeschichte," p. 380 (ET: *The Trinity*, p. 96), my emphasis.

82 Ibid., pp. 380–381 (ET: ibid., 96–98).

83 "Bemerkungen zum dogmatischen Traktat *De Trinitate*," *ST*, 4:126, n. 28 (ET: *TI*, 4:96, n. 28).

84 "Der dreifaltige Gott als transzendenter Urgrund der Heilsgeschichte," p. 389 (ET: *The Trinity*, p. 109).

85 See "*Theos* im Neuen Testament," *ST*, 1:143–167 (ET: *TI*, 1:125–148).

86 "Über den Begriff des Geheimnisses in der katholischen Theologie," *ST*, 4:95 (ET: *TI*, 4:70).

87 "Der dreifaltige Gott als transzendenter Urgrund der Heilsgeschichte," pp. 364–366 (ET: *The Trinity*, pp. 73–76).

88 "Über den Begriff des Geheimnisses in der katholischen Theologie," *ST*, 4:96 (ET: *TI*, 4:70).

89 *GG*, pp. 142–143 (ET: *FCF*, pp. 136–137).

90 "Der dreifaltige Gott als transzendenter Urgrund der Heilsgeschichte," p. 384 (ET: *The Trinity*, pp. 101–102).

91 *Wirklichkeit und Glaube*, 2:344.

92 *GG*, pp. 140–141 (ET: *FCF*, p. 135).

93 Ibid., p. 141 (ET: ibid.).

94 For a further discussion of this issue, along with a comparison of Rahner's and Karl Barth's views of the trinity, see Ch. IX of this study.

95 "Über das Verhältnis von Natur und Gnade," *ST*, 1:336 (ET: *TI*, 1:310). The term "actual" in this passage again points out that although in fact God has communicated Godself in love, God could have had other plans that might not have included love for the creatures.

96 "Christologie im Rahmen des modernen Selbst- und Weltverständnisses," *ST*, 9:237 (ET: *TI*, 11:226).

[97] "Natur und Gnade," *ST*, 4:222 (ET: *TI*, 4:176) and "Zur Theologie der Menschwerdung," *ST*, 4:148 (ET: *TI*, 4:114–115).

[98] Ibid. (ET: ibid.).

[99] "Christologie im Rahmen des modernen Selbst- und Weltverständnisses," *ST*, 9:231–232 (ET: *TI*, 11:220).

[100] "Immanente und transzendente Vollendung der Welt," *ST*, 8:600 (ET: *TI*, 10:280–281).

[101] *GG*, pp. 127–128 (ET: *FCF*, pp. 120–122).

[102] "Zur Theologie der Menschwerdung," *ST*, 4:148 (ET: *TI*, 4:115).

[103] "Immanente und transzendente Vollendung der Welt," *ST*, 8:601 (ET: *TI*, 10:281).

[104] *GG*, p. 128 (ET: *FCF*, p. 122).

[105] "Probleme der Christologie von heute," *ST*, 1:185 (ET: *TI*, 1:165).

[106] "Fragen der Kontroverstheologie der Rechtfertigung," *ST*, 4:266 (ET: *TI*, 4:213–214).

[107] I will consider Rahner's understanding of the incarnation in more detail in Ch. VI. For the moment, I only wish to indicate that the event of Jesus Christ is the historical culmination of the dynamism of human being (Ch. III) and the self-communicative activity of God (Ch. IV).

[108] "Probleme der Christologie von heute," *ST*, 1:186 (ET: *TI*, 1:165).

CHAPTER V
THE FREEDOM OF DIVINE LOVE

The previous chapter has shown that, for Rahner, love is the fundamental act of God. It is an act that grounds and encompasses all other divine activity. This love is communicated to all human beings as an immanent principle of their self-fulfillment. However, one would misunderstand Rahner's view of God if one were to forget that the love of God, although the primordial divine act, is, nevertheless, a freely chosen act. God could be God without bestowing love upon the spiritual creature. Likewise, although divine self-communication is an existential within human existence, it is a *supernatural* existential. Human being would still be possible without the presence of this supernatural existential, which is the offer of God's love. Further, while Rahner stresses the intrinsic character of grace in human existence, the important distinction between nature and grace for him must not be overlooked. Finally, it was stated above that the essential core of the Christian proclamation is an affirmation that God is love and not just unapproachably distant silence. Rahner also holds, however, that this New Testament proclamation would be lost if one were to understand the love of God as anything other than a wholly unexpected and unexacted act of free, personal love on God's part. The goal of this chapter is to demonstrate the radically free and gratuitous character of God's love in Rahner's theology.

God as Free Personal Actor

It has already been shown that, as Rahner understands it, the primary meaning of freedom is the self-actualization or self-realization of the free subject. A free act, for him, is not so much the production of a work that stands over against the actor, but is rather a taking possession and fulfilling of the essence of the free actor itself.[1] Freedom is the ability to constitute oneself as per-

sonal subject, not the ability to do this or that particular act.
Because a subject is free, first of all, in relation to itself, that is,
free in a transcendental sense (which includes a transcendental
relationship to God and to other persons), the subject can act in
relation to other persons and objects in a categorial sense.[2] The
categorial acts of a free agent, which mediate the subject's free
self-realization, are always novel events that cannot be deduced
or predicted ahead of time by others. Free persons must be
encountered. One must wait upon the free self-disclosure of
another subject.[3]

According to Rahner, the fullest self-disclosure of a free
person occurs in an act of love, where one gives or abandons
oneself to another. Freedom is a necessary condition of the
possibility of such an act of love. Only an agent who possesses
her- or himself, and thus can either give or refuse her- or
himself, has the requisite freedom to enter into a relationship of
personal love.[4] For, as was shown above, love, for Rahner, is

> . . . not a natural flowing out of the self, but is the free
> self-bestowal of a person . . . whose gift is always an
> event of wonder and grace. . . . Love in the full, per-
> sonal sense is . . . the abandoning and opening of one's
> innermost self to and for the other, who is loved.[5]

Rahner says that if the biblical understanding of grace is to
be maintained, then God must also be conceived as a free actor
capable of personal love. He distinguishes two senses in which
God is free relative to the creatures. On the one hand, God as the
mysterious horizon of human transcendence is free in the metaphysical sense of being existentially independent of finite reality,
while, on the other hand, the God of self-communicating love
proclaimed in the New Testament is free in the additional sense
of having entered into a personal relationship with human
beings that is necessary neither to divine nor to human being.
These two senses of divine freedom will be discussed in this and
in the following section of the present chapter.

Christianity, and theistic philosophy in general, Rahner
holds,

> . . . confess God as the "unchangeable one," who simply
> is—actus purus—who in blessed security, who in the self-
> sufficiency of infinite reality, from eternity to eternity in
> absolute, unmoved, serene fullness always already pos-

sesses what he is, without becoming, without having to achieve what he is.[6]

God is the absolute one.[7] As such, God is completely self-sufficient and self-subsistent. God is wholly independent of the world.

> He cannot, therefore, need finite reality, called "the world," for, otherwise, he would not be radically different from the world, but would be part of a larger whole. . . . On the other hand, the world must be radically dependent on God without making him dependent on the world as the master is dependent on the servant.[8]

Rahner affirms that God does not have real relations to the world, while maintaining the world is really related to God.[9] He argues that "God stands in connection with another and yet remains totally transcendent to this other, i.e., God is influential, although this state of affairs does not work reciprocally upon God himself and does not determine him anew."[10]

This nonrelativity of God is clearly revealed in Rahner's discussion of the divine knowledge. He understands human knowledge, in realistic fashion, to be the *Beisichsein* of the knower that is mediated by receptive being with another. The known is "in" the knower, giving the knower a new determination.[11] But divine knowledge is not receptive and does not entail any relativity on the part of God.[12] Rahner understands the knowledge God has of other reality as follows: "[God], as pure being, is from the outset *beisich* and grasps his own essence in the being reflected into itself of pure being. He knows himself thereby as the omnipotent, creative ground of finite beings, and thus knows these finite beings."[13] Whereas human persons return to themselves and possess themselves only through real relations to other objects and persons, just the opposite is the case with respect to the divine being: God is aware of other beings as a consequence of God's absolute self-knowledge and self-possession.

All of these assertions concerning the metaphysical freedom or strict nonrelativity of God are not to be affirmed simply because they are part of the scholastic tradition. Rather, Rahner argues, only the God who is wholly independent of creaturely reality can be the *Woraufhin* of human transcendence that is unthematically, but necessarily, affirmed in all human activity.

"Only if God is infinite fullness can the becoming of spirit and nature be more than a meaningless coming to itself of absolute emptiness, which collapses into the void that it itself is."[14] As was shown above, only if the human *Vorgriff* is directed toward the absolute fullness of the divine being, are the necessary conditions of human knowledge provided.

According the Rahner, the doctrine of creation *ex nihilo* thematizes the relation of the human subject to its *Woraufhin*, which is given in transcendental experience.[15] (This assumes, he says, that creation is not understood as referring to an earlier moment of time in which the world came into being. Creation refers, rather, to an actual, ongoing process. God's creative activity takes place in every moment as the grounding of time and temporal existence as such.[16]) God's act of creation is free. In innerworldly causal relationships, the cause is, in a certain sense, dependent on the effect, for a cause cannot be precisely *this* cause without causing just *that* effect.[17] In the case of the divine creation of the world this is not true. God as creator remains completely independent of the world.

Rahner argues that it is through God's willing and loving of God's own creative power that the finite world is willed and loved. God's primary act in creation is once again God's own free act of self-possession or self-constitution. On the basis of this self-love, the loving, and thus the positing, of the world is possible. The following passage is important in that it reveals quite clearly the manner in which Rahner understands the metaphysical freedom (even love) of God, which is necessarily affirmed in human experience as such.

> The finite has its ground in the free, illuminated act of God. The free act in which the actor is with itself [*die freie, beisichseiende Tat*] is love. For love is the illuminated will to the person in his underivable uniqueness. God exemplifies this type of will in the positing of finite being. For he intends himself in his free, creative power. . . . The finite, contingent being is illuminated in the free love of God for himself, and, thereby, for his freely posited work. . . . Inasmuch as God in love freely loves himself as the creative power of the finite, he lovingly apprehends the finite itself. In this love, that which is thrown [*das Geworfene*] is elevated into the light of being. Because and to the extent that God loves the finite, it participates in the luminosity of being.[18]

This passage indicates that God, considered solely as the *Woraufhin* of human transcendence (i.e., prescinding from the supernatural self-communication of God), is already more than an impersonal causal principle, and is affirmed to be a personal agent, at least in an analogous sense. Rahner argues that God, like all other persons, does not have attributes with respect to others, but rather freely adopted attitudes or modes of personal behavior.[19] For this reason, he holds that the Christian doctrine of God is more adequately understood as discourse concerning the character or structure of God's freely chosen relationships to the world, than as discourse concerning metaphysically necessary qualities or attributes of God.[20]

The *Woraufhin* and creative ground of human existence is affirmed unthematically within human experience to be a free, transcendent, personal agent.[21] The acts of God as this free agent, that is, the relationships with the creatures into which God freely chooses to enter, cannot be deduced as necessary metaphysical truths. God's activity must be freely revealed. Therefore, God is free over against the world not simply by virtue of the fact that God is the creator. God remains free in relation to the world God has created.[22] The act of creation does not impose any limitations upon the freedom of God's subsequent activity. Rahner remarks that the creature must say not only that God has posited it freely, but also that God disposes of it freely.[23]

> The possibility of [God's] positing the creature . . . must not be exhausted by this positing. God's previous creation [*die Schöpfung*] may not represent the exhaustion [*die Erschöpfung*] of his possibilities. God must still have an unlimited range of free action with respect to his creature.[24]

God's subsequent activity in relation to the world God creates cannot simply be the logical consequence of the original act of creation.

This means that God, known precisely as the *Woraufhin* of human transcendence, is experienced by human persons as having a freedom over against them that transcends God's metaphysical freedom as the creator. The knowledge of God given necessarily in human transcendental experience reveals *that* God is a free personal actor in relation to the created world. However, such metaphysical knowing cannot determine a priori *how*

God does in fact freely relate Godself to the world. Such divine activity is free in the sense of a personal relationship and cannot be determined prior to the relationship itself.

> Precisely because the God who is known from the world by the natural reason of man is a free transcendent person, . . . the concrete way in which God relates himself to man and wishes to act toward him cannot be calculated from human nature, from below. . . . This question cannot be answered by way of a metaphysical projection of the essence of God on the part of man, but can only be answered by God, in the event of his own free decision.[25]

In the following passage, Rahner distinguishes between "necessary revelation" (a disclosure of God as creator who is free in a metaphysical sense) and revelation in a theological sense (whereby God as a free person is disclosed).

> The one who stands over against another as free always shows himself. He shows himself precisely as the person he wishes to be in relation to the other: either the one who is concealed or the one who is disclosed. In this sense revelation occurs necessarily. And because revelation occurs necessarily in this sense (not just could occur), man must reckon with revelation in the usual theological sense: a possible speech of God that breaks his silence and manifests the divine depths to finite spirit. And precisely because revelation is necessary in the indicated metaphysical sense, because man is always confronted with it, revelation in the theological sense is free.[26]

Human being is characterized by this openness to the free revelation of God. The human person is a hearer of the word (*ein Hörer des Wortes*).

> Man always and essentially attends to the speech or the silence of the free God who is wholly self-sufficient. Otherwise, man would not be spirit. . . . As spirit, man stands before the free, living God, the one who either manifests himself or conceals himself.[27]

The Gratuity of Divine Self-Communication

Rahner holds that the actual character of the God who is free to enter into a personal relationship with the creature is finally revealed in divine self-communication: transcendentally in grace, historically in the incarnation. The ecstatic, self-giving of God Godself is the highest act of divine freedom, for it is the act in which Godself, and not a created quality, is communicated. In the act of self-communication, as in the act of creation, "God remains the one who is absolutely free, absolutely without need, and the one who is elevated above all creaturely reality, the addressee of such possible and free self-communication."[28]

All persons, according to Rahner, have a necessary orientation toward God as holy mystery. In the New Testament, the question of whether there is a God is not raised. God is affirmed, simply, to be there, given to human being as such. The question to which the New Testament does seek to respond is the question of "how this already given, self-evident God acts."[29] That God in fact loves us is not a self-evident proposition of metaphysics, but is an incomprehensible wonder that is to be proclaimed again and again.[30] The love of God is a spontaneous, free act that cannot be anticipated ahead of time. It must be made manifest in the actual history of the divine-human relationship.

Human being is necessarily open to God, for it is spirit. But the spiritual nature of human being, in itself, provides no guarantee that God will in fact reveal Godself as love. It is just as conceivable, from the standpoint of human being, that God could refuse Godself and remain the silent, mysterious *Woraufhin* of human transcendence.[31] In fact, because God has bestowed Godself in grace and incarnation, it can be seen that there is a teleology of divine activity, one that is oriented toward self-communication. But this self-communication, although the fundamental act of God's actual dealings with the world, must not be conceived as God's primordial necessity. Rather, it is to be viewed as a primordial possibility of God, which, in fact, has been realized.[32]

As Rahner argues in the following passage, our human experience requires that God be the existentially independent *Woraufhin* of our transcendence, but does not require that God enter into a personal, loving relationship with us.

> The faithfulness, the merciful kindness, the love, etc. that we factually experience and express [in the Christian doctrine of God] are not merely the (theologically attested) necessary "attributes" of the metaphysical essence of God, but are really much more than this. For God could refuse *this* faithfulness, love, etc., which he in fact

demonstrates to us, without thereby ceasing to be
faithful, loving, etc. in a metaphysical sense.[33]

That God through self-communication becomes an intrinsic
principle within human self-realization and not just an
asymptotic goal is solely the result of God's own free decision.
Further, says Rahner:

> Only when we know not only that God is more than we
> have conceived him to be in our human knowledge, as
> we have established it in an anthropology, but also that
> he can speak or remain silent, only then can a real
> speech of God, if it actually occurs, be conceived as that
> which it is: the uncalculable act of free personal love
> before which man sinks to his knee in prayer.[34]

On this basis, Rahner affirms the self-communication of
God to be a strictly gratuitous act of divine freedom. The divine
love is not exacted by human being, nor is it owed to human
being simply because persons have a necessary openness to God.
In the actual world order, divine self-communication is a supernatural existential within human being. But this order is not the
only possible world order. Human being is conceivable without
such a supernatural existential.[35] In the same way, he argues that
the creation of the world would have been possible even if God
had not in fact wished to communicate Godself to that creation
in a historically definitive fashion in the incarnation of the Logos
in Jesus Christ.[36]

Care must be taken to understand the radical nature of the
gratuity of the divine love for Rahner. The gratuity of God's love
is not simply a function of human sinfulness, that is, our failure
to merit grace because of sin. "That which we call 'supernatural
grace' in the Catholic doctrine of grace is already unmerited by
us in relation to our [nature] . . . prior to sin."[37] Nor is the love
of God free merely in the sense that human beings must either
accept or reject the offer of divine self-communication. God's
love is gratuitous because "God himself in his sovereignty bestows or refuses his merciful love that is received by man."[38]
Finally, Rahner argues that God's love is not merely gratuitous
relative to possible human beings, who, because they might not
exist at all, are not owed the self-communication of God. Rather,
God was free to withhold grace from actually existing persons,
although, in fact, God decided to bestow grace universally.[39]
Rahner states quite pointedly that:

> [God], for the sake of the pure sovereignty of his love with respect not just to the possible, but to the existing creature as such, can only create the creature, the *pre-*supposition of this act of personal, divine love, so that precisely as posited and created the creature must receive that for which it was created as free grace. Thus it must be said that the creature could also have been created without this [divine] communication.[40]

Human being, for Rahner, is created by God such that grace is received as a free gift from God and not as an essential aspect of human existence, similar to the necessary orientation of human spirit toward God as holy mystery. He states that human beings can and must receive divine self-communication as a free gift, by which he means:

> First of all, simply the fact: God desires to communicate himself in such a way that his self-communication to the creaturely subject is unexacted. Therefore, God must create man *so* that man can receive this self-communication only as grace. God must give man not only an essence, but must constitute him as "nature" (in opposition to an unexacted supernatural reality). But this formula indicates, secondly, that self-communication *could not* exist other than as unexacted; the will to a "pure," gratuitous self-communication is not only fact, but necessity: God could not constitute a creaturely essence for which this communication would be its necessarily given, normal, self-evident fulfillment.[41]

Just as in human love, where the ecstatic donation of the human self to another is always a free and wondrous event, so the bestowal of God's love upon human beings is an act of unexacted, unexpected grace. Rahner writes that the human relationship to God has a certain dual character because of the sheer gratuity of the divine love. On the one hand, humans have to do with God unavoidably in every act. Yet, on the other hand, he holds that from the perspective of a natural view of human being it is fundamentally unclear how God comports Godself toward human beings.

> If man is that particular being that must listen for a possible revelation in history, and if he experiences this personal self-manifestation of God not only as a free act of God but also as free grace to him as one who is already constituted (and this is the biblical and Christian meaning of revelation), then he must be, from the outset

("from nature"), that particular being that must reckon with a speech or a silence of God, a self-donation or a self-refusal of God. Only if the bivalence of such a relation to God belongs to his essence, can man be, on the one hand, the possible, receptive subject of revelation, constituted such that he can permanently refuse revelation sinfully and in conscious awareness of sin (because only in this way does he remain one who can accept [revelation]) and, on the other hand, the one who can experience revelation, in case it occurs, as free grace (because, in himself, he must also reckon with a silence of God).[42]

Because of this bivalent character of the human relation to God, Rahner holds to a view of the double gratuity of creation and grace. Human persons experience themselves to be contingent. They receive their existence as a free gift from God, who, as the creator, is existentially independent of, or free over against, the creature. But human persons also receive the self-communication of God as a gift, not from the distant creator, but from God as personal agent in intimate relationship to human persons. These two gifts are not the same gift of divine freedom.[43] The act of divine self-communication goes beyond God's act of creation, for in self-communication God does not posit the creature over against God through efficient causality, but, through quasi-formal causality, communicates Godself to the previously posited creature. Divine self-communication, because it is the ecstatic self-giving of God Godself, is the most radical act of divine freedom, and must be distinguished from God's (free) act of creation.

Rahner, in arguing for such a view of double gratuity over against "la nouvelle théologie," asks: "Can the one who *himself creates* the orientation toward the intimate, personal communion of love between two persons (in our case: man and God), . . . at the same time, refuse this communication without contradicting the meaning of this creation and his creative act itself?"[44] Rahner answers this question affirmatively. He asserts that God could have created human being solely as a *potentia oboedientialis* for a possible revelation of God, without actually revealing Godself in a personal sense. Human being is conceivable as oriented toward God as the distant, mysterious *Woraufhin* of its transcendence. Humans, in such a state, would indeed strive toward God as the horizon of all their knowledge and free activity. But God would remain fundamentally unattainable.

So, while, in fact, the self-communication of God is the fundamental act of God, which grounds the possibility of the act of creation, nevertheless, these two acts must be distinguished. Rahner argues that this assertion of a double gratuity of creation and self-communication is not merely an abstract and hypothetical expression concerning a *possible* world (namely, a world without self-communication), but, rather, "reveals something theologically important and meaningful for the religious understanding of our own actual situation."[45] For him, the theologically important and existentially significant concept that is expressed and defended by double gratuity is that of the radical freedom of God. He wishes to stress the fact that God remains free even in the act of communicating Godself in love to the creatures. In the words of Klaus Fischer, Rahner "adheres to the double gratuity of creation and grace because, in this way, the unexacted character of grace, that is, the absolute freedom of God, seems to be better defended."[46] The double gratuity of creation and grace is affirmed by Rahner in order to show that freedom is a necessary condition of the fundamental divine act (love), just as human love is only possible because human persons are free agents. At the same time, Rahner holds that the concept of gratuity is not brought to the phenomenon of divine self-communication as ready-made from some other context. Rather, he says: "We should not forget, in all this, that we know, finally, what 'gratuitous' means when we know what personal love is, not the other way around."[47]

The following passage illustrates well Rahner's view of the relationship between divine creation and self-communication: on the one hand, the self-communication of God is the fundamental divine act, while, on the other hand, this fundamental act derives from a free decision of God.

> We may calmly conceive that which we call creation as a partial moment within that process of God becoming the world in which God expresses himself factually, although freely, in his Logos, which has become worldly and material. We have the right not to think of creation and incarnation as two disparate acts of God *ad extra* which lie side by side and derive from two separate initiatives of God. Rather, we may think of creation and incarnation as two moments and two phases, within the actual world, *of the one* occurrence of the self-alienation and self-expression of God, even if these two moments are internally differentiated. . . . Such a conception in no way

denies that God could have created a world without the incarnation, i.e., that he could have refused to the self-transcendence of the material that final, crowning consummation that occurs in grace and incarnation.[48]

Nature and Grace

I claimed earlier that Rahner seeks to move beyond the traditional extrinsicist understanding of the relation of nature and grace. Only now that the divine love has been shown to be a supernatural existential in human existence can Rahner's own position on the problem of nature and grace be presented.

Rahner first expressed his understanding of the relation between nature and grace in an essay in the journal *Orientierung*, which appeared in 1950.[49] This essay is a response to an article by "D.," an anonymous representative of the so-called *"nouvelle théologie,"* which is associated with Henri de Lubac.[50] Rahner sums up the position of *"la nouvelle théologie"* on nature and grace as follows:

> . . . [the] orientation toward the blessed vision of God, in this recent view, is understood, on the one hand, as an inner constituent of the nature of man that cannot be forfeited, and, on the other hand, is conceived in such a way that the withholding of the goal of this orientation is incompatible with the wisdom and goodness of God and is, in this sense, unconditional.[51]

He asserts that *"la nouvelle théologie"* is right that the extrinsicism of classical scholastic theology must be overcome. The supernatural (grace) ought not to be viewed as an uncalled for superstructure imposed upon human nature by divine fiat. Rather, Rahner agrees, human being has an intrinsic orientation toward God. This orientation is more than a mere nonrepugnance of human being for grace. It is an active striving or unlimited dynamism for God as the blessed fulfillment of human existence.[52]

But despite this considerable agreement with *"la nouvelle théologie,"* Rahner argues that its understanding of the relation between nature and grace is unacceptable because the unexacted character of grace is not sufficiently defended. He writes that D., against his will, does not affirm any gratuitous act of God beyond that of the creation of the world itself. In relation to the position of D., Rahner asks: "is grace still to be conceived as unexacted if the existential of the inner, unconditioned orientation toward grace and the vision of God were a constituent of the 'nature' of man in the sense that man as such could not be thought of without it?"[53] He says the answer to this question must be no. Grace, for D., according to Rahner, is a constitutive element of human being. Human being is inconceivable without grace. Simply by virtue of existing as creatures of God, according to D., human beings are assured of being able to attain God as their final, blessed goal (provided, of course, that the natural orientation toward the grace of God is not sinfully denied). Such a view, in Rahner's mind, compromises the gratuity of the divine love.

Therefore, Rahner, in his own view of nature and grace, attempts to defend both the intrinsic character of grace in concrete human existence and its gratuitous or supernatural character. Although his way of doing this has already been indicated implicitly, his solution to the problem of nature and grace must now be laid out explicitly.

Human experience, for Rahner, in fact always has as an ingredient the grace of God (even if this grace is sinfully rejected). God has decided not to withhold from human persons that toward which they are oriented: namely, God Godself. Human existence has a supernatural existential, which is the offer of the divine love. This love of God is present universally and unfailingly in human existence. Therefore, there is no such thing as human "nature" if this is taken to refer to a state of human existence that is (or was) actually experienced.

> Factual [human] nature *never* is a "pure" nature, but is always nature within a supernatural order from which man cannot extricate himself (even as an unbeliever and a sinner). It is a nature that is permanently transformed (which does not mean: justified) by the offer of the supernatural grace of salvation.[54]

In our actual experience a state of pure nature is never given. In our actual experience no clear distinctions can be made between human nature and the supernatural existential, for grace is a divinization of the fundamental structures of human being in the world. For Rahner, wherever human being is present, the grace of God is also present as an intrinsic moment within the human spirit.

Yet, for Rahner, this factual condition of human being is not the only one that is conceivable. Human being could exist without the immediate, intrinsic presence of the grace of God. Such a mode of human being is what is meant by "nature" in the strict theological sense of the opposite of the supernatural. It is important to realize that the concept of nature, in Rahner's thought, does not refer to any actual state of human existence. "Nature" is a remainder concept *(ein Restbegriff)*. Human nature is the remainder that is left when the supernatural existential (grace) has been conceptually bracketed or removed from the concrete essence of human being.[55] Since grace is an existential in actual human being, "nature" is not experienced as such. Nature is not a preliminary stage in the history of human being, as if there were a time in the history of the human race, or in the personal history of any individual, in which there existed a wholly "natural" human being untouched by the grace of God. The history of the human appropriation of the grace of God is coextensive with human history as such.[56]

While human nature is not an experiential datum, nevertheless, for Rahner, "nature" is an absolutely crucial theological concept. Nature must have a genuine meaning and must be a mode of human being that could actually have been given if God had so willed. He holds that human being must really be conceivable without the supernatural existential if the unexacted character of grace is to be maintained. For if the supernatural existential and nature cannot be distinguished within concrete human being, then grace is a constitutive element of human being as such, and is exacted by or owed to human being simply by virtue of the fact that the human person exists.[57] Here a single, not a double gratuity is asserted and, for Rahner, the central affirmation of the Christian faith concerning the wonder and grace of God's love has been lost.

"Nature" is a remainder concept, but one that must be utilized in theological thinking if the radical freedom of God, above all, in God's fundamental act of self-communicating love, is to be defended. The concept of nature (human being as possible without the self-communicating love of God) is given when one distinguishes the gratuity of creation and the gratuity of the supernatural elevation of the creature.

> The concept of pure nature is legitimate. If one says: I experience myself as one who is unconditionally oriented toward the immediate possession of God, then he

need not have said something false. The proposition
would be false only if he claimed that this unconditional
longing were an essential moment of "pure" nature; or if
he said that such a pure nature (which does not exist)
simply *could* not exist. Where man knows of the *visio
beatifica* as grace through the revelation of the word and
experiences it as the wonder of free, divine love in his
desire for it, he must say that the *visio beatifica* is not owed
to him (as nature), and is not owed to him precisely as
one who exists (so that the gratuity of creation as an act
of the freedom of God and grace as a free gift to the
creature as already existing are not one and the same gift
of the freedom of God). In this the concept of "pure
nature" is already implicitly given.[58]

For Rahner, the distinction between nature and grace is not
demanded by the empirical existence of natural human being,
but rather is a consequence of giving full glory to the sovereignty
of the love or grace of God.[59]

Rahner, in his understanding of nature and grace, attempts
to chart a course between the extremes represented by
Thomistic extrinsicism and *"la nouvelle théologie."* He holds with
"la nouvelle théologie" that grace is not an alien imposition upon
nature. Indeed, nature is an inner moment within the order of
grace, just as God's creative activity is encompassed by God's
more fundamental activity of self-communication.[60] In the actual world order, grace is universally present in human existence
as a supernatural elevation of the person that orients the human
person toward the God who is disclosed to be free, self-giving
love. But, at the same time, Rahner asserts over against *"la
nouvelle théologie"* that if grace is to be experienced as grace, that
is, as the free event of God's sovereign love, then "man, in
principle, must have something to do with God at one point, at
least, which is not already grace."[61] That is to say, while grace is
an intrinsic moment in concrete human existence, grace is not an
essential characteristic of human being. Human being is conceivable without the bestowal of the supernatural grace of God and
such "natural" human beings *could have* existed had God not
chosen to communicate Godself in love. This must be the case,
for Rahner, if the freedom of God in the act of self-communication is to be adequately defended.

In summary, the one primordial act of God, for Rahner, is
love, just as love represents the final wholeness of human being.
However, this act of self-communication is radically free on

God's part, and must be distinguished from God's free act of the creation of the world. Because God "wished to express himself in his eternal word, because he is love, the world exists precisely in the difference of nature and grace."[62] God's love would not be the love of the transcendent, sovereign God if it were not received as a gift, unexacted by the essential structure of human being.

> Even that which is temporally prior [creation] can exist *because* it is the condition of the possibility of that which is temporally subsequent [self-communication], for both are given as supported by the one God who desires one thing: to communicate himself, and therefore must posit two things: the essential structure of the hearer who is to be graced by the message and the message itself. For these two must be distinguished if the message is to be the act of free love of the personal self-communication of God. The autonomy of the [human] spirit as "nature" is the condition of the possibility of that obedience through which revelation alone can be received as it must be received: in the free acceptance of grace.[63]

God's one goal is to communicate Godself as love to human beings. But the accomplishing of this goal requires the duality of nature and grace, creation and self-communication. "God has created the servant solely in order to make him a child [of God]. But he was able to create the child through grace . . . only by creating the servant, the addressee who has no claim to sonship."[64]

NOTES

[1] *HW*, p. 123.
[2] "Theologie der Freiheit," *ST*, 6:224 (ET: *TI*, 6:185).
[3] *HW*, p. 111.
[4] "*Theos* im Neuen Testament," *ST*, 1:141 (ET: *TI*, 1:123).
[5] Ibid. (ET: ibid.).
[6] "Zur Theologie der Menschwerdung," *ST*, 4:145 (ET: *TI*, 4:112).
[7] *GG*, p. 85 (ET: *FCF*, p. 77). Rahner writes that "the one who is absolute" *(der Absolute)* is preferable to "the (impersonal) absolute" *(das Absolute)* as a way of speaking of the divine reality.
[8] Ibid. (ET: ibid., p. 78). See G. W. F. Hegel, *Phenomenology of Mind*,

trans. J. B. Baillie (New York: Harper & Row, 1967), pp. 228–240, for the motif in which the master, finally, becomes dependent upon the servant.

[9] See "Überlegungen zur Methode der Theologie," *ST*, 9:119 (ET: *TI*, 11:107), "Zur scholastischen Begrifflichkeit der ungeschaffenen Gnade," *ST*, 1:356–357 (ET: *TI*, 1:328–329), and "Der dreifaltige Gott als transzendenter Urgrund der Heilsgeschichte," pp. 323, n. 11, 329, n. 19 (ET: *The Trinity*, pp. 15, n. 11, 24, n. 19). I will show in the next chapter that Rahner holds that classical theological assertions concerning God's aseity, immutability, and eternity (precisely God's "metaphysical freedom") must be understood in a dialectical fashion, because of the intimate nature of the God-world relationship established by divine self-communication (the fundamental act of God's personal or relational freedom).

[10] "Zur scholastischen Begrifflichkeit der ungeschaffenen Gnade," *ST*, 1:358 (ET: *TI*, 1:330).

[11] *HW*, p. 171.

[12] "Der dreifaltige Gott als transzendenter Urgrund der Heilsgeschichte," p. 387, n. 29 (ET: *The Trinity*, p. 107, n. 29).

[13] *HW*, p. 151.

[14] "Zur Theologie der Menschwerdung," *ST*, 4:146 (ET: *TI*, 4:112).

[15] *GG*, pp. 83–88 (ET: *FCF*, pp. 75–81).

[16] Ibid., pp. 84–85 (ET: ibid., pp. 76–77).

[17] Ibid., p. 86 (ET: ibid., p. 78).

[18] *HW*, pp. 125–126.

[19] "*Theos* im Neuen Testament," *ST*, 1:128 (ET: *TI*, 1:112).

[20] "Bemerkungen zur Gotteslehre in der katholischen Dogmatik," *ST*, 8:175–176 (ET: *TI*, 9:136).

[21] *HW*, p. 111.

[22] "Über die Verborgenheit Gottes," *ST*, 12:287 (ET: *TI*, 16:229).

[23] "Fragen der Kontroverstheologie über die Rechtfertigung," *ST*, 4:265 (ET: *TI*, 4:213).

[24] *HW*, pp. 111–112.

[25] "*Theos* im Neuen Testament," *ST*, 1:99 (ET: *TI*, 1:86).

[26] *HW*, p. 115.

[27] Ibid., p. 114.

[28] "Transzendente und immanente Vollendung der Welt," *ST*, 8:600–601 (ET: *TI*, 10:281).

[29] "*Theos* im Neuen Testament," *ST*, 1:108 (ET: *TI*, 1:94).

[30] Ibid., p. 131 (ET: ibid., p. 115).

[31] *HW*, p. 114.

[32] "Zur Theologie der Menschwerdung," *ST*, 4:148 (ET: *TI*, 4:115).

[33] "Gotteslehre," in *LTK*, vol. 4, col. 1123.

[34] *HW*, p. 102.

35 "Fragen der Kontroverstheologie über die Rechtfertigung," ST, 4:267 (ET: TI, 4:215).

36 GG, p. 197 (ET: FCF, p. 197).

37 "Fragen der Kontroverstheologie über die Rechtfertigung," ST, 4:265 (ET: TI, 4:213).

38 "Theos im Neuen Testament," ST, 1:132 (ET: TI, 1:115).

39 "Fragen der Kontroverstheologie über die Rechtfertigung," ST, 4:265 (ET: TI, 4:214).

40 Ibid., p. 267 (ET: ibid., pp. 214–215).

41 "Über das Verhältnis von Natur und Gnade," ST, 1:337, n. 1 (ET: TI, 1:310, n. 1).

42 "Theos im Neuen Testament," ST, 1:96–97 (ET: TI, 1:84).

43 "Natur und Gnade," ST, 4:233–234 (ET: TI, 4:185).

44 "Über das Verhältnis von Natur und Gnade," ST, 1:332 (ET: TI, 1:306). I will have more to say concerning Rahner's criticism of "la nouvelle théologie" later in this chapter.

45 "Fragen der Kontroverstheologie über die Rechtfertigung," ST, 4:264 (ET: TI, 4:212).

46 Der Mensch als Geheimnis, p. 250.

47 "Über das Verhältnis von Natur und Gnade," ST, 1:337 (ET: TI, 1:310).

48 GG, p. 197 (ET: FCF, p. 197).

49 "Eine Antwort," Orientierung 14 (1950):141–145. This article was subsequently published in a slightly revised form as "Über das Verhältnis von Natur und Gnade," ST, 1:323–345 (ET: TI, 1:297–317). With the one exception noted in the previous chapter, Rahner consistently maintains the view of nature and grace presented in this essay throughout his published works.

50 D.'s article is entitled "Ein Weg zur Bestimmung des Verhältnisses von Natur und Gnade," Orientierung 14 (1950):138–141. There seems to be little doubt that D. is Pierre Delaye: see William Shepherd, Man's Condition, p. 81, n. 2. De Lubac's key work on the relation of nature and grace is Surnaturel (Paris: Aubier, 1946).

51 "Über das Verhältnis von Natur und Gnade," ST, 1:330 (ET: TI, 1:304).

52 Ibid., pp. 328–329, 342 (ET: ibid., pp. 302–303, 315).

53 Ibid., p. 330 (ET: ibid., p. 304).

54 "Natur und Gnade," ST, 4:230 (ET: TI, 4:183).

55 "Über das Verhältnis von Natur und Gnade," ST, 1:340–342 (ET: TI, 1:313–315).

56 See GG, pp. 147–157 (ET: FCF, pp. 142–152).

57 "Über das Verhältnis von Natur und Gnade," ST, 1:340 (ET: TI, 1:314).

58 "Natur und Gnade," ST, 4:233–234 (ET: TI, 4:185).

[59] "Fragen der Kontroverstheologie über die Rechtfertigung," *ST*, 4:270 (ET: *TI*, 4:217).

[60] "Philosophie und Theologie," *ST*, 6:93 (ET: *TI*, 6:72).

[61] "*Theos* im Neuen Testament," *ST*, 1:96 (ET: *TI*, 1:83).

[62] "Weltgeschichte und Heilsgeschichte," *ST*, 5:134 (ET: *TI*, 5:114).

[63] "Philosophie und Theologie," *ST*, 6:97 (ET: *TI*, 6:76).

[64] Ibid., p. 96 (ET: ibid., p. 75).

CHAPTER VI
DIVINE LOVE AND THE GOD-WORLD RELATIONSHIP

In the preceding three chapters I have sought to show what Rahner understands the assertion "God is love" to mean. The purpose of this chapter is to explicate the nature of the God-world relationship that he holds to be implied by the divine love for others. It is my conviction that Rahner takes a significant step beyond the classical view of the God-world relationship, precisely because his starting point in such matters is a concept of God as a person who can enter into genuine, loving relationships with others.[1]

In particular I want to show that Rahner holds the God-world relationship to be a personal dialogue between God and the world; that he seeks to find a middle way between two extreme positions on the God-world relationship, namely, dualism and pantheism; that he further specifies the God-world relationship or dialogue to be a dialectic of identity and difference in which the dependence of the world upon God and the world's autonomy are directly, and not inversely, proportional; that the fullest exemplification of this dialectic is to be found in the self-expression of God in God's real symbol, Jesus Christ; and that Rahner, on the basis of the historical self-expression or incarnation of God, holds that classical affirmations concerning God's aseity, immutability, and eternity must be understood dialectically, so that it can be said truly that the God who is immutable in Godself changes in God's other (the real symbol).

The God-World Dialogue

Because he holds that the fundamental act of God is the loving communication of Godself to the world, Rahner is led to understand the relationship that obtains between God and the world in a revisionary way. He warns that the usual concept of divine creation is oriented toward the model of innerworldly causality in too primitive a fashion and thus distorts the true God-world relationship.[2] In the traditional view of creation, the duality of God and the world is seen as a presupposition of the creator-creature relationship. God is conceived simply as the one who establishes the world as something separate from Godself. This view cannot capture the uniquely personal and mutually participatory relationship between God and the spiritual creature affirmed in the Christian doctrine of grace.

As I have already argued, Rahner does not understand the creation of the world to be God's fundamental act. Creation, although grounded in God's love for Godself, does not represent a fully personal act of love on God's part. Such an act of divine *ecstasis* occurs only in the act of divine self-communication. The act of self-communication, according to Rahner, encompasses the act of creation. Indeed, he says that the world has its origin in the event of God's self-communication. Because he holds this to be the case, it is not surprising that he asserts that the God-world relationship cannot be adequately understood in terms of divine creation alone. On the contrary, the proper *topos* for a theological understanding of the relationship of God to the world is not "an abstract metaphysical doctrine of God, but is the doctrine of grace, this being understood, of course, not as a doctrine concerning the creative production of a created quality of grace, but rather as the doctrine concerning a quasi-formal relationship of the being of God to the world, in which the reality of God is itself communicated to the world as its highest determination."[3] Rahner makes this claim with the assumption that the doctrine of grace that is to be used as such a *topos* for an understanding of the God-world relationship itself will make use of personal categories such as love, intimacy, personal closeness, and self-communication.[4]

So, for Rahner, the God-world relationship is to be conceived on the basis of our own interpersonal experience, using personal categories, and taking the self-communication of God rather than divine creation as a paradigm. Because the final goal of the dynamism of finite reality is immediacy to God and because the *telos* of all divine activity is the loving immediacy of God to the creatures in self-communication, the first word that must be said concerning Rahner's view of the God-world relationship is that it really is a personal relationship or communion between God and the creatures.

Rahner holds that the God-world relationship is a dialogue.[5] It must be noted immediately that when he speaks of the God-world relationship he refers first of all to the relationship between God and human being. What is true of the God-human relationship is true, in a derived sense, for the God-world relationship in general because the whole material cosmos is fulfilled in human being. Rahner says, for instance, "above all, we must attend in a special, existential-philosophical way to the relation of the spiritual creature to God. For it is the spiritual creature that is related to God in a special way, as a person constituted by transcendence and freedom."[6] With this proviso, he asserts that both participants in the God-world dialogue are persons. There is in this dialogue free decision on the part of God as well as on the part of human being.[7] God, in self-communication, establishes a genuine interpersonal relationship between Godself and human being. God gives Godself as an intimate partner of human persons, not just as the distant creator who sets the world over against Godself as that which is other.[8] This interpersonal relationship between God and the creatures, which God initiates, makes possible the interpersonal nature of human being, as well as the interrelated character of the material cosmos as a whole.

Rahner holds that this God-world dialogue is to be taken quite seriously as meaning that both parties to the dialogue are genuinely qualified by the actions and responses of the other. What is significant is that this is affirmed to be true of the divine being. According to Rahner, all New Testament affirmations concerning the relationship between God and human beings:

> Presuppose the same dual, personal relationship between God and man. Only in this way is the peculiarity of the free activity of God in history to be conceived. God's activity in the course of salvation history is not simply a monologue that God undertakes for himself alone. It is rather a long dramatic dialogue between God and his creature in which God grants to man the possibility of genuinely responding to his word. Thus, in fact, God makes his own further word dependent upon the outcome of man's free response.[9]

It is Rahner's intention to describe a genuine personal dialogue between God and the world that is established by divine self-communication. In this dialogue both parties encounter one another as persons whose freedom must be respected. Since the relationship is a dialogue, God and the world are each dependent upon the free response of the other. As Rahner puts it,

> . . . the free act of God is again and again kindled by the activity of man. History is not merely a play that God himself performs and in which the creatures are simply what is performed. Rather, the creature is a genuine co-performer in this divine-human drama of history.[10]

Beyond Dualism and Pantheism

Rahner holds that his view of the God-world relationship, which is centered around the personal love of God, provides a mediating position between the extremes of dualism and pantheism.[11] The error of dualism (or deism or vulgar theism), according to him, lies in its wholly external view of the relationship of God to the world.[12] Dualism fails to grasp adequately the nature of God. It understands God to be a part within a larger whole. This is both a conceptual and an existentiell error. Rahner claims that

> . . . the God who is influential and who holds sway as an individual being alongside of other beings, and so to a certain extent is himself once again present within the larger house of reality, just does not exist. If one sought for such a God, then one would have sought for a false God.[13]

He tries to show, by way of his understanding of the Christian doctrine of God's grace, that God cannot be viewed simply as a supreme causal principle independent of, and external to, the world. On the contrary, God is "present within the world as an inner constituent of the becoming [of the world] and bears this becoming, although God himself is free from becoming."[14] Because God's fundamental act is the bestowal of Godself upon the creatures in love, God cannot be related to the world in a merely external fashion as dualism would assert.

Rahner argues that the moment of truth in pantheism lies in its refusal to conceive God and the world as two objects lying side by side, both of which are part of a larger whole, namely, reality as such. Pantheism is rightly designated as "the feeling (better: the transcendental experience) that God is the absolute reality, the primordial ground, the final *Woraufhin* of transcendence."[15] Pantheism refuses to view God and the world dualistically. It affirms the final totality of reality to be the divine reality itself. The nondualistic image of God as the totality of reality, the all in all of 1 Corinthians 15:28, appears a number of times in Rahner's works.[16] God as the all in all is the one who "silently encompasses everything. . . . All ways become lost in him, the one in whom we live, move, and have our being, who is not far from any one of us, who supports and surrounds all, and who is comprehended and surpassed by none."[17]

But Rahner does not believe that pantheism provides an adequate understanding of God and the world either. He asserts that God is completely different from the world. God and the world cannot be identified. He argues that "God must be absolutely distinguished as the absolute and infinite one. . . . Therefore he cannot need finite reality, called 'world,' for otherwise, he would not be radically different from the world."[18] As was shown above, a properly expressed doctrine of creation *ex nihilo* affirms precisely this difference between God and the world. A Christian view of God confesses, as pantheism does not, the creatureliness of the world, by which Rahner means:

> Its permanent being given to itself from the personal God who posits it freely. This positing [*die Setzung*], therefore, does not have as its presupposition [*die Voraussetzung*] any material that is already present at hand. It is in this sense *ex nihilo*. Creation *ex nihilo* means, in essence: creation totally from God, precisely such that in creation the world is radically dependent on God, while God is not dependent on the world, but remains the self-sufficient one who is free over against the world.[19]

This shows that although Rahner asserts the existence of a genuine, personal dialogue between God and the world, nevertheless, for him, "the dialogical relationship between God and us, which has the character of a partnership, is a unique and incomparable relationship. It cannot simply be conceived univocally according to the model of a dialogical relationship between human partners."[20] Here is a clear indication of the limitations Rahner wishes to place upon the use of concepts derived from human experience when such concepts are applied to the divine reality. God's fundamental act, for him, is indeed to be understood in terms of the fundamental human experience of love, but divine love must be understood as a radically free love that is not necessary to the being of God. In the same way, Rahner characterizes the God-world relationship as a personal dialogue, but a unique type of dialogue in which God's transcendence and independence are maintained.

It is interesting and significant that when Rahner stresses the intimate nature of God's love he is led to affirm the truth of pantheism, namely, that the final totality of reality is nothing other than the God of love who unites the world with Godself. But when he stresses the freedom of this divine love, he affirms the truth of dualism with its distinction of God and the world expressed in the doctrine of creation.

Rahner grants that God and the world must be differentiated. But he urges caution when we try to state precisely the nature of this difference. The legitimate Christian denial of pantheism does not entail a dualistic view of the God-world relationship. Rahner asserts that

> . . . this nonidentity [of God and the world] does not mean that God is a particular discrete entity alongside of the entities of the world. Rather it indicates a differentiation of a unique kind, the expression and realization of which belongs to the most difficult tasks of Christian theology.[21]

The mistake of dualism, one that is also presupposed uncritically by many Christians, lies in its understanding the God-world relationship to be similar to the difference between two categorial objects. Rahner argues:

> When we say against pantheism that God and the world are different, this proposition is radically misunderstood if it is meant in a dualistic fashion. The difference between God and the world is of such a nature that the one [God] itself is and posits the difference between the other [the world] and itself, and, for this reason, establishes the greatest unity precisely in the differentiation. For if the difference itself originates from God and is itself once again identical to God—if we can say such a thing—then the difference between God and the world is to be conceived as completely different from the difference between two categorial realities. A difference precedes two categorial realities because they already presuppose in a certain sense a space that encompasses and differentiates them. Neither of these distinct cate-

gorial entities itself posits the difference from the other nor is it this difference.[22]

For Rahner, there is no further horizon against which God and the world can be differentiated. God Godself, as pantheism rightly sees, *is* this final horizon which makes possible all other distinctions among finite realities.[23] "The creation of finite being by God does not presuppose the difference between God and creature, nor does it create this difference. Rather, from God's point of view, God himself in his own being *is* this difference."[24]

This is an important point, for it means that the God-world distinction is internal rather than external to God. The world's radical difference from God is grounded in an equally radical unity of God and world. God is experienced as different, as transcendent and infinite precisely in the experience of the radical presence or immanence of God in the world. God and the world, according to Rahner, are distinct, but this distinction is a consequence of the true communion God and the world share with one another. He argues that Christian theology must come to view God in a nondualistic way if the gospel is to be proclaimed credibly in the contemporary situation. This is the case because even the average person today does not and cannot believe in the God who is viewed as an individual being, a part of reality, even if the most perfect individual being.[25] This image of God has genuinely died, precisely, Rahner hopes, so that the God who is the totality of reality, the final horizon of the real, may be God. Only if God is radically different from the world, as the final source and goal of finite reality, can God become an intrinsic principle within finite reality without ceasing to be infinite or abrogating the freedom and integrity of the finite. As will be shown more clearly below, the radical identity and difference of God and world imply one another necessarily in Rahner's thought.

The Activity of God in the World

This understanding of the God-world relationship has important consequences for Rahner's view of the divine activity in relation to the world. His basic position is that God is not an actor within the world at all, if this activity is understood to be similar to that of any other worldly agent. Just as God's relationship to the world is unique, so the activity of God is different from all forms of innerworldly activity.

On the one hand, Rahner asserts, the average contemporary person understands her- or himself to be in a Godless world. The world has been radically de-divinized. God is no longer invoked to explain the functioning of the world.

> The world has become a self-contained quantity that is not really open to God at particular points and that does not lead to God. The causal impact of God within the world is not experienced at specific individual points that are observable by us.[26]

No room seems to be left for God as an agent within the world.

And yet, on the other hand, Christian theology affirms with Thomas Aquinas that God works through secondary causes.[27] According to Rahner, if this maxim is properly understood it is possible for a contemporary person to see that the world as a whole, not any particular worldly state of affairs, points to God as the condition of its possibility. The proposition concerning God's activity through secondary causes, if it is not to be rendered wholly innocuous, must mean that:

> God causes *the* world and does not really act causally *within the* world. It means he supports the causal chain but, in his activity, is not interposed as a member of the chain of causes, as one cause among others. The chain as a whole, that is, the world in its interconnectedness, not only in its abstract, formal unity but also in its concrete differentiation and in the fundamental distinction among the moments within the totality of the world, is the self-revelation of the ground. For the ground is not present within that which is grounded if it really is the radical, thus divine, ground and not a function within a network of functions.[28]

God, for Rahner, is not a moment within the totality of reality. God is not a particular cause or center of activity within the world. Rather, God is the active, transcendent grounding of the plurality of reality.

> Therefore, for a pure metaphysics, God cannot be present among and between other entities. God's activity is not a moment within our experience, but rather is always present only through the mediation of the finite as the implicitly co-affirmed ground of every reality that is

> encountered and affirmed, that is, as being [*das Sein*],
> which is the ground of that which is [*das Seiende*].29

This does not mean that "God" simply refers to the unity of
reality that is postulated as a result of empirical experience.
Indeed, God is the antecedent, transcendental ground of the
unity of reality that we do, in fact, experience.30 But this view of
divine activity does mean that God does not intervene in the
world process in any traditional sense of the word. The immediate presence of God in the world, which the doctrine of grace
affirms, does not require that God be inserted into the world at
some particular point. Rahner argues, to the contrary, that:

> The immediacy of God, if it is not to be an absolute
> contradiction from the outset, cannot depend upon the
> fact that the nondivine completely disappears when God
> approaches. God does not need to find a place by having
> another, which is not God, make room. For the presence
> of God as the transcendental ground and horizon of all
> that is and knows (which indeed is a presence of God, an
> immediacy to him) occurs precisely through and in the
> givenness of finite being.31

Rahner asserts, therefore, that the particular, historical "interventions" of God that are proclaimed by the historical religions, including Christianity, must be understood to be
categorial thematizations of the transcendental immediacy of
God to the world given in existence as such. Any other sort of
intervention on God's part would be viewed as an incredible
myth by modern persons. The following passage indicates how
Rahner himself understands the special, revelatory acts of God
within history.

> A special intervention [*ein Eingreifen*] of God can only be
> understood as the historical concreteness of the tran-
> scendental self-communication that is always already in-
> trinsic to the concrete world. Such an intervention of
> God occurs, first of all, on the basis of the fundamental
> openness of a finite material and biological system to
> spirit and its history and, secondly, on the basis of the
> openness of spirit to the history of the transcendental
> relationship between God and the creaturely person in
> mutual freedom. As a result, each actual intervention of
> God into his world, despite its free, nondeducible
> character, is always only the historical concretization of
> that intervention in which God, the transcendental

ground of the world, has established himself from the
outset in this world as the ground that communicates
itself.[32]

This passage is important, I think, because it shows that Rahner's
basic principle concerning God's activity "in" the world, namely,
that God effects the world as a whole rather than any particular
state of affairs within the world, applies to God precisely in the
act of loving self-communication. One might be tempted to view
this stricture as applying only to the metaphysically free creator
and not to the God of self-communication who is free in a
personal sense of being able to enter into a relationship of love
with the creatures. While I will show later that Rahner, in fact,
does reveal a different understanding of the nature of the divine
activity when he speaks of the self-expression of God in the
incarnation, it is crucial to realize at this point that he does
maintain, at least formally, that God does not and cannot act as a
categorial agent within the world. God acts rather as the transcendental ground of reality that communicates itself freely to
the reality it grounds. As such a self-communicating or loving
ground, God is immediately related to all the creatures in a
unique way. All of the particular acts of God within the world,
which are asserted by the world religions, must be viewed as
historical mediations or thematizations of the one fundamental
God-world relationship or dialogue established by the self-communication of God to the world.

The God-World Relationship as a Dialectic of Identity and Difference

In providing a mediating position between dualism and
pantheism, Rahner asserts that the God-world relationship is a
dialectic of identity and difference. The world process as a
whole demands both the immanence (or identity) of God in the
world and the transcendence (or difference) of God over against
the world.[33] The divine being must be immanent in the world to
such a radical extent that the process of worldly becoming, which
is made possible by God's presence, is truly an act of *self*-tran-
scendence on the part of nondivine reality. At the same time,
God must remain a transcendent ground and goal of worldly
becoming so that this process is one of self-*transcendence* and not
simply the replication of the one, eternal, divine essence.[34]

Rahner explicates his understanding of the dialectic of God's immanence and transcendence, or identity and difference with respect to the world, more fully in the following passage.

> This self-transcendence [of the world] can only be thought of as an event by virtue of the power of the absolute fullness of being [God]. This fullness of being, on the one hand, is to be conceived as so interior to the finite being, which moves itself toward its fulfillment, that this finite reality is empowered to a genuine, active self-transcendence. Finite being does not simply receive this new reality passively as produced by God. On the other hand, the innermost power of self-transcendence is, at the same time, to be understood as distinct from the finite agent so that the power of the dynamism that is intrinsic to finite being nevertheless is *not* to be conceived as constitutive of the essence of the finite. For if the absoluteness of being that imparts and empowers this efficacy were itself the essence of the finite agent, then this agent would no longer be capable of a genuine becoming in time and history at all because it would already possess from the outset the absolute fullness of being as its very own.[35]

To develop further the nature of this dialectic of identity and difference that is characteristic of the God-world relationship, Rahner formulates what he calls variously "the axiom of all relations between God and creature," "the foundational truth of the creator-creature relationship," or "the Christian statute concerning the basic relationship of God and creature."[36] This axiom runs as follows: "the radical dependence and genuine reality of the being that has its origin in God increase in direct, and not in inverse, proportion."[37] In other words, the existential dependence of the creature upon God and the genuine selfhood and autonomy of the creature are not mutually exclusive. They increase in direct proportion to one another. The creature is an autonomous center of value and activity precisely because it has God as its final ground and goal.

Rahner's affirmation that God is the final totality of reality does not in any sense imply a denial of the genuine reality of the non divine. In a very colorful passage, he seeks to distinguish his view of God from a pantheistic one in which God alone is real and the reality of the world is merely apparent.

> The true God is not one who kills in order to live himself. He is not "the only real one," the one who, like a

vampire, draws to himself and, to a certain extent, sucks
out the reality of the things that are distinct from him.
He is not the *esse omnium*. The nearer one draws to God,
the more God grows within and before one, the more
autonomous one becomes in one's own right.[38]

Once again, Rahner stresses that this dialectical relationship
between dependence upon God and autonomy over against God
is a function of the unique dialogue that obtains between God
and the creature. In our ordinary experience we discover just
the opposite relationship between dependence and autonomy.
We find that the more something or someone is dependent upon
us, the less that thing or person is different from us. The more
radically a finite effect depends upon its cause, the less genuine
autonomy it has, for within finite reality dependence and autonomy are inversely related. But, says Rahner,

> If we reflect upon the genuine transcendental rela-
> tionship between God and the creature, then it is appar-
> ent that here true reality and radical dependence are
> only two sides of one and the same phenomenon and
> therefore increase precisely in the same, and not in in-
> verse, proportion. We and the particular beings of our
> world are genuinely and truly different from God not in
> spite of the fact but because we are posited by God and
> no one else.[39]

The God-world relationship is unique. God's radical immanence
in the world is transcendental in character and thus provides no
threat to the autonomy of the creatures.

This axiom concerning the nature of the God-world relationship is valid, in Rahner's view, relative to both divine creation
and divine self-communication. He holds that the mystery of
active creation, which applies to God alone, consists of the ability
to create a creature that is both wholly dependent upon God for
its being and yet fully autonomous.

> It is only conceivable with respect to *God* that he himself
> can constitute the differentiation [of other entities] from
> himself. This is a predicate of his divinity and his own
> creativity: the possibility of constituting something
> through himself and through his *own* act *as such*, which,
> at one and the same time, is radically dependent (be-
> cause it is *totally* constituted) and yet attains a genuine
> autonomy, validity, and truth, indeed, precisely with re-
> spect to the God that constituted it (because it is con-

stituted by the one, unique *God*). God alone can make
something that has validity even with respect to God
himself.[40]

But it is also the case that the spiritual creature is simultaneously dependent upon, and autonomous with respect to,
God in the event of God's loving self-communication to the
world. As was shown above, the love of God, the gift of Godself,
is an intrinsic moment within concrete human existence. Grace is
an existential that transforms all of the essential structures of
human being. At the same time, however, the love of God is
addressed to the human subject as a free person. Grace must be
appropriated freely by human beings. Human freedom is so
genuine and inviolate that an ultimately self-contradictory act of
refusing the offer of God's love through the employment of the
power of self-disposition that is grounded in the self-communication of God is a real possibility for human being.[41]

Rahner argues that our usual models of causality, derived
from the experience of innerworldly events, cannot illuminate
this unique dialectical relationship of identity and difference,
dependence and autonomy, which obtains between God and the
world. For reasons already cited, the efficient causality operative
in the divine creation of the world is radically different from any
innerworldly efficient causality. Even an appropriately divine
form of efficient causality cannot do justice to the God-world
relationship established by the self-communication of God. By
efficient causality, according to Rahner, God posits that which is
other than Godself. But in the self-communication of God, God
bestows Godself upon the nondivine, becomes an intrinsic moment within human being, and initiates a unique God-world
relationship.

The nature of this God-world relationship is clarified adequately only if a model of quasi-formal causality is used. Indeed,
quasi-formal causality is nothing but a thematization of the love
relationship that exists between God and the world through
God's grace.[42] In quasi-formal causality, God is radically united
with the spiritual creature, as a form is united to the matter it
informs. As Rahner argues in the following passage, an identity
of God and the world is brought about in divine self-communication that surpasses that brought about by God's efficient
causality relative to the world.

We have already said that creation can and should be conceived as a moment within, and a presupposition of, the self-communication of God in which he does not create and set over against himself that which is other than himself, but rather communicates his own reality to the other. If and insofar as the created world is understood as an addressee of divine self-communication, as the condition of the possibility that the self-communication itself presupposes, if—in other words—the world originates in the event of the self-communication of God, then, of course, there is given an immanence of God in the world . . . that is not merely the immanence of the creator in the creature, but which is the immanence that Christian theology explains by way of the indwelling of God in the spiritual creature. This indwelling is no longer to be understood merely as a particular occurrence given here and there within the world. Instead, it is a fundamental relationship of God to the world in general.[43]

However, God does not lose Godself in the communication of Godself to the spiritual creature. The transcendence or difference of God with respect to the world is maintained. Further, the immanence of God in human being as the supernatural existential does not cancel, but radicalizes the freedom and autonomy of the human being.

The highest exemplification of the axiom concerning the God-world relationship is to be found, according to Rahner, in the incarnation of the divine Logos in Jesus Christ. This means, on the one hand, that the docetic and monophysite tendencies of the average Christian understanding of the incarnation must be overcome. The view of many Christians is that, in the incarnation,

God disguises himself as a man, or makes gestures with a human reality, in order to make himself noticable (because he himself is invisible). This human reality, because it is used in this manner, however, is not really a genuinely independent and free man any longer, but is a marionette through which the real player behind the stage makes himself known.[44]

This understanding of the humanity of Jesus Christ as a disguise of God is mythological. The true dogma of the incarnation, Rahner says, entails the view that "the 'human nature' of the Logos possesses a genuine, spontaneous, free spiritual center of activity, a human self-consciousness that stands over against the eternal word as a creature in the genuine human attitude of prayer, obedience, and the radical awareness of being a creature."[45] The autonomy of the human nature of Jesus Christ is not violated even though that human nature is uniquely united to the divine being.

And yet, on the other hand, Rahner affirms that this autonomous human subject, Jesus, who is related to God in grace just as we are, is precisely *as such* the real self-expression or self-revelation of God, the irrevocable promise of God's love for us. This promise, in its historical manifestation, is "not just posited by God, but is God himself."[46] Speaking of the life of Jesus, Rahner argues that

> . . . this human one is not human (and as such uninteresting to us) and "in addition" God (and only important in this respect, although this characteristic [the divinity of Christ] is always simply suspended above the human one and frames it from the outside), rather the ordinary humanity of this life is the ex-istence [*die Ek-sistenz*] of God.[47]

Elsewhere he says that human being is the grammar of God's self-expression.[48] When God decides to step out from Godself into the world, it is human being that results. Jesus Christ is most radically and fully human, precisely because he is the historical self-expression of God's Logos.

It is in this sense that the incarnation represents the highest exemplification of the axiom of the God-world relationship.

> The relationship of the person of the Logos to its human nature is to be conceived precisely such that autonomy *and* radical nearness [to God] correspondingly come to their unique highpoint, which is qualitatively incommensurable with all other cases, but which is still the unique highpoint of the creator-creature relationship.[49]

Because this is the case, Rahner asserts that the characteristics of the God-world relationship in general can be seen as fully exemplified in the particular relationship between God and the world given in the incarnation. He lists the four pairs of categories applicable to the God-creature relationship: closeness/distance, image/veil, time/eternity, dependence/autonomy, and illustrates their supreme application in the incarnation as follows:

> The movement of creation appears from the outset as oriented toward the point at which God attains simultaneously the singularly greatest *closeness* and *distance* to that which is other than him. God accomplishes this by objectifying himself most radically in his *image*, in which, therefore, he is given most truly *as himself*, and by accepting that which is created by him as that which is most radically his own. God is no longer merely the *ahistorical* founder of a history that is alien to him, but is the one whose own *history* is at issue.[50]

Conversely, Rahner writes that the relationships between all other finite beings and God can be viewed as deficient modes of the primordial, christological relationship.

> Indeed, christology as a whole could appear as the unique, most radical realization of this primordial relation of God to that which is other than himself, against which all of the rest of creation would be only a deficient mode, the hazy area around the clearest realization of this primordial relation that lies in the self-alienation of the God who remains radically with himself, and thus is immutable.[51]

He speaks of a retrospective use of christological categories in ontology and anthropology in general. The point of such a retrospective ontological employment of the categories that illuminate the relationship of the Logos to its human nature is to show, once again, that the God-world relationship is a dialectic of identity and difference in which the existential dependence of the world upon God increases in direct proportion to the autonomy of the world.

The Real Symbol and God's Self-Expression

As I indicated above, for Rahner, the incarnation does not represent just the highpoint of the creature's relationship to God, in which dependence upon God and genuine creaturely autonomy are uniquely co-present. The incarnation is also a unique event in the life of God, for it is the self-expression or self-alienation of God in the world. The self-communication of God to the world as the intrinsic supernatural principle of the world's dynamism is, at the same time, the act in which God becomes the nondivine reality God has posited. The following passage indicates the seriousness with which Rahner takes such a claim.

> The absolute [*das Absolute*], more correctly: the one who is absolute [*der Absolute*] has, in the pure freedom of his infinite nonrelativity, which he always preserves, the possibility of becoming the other, that which is finite; the possibility of positing the other as his own reality in that and because he alienates *himself* from himself and gives *himself* away. . . . The primordial phenomenon that is given in faith is precisely the *self-alienation*, the becoming, the *kenosis* and *genesis* of God himself.[52]

Much could be said about Rahner's christology. What is of importance in this study, which is primarily concerned with the concept of God, in the sense in which the incarnation represents the radical self-expression of God in the nondivine realm. The concept of the real symbol is crucial to his understanding of the meaning of this self-expression. And so, in this section, I will seek to clarify the notion of the real symbol and to show how Rahner understands the divine act whereby God, through God's real symbol, takes finite reality as a determination of Godself.[53]

Rahner distinguishes between a representational symbol (*ein Vertretungssymbol*) and a real symbol (*ein Realsymbol*). A representational symbol is a figure, a sign, a cipher that accidentally indicates another reality. Both the reality or the concept that serves as a representational symbol and that which it symbolizes are already intelligible in themselves and could exist without the symbolic relationship between them. This relationship is extrinsic to the essence of both realities. Rahner says that the representational symbol represents only a secondary, derived type of symbol. A real symbol, on the other hand, is the highest form of representation in which "a reality makes another reality present and lets it be there [*dasein lässt*]."[54] In the case of a real symbol, there is a much more intrinsic or essential mediation of a reality on the part of some other reality (the symbol). Symbolism in this sense is an ontological phenomenon and not just the product of an arbitrary decision by a human person that *x* should be viewed as symbolizing *y*.

Rahner formulates two basic principles (really a single principle and its converse) of what he calls an "ontology of the real symbol." First, he says, "that which is [*das Seiende*] is in itself symbolic because it necessarily expresses itself in order to attain its own essence."[55] And second, "the genuine symbol (real symbol) is the self-fulfillment of a particular being [*ein Seiendes*] in another, which is constitutive of the essence of that particular being."[56] My goal, in what follows, is to elucidate the meaning and significance of these two principles.

The first thing to notice is that a particular being is symbolic primarily for its own sake. That is to say, an entity has its appropriate real symbol not in order to disclose itself to other "observers," but in order to realize itself. On the basis of this primordial symbolization for its own sake, an entity is knowable by other entities.

A condition of the possibility of such a self-expression (symbolization for the sake of that which is symbolized), Rahner says, is the intrinsic plurality of all that is. Individual entities are not absolutely simple. Their self-actualization is always mediated. Their unity is always a unity of distinct moments that exist within the particular entities.

Rahner says that this is obviously the case for finite reality. Finite beings are not fully self-possessed. Finite beings are material and thus attain to actuality only through a mediation of the particular being to itself. A finite entity is not perfectly self-identical but is composed of a unity of plural moments. However, Rahner argues, this plural nature of reality applies also to God, for it is an ontological characteristic. As the doctrine of the trinity indicates, the being of God itself is composed of (three) distinct moments that mediate the one divine subject to itself. This unity in plurality is a pure perfection and not a limitation. The unity that results from the self-differentiation and self-mediation of a living being is a higher form of unity or integrity than a mere "dead identity that collapses in upon itself."[57] Thus, the first principle of an ontology of the symbol, namely, "that which is is in itself symbolic," is an ontological proposition, one having universal validity.

All beings, from the smallest bit of matter to God, are internally plural, composed of distinct moments, although in different degrees corresponding to the level of being of each entity. How, Rahner asks, are the various moments within a particular, unitary being related to one another? He argues, on the basis of the Thomistic maxim that runs: *non enim plura secundum se uniuntur* (there can be no union of things that are in themselves multiple), that the plural moments within a particular being cannot simply be coordinate with one another, related only in terms of juxtaposition.[58] If the various moments of a particular being were equiprimordial, then they could no longer be the moments of a single unified being. At best, these moments might be joined together externally and subsequently. For Rahner, such a unity would not be an essential unity, but only an accidental uniting of that which is essentially separate. Therefore, he argues,

> . . . a plurality in a primordial, and primordially superior, unity can only be conceived as the unfolding of the one [i.e., the originally unitary being]. The plural originates from out of a primordial "one" in a relationship of origination and consequence. The most primordial unity, which also forms the unity that unites the plural, releases and "dis-closes" [ent-schliesst] itself into a plurality, while remaining the master of itself, precisely in order to find itself.[59]

The multiple moments that compose the actuality of all particular beings must be understood, according to Rahner, as the unfolding or the self-expression of the unity of the particular being itself. The one, unified particular being actualizes itself or exists only by expressing itself, by positing a moment of itself that is distinct from its primordial identity. This distinct moment or "other" is a real symbol. It is the means by which a being mediates itself to itself and takes possession of itself. The real symbol is the self-expression of the being as it actualizes itself. Rahner states the meaning of the first principle of an ontology of the symbol in the following passage.

> A plurality belongs to each particular being as such, as an inner moment of the unity that provides its meaning. This plurality is one that constitutes itself, through its origin in a primordial unity, as the fulfillment of the particular being (or, because of its perfection [i.e., in the case of God]), in such a way that that which is posited as different has an agreement with its origin and thus the character of an expression or a "symbol" in relation to its origin (at least in the sense of specifying, if not always duplicating, its origin).[60]

There is a unique relationship of identity between a being (that which is symbolized) and its symbol. It is, for Rahner, more primordial and intimate than the relation of an efficient cause to its effect. A real symbol, is not simply posited as an alien reality over against its origin. Rather, the original being expresses itself in the real symbol by way of formal causality.[61] In the words of Peter Eicher, "the symbol, therefore, is not simply an external sign for a real, distinct thing, but a being's own self-mediation."[62] The relationship between a real symbol and that which it symbolizes is characterized as a dialectic in which identity and difference are directly proportional.[63] The being that is symbolized communicates or imparts itself to the real symbol, is genuinely present in the real symbol, and realizes itself through the process of expressing this real symbol. The original being is its own effect in the real symbol. It gives itself away, alienates itself from itself in order to find itself in a fuller mode of being in the mediated possession of itself in the real symbol.

While I want to reserve my critical analysis of Rahner's ontology of the symbol until the next chapter, it should be noted at this point that Rahner's view of the symbolic nature of reality represents one of the more difficult aspects of his thought to understand and appropriate. It seems to me that the examples he cites to elucidate his ontology of the symbol, namely, the trinity, the incarnation, and the relation of the human soul to its body, are special cases that are of dubious value in the attempt to show that reality as such is internally plural or symbolic. I must confess that I simply do not believe Rahner has given sufficient evidence to show that all actual beings necessarily form for themselves a real symbol. However, this is not Rahner's main task in the essay on the real symbol. His purpose is to investigate a theology of the symbol. He admits that his discussion of the ontology of the symbol is incomplete.

> We choose a method that leads us as quickly and simply as possible to our goal, even though it oversimplifies the problem in that we presuppose ontological and theological starting points, which, in a genuinely worked out ontology of the symbol, would have to be proved, not presupposed. However, for the reader who is primarily intended here, these presuppositions may be made without hesitation.[64]

I will not try to evaluate the validity of Rahner's final claim in this passage. But I do wish to suggest that Rahner's largely presupposed ontology of the symbol can fruitfully be approached from the perspective of the philosophy of Hegel.

Now, whether a reference to Hegel will serve to illuminate or only further to obscure Rahner's concept of the real symbol, depends on one's own appraisal of Hegel. One critic says that Rahner's thought is least helpful when it is most Hegelian.[65] Yet, Rahner's relation to Hegel has been the topic of several recent articles.[66]

That Rahner's writings are reminiscent of Hegel at a number of points cannot be denied. Indeed, in the few places where he refers to Hegel by name, Rahner attempts to show that although some of his formulations are similar to Hegel's, one need not be a Hegelian to affirm them.[67] I think Klaus Fischer best expresses the relation of Rahner to Hegel when he says that Rahner employs Hegelian terms and concepts for his own purposes without taking over from Hegel the presuppositions and original contexts of those terms and concepts.[68]

In the essay "Zur Theologie des Symbols," the influence of Hegelian thought upon Rahner is most evident. His ontology of the symbol, which I have tried to outline above, seems to express a view of the real that is similar to Hegel's phenomenology of spirit. For Hegel, reality is a dialectical process of self-possession or self-realization through self-alienation. In the first moment of this dialectic there is given what Hegel calls the in itself *(an sich)*. The in itself is indeterminate. It is substance or consciousness. However, the in itself develops. It alienates itself from itself by positing an "other" that is particular and determinate. This "other" is characterized as for itself *(für sich)*. It is subject, not substance and self-consciousness, not simply consciousness. By grasping the other precisely as its own reality, the original moment overcomes its self-alienation and effects a return to itself as concrete and actual. The similarity between this view and Rahner's understanding of the real symbol is obvious. Compare the following two passages in which Hegel defines spirit (which most fully exemplifies this dialectic) and Rahner summarizes his understanding of the symbolic character of reality.

Hegel:

> Spirit is the knowledge of self in alienation [*die Ent-
> äusserung*]; it is the process of maintaining identity with
> self in otherness. . . . Spirit has shown itself to us to be
> neither simply the retreat of self-consciousness into its
> pure interiority, nor the submersion of self-con-

sciousness into the substance and nonbeing of its distinction [from itself]. Rather, spirit is the movement of the
self that alienates [*entäussern*] its own self and submerges
itself in its substance and so, as subject, has emerged
from substance into an object and a content as it preserves, cancels, and elevates [*aufheben*] this distinction of
objectivity and of content.[69]

Rahner:

That which is [*das Seiende*] (to the degree that it has and
realizes being) is, first of all, *itself* "symbolic." It expresses
itself and thereby possesses itself. It gives itself away to
that which is other than itself and finds itself in the other
through knowledge and love. This is the case because
that which is, in the positing of the inner other, comes to
(or from) its self-fulfillment, which is the presupposition
or the act of being given to oneself in knowledge and
love.[70]

In both cases, an entity exists or is actual by virtue of the fact that
it returns to itself through a process of self-alienation. It posits
an other and in grasping that other as its own reality, despite its
genuine otherness, truly possesses itself for the first time. Peter
Eicher's statement, which is made in reference to Rahner's ontology of the symbol, could apply just as well to Hegel's understanding of spirit: "that which is is *bei sich* only in that it puts out
from itself as its own reality an other which is alien to itself."[71]

With this background we can now approach the concept of
the real symbol more directly by considering the symbolic
character of human being and divine being. Although Rahner
does indeed hold that that which is, as such, is symbolic, that is to
say, the positing of a real symbol is a transcendental category
applicable to all reality, there can be no doubt that what he
means by the real symbol is revealed most clearly when he
discusses human being and God.[72] This reflects Rahner's basic
position that it is human being that is to be interrogated first and
foremost in all metaphysical questions and his view that God
eminently exemplifies all pure perfections.[73] Therefore, as one
interpreter of Rahner puts it, "the ontology of the symbol is first
of all the ontology of man."[74]

While all particular beings necessarily posit an appropriate
real symbol, each being does this in a manner corresponding to
its level of being. As was shown in Chapter III, the content of the

concept "being" is, for Rahner, self-possession, subjectivity, *Beisichsein*. The higher on the scale of being a particular being is, the higher its degree of being reflected upon itself, that is, its subjectivity. The inner plurality or symbolic character of a being is a condition of the possibility of such subjectivity. For Rahner, as for Hegel, a being can return to itself and possess itself as a subject only if it has first alienated itself from itself, or gone out from itself. As Rahner argues:

> All doing and acting, from that which is merely material to the inner life of the triune God, is simply an application of this one metaphysical theme, an application of the one meaning of being: self-possession. However, self-possession has two phases: a flowing outward, a setting out of one's own essence from one's own ground, an emanation; and a taking back into oneself of this essence that has been set out, revealed, as it were, from one's ground. The more inward both phases are to the particular being that emanates and flows back to itself, the more a particular being can express itself and can, thereby, keep to itself that which is expressed and perceive the expressed essence itself, the more it participates in being [*das Sein*], which is *Beisichsein*.[75]

Pure matter represents the zero point on the scale of *Beisichsein*, for it is wholly given over to another and does not return to itself. But in human being there is a *reditio completa in seipsum*, a full return to self. In discussing the emanation of human being that makes the return to self possible, Rahner, in *Geist in Welt*, expresses the conceptuality that he later identifies with the real symbol.[76]

Because human being is material spirit, spirit in world, the self-possession or self-realization of the human person always necessarily involves a *conversio ad phantasma*. The self-possession of human spirit occurs through the mediation of the material world. Rahner is concerned to show that this orientation to matter is not simply a limitation or a burden to human spirit, but is in fact the means by which human spirit is realized. Human spirit comes to itself only by encountering another receptively. But human spirit "must . . . from itself create the possibility of its being able to encounter another objectively as that which it knows first [*das Erstgewusste*]."[77] Human spirit posits its own materiality. The intellect, in order to know being, posits sen-

sibility and the knowledge of particular beings given thereby.
The human subject possesses itself as spirit precisely by positing,
as its own reality, that which is not spirit.

> The possible intellect can establish itself in the real pos-
> sibility of being spirit only by becoming sensibility. But,
> on the other hand, because the possibility of a *reditio
> completa*, in which the essence of being spiritual lies,
> demands essentially that the intellect as returning into
> itself not be sensible, but rather free from matter, sub-
> sisting in itself, this becoming sensible of the (possible)
> intellect can only be understood such that the intellect
> allows sensibility to arise out of itself as the intellect's own
> faculty. This must take place in such a way that the
> intellect does not completely lose itself, in such a way,
> therefore, that it holds with itself the sensibility that
> arises from out of the intellect as its very own, although
> subordinate, faculty. The intellect appears as a nonsensi-
> ble faculty that acts as such alongside of sensibility. Thus
> the (possible) intellect appears as the origin of sen-
> sibility. . . . But sensibility, because it arises out of the
> intellect, and thus is the intellect's own reality, is the
> always already realized turning of the intellect itself to
> the other, i.e., *conversio ad phantasma.*[78]

Using Rahner's later conceptuality, one can say that sensibility (and thus the human body as a whole) is the real symbol
of the human intellect (or soul). The body is posited as the
means by which the intellect realizes itself. This occurs by means
of formal causality, for the positing of the body as a real symbol
of the intellect represents "an extension or diffusion of [the
intellect's] own essence in the otherness of the other."[79] The
body, as a real symbol, is genuinely other than the intellect. And
yet it is an expression of the intellect, without which the intellect
could not realize itself. As a formal cause, the intellect does not
posit the body as something wholly other, but communicates
itself to the body, informs the body, and thus posits the body as
its own reality.[80]

With this understanding of a particular instance of the
positing of a real symbol, the second proposition of Rahner's
ontology of the symbol should be more readily understandable:
"the genuine symbol (real symbol) is the self-fulfillment of a
particular being in another that is constitutive of the essence of
that particular being."[81] The expression of a real symbol is a
necessary moment within the process of self-discovery, self-pos-

session, and self-realization on the part of a particular being. An
other must be posited so that in distinguishing itself from this
other and in possessing this other as itself, a being becomes a
subject for the first time.

> That which is (to the extent that it is and has being) is,
> first of all, *itself* "symbolic." It expresses itself and thereby
> possesses itself. It gives itself away to that which is other
> and finds itself in the other through knowledge and love.
> This is the case because that which is, in the positing of
> the inner other, comes to (or from) its self-fulfillment,
> which is the presupposition or act of being given to
> oneself in knowledge and love.[82]

Now that this lengthy, but necessary, discussion of the ontology of the symbol has been completed, we can turn our
attention once again to christology and God's self-expressive
activity in the world. God, for Rahner, is absolute being and thus
possesses the highest degree of *Beisichsein*. As the doctrine of the
trinity indicates, God also is most perfectly symbolic.[83] God
would not be more ontologically simple and perfect if there were
no intradivine distinctions. The divine plurality is a pure perfection, not an indication of imperfection or limitation. Nor do the
relative trinitarian distinctions within God represent any weak-
ening of the divine unity.

According to Rahner, the theology of the Logos represents
the highest application of the ontology of the symbol. "The
Logos is the 'word' of the Father, his perfect 'likeness,' his im-
print, his reflection, his self-expression."[84] The Logos is the real
symbol of God the unoriginate source. Rahner means this in
precisely the same sense in which the real symbol was described
above: as the "inner symbol, which is expressed by the one who is
symbolized himself and yet is different from him, in which the
one who is symbolized expresses himself and thus has himself."[85] In the expression of the Logos and in grasping the Logos
as God's own other, God possesses Godself. Rahner does not
understand this to mean that God *becomes* perfect *Beisichsein*
through the process of positing the Logos as God's real symbol.
The self-expression of God in the Logos is the act of the divine
self-possession itself.

> The Logos (as reality of the immanent divine life) is
> "generated" from the Father as *"likeness"* and *"expression"*
> of the Father. This process is an event that is given

necessarily with the divine self-knowing, without which the absolute act of the knowing divine self-possession cannot be.[86]

This innerdivine plurality in which God expresses Godself *ad intra* in the Logos is a condition of the possibility of the divine self-expression *ad extra* in the world. The intradivine self-expression occurs necessarily, for it *is* the event of God's self-possession. God would not be God if God did not posit the Logos as real symbol. But the self-expression of God in the world is a free act on God's part, not required for God to be God.

> Because God "must express" himself in an innerdivine way, he can express himself *ad extra;* the creaturely, finite expression *ad extra* is a continuation of the innerdivine establishment of an "image and likeness" and genuinely occurs . . . *"through"* the Logos (John 1:3).[87]

In the incarnation of the divine Logos in Jesus Christ, God expresses Godself in the world, in the nondivine realm. This is a true *self*-expression for Rahner. Therefore, it involves a real symbol. God (in the Logos) takes the world (in a human being) as God's own other, God's real symbol.

> The incarnate Logos is the absolute symbol of God in the world. The incarnate Logos is unsurpassibly filled with the one who is symbolized. The incarnate Logos, therefore, is not only the presence and revelation, in the world, of what God is in himself, but is also the expressive being-there [*das ausdrückende Da-sein*] of that which (or better; the one whom) God in free grace wishes to be in relation to the world.[88]

This means that the human nature of Jesus Christ is not borne by the Logos as if it were a uniform or a mask. Such a docetic view of the incarnation asserts merely that "the Logos makes itself known and lets itself be perceived through a reality that is alien to the Logos, that is adopted accidentally in an external way, and that, in its inner essence, has nothing to do with the Logos."[89] On the contrary, Rahner asserts that the human nature of Jesus is an appropriate expression of the Logos, its real symbol. He makes some very striking claims at this point. He says, for instance, that the humanity of Jesus is the very existence of God in the world.[90] He calls human being the abbreviation or cipher of God. When God wills to be nondivine, it is human being that appears. Human being is created as the grammar or the syntax of a possible self-expression of God. For Rahner, "man could be defined as that which arises when the self-expression of God, his word, is lovingly uttered into the emptiness of the Godless void."[91]

Because human being is a real symbol of God, and not just an accidental sign of the divine reality, the relationship between God and the human nature of Jesus is one of quasi-formal causality. The very being of God itself is communicated to the nondivine. In this act of self-expression or self-communication, God adopts the reality of the world as God's own reality, as God's environment.[92] The world, for Rahner, belongs to God as God's own substantial determination.

> The being of the Logos (of course *as* that which is retained through a procession from the Father) must be thought of as externalizing itself in such a way that (without detriment to its immutability in and of *itself*) it *itself* in truth becomes the existence of a created reality.[93]

The self-expression of God in the world through God's finite real symbol (human being) is the event in which God becomes, in a real sense, a creature. God is no longer the horizon of the world, but the innermost, loving heart of the world. As has been shown, the existence of the world as such is, for Rahner, grounded in God's ability to communicate Godself to the world and thus to take the reality of the world as God's own.

> God goes out of himself, he himself, he as the fullness which gives itself away lavishly. Because he can do this, because this is his free, primordial possibility (for which reason he is defined as love in Scripture), his ability to be the creator, the ability merely to posit that which is other without giving himself away, is only the derived, limited, secondary possibility. The possibility of being a creator is finally grounded in this genuine primordial possibility of God, namely the ability to give himself away to the nondivine and thereby to have, as his own history, a genuine, proper history in that which is other. . . . God projects the creature creatively, establishing it, *ex nihilo*, in its own reality that is distinct from God, as the grammar of a possible self-expression of God.[94]

All of this indicates the presence, in Rahner's thought, of a somewhat different understanding of the divine activity in the world from that outlined above. I said earlier that God, for Rahner, is not an agent within the world at all, but is the ground of the whole world process. Here, in Rahner's christology, one must say that God does act within the world. Of course, this activity of God in the world is an activity in God's real symbol. But I have tried to emphasize the radical unity of a real symbol and that which it symbolizes in Rahner's thought. A real symbol makes present that which it symbolizes. Thus, God is present and active in the world through God's real symbol.

In the event of the incarnation a mode of divine activity is implied that surpasses the activity of God as a creator and sustainer of the finite world.

> It follows from what has been said that the Logos, as the son of the Father, *in* his *humanity* as such, is in all truth the revelatory symbol in which the Father utters himself to the world in this son, because the Logos is the symbol that makes present that which is symbolized itself. . . . From this perspective, we must consider that the natural depth of the symbolic reality of all things (which in itself transcends to God in an innerworldly or purely natural way) has received, ontologically, an infinite widening in that this reality has also become a determination or the environment of the Logos itself. Each reality that originates from God . . . expresses much more than merely itself. Each one always indicates and resonates, in its own way, the totality of reality itself. If the individual reality, in allowing the totality to be present, also refers to God (finally through a transcendental orientation to him as the exemplary, efficient, and final cause), then this transcendence receives a radicality in that in Christ these realities no longer merely refer to God as the cause, but to the God to whom these realities belong as his substantial determination or his very own environment (even if this can be grasped only by faith).[95]

The transcendent divine horizon, which is the creative ground of finite reality, becomes intrinsic within that finite reality by making it its own environment. The divine self-expression in the incarnation, as Rahner asserts in the following passage, is the event in which God in some sense becomes an entity and agent within the world. God no longer simply acts on the world, but acts within the world through God's real symbol.

> One could still say, with Old Testament scripture, that the creator is in heaven and we are on the earth. But one must say of the God whom we confess in Christ that he is precisely where we are and can only be found there. And though he remains infinite, this does not mean that he is

elsewhere and in addition something else, but rather than the finite itself has received an infinite depth and is no longer the antithesis to the infinite. Instead, the finite is that which the infinite itself has become in order to open an entrance into the infinite for all that is finite, of which God himself has become a part. God has made himself this entrance, this door. God has become the reality of that which is void [*das Nichtige*].[96]

God Changes in God's Other

Rahner's portrayal of the self-expression of God in the non-divine realm, which takes place through God's real symbol, raises the question of whether he still maintains the nonrelativity of God expressed in the traditional language concerning God's aseity, immutability, and eternity. In what sense, for Rahner, is the God who enters into a genuine relationship with human beings, who expresses Godself in the world and who communicates Godself to the world by becoming worldly, nevertheless, radically *a se*, immutable, and eternal?

This question, Rahner says, is already unavoidably raised by the Johannine claim that the word (the Logos) became flesh.[97] Does this proposition mean that God can become? The answer to this question in pantheism is a simple yes, for in such a view God exists historically. But the Christian theologian finds her- or himself in a difficult situation when confronted with this question. On the one hand, Rahner says, the Christian must confess God to be genuinely nonrelative to the world: the immutable, eternal *actus purus*, who is already fully self-possessed and has no need to become. On the other hand, "it remains true: the word has *become* flesh."[98]

Rahner asserts without hesitation that at this point "the traditional scholastic theology and philosophy begins to blink and stammer."[99] While affirming verbally that the Logos became flesh, scholastic thought understands this to mean that all change and becoming in the incarnation is on the part of the human nature and not on the part of the divine person. For scholastic thought,

> . . . all is clear: the Logos assumes, without alteration, that which as a *creaturely* reality is subject to becoming, including its being assumed. Thus, all becoming and all history with its hardship are on this side of the absolute

> abyss that separates the immutable, necessary God and
> the mutable, conditioned world and that prevents them
> from mixing.[100]

This traditional view of the incarnation, according to
Rahner, neither takes seriously the claim that the divine Logos
itself became flesh, nor is credible in the contemporary world.
Such a view is understood by modern persons to be nothing
more than a myth in which God appears in the world disguised
as a human being, one who is nothing more than a puppet that
God manipulates.[101] For Rahner, the central Christian claim is
precisely that God has assumed our own worldly, human reality
and has become subject to the finitude of our reality and our
world. "It remains true, however, that the *Logos became* man; that
the history of the development of this human reality is [the
Logos'] history; our time became the time of the eternal one, our
death became the death of the immortal God himself."[102]

The radical nature of God's presence in the world in the
event of the incarnation means, for Rahner, that the traditional
assertions concerning God's nonrelativity to the world cannot be
made without qualification. He indicates something of the problem of an unqualified assertion of the nonrelativity of God in the
following passage.

> We scholastics often say, for example, that God does not
> have real relations *ad extra*. This formula expresses some-
> thing true, and yet, who is the God who does not have a
> real relation to me? This is absurd. God really loves me,
> really is made flesh, and really is the one [Jesus Christ]
> who exists on the earth, who not only exists within God's
> view, but who is himself divine.[103]

To take the incarnation seriously means, for Rahner, to assert a
certain relativity of God to the world. God is related to the world
as a person, as one who can really be said to be love. The
Christian theologian must say that "God can become something,
the one who is immutable in himself can *himself* be mutable *in the
other*."[104]

On the basis of this maxim, which recurs frequently in his
writings, Rahner understands the traditional theological assertions concerning God's nonrelativity to be dialectical assertions.
He writes:

> It follows that the statement concerning the "immu-
> tability" of God, the lack of a real relation of God to the

world, is, in a true sense, a dialectical assertion. One can, indeed, must say this without thereby being Hegelian. For it is both true and dogma that the Logos himself has become man. He himself has become something that *(formaliter)* he has not always already been. Therefore, what has become in this manner itself and through itself is precisely the reality of God. However, if this is the truth of faith, then ontology must conform itself to this truth, allow itself to be enlightened and admit that God is immutable "in himself," yet can change in the other, and that *both* assertions really and truly must be made of the same God himself.[105]

The situation is similar, Rahner holds, with regard to the eternity or atemporal nature of God.[106] In Godself, God is eternally atemporal. But at the same time, because of the incarnation, Christian theology must affirm that God Godself, in God's other, experiences history, change, and time. God not only creates time, but accepts it as God's own determination. God "makes his own eternity into the true content of time. He creates his own time in order to communicate to it his eternity, the radical validity of his free love."[107] Temporal becoming is not just a characteristic of the nondivine but, precisely as different from God in Godself, has been made by God a characteristic of God. This is possible, Rahner argues:

> Because the difference between the time of the creature and the eternity of God sets time apart from eternity, but does not really set eternity apart from time. For if God himself creates the difference, then he sets that which is created apart from himself, but does not set himself apart from that which he created. Difference from eternity is a predicate of created time; eternity of the God who creates time, however, implies through and through the temporal as a moment within eternity itself. Therefore, God can create time as his own time by assuming it and can assume it by creating it.[108]

Rahner says that both poles of this dialectic, the aseity, immutability, eternity of God and the relativity, mutability, temporality of God, must be affirmed, not only for metaphysical, but also for soteriological reasons. On the one hand, God must be radically identified with human beings if *human being* is to be redeemed. A wholly unrelated God cannot be *our* savior. Yet, on the other hand, if the savior is not also the eternal, immutable God who is radically *a se*, then the savior would simply be one of us, likewise in need of redemption. God must be radically other than human beings if human being is to be *redeemed*. A finite God cannot be our *savior*.[109]

The question, of course, is how relativity and nonrelativity are both compossible within one and the same divine being.[110] What does the proposition that God changes in God's other while remaining immutable in Godself mean? Rahner argues that "this 'altering oneself *in* another' may neither be viewed as a contradiction of the immutability of God in himself, nor be allowed to revert into the assertion of an 'alteration *of* the other.'"[111] At this point ontology must orient itself to the message of faith. Just as the unity of God is not denied by the doctrine of the trinity, while this concept of unity cannot simply be used to determine the meaning of the trinity, so, too, the immutability of God must be maintained in such a way that the mystery of the incarnation is not dissolved. No finite analogues of the dialectic of relativity and nonrelativity within the divine reality can be found, for the event in which this dialectic is revealed, the incarnation, is a mystery in the strict sense. This dialectic of relativity and nonrelativity is the mystery of God's reality itself. Both poles of the dialectic must be maintained and neither can be thought of as prior to the other. "We learn from the doctrine of the incarnation that the immutability of God (without being cancelled) does not alone characterize God. Instead, we learn that *he* in and despite his immutability can truly *become* something."[112] This possibility is an indication of God's perfection, "which would be inferior if he could not, in addition to his infinity, become less than he (always) is [i.e., become finite]."[113]

At this point, many of the themes within Rahner's understanding of God that have been discussed previously can be linked together. For Rahner, the becoming of God in God's real symbol, the finite reality in which God expresses Godself, does not contradict the divine immutability because the self-expression of God derives from God's freedom as a person not from God's metaphysical essence. In his view, God *can* change, *can* assume finite reality as God's own environment, but need not do so in order to realize Godself. Because God is fully self-possessed and has no need of finite reality, God can freely add finitude to Godself. The relativity of God is a function of God's loving freedom not of God's essential nature. Indeed, the relativity of God *is* God's love.[114]

Since the self-expression of God, in which God genuinely

becomes, arises out of a free decision of God as a person, this act remains fundamentally mysterious. As was shown earlier, for Rahner, the acts of a free person cannot be anticipated or calculated. They must be encountered by those who are related to the free agent and accepted in an attitude of love. In love, one gives oneself over to the mystery of the freedom of the other person.

In an article on God in the *Lexikon für Theologie und Kirche*, Rahner reveals quite clearly his understanding that the relativity of God is grounded in the personal freedom of God.

> The doctrine of salvation history, trinity, and incarnation is concerned to show that God, despite all ontology, is for faith more than the transcendent source of the world that remains unchanged, enclosed in dead solitude. Over and over again this teaching leads the doctrine of the transcendence [*die Überweltlichkeit*] of the *immutable* God in his *historical* self-communication to the creature back into the mystery of the greater God, where the dialectical comparison between the immutability of God (timelessness, nonrelativity, graduated mediation of his own efficacy through the creatures) and his historical might and immediacy does not succeed . . . because this comparison on the part of the creature cannot be fully successful . . . and, therefore, is a necessarily unrealizable task.[115]

The act by which God assumes finite reality as God's own reality is, for Rahner, the most fundamental act of the divine freedom. It cannot be anticipated ahead of time, nor even fully understood after the fact. And yet it is precisely this act that indicates that God is love, for love is the most authentic realization of a free agent.[116] By communicating Godself to the world, by taking the world (in human being) as God's own real symbol, God reveals Godself to be a personal agent related to the world in love. This ecstatic, self-giving, self-alienating love for others is the fundamental act of God. Precisely because God is, in principle, free not to give Godself in love, the actual love of God for the creatures can only be experienced as the most profound mystery and gift of existence.[117]

NOTES

[1] It should be noted here that there are tensions within Rahner's understanding of the God-world relationship. He does not seem to

carry through fully the revisionary thrust of his basic insight. I will try to demonstrate this in Part II of this study.

2 "Fragen zur Unbegreiflichkeit Gottes nach Thomas von Aquin," *ST*, 12:311–314 (ET: *TI*, 16:249–251).

3 "Christologie im Rahmen des modernen Selbst- und Weltverständnisses," *ST*, 9:237 (ET: *TI*, 11:225).

4 "Über das Verhältnis von Natur und Gnade," *ST*, 1:343 (ET: *TI*, 1:316).

5 "*Theos* im Neuen Testament," *ST*, 1:126 (ET: *TI*, 1:110).

6 "Probleme der Christologie von heute," *ST*, 1:184, n. 1 (ET: *TI*, 1:164, n. 1).

7 "Weltgeschichte und Heilsgeschichte," *ST*, 5:123–124 (ET: *TI*, 5:104).

8 "Der eine Mittler und die Vielfalt der Vermittlungen," *ST*, 8:228 (ET: *TI*, 9:178).

9 "*Theos* im Neuen Testament," *ST*, 1:126–127 (ET: *TI*, 1:110–111).

10 Ibid., p. 127 (ET: ibid., p. 111).

11 *GG*, pp. 71–72 (ET: *FCF*, pp. 62–63).

12 "Marxistische Utopie und christliche Zukunft des Menschen," *ST*, 6:78 (ET: *TI*, 6:60).

13 *GG*, p. 72 (ET: *FCF*, p. 63).

14 "Marxistische Utopie und christliche Zukunft des Menschen," *ST*, 6:78 (ET: *TI*, 6:60).

15 *GG*, pp. 71–72 (ET: *FCF*, p. 63).

16 See "Probleme der Christologie von heute," *ST*, 1:186 (ET: *TI*, 1:165); "Über die Möglichkeit des Glaubens heute," *ST*, 5:32 (ET: *TI*, 5:22); "Immanente und transzendente Vollendung der Welt," *ST*, 8:609 (ET: *TI*, 10:289).

17 "Über die Möglichkeit des Glaubens heute," *ST*, 5:30 (ET: *TI*, 5:21).

18 *GG*, p. 85 (ET: *FCF*, pp. 77–78). This passage continues: "but [God] would rather be a portion of a higher whole as is understood in pantheism." Here it is pantheism, and not dualism, that is purported to view God and the world as parts of the larger totality of reality. This is a reversal of Rahner's usual understanding of dualism and pantheism.

19 Ibid., p. 86 (ET: ibid., p. 78).

20 "Zwiegespräch mit Gott?" *ST*, 13:154.

21 "Die theologische Dimension der Frage nach dem Menschen," *ST*, 12:393 (ET: *TI*, 17:58).

22 *GG*, p. 71 (ET: *FCF*, pp. 62–63).

23 "Über den Begriff des Geheimnisses in der katholischen Theologie," *ST*, 4:71 (ET: *TI*, 4:51). Elsewhere, Rahner remarks: "the differentiation of the individual creatures *amongst* themselves is encompassed by their *common* difference from God" ("Zum theologischen Begriff der Konkupiszenz," *ST*, 1:386, n. 1 (ET: *TI*, 1:356, n. 1)).

24 "Christologie im Rahmen des modernen Selbst- und Weltverständnisses," *ST*, 9:236 (ET: *TI*, 11:224).

25 "Gotteserfahrung heute," *ST*, 9:172–173 (ET: *TI*, 11:160–161).

26 "Glaubende Annahme der Wahrheit Gottes," *ST*, 12:215 (ET: *TI*, 16:169–170).

27 *GG*, p. 93 (ET: *FCF*, p. 86).

28 Ibid., p. 94 (ET: ibid.).

29 "Die Hominisation als theologische Frage," p. 58 (ET: *Hominization*, p. 65).

30 "Die Einheit von Geist und Materie im christlichen Glaubensverständnis," *ST*, 6:189 (ET: *TI*, 6:156).

31 *GG*, p. 91 (ET: *FCF*, p. 83).

32 Ibid., p. 94 (ET: ibid., p. 87).

33 "Christologie im Rahmen des modernen Selbst- und Weltverständnisses," *ST*, 9:236 (ET: *TI*, 11:224).

34 "Die Einheit von Geist und Materie im christlichen Glaubensverständnis," *ST*, 6:210–211 (ET: *TI*, 6:174–175).

35 *GG*, p. 186 (ET: *FCF*, p. 185).

36 See "Zur Theologie der Menschwerdung," *ST*, 4:151 (ET: *TI*, 4:117); "Probleme der Christologie von heute," *ST*, 1:183 (ET: *TI*, 1:162); "Über den Versuch eines Aufrisses einer Dogmatik," *ST*, 1:29, n. 1 (ET: *TI*, 1:19, n. 1) respectively.

37 *GG*, p. 86 (ET: *FCF*, p. 79). See, in addition to those passages indicated in note 36, "Über die Möglichkeit des Glaubens heute," *ST*, 5:21 (ET: *TI*, 5:12); "Immanente und transzendente Vollendung der Welt," *ST*, 8:601 (ET: *TI*, 10:281).

38 "Die ewige Bedeutung der Menschheit Jesu für unser Gottesverhältnis," *ST*, 3:53 (ET: *TI*, 3:40).

39 *GG*, p. 86 (ET: *FCF*, p. 79).

40 "Probleme der Christologie von heute," *ST*, 1:182–183 (ET: *TI*, 1:162).

41 *GG*, pp. 104–110 (ET: *FCF*, pp. 97–104).

42 Klaus Fischer argues that "nearness is an existentiell concept for the (analogous) formal causality of God" (*Der Mensch als Geheimnis*, p. 249).

43 "Christologie im Rahmen des modernen Selbst- und Weltverständnisses," *ST*, 9:236–237 (ET: *TI*, 11:225).

44 "Zur Theologie der Menschwerdung," *ST*, 4:152 (ET: *TI*, 4:118).

45 "Probleme der Christologie von heute," *ST*, 1:178 (ET: *TI*, 1:158).

46 *GG*, p. 202 (ET: *FCF*, p. 202).

47 "Probleme der Christologie von heute," *ST*, 1:212 (ET: *TI*, 1:191).

48 "Zur Theologie der Menschwerdung," *ST*, 4:149–150 (ET: *TI*, 4:115–116).

49 "Probleme der Christologie von heute," *ST*, 1:183 (ET: *TI*, 1:162–163).

50 Ibid., p. 185 (ET: ibid., p. 165), my emphasis.

51 Ibid., p. 196, n. 1 (ET: ibid., p. 176, n. 1).

52 "Zur Theologie der Menschwerdung," *ST*, 4:148 (ET: *TI*, 4:114).

53 The key essay in which Rahner's understanding of the real symbol is presented, and which will be the primary focus of my attention in this section, is: "Zur Theologie des Symbols," *ST*, 4:275–311 (ET: *TI*, 4:221–252). The English translation of this essay is quite confusing, for *"das Seiende," "das Sein"* (and even *"das Wesen"*) are all rendered by the English "being."

54 "Zur Theologie des Symbols," *ST*, 4:279 (ET: *TI*, 4:225).

55 Ibid., p. 278 (ET: ibid., p. 224).

56 Ibid., p. 290 (ET: ibid., p. 234).

57 Ibid., p. 280 (ET: ibid., p. 226).

58 Ibid., pp. 282–283 (ET: ibid., pp. 227–228). This maxim of Thomas' appears a number of times in different contexts in Rahner's work.

59 Ibid., p. 282 (ET: ibid., p. 227).

60 Ibid., p. 284 (ET: ibid., p. 229).

61 Ibid., pp. 287–288 (ET: ibid., pp. 231–232).

62 *Die anthropologische Wende*, p. 307.

63 "Zur Theologie des Symbols," *ST*, 4:283 (ET: *TI*, 4:228).

64 Ibid., p. 280, n. 4 (ET: ibid., pp. 225–226, n. 4).

65 Anne Carr, *The Theological Method of Karl Rahner*, p. 84.

66 Thomas Pearl, "Dialectical Panentheism: On the Hegelian Character of Rahner's Key Christological Writings," *Irish Theological Journal* 42 (1975):119–137; Denis Bradley, "Rahner's *Spirit in the World: Aquinas or Hegel?*" *Thomist* 41 (1977): 167–199; Winfried Corduan, "Hegel in Rahner: A Study in Philosophical Hermeneutics," *Harvard Theological Review* 71 (1978):285–298.

67 "Probleme der Christologie von heute," *ST*, 1:196–197, n. 2; 202, n. 2 (ET: *TI*, 1:176, n. 2; 181, n. 3); "Zur Theologie der Menschwerdung," *ST*, 4:147, n. 3 (ET: *TI*, 4:113–114, n. 3).

68 *Der Mensch als Geheimnis*, p. 346.

69 *Sämtliche Werke*, vol. 2: *Phänomenologie des Geistes* (Stuttgart: Frommanns Verlag, 1951), pp. 577, 616.

70 "Zur Theologie des Symbols," *ST*, 4:285 (ET: *TI*, 4:229–230). Rahner says "to *(or from)* its self-fulfillment" and "the presupposition or the *act* of being given to oneself" to indicate that the symbolic nature of God, whereby God posits a divine other (namely, the Logos), does not represent a process in which God attains self-fulfillment, but is rather the act or self-expression of the God who is self-fulfilled.

71 *Die anthropologische Wende*, p. 307.

72 The same could be said of Hegel's phenomenology of spirit.

73 See *HW*, p. 48 and "Zur Theologie des Symbols," *ST*, 4:282 (ET: *TI*, 4:227–228).

74 Eicher, *Die anthropologische Wende*, p. 305.

75 *HW,* pp. 63–64.

76 Ch. 4, "Conversio ad phantasma," pp. 169–280. This discussion is briefly summarized in "Zur Theologie des Symbols," *ST,* 4:304–306 (ET: TI, 4:245–247). That Rahner's understanding of formal causality and the way in which self-possession involves both an emanation from, and a return to, self is already formulated so clearly in this early work is some indication, I think, of how central these conceptualities are to his thought.

77 *GW,* p. 176.

78 Ibid., p. 176.

79 Ibid., p. 261.

80 Ibid., p. 258.

81 "Zur Theologie des Symbols," *ST,* 4:290 (ET: *TI,* 4:234).

82 Ibid., p. 285 (ET: ibid., pp. 229–230).

83 Ibid., pp. 280–281 (ET: ibid., pp. 226–227).

84 Ibid., p. 292 (ET: ibid., p. 236).

85 Ibid. (ET: ibid.). Once again, at this point, Rahner's and Hegel's views are quite similar. For Hegel, as for Rahner, the dynamic of the inner life of the triune God always forms the background for his view that the real as such is constituted by a dialectical process of self-possession through self-alienation. Compare Hegel's view of the divine trinity with the one expressed in the passage just cited from Rahner: "There are thus three moments to be distinguished [within God as absolute spirit]: the essential being; the being for itself that is the otherness of the essential being and for which the essential being exists; and the being for itself or the knowing of self of the essential being in the other. The essential being views itself only in its being for itself. It is *bei sich* only in this alienation from itself. The being for itself which excludes itself from the essential being is the self-knowing of the essential being itself; it is the word, which, when expressed, alienates the one who expresses it and leaves this one behind emptied. But it is immediately perceived and this self-perceiving alone is the existence of the word. Thus the distinctions that are made [i.e., between the essential being, the word, and the essential being's knowledge of itself in the word] are resolved immediately upon being made and made again immediately upon being resolved. That which is true and real is constituted precisely by this movement that revolves within itself" (*Phänomenologie des Geistes,* pp. 584–585).

86 "Zur Theologie des Symbols," *ST,* 4:292 (ET: *TI,* 4:236).

87 Ibid., p. 293 (ET: ibid., pp. 236–237).

88 Ibid., pp. 293–294 (ET: ibid., p. 237).

89 Ibid., p. 294 (ET: ibid., pp. 237–238).

90 "Probleme der Christologie von heute," *ST,* 1:212 (ET: *TI,* 1:191).

91 "Zur Theologie der Menschwerdung," *ST,* 4:150 (ET: *TI,* 4:116).

92 "Zur Theologie des Symbols," *ST,* 4:297 (ET: *TI,* 4:239).

93 Ibid., p. 295 (ET: ibid., p. 238).

94 *GG*, pp. 220–221 (ET: *FCF*, pp. 222–223).

95 "Zur Theologie des Symbols," *ST*, 4:296–297 (ET: *TI*, 4:239).

96 "Zur Theologie der Menschwerdung," *ST*, 4:151 (ET: *TI*, 4:117).

97 Ibid., p. 145 (ET: ibid., p. 112).

98 Ibid., p. 146 (ET: ibid.).

99 Ibid. (ET: ibid., p. 113).

100 Ibid. (ET: ibid.).

101 Ibid., p. 152 (ET: ibid., p. 118). Elsewhere Rahner expands a little on the mythological character of such a view. "One could define mythology in this connection as follows: The representation of the incarnation of a god such that the 'human' moment is only the clothing, the livery of the god, which he uses in order to signal his presence here with us, while, at the same time, the human moment does not attain its highest spontaneity and self-control precisely by being assumed by God, is mythological. Viewed from this perspective, there is one idea and fundamental conception that runs through the christological heresies from Apollinarianism to Monothelitism, sustained by this same basic mythological feeling. That this mythological view had such a tenacious life, even in theoretical formulations, should call our attention to the fact that it probably still lives on today (foregoing such a theoretical self-confession) in what countless Christians actually understand 'incarnation' [to mean], whether they believe in it or reject it" ("Probleme der Christologie von heute," *ST*, 1:176–177, n. 3 (ET: *TI*, 1:156, n. 1)).

102 "Zur Theologie der Menschwerdung," *ST*, 4:146 (ET: *TI*, 4:113).

103 "Débats sur le rapport du P. Rahner," in *Problèmes actuels de christologie*, ed. H. Bouessé (Paris: Desclée de Brouwer, 1965), p. 407.

104 "Zur Theologie der Menschwerdung," *ST*, 4:147 (ET: *TI*, 4:113).

105 "Probleme der Christologie von heute," *ST*, 1:202, n. 2 (ET: *TI*, 1:181, n. 3).

106 "Theologische Bemerkungen zum Zeitbegriff," *ST*, 9:321–322 (ET: *TI*, 11:307–308).

107 Ibid., p. 321 (ET: ibid., p. 308).

108 Ibid., pp. 321–322 (ET: ibid., p. 308).

109 "Probleme der Christologie von heute," *ST*, 1:194–200 (ET: *TI*, 1:174–179).

110 I will deal with this question in depth in Chapter VII of this study.

111 "Zur Theologie der Menschwerdung," *ST*, 4:147, n. 3 (ET: *TI*, 4:113–114, n. 3).

112 Ibid. (ET: ibid.).

113 Ibid. (ET: ibid.).

114 See Fischer, *Der Mensch als Geheimnis*, pp. 347–349.

115 Vol. 4, cols. 1083–1084.

116 See William Shepherd, *Man's Condition*, p. 187.

117 "Zur Theologie der Menschwerdung," *ST*, 4:148 (ET: *TI*, 4:114).

PART II
A CRITICAL APPRAISAL OF RAHNER'S CONCEPT OF GOD

CHAPTER VII
LOVE AND THE RELATIVITY OF GOD

This study seeks to contribute to a solution to the contemporary problem of the concept of God through an analysis of the meaning and truth of the assertion "God is love." Hopefully, the preceding part of the study has made Rahner's solution to this problem clear. I have tried to show that love, for him, is the ecstatic giving away of oneself to another person. In the act of love, the fullest realization of a free person is given. "God" refers to the nameless, unlimited, uncontrollable *Woraufhin* of the transcendentality of human knowledge, freedom, and love. But God, in Rahner's view is not just the ground and goal of human love, but is Godself love. This means that God gives or communicates Godself ecstatically to the spiritual creature in grace and incarnation. Just as love is the fundamental human act, so love is the fundamental act of divine being. All divine activity, according to Rahner, finds its *telos* and final significance in the act of divine love. The divine love is radically free. It is necessary neither to the divine being nor to human being. Both are conceivable without the divine love for the creatures. The love of God for the creatures, which is freely bestowed, establishes a unique relationship or dialogue between God and the world. Rahner holds that by conceiving the God-world relationship to be a personal dialogue of love, he has provided a revisionary alternative to the classical positions of dualism and pantheism. He asserts that a necessary implication of the assertion that God is love is that Christian theology must understand traditional affirmations of God's nonrelativity dialectically. He says that God is genuinely related to the world in God's other, while remaining strictly nonrelative or absolute in Godself.

Rahner's concept of God, which is based on the assertion that God is love, is summed up in one amazing passage in his *Schriften zur Theologie*. I wish to quote this passage in full, for it both restates clearly and succinctly the results of Part I of this study and provides a nice starting point for the critical appraisal of Rahner's concept of God undertaken in this second part of the study.

> God is not just the creator of a world that is different from him. In that which we call grace, in genuine, imme-diate self-communication, he has made himself an inner principle of this world in the spiritual creature that is a moment of this one world. This grace can be conceived in such a way that God's possibility of creating out of nothing is a moment of the higher and more encompass-ing possibility of God as the one who can communicate himself in free love. Likewise, grace can be conceived such that God has factually willed the creation *because,* in free love, he wanted to give himself away, alienate him-self, step out from *himself.* Thus, in the actual order, "nature" is willed from the outset for the sake of "grace," and "creation" for the sake of the covenant of personal love. In this self-communication, which arises from free love, God remains, on the one hand, the absolutely free and unneedy one, the one who is infinitely elevated above all creatures, the addressees of such a possible and free self-communication in uncreated grace. But in this self-communication, the God who remains absolutely transcendent becomes the innermost principle, the in-nermost ground, and the most proper goal of the (spir-itual) creation. God is not only the "efficient cause," but also the "quasi-formal cause" of what the creature con-cretely and genuinely is. The essence of the spiritual creature consists in the fact that its innermost moment, that *from which, to which,* and *through which* it exists, is precisely *not* a moment of this its essence and its nature. Rather, its essence is based on the fact that that which is superessential and transcends it is that which gives the spiritual creature its stability, meaning, future, and final stimulus. This, of course, in such a way that the essence of the spiritual creature, which belongs to it as such, does not thereby diminish, but rather receives its final validity and consistency and thus grows and develops. Proximity to the self-communication of God and the selfhood of the creature increase in direct, and not in inverse, pro-portions. This self-communication of God, in which God communicates himself precisely *as* the absolutely tran-scendent one, is the most immanent element in the crea-ture. The conveyance of the creatures' essence to itself [i.e., the creation of the creature], the immanence of essence in this sense, is at one and the same time, the presupposition and the consequence of the transcen-dence of God in the spiritual creature as blessed with the

uncreated grace of God. The model of thought which is built upon the distinction between "within" and "without" breaks down here. The orientation to the self-communication of the God who is radically different is that which is most internal, and precisely the possibility of the immanence of that which is most external.[1]

This then is Rahner's basic concept of God. The purpose of this part of the study is to analyze critically the adequacy of this concept of God for Christian theology through an appraisal of Rahner's account of the meaning and truth of "God is love." The criteria for this critical evaluation are themselves the criteria Rahner proposes for the adequacy of theological statements in general, as outlined in the introduction to this study. On the one hand, all theological statements must be congruent with the apostolic witness of scripture, which is the *norma non normata* of theology. On the other hand, all theological statements must interpret the scriptural witness in a way that is credible to contemporary persons. Because theology is *critical* reflection, Rahner says, theological statements must be evaluated in terms of the same standards of meaning and truth that apply to any statements of a similar logical type.[2] This is to say that theological statements must be logically consistent and must appeal finally to the common experience we share as persons.

In spite of Rahner's significant contribution to a solution of the problem of the concept of God in Christian theology, I must conclude, finally, that his solution to this problem is not wholly adequate when judged by the criteria of meaning and truth he proposes. The central thrust of my critical appraisal will be to argue that at a number of crucial points Rahner's concept of God and his account of the meaning and truth of the assertion "God is love" are inadequate because they lead to a conceptual impasse. I will attempt to demonstrate this through an immanent criticism of Rahner's thought.

In this chapter I want to examine Rahner's understanding of the God-world relationship that he holds is necessarily implied by the assertion "God is love." Then, in the next two chapters, I will evaluate the adequacy of his account of the meaning and truth of the assertion that God is love itself. And in the final chapter of this part of the study, the adequacy of Rahner's attempt to inform the doctrine of God with a methodological "turn to the subject" will be considered.

How Does God Act in the World?

The assertion that God is love means, for Rahner, that God communicates Godself ecstatically to the world. This implies that God is in some sense a personal agent with respect to the world. However, it seems to me that Rahner's understanding of the activity of God in the world is self-contradictory. On the one hand, he holds, as was shown in Chapter VI above, that "God causes *the* world and does not really act causally *within the* world. [This] means he supports the causal chain but, in his activity, is not interposed as a member of the chain of causes as one cause among others."[3] This principle applies to God's activity both in creation and in self-communication. Thus, all particular interventions of God in the world, such as those affirmed by the historical religions, are to be understood as thematizations of the one transcendental activity of God. On the other hand, Rahner understands the incarnation of the divine Logos in Jesus Christ to be, in the strictest sense of the word, the self-expression of God in the world. In this self-expressive act the infinite God becomes a part of the finite world. This would seem to indicate a presence and activity of God in the world that is more than the presence and activity of God as the ground and goal of the finite world. Here an intervention of God in the world is asserted that is not simply a particular thematization of the universal human experience of God, but is, instead, the absolute, irreversible gift of Godself to the world.[4]

The charge that Rahner's view of God's activity in the world is self-contradictory is central to two interpreters' criticisms of his theology. It will be helpful to look briefly at their discussions of this issue.

Bert van der Heijden offers the following summary of his detailed analysis of Rahner's theology:

> . . . we attempted to examine Rahner's twofold presupposition that it is unacceptable "mythology" to hold an "intervention" of God in history, conceived in the manner of a human (interpersonal) intervention, to be possible, while, on the other hand, holding unreflectively a personal relation of God to us to be possible and actual.[5]

Van der Heijden argues that Rahner's theology is inadequate because it cannot do justice to the biblical understanding of revelation. He says that revelation, in Rahner's scheme, reduces to the natural, universal givenness of God as the *ipsum esse*.[6] God does not effect any particular states of affairs within the world *(entia)*, but only grounds the being *(esse)* of the world as a whole.[7] Such a God, van der Heijden claims, is incapable of entering into a personal relationship with human beings. Therefore, there can be no room left for a categorial revelation of God as a person in Rahner's scheme. All that is possible is a transcendental revelation of God as the ground of being.[8]

Alexander Gerken makes similar claims concerning the role of categorial revelation in Rahner's theology. He asserts that Rahner cannot distinguish "genuine revelation" (i.e., the particular revelation attested to in the Judeo-Christian tradition) from the general history of religion.[9] Gerken holds, as does van der Heijden, that God, for Rahner, can be nothing more than the ground of being. He says that Rahner concludes from the "incontrovertible fact that God is 'not an object alongside others,' . . . that he cannot become objective at all, but is only the primordial ground and absolute future of all reality."[10] Gerken urges that the biblical view of revelation is precisely that God Godself, in decisive moments in salvation history, enters into human history. Rahner, according to Gerken, cannot account for such a historical activity or intervention of God. "If God gives himself categorially (to Israel, to the prophets, to the human nature of Jesus), then . . . a *historical* efficacy on the *part of God* is necessary and not just a transcendental efficacy."[11]

It seems to me that, as illuminating as both of these criticisms of Rahner are, neither accurately portrays his actual position. Both van der Heijden and Gerken interpret Rahner in a onesided fashion, and thereby cause his position to appear to be more consistent than it is. Rahner, in fact, not only holds the position that van der Heijden and Gerken find inadequate (i.e., that God is active in relation to the world solely as the ground of being), but also explicitly argues for the very understanding of the divine activity that van der Heijden and Gerken espouse (namely, that in the particular salvation history recounted by the Jewish and Christian scriptures, and above all in the Christ event, God is revealed as active categorially within history).

Van der Heijden asks rhetorically, with respect to Rahner's view of God, "must not revelation, in as much as it expresses God himself and is his own expression (and not merely a new *modus cognoscendi* of natural revelation) necessarily become reduced to

the metaphysical *ipsum esse* and the natural givenness of God?"[12]
To the contrary, Rahner argues that in the self-communication
of God to human persons a new relationship between human
beings and God as a person is established. As I tried to show in
Chapter IV of this study, Rahner characteristically distinguishes
the natural mode of God's givenness, in which God is experienced as the distant *Woraufhin* of human transcendence, from
the supernatural presence of God in self-communication, in
which God is experienced as that most intimate, loving partner
of human being. One need only recall the following passage to
see that van der Heijden has not adequately presented Rahner's
understanding of the presence of God in revelation:

> The man who has anything at all to do with his transcen-
> dental experience of holy mystery makes the discovery
> that this mystery is not only the distant horizon, the
> repelling, distancing and condemning judgment of his
> consciousness and environment and co-world, that
> which is uncanny, which frightens him back into the
> home of everyday life, but that this holy mystery is also
> the sheltering nearness, the forgiving intimacy, home
> itself, the love that communicates itself, that which is
> familiar, which one can approach and to which one can
> flee from the uncanniness of the empty and threatened
> character of his own life.[13]

The experience of God as a loving person is not, for Rahner, a
new human *modus cognoscendi* of the natural revelation of God,
but is the experience of a self-expression of God that is in no
sense required by human "nature."

In divine self-communication God is no longer simply the
ipsum esse, but becomes an immanent principle within the spiritual creature. And in the historical highpoint of this self-communication of God, God takes the reality of the world as God's
own reality. Rahner does hold, contrary to Gerken's judgment,
that in the incarnation God can become objective. In the Christ
event there is a categorial givenness of God and a genuinely
historical efficacy on God's part.

Indeed, Gerken is correct when he says that

> . . . it would be more consistent if one drew the con-
> clusion from Rahner's view that every historical event,
> with respect to its ability to bring the graciously elevated
> transcendentality of man to self-realization, is of equal
> value and that, therefore, even the Christ event and the
> form of Christ [*die Gestalt Christi*] are replaceable.[14]

But Rahner's position is not consistent at this point. He proposes, as a general principle governing all divine activity, including self-communication, that God does not act within the world process at all, but rather makes possible the world process as a whole. He argues that a consequence of the de-divinization of the world, effected largely by the modern scientific world-view, is that any statement to the effect that God acts within the world by intervening in the causal chain of worldly events can only be understood today to be a mythological statement. Rahner writes that if we speak of particular acts or interventions of God within history we can only mean that certain events mediate to us thematically the relationship of God to the world as the transcendent ground and goal of the entire world process.[15]

Yet, Rahner asserts that in the event of Jesus Christ a unique presence of God is given. Indeed the Christ event is the event in which God adopts the reality of the world as God's own reality. He argues that the humanity of Jesus Christ must be precisely the reality of God, if the incarnation is to be the absolute, historical self-communication of God.

> As long as the finite mediation of the divine self-expression does not represent a reality of God in the strict and proper sense, it is always still fundamentally precursory and surpassible because it is finite. In this finitude, it is not simply God's reality itself and so can be surpassed by God himself through a new positing of something finite.[16]

In the assertion that God makes finite reality God's own reality in Jesus Christ, Rahner is not simply claiming that the Christ event is a historical thematization of our common, human transcendental experience of God. Here, his general principle that God is not a categorial actor within the world seems no longer to apply. While he continually seeks to dissociate his christology from all mythological interpretations of the Christ event, he seems to assert, in his understanding of the incarnation, a mode of divine activity that he elsewhere states to be, at least formally, mythological. This is a serious inconsistency in Rahner's thought.

If Rahner's position on the divine activity in the world is to be consistent, then either his general principle of divine activity must be amended in order to reflect the possibility that God, by adopting the reality of the world as God's own reality, can be present and active within the causal network of the world at some particular point, or his understanding of the Christ event must be altered so that the divine activity affirmed in this event itself obeys the principle that God cannot plausibly be conceived as a categorial actor within the world. Rahner would seem to be fundamentally opposed to either of these two options, and thus his view, as it stands, cannot provide an adequate theological understanding of the divine activity since it is flawed by a basic self-contradiction. Some alternative account of the divine activity is called for.

I want to make clear that my disagreement here is not with Rahner's motives for holding the position he does. Indeed, the tension in Rahner's thought between his basic understanding of divine activity and his view of the peculiar nature of the Christ event seems to be traceable to an attempt, on his part, to maintain what any adequate Christian theology must maintain. On the one hand, Christian theology, if its message is to be credible to modern persons, cannot simply assert that God is one particular agent among the other worldly agents. This would be to lapse into a mythological mode of representing the divine reality, which would ignore that fact that God's presence and activity in the world must be infinitely qualitatively different from the presence and activity of all finite individuals, if God is to be God. And yet, on the other hand, an adequate Christian theology must maintain the centrality, uniqueness, and irreplaceability of the confession that Jesus is Christ, if that theology is to remain *Christian* theology. The problem is not that Rahner seeks to respond to both demands, but that he does so only at the cost of a fundamental logical inconsistency in his thought. And, as I have argued, the demand of logical consistency is an integral part of the demand that the assertions of Christian theology be credible to contemporary persons on purely secular or public grounds of meaning and truth. The conclusion to be drawn from all this is that some alternative to Rahner's view of the divine activity is needed.

In What Sense is God Both Relative and Nonrelative?

A second implication of the assertion "God is love," for Rahner, is expressed in the following statement: "God can become something, the one who is immutable in himself can *himself* be mutable *in the other*."[17] Rahner believes that the traditional scholastic denial of a real relativity of the divine being to the world must be understood dialectically, in order that the gen-

uine relativity of God, a relativity implied by the Christian doctrines of incarnation and grace, be recognized. He holds that the
statement that God Godself is relative in the other while remaining nonrelative in Godself must be construed neither as a denial
of God's essential nonrelativity nor as a mere affirmation of the
relativity of the (finite) other.[18] The key question, of course, is
what this claim means. It seems to me that as Rahner argues this
claim it has no clear, consistent meaning. Rahner provides no
coherent understanding of how God can be both nonrelative in
Godself and yet genuinely relative in God's other.

As I tried to show above, one must recognize that Rahner's
defense of how one and the same God can be both in some sense
nonrelative and in some other sense relative, is offered with the
understanding that no final, adequate explanation of this notion
is possible. Rahner says that because the event in which the
dialectic of the relativity and nonrelativity of God is presented to
us involves a mystery in the strict sense of the word (i.e., a self-
communication of the divine being), ontology must cease being
the schoolmaster of faith and orient or submit itself to faith.[19]
How God is both relative and nonrelative is for him finally a
mystery, or rather, is identical with the mystery of the divine
being itself. While I would not want to minimize the importance
of the concept of the mysterious character of the divine being, or
to deny that the Christian doctrine of the incarnation expresses
truths that cannot simply be reduced to the literal assertions of
transcendental metaphysics, I must say that Rahner's appeal to
mystery in this case seems to be a convenient way of excusing
real conceptual incoherence.[20] Here Rahner seems, unwittingly,
to be sure, to lapse into an understanding of mystery he
elsewhere calls decisively into question, namely, a view in which
mystery is a function of the finitude of the human *ratio*. Thus,
Rahner's own admission that the dialectic of relativity and nonrelativity in God is ultimately a mystery must, from the outset,
raise doubts as to whether his concept of God at this point is
internally coherent.

Be that as it may, Rahner does offer three closely related
explications of how the claim that God Godself is relative in the
other yet nonrelative in Godself is to be understood and defended, namely, by way of the concept of the real symbol, the
distinction between God's necessary essence and God as a free
person, and the model of quasi-formal causality.

Rahner's first defense of the claim that God is relative in the other while nonrelative in Godself, which involves the concept of the real symbol, focuses on the meaning of the phrase "in the other." God, for Rahner, is relative to the finite world through or in God's real symbol, while God in Godself remains essentially nonrelative. Recall how he understands the relationship between an entity and its real symbol: the entity posits an other, gives itself away to this other, and yet finds itself or returns to itself precisely through this process of self-alienation.[21] The real symbol is genuinely other than that which is symbolized. However, the real symbol is an expression of that which is symbolized. The real symbol is not posited as wholly other by way of efficient causality. Rather, that which is symbolized communicates itself to the real symbol, which is functionally other, by way of formal causality.[22]

In the context of the incarnation, this means that God, or more precisely, the divine Logos, takes as God's real symbol a finite, and thus relative, mutable, temporal, creature. Because this real symbol (the human nature of Jesus Christ) is genuinely distinct from God and is God's other, the strict nonrelativity of God in Godself is maintained. It is God's *other* that is relative. And yet because this other is not just a creature posited by God the creator through efficient causality, but is God's own self-expression through quasi-formal causality, Rahner claims that one can legitimately say that *God* is relative, mutable, and temporal in this other. He says,

> . . . the being of the Logos (of course *as* that which is retained through a procession from the Father) must be thought of as externalizing itself in such a way that (without detriment to its immutability in and of *itself*) *it itself* in truth becomes the existence of a created reality.[23]

Unfortunately, the concept of the real symbol does not seem to offer much clarification of how God can be relative in God's other while remaining in Godself nonrelative. Far from explicating this dialectic, the concept of the real symbol is a restatement of it. As Rahner himself admits, much is simply presupposed in his ontology of the symbol that really ought to be proven. Chief among such presupposed elements, I would argue, is precisely the sense in which the concept of the symbol expresses a dialectic of identity and difference within a unified entity, rather than a mere juxtaposition of two entities having no intrinsic relation to one another. When Rahner stresses the genuine otherness of the real symbol he seems close to speaking of a representational symbol, in which that which is symbolized is merely externally or nominally related to its symbol.[24] When he emphasizes that the real symbol is the self-expression of that which is symbolized, the distinction between them is less than apparent.[25] In the christological case, this means that his view seems to vacillate between the extremes of asserting a relativity of the human nature that, because it is merely a representational symbol, implies no relativity of God, and of asserting that God in Godself is relative because the human nature is a genuine expression of God's own being. Clearly, Rahner does not wish to affirm either of these extreme positions, but his concept of the real symbol, as it stands, provides no clear indication of how this dilemma can be avoided.

It has been suggested that one way of overcoming the seeming contradiction within the claim that God is both nonrelative and relative is provided by Hegelian thought.[26] Thus, one might seek to augment Rahner's ontology of the symbol with Hegelian concepts. While I argued, in the previous chapter, that Rahner's ontology of the symbol can indeed be illuminated by Hegel's phenomenology of spirit, it seems to be that Hegel's thought finally cannot be used to overcome the lack of clarity in Rahner's notion of the real symbol, and thus the lack of clarity in the claim that God is both relative in God's other and nonrelative in Godself. There are two reasons for this judgment. First, it seems to me that Rahner is much more careful than Hegel to avoid language that implies that the distinction between that which is symbolized and the real symbol is a temporal distinction. One gets the clear impression in Hegel that the *an sich*, the being in itself, enjoys not only a logical, but also a temporal, priority in relation to the other it posits, the *für sich*. Hegel's phenomenology describes a temporal process whereby substance becomes subject and consciousness becomes self-consciousness.[27] Rahner, on the other hand, argues that the real symbol is a logically, but not a temporally, distinct moment within the self-realization of an entity.[28] Thus, for example, intellect is never without its real symbol, sensibility.[29] Rahner's ontology of the real symbol is, therefore, less clear than Hegel's phenomenology of spirit precisely because Rahner understands the inner plurality of an entity to be a characteristic of each moment of that entity's self-realization.

Second, Rahner distinguishes much more clearly than does Hegel, the intra-divine plurality, whereby God the unoriginate source expresses Godself in the Logos, from the self-expression of God *ad extra* in the world. Rahner states that God's positing of the Logos (God's self-expression *ad intra*) is a necessary event that in no way implies, but rather is implied by the free, contingent decision of God (the Logos) to posit as God's real symbol *ad extra* the human nature of Jesus Christ.[30] Hegel holds that the self-expression or self-alienation of God in the world is necessary to God's self-actualization.[31] Indeed, at times, Hegel equates the generation of the Logos with the creation of the world, both as the self-expression of God *ad extra*.[32] Once again, at this point, it would seem that one could make use of Hegel's phenomenology of spirit to make Rahner's ontology of the symbol more internally consistent only at the cost of fundamentally misconstruing Rahner's concept of God. Thus, the question concerning the coherence of Rahner's concept of the real symbol remains unanswered.

The second way in which Rahner seeks to show that his claim that God is both relative and nonrelative is not simply a contradiction in terms involves drawing a distinction between God's necessary, metaphysical nature or essence and God's activity as a free person. As was shown above, the Christian doctrines of the trinity, grace, and incarnation, which arise out of salvation history, reveal God to be more than the immutable, self-enclosed God of metaphysics.[33] In a metaphysical view of God, Rahner says, the necessary essence of God is attained, while in reflection upon salvation history the free activity of God as a person is illuminated.[34] On the one hand, one is presented with fixed, metaphysical characteristics of the divine essence; on the other hand, the personal activity or the concrete behavior of God. This distinction also applies to God's self-expression in God's real symbol. God must express Godself *ad intra*. The intradivine real symbol is a necessary moment of the divine identity. Because God is internally self-expressive, God can freely express Godself *ad extra*, by taking a finite, creaturely reality as God's own determination. This event of divine self-expression in the world is a wholly free and gratuitous act of the divine love, one that is not necessitated by the divine essence, even if this act of love is the *telos* of the factual divine activity as such. Thus, in Godself, in God's essential nature, God is strictly nonrelative:

eternal, immutable, *a se*. But as a free person, as one who has chosen to communicate Godself in love to the creatures by adopting the creatures' own finite reality, God is genuinely relative, mutable, and temporal.[35]

A number of thinkers develop this line of thought suggested by Rahner. Bert van der Heijden distinguishes the communication of the divine being and the communication of the divine self. This enables him to understand Rahner's claim concerning the relativity and nonrelativity of God as follows:

> If the formula "God himself changes in the other without himself changing" is not to be a contradiction, the "himself" cannot mean the same thing in both cases. . . . The second part of the formula ("without himself changing") is intended to express that immutability of God that follows from the perfection of God that is affirmed by philosophy and theology. "Himself" means, consequently, God as distinct from everything that is finite and imperfect, it indicates the divine "essence": fullness of being. . . . The first part of the formula relates not to the essence of God, but to a personal relation. . . . It expresses a relation, one that is other than the relation that must always and essentially obtain between being and a particular being, creator and creature, God himself and a human nature. The otherness of the relation is formulated in personal categories: God adopts "personally" human categoriality, which thereby becomes his self-communication and expresses his personal behavior. . . . What is meant is a relation of God to us that corresponds in a particular way to our mode of personal being.[36]

Several British and American Roman Catholic thinkers have used this distinction between the freely chosen relativity of God as a person and the necessary nonrelativity of God in Godself to develop a Thomistic response to process thought, one that is more sensitive to the contribution process thought makes to a conception of the divine being.[37] For instance, William Hill argues that God, on "the level of God's freedom and personhood" is willing to enter into relationships with, and thus to be determined by, the creatures without thereby being determined on "the level of God's nature."[38] He says, "these relationships do 'determine' God (although only because he has so willed to be determined by creating finite persons in the first place) in the sense that such relationality is in part determined by the 'other' to which it relates."[39] Anthony Kelly also asserts that God has freely decided to be related to the creatures. He proposes that this relationship be understood as a *relatio conscientiae personalis* (a relationship of intersubjectivity), rather than as a nominal relation (which might be viewed as a relation wholly extrinsic to God) or a real relation (which, Kelly claims, would imply the absurdity of an increment in the divine perfection).[40]

It is Norris Clarke who presses this line of thought the farthest in his detailed reexamination of the Thomistic view of the immutability of God. Clarke affirms that God is genuinely related to the world. The world does make a difference to God in the realm of God's personal relations.[41] Because God has chosen to create this actual world, rather than some other world or no world at all, the content of God's intentional consciousness is contingently different from what it would have been if another world existed or if no world existed at all. But this relativity of God's consciousness does not imply any relativity or alteration of God's essential being, for God would be God no matter what the actual content of God's intentional consciousness might be. Clarke specifies further the way in which the creatures determine God:

> The kernel of my solution is that there are *two ways* in which one's knowledge can be determined by another. In the first way the object known acts causally on the knower as on a passive recipient. This way is, of course, excluded in the case of God. In the other way a superior agent freely offers its indeterminate abundance of power to a lower agent, allowing the latter to channel, or determine—which means here to delimit (partially negate)—the flow of the former's power along lines determined by the lesser agent, to help him execute his own limited operation. In this case the determination contributed by the lower agent does not add any new being to the power of the higher agent. It "adds on" only a partial negation or determination of the higher plenitude, hence does not introduce any change in, or addition to the real being of the higher agent. In this situation the higher agent knows what the lower is doing, not by being positively acted on to receive new real being from the lower, but precisely by knowing *its own action*, by knowing just how its own power is allowed to flow through the lower agent, along the channel which the lower agent determines. So God can know my free action by knowing just how I allow His freely offered power, always gently drawing me through the good, to flow through me. He knows my choice by knowing His own

active power working within me, as thus determined or channeled determinately here and now by me. Hence He knows by acting, not by being acted upon, but I supply the inner determination or limit of this power at work—which I repeat is not a new positive being at all but only a limiting down of an indeterminate plenitude. Clearly I am not limiting the real being of God or the inner plenitude of His power as in Him, but only the exercise of it to me.[42]

In this way, Clarke holds he has shown how God can be strictly nonrelative in Godself, in God's essence, and yet relative as a free person.

That these understandings of how God can be said, without contradiction, to be both relative and nonrelative are based on Rahner's thought is clear. Van der Heijden, Hill, Kelly, and Clarke all acknowledge the contribution Rahner's thought makes to an attempt to conceive a genuine relativity of God within the framework of Thomistic thought. In the words of Walter Stokes,

> . . . between a philosophy of creative act which excludes the possibility of the real relation of God to the world [traditional Thomism] and a modal philosophy which demands reciprocal relations between God and the world [process thought], it is possible to posit a "third position": a philosophy of creative act with real but asymmetrical relations between God and the world.[43]

But while Rahner's thought may suggest such a third position, it cannot, it seems to me, itself provide a genuine alternative simply because it is not clear exactly what Rahner means. Martin D'Arcy is right, I think, when he says

> . . . it is high time that God's immutability be reexamined, Karl Rahner does this provocatively; but though he breaks through the shell, no chicken so far as I can see emerges. He leaves us with the cryptic saying: "God is immutable in himself, but mutable in another." In the context of a Hegel and perhaps a Heidegger this might be informative, but if it is meant to be a new insight it is too cloudy.[44]

Van der Heijden is correct when he says that the term "Godself" cannot mean, for Rahner, the same thing in both parts of the assertion that God is nonrelative in Godself and yet is Godself relative to the world in God's other. But Rahner himself never clearly indicates what this difference is. Van der Heijden recognizes this when he charges that Rahner's notion of self-communication is ambiguous in that Rahner does not distinguish the communication of the divine being from the communication of the divine self. In fact, as I pointed out earlier, Rahner explicitly identifies the two senses of divine self-communication: "if God is really God, absolute reality in personal spirituality, then communication of divine being and divine self-communication [*Seinsmitteilung und Selbstmitteilung Gottes*] must be the same."[45] Thus van der Heijden's account of the relativity of God contains elements not found in Rahner's own understanding of the matter.

Rahner does state that God's relativity to the world results from God's free decision to communicate Godself to the creatures. He writes, for example, that the incarnate Logos as the real symbol of God in the world "is not only the presence of what God is *in himself*, but is also the expressive being there of that which (better: the one whom) God in free grace wishes to be *in relation to* the world."[46] But Rahner never clearly distinguishes the "level of God's nature" and the "level of God's freedom and personhood" (Hill) or God's "natural being" and God's "intentional being" (Clarke). Rahner does not attempt to formulate a new understanding of the divine relativity, such as Kelly's *relatio conscientiae personalis*. He simply says, "the 'immutability' of God, the lack of a real relation of God to the world, is, in a true sense, a dialectical assertion."[47]

Finally, Rahner does assert that the possibility of God adopting finite reality as God's own reality "is not to be thought of as a sign of [God's] neediness, but rather as the height of his perfection, which would be more inferior if he could not, in addition to his infinity, become less than he (always) is."[48] This sounds like Norris Clarke's argument that God can be said to be relative to the world in that God allows God's infinity to be limited by the creature. But nowhere does Rahner explicate, in the way that Clarke does, how this self-limitation of God is to be understood.

All of these attempts would seem to be more or less appropriate ways of making Rahner's position on the relativity and nonrelativity of God more clear and explicit. The point is, however, that in and of itself Rahner's thought does not offer an adequate, revisionary understanding of the relativity of God. He indicates this to be a task for theology, but some alternative account of the divine relativity is required if this task is to be accomplished in an adequate fashion.

Yet there is an even more serious problem with regard to the internal coherence of Rahner's claim that God is both in some sense relative and in some other sense nonrelative to the world. This further problem is raised both by Rahner's defense of his claim based on the concept of the real symbol and by his defense based on the distinction between the essential nature of God and the free, personal activity of God. What is more, this problem would still be present in Rahner's thought even if his thought were made more consistent than it actually is through the use of concepts and distinctions introduced by other thinkers. This further, more serious difficulty can be stated as follows: either Rahner's position entails a real relatedness of God *in Godself* to the world, or Rahner's solution to the problem of how God can be both relative and nonrelative to the world is merely a verbal solution. Rahner clearly holds that the assertion of a genuine relativity of God to the world is demanded if the incarnation is to be presented in a credible manner to contemporary persons. Thus, he intends to offer a real, and not merely a verbal, solution to the problem. But, at the same time, he resolutely maintains that to assert a real relatedness of God in Godself to the world would be to forfeit the strict nonrelativity of God that is demanded both by the Christian proclamation and by our common human experience of ourselves as finite creatures oriented toward an infinite *Woraufhin*. Therefore, his position, as it stands, is not a coherent position at all, but must reduce to one or the other of two views of the relativity of God, neither of which he intends to espouse. Because Rahner's position is incoherent, it is less than a fully adequate resource for a theological appraisal of the meaning and truth of the assertion "God is love," of which the relativity and nonrelativity of one and the same God are necessary implications.

Before I give evidence for this judgment, I want to emphasize again my fundamental agreement with Rahner with respect to the motives that lie behind the formulation of his view of the relativity and nonrelativity of God. He is correct that an adequate Christian theology must affirm both the relativity and nonrelativity of God. He argues convincingly that a necessary condition of the possibility of our own self-realization, and of the development of the cosmos as a whole, is the divine reality

precisely as the absolute, nonrelative ground of worldly becoming. If God were not qualitatively different from the finite world,
in some sense unthreatened by the vicissitudes of the world, and
not subject to the mortality that characterizes all that is finite,
then "the becoming of spirit and nature [would] be . . . a meaningless coming to itself of absolute emptiness, which collapses
into the void that it itself is."[49] If God is not in some sense free
from the corruption, mortality, and futility of the world, then
God could be, at best, one who felt, understood, and perhaps
commiserated with our plight. But God, under such conditions,
could not be the source of our hope, the rock of our salvation,
the one whose love is steadfast and endures forever.

At the same time, Rahner rightly sees that our existence and
our affairs must make some difference to God if God is to be one
to whom it would make sense to entrust our lives. It is clear that
if the biblical proclamation that salvation history is a genuine
divine-human dialogue is to be maintained, the human participants in this dialogue must be real participants who can genuinely respond to God and upon whom God, in some sense,
must wait. Further, if the constitutive element of Christianity,
the incarnation, is to be presented as more than a myth, then the
identification of God with the world must be taken to indicate a
genuine relativity of God to the world.

So, the question, in Christian theology, cannot be whether
God is to be understood as wholly nonrelative to the world or as
wholly relative. A wholly nonrelative God would be superfluous
to our concerns, while a wholly relative God would not be God at
all, but would be just another creature. A necessary implication
of the Christian affirmation that God is love is that God must in
some genuine sense be both relative and nonrelative. The only
question is how this is to be understood as more than a simple
contradiction in terms. The purpose of my critical analysis here
is to suggest that while Rahner has a clear sense *that* Christian
theology must affirm the relativity and nonrelativity of one and
the same God, he does not give a coherent account of *how* one
and the same God can be both relative and nonrelative to the
world.

Thus far, two of the three ways in which Rahner seeks to
show that his affirmation that God is both relative and nonrelative is coherent have been discussed. He argues that God in
Godself is nonrelative while God is relative in and through God's

real symbol, and that God, when viewed in terms of God's necessary, essential nature, is nonrelative, while God viewed as a personal agent is one who freely adopts a relativity to the world. In each case, the relativity of God is seen as applying to one aspect of God and the nonrelativity of God to another aspect. The question can be raised concerning the adequacy of Rahner's account of the unity of these two aspects of the one God.

If there are two terms, *a* and *b*, that are related to one another in some fashion, logically, there are three and only three possible ways of accounting for that relation: (1) *a* includes *b*, that is, *a* is the inclusive term of the relation between *a* and *b;* (2) *b* includes *a*, that is, *b* is the inclusive term of the relation; or (3) *a* and *b* are both included in some third term *c*, in which case, *a* and *b* are related to each other merely in an external or nominal way.[50] For example, in a realist view of knowledge, *a* is the inclusive term of the relationship described by "*a* knows *b*." Here, *a* includes *b*, *a* is really related to *b*, *a* grounds or provides the unity of *a* and *b*. In the case of the relation *a* is to the left of *b* (or *b* is to the right of *a*), neither *a* nor *b* is the inclusive term. "To the left of" and "to the right of" are relations that are internal to neither term. It is my knowledge, *c*, that *a* is to the left of *b* that provides the unity of *a* and *b*. This is simply to say that there must be an inclusive term in any relation, even if the inclusive term is a third term that includes both of the two original terms.

Rahner's utilization of the Thomistic maxim *non enim plura secundum se uniuntur* (there can be no union of things that are in themselves multiple) shows that he too would grant that this trichotomy is an exhaustive one, at least with respect to an individual entity.[51] That is to say, for him, two genuinely plural moments within a single entity (two genuinely distinct terms) cannot simply be juxtaposed or nominally related to one another. One of these plural moments must include, or be really related to, the other, or, they both must be included within a more primordial moment of the entity. One term, or the other, or a third term, must provide the unity of the two terms, the unity that constitutes them as two moments of a single entity in the first place. For example, Rahner argues that a real symbol is the self-expression of the entity it symbolizes. The unity of an entity and its real symbol is provided by the original entity itself. The entity that is symbolized is the inclusive term of the relation between it and its real symbol.

It is illuminating, I think, to evaluate Rahner's account of the unity of the relative and nonrelative aspects of God in terms of this trichotomy. It must be made clear from the outset that Rahner himself never explicitly does this. I would argue, however, that this is an appropriate question to put to him, precisely because of his affirmation of the principle *non enim plura secundum se uniuntur*. But the reader must bear in mind, in what follows, that I am putting to Rahner questions that he never raises, in order to be better able to evaluate his concept of God.

It can be said, first of all, that this trichotomy must be applicable to the relation between God as relative and God as nonrelative, since these are two aspects of the one God for Rahner. These two aspects must be united in some fashion, there must be an inclusive term of this relation. Further, it is apparent that the inclusive term of this relation, which provides the unity of these two aspects of the divine being, must itself be something divine. It would be absurd to suppose that any creaturely reality could provide the unity of two aspects of the divine being. Therefore, there are only three possible ways of accounting for the unity of these two aspects of the one God: (1) God as relative is inclusive of God as strictly nonrelative; (2) God as strictly nonrelative is inclusive of God as relative; or (3) God as relative and God as nonrelative both are included within a third, more primordial, aspect of the divine being.

The third possibility can be ruled out immediately, for there is no evidence in Rahner's writings to suggest that he understands there to be a third aspect of the divine reality beyond God as absolute or strictly nonrelative (God in Godself, God in God's essential nature) and God as relative (God in God's other, God in God's free personal activity). The question, therefore, is which of these two aspects of God, God as nonrelative or God as relative, can be understood to include within itself the other aspect, thereby providing or grounding the unity of these two aspects of the divine being.

It would seem that Rahner, almost by default, would have to respond to this question by saying that God as nonrelative, God in Godself, God in God's essential nature, must be the inclusive aspect of the divine reality. That is, God as nonrelative must be inclusive of God as relative.[52] This would have to be Rahner's response because of his understanding that the nonrelativity of God is necessary to the divine being, while the relativity of God is a consequence of God's free, contingent decision to communicate Godself in love to the creatures. God could be God without communicating Godself to the world, without adopting the reality of the world, including real relatedness to others, as God's own reality. But God, for Rahner, would not be God if God were not absolute being, existentially independent of the world, self-sufficient, in short, strictly nonrelative to others. God as related to the world is a free self-expression of God in Godself, God in God's essential nature. It would be impossible, given these presuppositions, to assert that God as relative could be inclusive of God as nonrelative. This would be to say that the ground of the unity between what God necessarily must be (God as absolute in Godself) and what God freely chooses to be (God as relative in God's other) is provided by the aspect of God that is not necessary to the divine being. It can only be the necessary, nonrelative aspect of God that provides the unity between this aspect of God and God's freely adopted relativity to the world. The freely adopted relativity of God, for Rahner, must be understood to be derived from the nonrelative, essential nature of God, for the essential nature of God is more primordial. Therefore, the essential nature of God, God in Godself, alone can be the inclusive term of the relation that obtains between God in Godself and God as freely related to the world in God's other.

Recall Rahner's understanding of the relation between an entity and its real symbol. He says:

> . . . a plurality in a primordial, and primordially superior, unity can only be conceived as the unfolding of the one. The plural originates out of a primordial "one" in a relationship of origination and consequence. The most primordial unity, which also forms the unity that unites the plural, releases and "dis-closes" itself into a plurality, while remaining the master of itself.[53]

Obviously, the unity of the divine being is just such a primordial unity, for God is one. But there is also a certain "plurality" within the divine being: God as absolute being has communicated Godself to the world, and has adopted, in God's other, the reality of the creature as God's own reality. These two moments or aspects, which seem to be mutually exclusive, are united, nevertheless, in the divine being, whose absolute perfection is revealed precisely in the fact that the infinite God can become less than God is, that is, can become finite.[54] Because God in Godself, for Rahner, is

absolute being, God can limit God's infinite essential nature by
expressing Godself in a worldly real symbol, thus adopting the
world, and real relatedness to others, as a determination of God's
own reality. The nonrelativity or absoluteness of God, therefore,
is inclusive of the relativity of God, for God as related to others is
a free, contingent, loving self-expression of the God who requires no relatedness to this world, or to any world at all, in
order to be God.

> The absolute, more correctly, the one who is absolute,
> has in the pure freedom of his infinite nonrelativity,
> which he always preserves, the possibility of becoming
> the other, that which is finite; the possibility of positing
> the other as his own reality in that and because he alien-
> ates himself from himself and gives *himself* away. . . . The
> primordial phenomenon that is given in faith is precisely
> the *self-alienation*, the becoming, the *kenosis* and *genesis* of
> God himself, who can become by coming to be that
> which is [other], . . . without having to become in his
> own self, in that which is primordial.[55]

This passage shows clearly that the inclusive term of the relation
that obtains between a self and its own state of self-alienation
must be the "original" or "primordial" self. The primordial self is
the inclusive ground from which the alienated self arises. God as
absolute being, as *actus purus*, as strictly nonrelative to others,
must be inclusive of God as a free person really related to others
in God's other. The aspect of God in which God is relative is a
self-alienating, kenotic possibility of God as the absolute and
thus can only be the included, not the inclusive, aspect.

It seems to me, however, that such an understanding of the
relation between God as relative and God as nonrelative is self-
contradictory. It is impossible for the absolute or nonrelative
aspect of God to be inclusive of the relative aspect of God.
Rather, that which is relative alone can include that which is
nonrelative as a moment within itself.

For a demonstration of this claim one could turn to Charles
Hartshorne, who argues that God conceived of as supremely
relative is inclusive of God conceived as supremely nonrelative.
Hartshorne remarks, for instance, that

> . . . it is often said that God as personal can only be an
> appearance or expression of the Absolute. And usually
> the implication is conveyed that the Absolute is more
> than God, or that God is a self-limitation or even a

> descent of the Absolute into a lower region. These are
> somewhat confused notions at best. . . . It is the divine
> Person that contains the Absolute, not vice versa.[56]

While I think that Hartshorne is right at this point, it is important to realize that on scholastic grounds alone the assertion that God as absolute includes God as relative as its self-expression or self-limitation is incoherent.

A basic Aristotelian principle is that form is given only as it informs some particular bit of matter. The unity of form and matter, the inclusive term of the relationship that obtains between form and matter, is not the form in itself, but rather the informed matter. Informed matter, that is, an individual entity, is concrete, particular, actual, and relative. It includes within itself that which is abstract and nonrelative, the form. An actual chair, in this scheme, is characterized by a set of abstract qualities, "chairness" if you will, that enable us to distinguish a chair from a couch, a bench, a table, an oak tree, and so forth. It makes sense to say that an actual, concrete chair includes the abstract qualities of "chairness," for these are the qualities that we abstract from this particular artificially produced object that has four legs, a back, and a seat when we recognize it to be a chair. It would not make sense to say that the abstraction "chairness" is inclusive of a particular chair. The concrete chair is more that the set of abstract qualities that constitute "chairness." It is more than just an instance of the form "chair." This particular chair was given to me by my grandmother, has been carelessly splashed with blue paint, sits in my kitchen, and is scarred with my daughter's teeth marks. One can derive the abstract, the nonrelative, "chairness" from the concrete chair, indeed one must be able to do this if we are to know this particular object as a chair. But one cannot derive a particular chair from the abstraction "chairness," for "chairness" abstracts precisely from the particular, contingent, relative details that make this particular chair what it is. Thus, for Aristotle, one can say that a particular entity is inclusive of its form. But one cannot coherently affirm that the form, that which is nonrelative and abstract, is inclusive of any particular entity.

A more relevant example of the same principle is suggested by a consideration of the relation between a person and her or his personality. The term "personality," at least in the admittedly restricted sense in which I am using it here, refers to the set of

abstract qualities that are revealed in the actual behavior of a
person over a period of time. I can derive this "personality" by
abstracting from the person's actual behavior. The person is
concrete, actual, and related to other persons, while the personality, the set of qualities that enable us to identify a particular
person and that characterize her or him at any given moment, is
abstract. The personality is not anything actual at all; it is strictly
nonrelative. It makes sense to say that a person has or includes
within her- or himself a personality.[57] It would be absurd, however, to say that a personality had or was inclusive of a person.
The personality can be said to be an aspect of an actual person,
namely, the abstract qualities that characterize that person in all
of her or his actual states. But it would make no sense to say that
a person was an aspect of her or his personality. The person, as a
concrete, actual, relative entity, is inclusive of that which is nonrelative and abstract, the personality.

Now this is precisely the way in which Rahner normally
understands the relation of the abstract and the concrete. That
is, he holds that the concrete is inclusive of the abstract. He
argues, for instance, that "historicity is something less than actual history; concrete love is something more (not less) than
formally analyzed subjectivity (ability and need to love); experienced dread is more (not less) than the concept of the basic
situation of man."[58]

Rahner describes the relative and nonrelative aspects of the
divine being in terms of this distinction between the concrete
and the abstract. He says, for instance:

> The faithfulness, the merciful kindness, the love, etc.,
> that we factually experience and express [in the Christian
> doctrine of God] are not merely the theologically at-
> tested, necessary "attributes" of the metaphysical essence
> of God, but are really much more than this. For God
> could refuse *this* faithfulness, love, etc., which he in fact
> demonstrates to us, without thereby ceasing to be
> faithful, loving, etc., in a metaphysical sense.[59]

In another essay he contrasts a "metaphysical contemplation of
that which is absolute and, thereby, impersonal and abstract" in
God, with the biblical proclamation of "the personal God in the
concreteness of his free activity."[60]

God in God's essential nature, for Rahner, is characterized
by a certain indeterminateness. Human experience necessarily

demands God as its nameless, unlimited, uncontrollable *Woraufhin,* that is, God as absolute being, God in God's essence. But it remains fundamentally unknown and unknowable, prior to God's self-disclosure, how this God who is necessarily implied by all human experience acts toward human persons. Indeed, God could have remained simply the aloof *Woraufhin* of human experience by refusing to give Godself in love to human beings. The free self-disclosure of God adds a further determination to God. God as related to the world in free self-giving love is "more" than God conceived strictly in God's essential nature (even if this "more" is understood to refer to an addition to God's intentional being, rather than to God's natural being, to use Clarke's distinction).

But, although he understands the concrete to be inclusive of the abstract in nondivine cases, and although he understands the essential nature of God to be relatively abstract and indeterminate and God as a free person related to others to be relatively concrete and determinate, Rahner implies that it is the abstract aspect of the divine being, and not the concrete aspect, that is the inclusive aspect of God. In effect, he seems to be saying that the unity of abstract and concrete, of nonrelative and relative in God is to be found in the nonrelative aspect of God, not in the relative aspect. This is the case, again, because Rahner views the concrete aspect of God, God as related to the world, to be the self-expression or self-alienation of the abstract and nonrelative aspect of God, God in God's essential nature. As I argued above, an entity that expresses itself in a real symbol, for Rahner, alone can be the inclusive term of the relation that exists between it and its real symbol. Because God must exist as the absolute or nonrelative one in order to be God, but need not relate Godself to the world at all, God as nonrelative, according to him, must be the inclusive aspect of God, the aspect that provides the unity of the divine being who is both relative and nonrelative.

This is, however, a self-contradictory way of relating the relative and the nonrelative, the abstract and the concrete. For if *a* represents God as nonrelative, God in God's essential nature, and *ab* represents God as a free, personal agent related to the world (*ab,* not just *b,* because, for Rahner, God retains God's strict nonrelativity even in the free act of relating or communicating Godself in love to the creatures), then it is apparent that *ab,* God as a free person related to the world, includes the

nonrelative, essential nature of God, *a*, within itself, and, therefore, cannot be included within it. Rahner seems to claim just the
reverse, that is, that the inclusive aspect of the divine being,
which grounds God as a free person related to others, is God in
Godself, God as the absolute or nonrelative one.

This same point can be made in an even more direct way.
Rahner argues that God as a free person related to others is an
expression of God in Godself, God as strictly nonrelative. The
divine being in all its "states," in all its activity, is characterized by
certain qualities that make it the divine being: transcendence,
nonrelativity, eternity, etc. This is the necessary nature or essence of God, the divinity of God. One could say that this
nonrelative, essential nature is the "personality" of God, in the
sense of "personality" indicated above. The divine personality is
the set of abstract qualities of God that enable us to recognize
God as God in all particular moments of the divine actuality.
Rahner claims that it is this God, this divine essence, that expresses or communicates Godself, revealing God to be not only
an asymptotic horizon of human transcendence, but Godself a
person who is intimately related to human persons.

Consider what this means. Rahner's view implies that God as
a person who is genuinely related to others is a free self-expression of the personality, divinity, or essence of God. God's
divinity is conceivable as existing even if God had chosen not to
reveal Godself as a person in relation to the world. Indeed, it
must exist necessarily. Rahner implies that God as person is a
self-expression of the essential nature or divinity of God. God as
relative to others is a moment within the more inclusive reality
that is God in Godself, God in God's essential nature. Here the
personality, the abstract, is viewed as inclusive of the person, that
which is concrete. But this is a complete reversal of the way in
which the terms "person" and "personality" can meaningfully be
used. The personality is the set of abstract qualities that are
revealed in a person's actual behavior. But it is a person who *has*
a personality. It would be absurd to say that a personality had a
person or that the person was included within her or his personality as an aspect of that personality. The abstract (the personality) is an element within the concrete (the person). God's
divinity is the abstract nature that characterizes God as God. But
this abstract nature itself cannot be understood as the inclusive

aspect of the divine being. Rather, the divine being as a person *has* the unique, divine personality.

At this point Rahner's thought is genuinely incoherent. Although he correctly sees that God in Godself, God in God's essential nature, God as strictly nonrelative, is abstract, and that God as a free person related to others in love is concrete, he is forced to view the abstract, nonrelative aspect of God as inclusive of the concrete, relative aspect of God, because he understands God as relative to be a free self-expression of God as nonrelative. This is to say, in effect, that the divinity of God expresses as its real symbol and, therefore, is inclusive of, God as person, God as related to others. The divinity of God, Rahner implies, could exist without God as a person related to others. This is precisely a role that the abstract divinity of God cannot play, for the abstract and nonrelative are always the set of abstract qualities belonging to some concrete individual that is related to others.

Two objections might be raised with respect to my criticism of Rahner's understanding of the relationship between the divine essence and God as a free personal agent related to others. The first objection is that Rahner does not understand God in Godself or in God's essential nature to be abstract at all, but rather understands God in Godself to be *actus purus,* the full actualization of all positive perfections. If God in Godself is concrete and not abstract, it might be objected, then my criticism is groundless. Indeed, Rahner does understand God in Godself to be the fullness of being, *actus purus.* But, it seems to me, a defense of Rahner's position based on this understanding simply points out the same incoherence in his concept of God that I am trying to demonstrate in this section, namely, that Rahner's position concerning the relativity and nonrelativity of God can represent more than a merely verbal solution to the problem only if, contrary to his most fundamental convictions, he admits a real relatedness to others of God in Godself. For if God as *actus purus* expresses Godself in a finite real symbol, then God as fully actual or fully concrete has somehow become more concrete, since, prior to the incarnation, God did not have finite reality as God's own reality. But this is absurd. If God is conceived as *actus purus,* then, by definition, God is incapable of becoming, of attaining any additional actuality. Under these conditions, the assertion that God is mutable in God's other can at best only verbally assert a relativity of God. The only way in which such a claim could be more than verbal is if God in Godself is already constituted by real relatedness to others. But such a view of the divine reality is excluded from the outset by the notion of God as *actus purus*.

The other objection that might be raised is that while it is true that a person is inclusive of her of his personality, just as the concrete is inclusive of the abstract, these principles do not apply to the matter at hand, namely the relationship between God as related to the world and God as unrelated, because in this case we are dealing with the self-limitation of God as absolute being. In other words, Rahner is correct that the relative or determinate aspect of God cannot be the inclusive aspect of the divine being, for it arises as a self-limitation of God as nonrelative or absolute. I think, however, that this line of argument also leads to self-contradiction.

Rahner claims that God in Godself, God as *actus purus*, God as unlimited, absolute being, limits Godself by adopting finite reality as God's own reality and thus, through this self-limitation, becomes relative to the world. On analysis, it seems to me, this position does not involve a limitation of the absoluteness or nonrelativity of God at all, but rather a real alteration of God as absolute being. I can speak coherently, for instance, of limiting myself only if I mean that in such self-limitation I choose not to employ some capacity or power that I already possess, at least as a real possibility for me. That is, I can meaningfully claim to limit my attention in this study to Rahner's concept of God only if it would be possible for me to consider also his understanding of the sacraments, Ignatian spirituality, or any number of other topics. I could investigate these areas, but I choose not to: I limit myself. The point of this mundane example is to show that talk of self-limitation is meaningful only if it refers to a partial negation of some positive capacity within an individual. For if I do not possess capacity x, then my not employing x is not a limitation of myself, but is simply the only way in which I can actualize myself since the actualization of x is not a possibility for me.

But Rahner's assertion that God, as infinite or nonrelative, limits Godself and becomes finite or relative, on these grounds, has no coherent meaning for no positive capacity of God has been limited or partially negated. The nonrelativity of God, for him, is a wholly negative characterization of God. It is a denial that God has any need of relations to others in order to be God. As absolute being, God is the *actus purus*, the completely self-subsistent individual who is free of all relatedness to others. Indeed, God as absolute cannot be really related to others or God would no longer be wholly self-subsistent and absolute. This nonrelativity of God is part of God's necessary essence. To talk of this nonrelativity of God being limited is confused at best. There is simply no positive quality to be limited. Thus, given Rahner's presuppositions, God's becoming relative to the world cannot be the self-limitation of God, but rather must be God adopting some new, positive determination (relatedness to others), which is not already part of God's essential nature.

Hence, Rahner's view that the relative aspect of God is to be understood as the self-limitation of God's necessary, nonrelative essence is not free from the internal incoherence of his understanding of the relationship between the concrete and abstract aspects of God. He attempts to derive a positive determination of God (relatedness to others) from a wholly negative and indeterminate aspect of God (God as strictly and essentially nonrelated to others). But the concrete, the positive, the determinate, cannot be derived from the abstract, the negative, and the indeterminate. Cyril Richardson's comments on the error of a "trinity of mediation" (a view that it is through the Logos that the wholly transcendent God is mediated to the finite world) apply to Rahner's understanding that the relativity of God is a consequence of the self-limitation of God as absolute being:

> The second problem of this Trinity of mediation is the assumption that the Absolute can beget the mediator. . . . [It] stems from the attempt to compose an essential paradox. It goes back to the idea of the fecundity of the Absolute, which by its overflowing nature produces the Logos, and, in turn, the world. But this is to deny the very quality of the absolute, which cannot have anything "left over," and which ever stands in a paradoxical relation to the world. Every attempt to do justice to the absolute character of God cannot overcome this paradox; and every attempt to relate his beyondness to his relatedness is doomed to failure by the very nature of these terms. If the one is in any sense begotten of the other, then the other is no longer absolute. The result of deriving God in his visible and encountered nature from God in his invisibility and self-sufficiency is to compromise the latter.[61]

Rahner seeks to accomplish something logically impossible: to include God as related within God as nonrelated. This is impossible because it is a contradiction in terms. The only coherent way of relating nonrelative or absolute and relative aspects of a single individual is to conceive the nonrelative aspect as the set of abstract qualities that characterize the actual, concrete individual in its relations to others.

If I am right that the concrete and relative is inclusive of the abstract and absolute, and that the relative cannot be a self-limitation of the absolute, then Rahner's position that the genuine relatedness of God (which Christian theology must affirm) is to be understood as the free self-expression, self-limitation, even self-alienation of God as absolute being is not a coherent, tenable position at all. It must reduce to one of two other positions.

First, Rahner's position could reflect merely a verbal solution to the problem of the relativity and nonrelativity of God. That is, the relatedness of God that is asserted is not really a relatedness *of God*. Any relatedness of God to the world resulting from God's free self-expression in a finite real symbol would appear to be totally superfluous to God in God's essential nature. God could be God, indeed *must* be God, even without such relatedness to others. Further, if God really is *absolute* being, *actus purus,* then any relatedness to others implied in God's self-expression *ad extra* cannot be a relatedness of God or God would no longer be the absolute one. Thus, the other, the real symbol, is not really God's reality.

Second, if Rahner's position is to be more than a verbal solution to this problem, then it must entail a real relatedness of God in Godself after all. To claim that God is related to others in God's real symbol would seem to be an empty assertion, for the only way in which a relatedness of God to the world in some particular instance can be meaningfully affirmed is if God in Godself is already really related to others prior to God's self-expression. If the relativity of God cannot be derived from the nonrelativity of God, even as a self-limitation of the latter, and yet if God is affirmed to be genuinely related to others, then the inclusive aspect of the divine being must already be God as really related to others. Contrary to Rahner's explicit claim, God in Godself must be God precisely as a personal agent, one who is really related to others. Then, the strict nonrelativity of God (which, I repeat, must be affirmed by any adequate Christian theology) would have to be understood as the abstract personality or divinity of God.

That Rahner intends to offer more than merely a verbal affirmation that God is both relative and nonrelative, and yet fails finally to make clear how this is to be done, is illustrated beautifully in a public exchange Rahner had with L. Malevez concerning Rahner's claim that "God can become something, the one who is immutable in himself can *himself* be mutable in the other."[62] Malevez asks rhetorically, "is this capacity that God has of becoming the finite grounded precisely upon the immutability of God?"[63] Rahner responds negatively. But then Malevez presses the issue as follows:

> However, this relation is implied, for the ability to create is only a limited form of the original ability to assume the other. That which would have to be the most profound in God is the ability to become the other (he becomes the other in the incarnation). He only creates the lesser in view of the greater, hence the ability to create is grounded upon the more profound ability to incarnate himself. Is this ability to incarnate himself—rendered by "God was made man"—grounded precisely upon the transcendence [*sic* of God]? Do you maintain this paradox: God is capable of becoming the mutable precisely because he transcends even our representation of immutability? Would you challenge our way of expressing immutability? Do we not take enough precaution in saying that we must dialectically surpass our representation of immutability? If we were to hold immutability at the level of pure affirmation, then we would render impossible the God made man. But we must recall that our affirmation of immutability is patient of a dialectical correction. It is necessary to transcend the affirmation by a negation, or, rather, it is necessary to synthesize an affirmation and a negation. This synthesis, although impossible at the level of understanding, all the same is the expression of something real.[64]

Rahner replies:

> No, I do not want to deduce the possibility of God becoming the other from the concept of the divine immutability, as we obtain it philosophically. However, I am saying, in fact, that these two things can be reconciled: *God* is made man, *creature*. Here is what I want to maintain: the affirmation of immutability concerns God in

himself, but it does not deny a real mutability of God in another. The dialectical formula "God immutable in himself, mutable in another," cannot be surpassed. If we say solely "God is immutable," and if we seek the means of reconciling the fact of the incarnate word by limiting the change simply to the created entity, then the problem would not be solved. The only satisfactory formula is "God immutable in himself, mutable in another."[65]

Clearly, Rahner understands his claim that God is nonrelative in Godself and relative in God's other to be more than the simple paradox Malevez suggests. But Rahner gives no indication of how his assertion is more than a contradiction in terms. He simply repeats his formula, adding "I refuse, in the name of faith, to allow one or the other term [the mutability or the immutability of God] to be dropped."[66]

There is still a third way in which Rahner seeks to defend the meaning of his claim that God freely adopts the relativity of the world as God's own while remaining in Godself strictly nonrelative. This defense involves his understanding of quasi-formal causality. It seems clear that Rahner appeals to the model of quasi-formal causality because he is dissatisfied with the merely extrinsic or nominal relatedness of God to the world presented in the usual models of efficient causality.[67] In grace and incarnation God does not simply posit finite reality as that which is wholly other than God, but communicates Godself to the creatures in quasi-formal causality. In quasi-formal causality God is God's own effect in the creature. The relationship between God and the world established by quasi-formal causality is much more intimate than the relationship between an efficient cause and its effect, for in quasi-formal causality God becomes immanent within the world and, in the incarnation, takes the reality of the world as God's own reality. Thus, one could argue that it is as a quasi-formal cause that God, for Rahner, is both relative to the world while retaining God's essential nonrelativity.

But here too Rahner's position is characterized by a certain inner tension. The problem at this point is that he seeks to advance beyond the unsatisfactory position of traditional scholasticism, which denies any real relatedness of God to the world, by proposing a new understanding of God as a causal agent over against the world. It seems to me that the issue involved in the question of God's relativity to the world cannot be settled simply through a modification of one's view of divine causality.

Here again I want to try to illustrate this tension in Rahner's thought by appealing to the scholastic philosophical tradition itself. For on classical grounds the attempt to explicate a relativity of God to the world on the basis of a theory of divine causality would seem to be doomed to failure from the outset. Consider the following statement by Norris Clarke.

> Recall the classic metaphysical position of both Aristotle and St. Thomas—still as valid and as profound as ever, it seems to me—that efficient causality "takes place," or is ontologically "located," in the effect, not in the agent as such: *actio est in passio*. For to cause is precisely to make *another* be (in whole or in part), to enrich *another*. It affirms nothing at all about enriching (or impoverishing) the agent. Change, on the other hand, is the exact opposite: it is enriching *oneself*, acquiring something new for *oneself*, and it says nothing at all about enrichment of another. Hence the affirmation of causal action, taken strictly and solely as such, gives no grounds for affirming any new intrinsic being in the agent. There is only the new reality resulting from a causal situation: this is in the subject or receiver of the action.[68]

If this account of causal action and change is accurate, and fundamentally, I think it is, then despite the differences Rahner points out between efficient and quasi-formal causality, in both cases God remains solely an agent over against the world. God, considered solely as a causal agent, cannot, in any metaphysics (whether classical or neoclassical), be conceived to be relative to the world. To be a causal agent is to be strictly nonrelative to one's effect. It is impossible to show God to be relative to the world if God is considered exclusively as a causal agent, even an agent who acts through quasi-formal causality. The relativity of God can be more than verbally affirmed only if God is conceived not only as a causal agent but also as a patient, in some sense, in relation to the world.

Once again, Rahner seems to attempt to derive God as a person genuinely related to other persons, one who can be said to be affected by others (even if there is no change in God's essential nature), from God as absolute being who, by definition, cannot be affected by others. The discussion of the incoherence of Rahner's understanding of the relationship between the absolute and the relative, the abstract and the concrete, could be repeated here with respect to the model of the divine quasi-formal causality. As was implied in the passage from Norris Clarke, a causal agent as such is the abstract, absolute, non-affected term of a causal relationship, while the effect as such is the concrete, relative, affected term.

So, Rahner's attempt to show that his statement that one and the same God is both relative and nonrelative is not simply a contradiction in terms must be judged unsuccessful. He rightly seeks to affirm both the relativity and the nonrelativity of God. Yet his position is incoherent. Either it reflects a merely verbal solution to the problem or it affirms something that Rahner has no intention of affirming (a real relatedness of God in Godself). At this point his thought leads us to an impasse. Some alternative is needed, for, evidently, there are no conceptual resources in Rahner's thought that would enable one to accomplish what he intends to accomplish, but does not, namely, a view of the divine being in which the relativity and nonrelativity of God can both be coherently affirmed.

Does Rahner Provide an Alternative to Dualism and Pantheism?

If the argument of this chapter has been sound and if Rahner does not, in fact, offer a coherent account of how one and the same God can be both relative and nonrelative, then it is doubtful that his thought can provide a genuinely alternative understanding of the divine reality, one that maintains the truth of both dualism and pantheism while avoiding the errors of each position. For his position can be more than a verbal solution to the problem of God's relativity and nonrelativity only if it entails a real relatedness of God in Godself, something he explicitly rejects. And yet if it does not admit a real relatedness of God in Godself, then his position is only verbally different from that of traditional scholasticism with its dualistic understanding of God and world. As I tried to show in the previous section, without an admission of a real relatedness of God in Godself, Rahner's understanding of the divine being reduces to the view that all relativity and change in God's self-expression *ad extra* is on the part of the finite other, the creature, while God remains strictly unaffected. Rahner's criticism of scholastic thought can be applied to his own position:

> . . . all is clear: the Logos assumes, without alteration,
> that which as a creaturely reality is subject to becoming,

including its being assumed. Thus all becoming and all
history with its hardship are on this side of the absolute
abyss that separates the immutable, necessary God and
the mutable, conditioned world and that prevents them
from mixing.[69]

Such a view, according to Rahner himself, is fundamentally
inadequate for it neither appropriately interprets the biblical
proclamation of a genuinely dialogic salvation history, nor credibly presents the divine reality to contemporary persons as an
existentielly significant aspect of their experience.

Rahner clearly intends to offer an understanding of the
divine reality that is more than merely verbally distinct from that
of traditional scholasticism. He correctly argues that an adequate
Christian theology can no longer view God as a particular individual (even if a supreme individual) who exists alongside of the
world, related to the world in a wholly external fashion.[70] The
moment of truth in pantheism must be affirmed, namely, that
God and the world are not parts within a larger whole, the
totality of reality. God, in some real sense, must be the totality of
reality, for the God-world difference is not a categorial, but a
metaphysical or transcendental, difference. Or, as Rahner says,
God *is* the difference between God and the world. This difference is internal to God, for God is the final horizon that
makes possible all categorial differences.

But Rahner is just as careful to point out the inadequacy of
pantheism, which lies in its identification of God and the world.
Such an identification would make God finite and relative. This
finite God could not be the infinite *Woraufhin* that is demanded
as a condition of the possibility of all human spiritual activity. An
adequate Christian theology must affirm a doctrine of creation
ex nihilo, Rahner says, in order to express the radical, qualitative
difference between God and the world.[71]

As was shown in the previous section, a number of thinkers
have found Rahner's thought to be helpful in developing an
understanding of the transcendence and immanence, nonrelativity and relativity of God that provides a mediating position
between classical dualism and what these interpreters take to be
pantheism. One writer has even suggested that his theology,
because of its understanding of the God-world relationship implied by the incarnation, can be viewed as "a type of dialectical
panentheism" similar to Hegel's.[72]

Is there really any justification for calling Rahner's understanding of the God-world relationship panentheistic? At first
glance it seems there might be. Rahner argues that God is the
totality of reality, that all categorial differences are grounded in
the transcendental difference between God and the world. The
imagery of God as the one who "silently encompasses everything," the one in whom "all ways become lost, . . . the one in
whom we live, move, and have our being, who is not far from
any one of us, who supports and surrounds all and who is
comprehended and surpassed by none," is not uncommon in his
works.[73] Further, it is instructive to note that while he dismisses
pantheism as an erroneous identification of God and world, he
speaks more positively of the panentheistic position:

> This form of pantheism does not intend simply to iden-
> tify the world with God in a monistic fashion (God = the
> "all") but intends to conceive the "all" of the world "in"
> God as an inner modification and appearance of God,
> even if God is not absorbed into the world. The doctrine
> of such a "being-in" of the world in God is false and
> heretical (*Denziger,* 1728) if and only if it denies the
> creation of the world by God and the distinction of the
> world from God (not only the distinction of God from
> the world); otherwise panentheism is a challenge ad-
> dressed to ontology to think through more deeply and
> exactly the relationship between absolute and finite
> being (i.e., by grasping the reciprocal conditioning of
> unity and difference that increase in direct propor-
> tion).[74]

Joseph Donceel is right, I think, when he says that Rahner
himself is one of those thinkers who seeks to respond to this
challenge to think through more deeply and exactly the relationship between absolute and finite being.[75] Donceel goes on to
remark, however, that Rahner's thought does not thereby
qualify as panentheistic. It seems to me that one could construe
Rahner's position concerning the God-world relationship to be a
form of panentheism only by ignoring the real inner tension
within his understanding of the relativity of the divine being.
While it seems that Rahner's view must entail a real relatedness
of God to the world if it is to be more than a merely verbal
solution to the problem it attempts to solve, it is not at all clear
how such a real relatedness of God could be possible given his
metaphysical presuppositions. Rahner can provide a genuine

solution to the problem of the relativity of God only by denying something that he explicitly states to be essential to a Christian concept of God, namely, that God in Godself is strictly non-relative.

Rahner claims to have surpassed the dualism of the classical scholastic understanding of God and world by conceiving God to be the totality of reality. But the meaning of this claim, for him, is not clear. Certainly God is not the totality of reality in the pantheistic sense of *deus sive natura*. I showed earlier that the affirmation that God is the totality of reality does not imply that God must "kill in order to live himself. He is not 'the only real one,' the one who, like a vampire, draws to himself and, to a certain extent, sucks out the reality of the things that are distinct from him. He is not the *esse omnium*."[76] God's being the totality of reality cannot cancel or abrogate the autonomy or reality of the nondivine individuals.

But if God is not the totality of reality in this pantheistic sense, then it seems to me, the only other meaning "God is the totality of reality" can have is that God somehow is inclusive of all reality, assuming the phrase "God is the totality of reality" is more than verbally different from an affirmation that God is the final horizon or *Woraufhin* of all reality. Thus, a necessary condition of the possibility of God being the totality of reality is that God is really related to the world. But once again, it is not clear how such a view of God is possible in Rahner's thought, since a real relatedness of God to others is already excluded by the notion of God as *actus purus*. God seems to "include" finite reality within the divine reality only in the sense that God, in the incarnation, limits God's nonrelativity and adopts the whole of finite reality by adopting the human nature of Jesus as God's own reality. But in this self-expressive or self-alienating act, God remains solely a causal agent in relation to the world. And, as I have argued, causal agents as such are not inclusive of their effects. Even in the incarnation, which for him is the historical highpoint of God's self-communicative activity in the world, Rahner does not assert an inclusion of the world in God as the totality of reality, but only a more radical immanence of God in the world.

Now it is true that at times Rahner suggests a receptivity to the world on God's part. He remarks very briefly and in passing, at one point, that an analogous attribution to God *per viam negationis et eminentiae* of materiality might be possible.[77] In another place, he says that a more adequate view of "an immanence of God in the world or an *immanence of the world in God* would be attainable" by conceiving the God-world difference to be God Godself rather than a creation of God or a presupposition of God's creative activity.[78] Unfortunately, Rahner never spells out clearly what these suggestions of a receptivity of God or of an immanence of the world in God might mean. And, indeed, there are many more statements in which Rahner unequivocally denies that God is essentially receptive or relative to the world.

But if Rahner's claim that God is the totality of reality is to mean anything more than that God is the final horizon of reality, or the source of all, then some receptivity of God must be admitted and God must be conceived not only as an agent but also as a patient in relation to the world. Since one cannot be sure exactly what Rahner's position is regarding the meaning of the claim that God is the totality of reality, this position cannot plausibly be held to represent a genuine alternative to dualism or pantheism. It is clear that his position is not pantheistic, but it is unclear to me whether his view of the distinction between God and world is more than merely verbally different from that of the dualistic view of classical scholastic thought. Rahner seems to be caught in the dilemma either of having to deny the nonrelativity of God in Godself in order to provide a genuine advance beyond the classical dualistic understanding of God's relationship to the world, or of maintaining the strict nonrelativity of God at the cost of perpetuating a dualistic view of God and the world.

In this first chapter of my critical appraisal of Rahner's concept of God I have tried to expose several inconsistencies within Rahner's view of the God-world relationship that he takes to be a necessary implication of the assertion that God is love. I first argued that his account of the divine activity in the incarnation (the historical highpoint of the self-communication of God in love to the creatures) seems to contradict his general principle concerning the nature of the activity of God in the world. Next I tried to show that while Rahner holds that God must be both relative to the world and nonrelative if God is to be said truly to be love, this claim is fundamentally incoherent, for either his solution to the problem of how God can be both relative and nonrelative is a merely verbal solution, or his solution entails a real relatedness to the world of God in Godself, something he characteristically denies. Finally, I argued that because his understanding of the relativity and nonrelativity of God is incoherent, he does not provide the genuine alternative to dualism and pantheism that he claims to have provided.

Rahner's argument that an alternative to dualism and pantheism is demanded by the Christian assertion that God is love seems to me to be convincing. But, as I have tried to show, he is unable to provide this alternative. He cannot maintain, at one and the same time, the relativity and nonrelativity of God. He either affirms a real relatedness of God in Godself, which, for him entails a pantheistic understanding of God and the world, or he maintains God's strict nonrelativity only at the cost of failing to move beyond the dualistic position of scholasticism he so clearly shows to be inadequate. Rahner's thought, at this point, leads us to an impasse. Some alternative view of God is needed in which a real relativity of God in Godself can be affirmed without obscuring the infinite, qualitative difference between God and the world.

NOTES

[1] "Immanente und transzendente Vollendung der Welt," *ST*, 8:600–601 (ET: *TI*, 10:280–281).

[2] The proviso "of a similar logical type" is crucial. The empirical, historical claims of theology are to be evaluated in terms of the accepted standards of historiography. But it would be inappropriate to apply such empirical standards to the transcendental or metaphysical claims of theology. The latter must be judged according to criteria of meaning and truth appropriate to metaphysical statements.

[3] *GG*, p. 94 (ET: *FCF*, p. 86).

[4] Ibid., pp. 196–202 (ET: ibid., pp. 195–203).

[5] *Karl Rahner*, pp. 452–453.

[6] Ibid., p. 181.

[7] Ibid., pp. 110–112.

[8] Ibid., p. 217.

[9] *Offenbarung und Transzendenzerfahrung*, p. 22.

[10] Ibid., pp. 33–34.

[11] Ibid., pp. 17–18.

[12] *Karl Rahner*, p. 181.

[13] *GG*, pp. 122–123 (ET: *FCF*, p. 116).

[14] *Offenbarung und Transzendenzerfahrung*, p. 35.

[15] *GG*, pp. 93–96 (ET: *FCF*, pp. 86–89).

[16] Ibid., p. 202 (ET: ibid., p. 202).

[17] "Zur Theologie der Menschwerdung," *ST*, 4:147 (ET: *TI*, 4:113). As Rahner indicates, similar claims can and must be made concerning God's temporality and aseity. Therefore, in what follows, I will speak generally of God's relativity and nonrelativity, intending to include therein all of these particular topics.

[18] Ibid., p. 147, n. 3 (ET: ibid., pp. 113–114, n. 3).

[19] Ibid. (ET: ibid.).

[20] I will have more to say concerning the mystery of God in Ch. XI of this study.

[21] "Zur Theologie des Symbols," *ST*, 4:285 (ET: *TI*, 4:229–230).

[22] *GW*, pp. 258–262.

[23] "Zur Theologie des Symbols," *ST*, 4:295 (ET: *TI*, 4:238).

[24] Ibid., pp. 278–281 (ET: ibid., pp. 224–227).

[25] Ibid., pp. 281–285 (ET: ibid., pp. 227–230).

[26] See Joseph Donceel, "Second Thoughts on the Nature of God," *Thought* 46 (1971):365–370.

[27] See *Phenomenology of Mind*, esp. pp. 68–130.

[28] "Zur Theologie des Symbols," *ST*, 4:285–290 (ET: *TI*, 4:230–234).

[29] *GW*, pp. 169–210.

[30] "Zur Theologie des Symbols," *ST*, 4:293 (ET: *TI*, 4:236–237).

[31] *Phenomenology of Mind*, pp. 789–808.

[32] "God as Spirit or as love means that God particularizes himself, generates the Son, creates the world, an other to himself, and has himself and is identical with himself in this other" (*Sämtliche Werke*, vol. 16: *Vorlesungen über die Beweise vom Dasein Gottes* (Stuttgart: Fr. Frommanns Verlag, 1959), p. 542).

[33] "Gott," *LTK*, vol. 4, cols. 1083–1084.

[34] See "Bemerkungen zur Gotteslehre in der katholischen Dogmatik," *ST*, 8:175–176 (ET: *TI*, 9:136); "*Theos* im Neuen Testament," *ST*, 1:99, 131 (ET: *TI*, 1:86, 114); *HW*, p. 115.

[35] "Zur Theologie der Menschwerdung," *ST*, 4:148 (ET: *TI*, 4:114).

[36] *Karl Rahner*, pp. 380–382.

[37] W. Norris Clarke, "A New Look at the Immutability of God," in *God Knowable and Unknowable*, ed. Robert Roth (New York: Fordham University Press, 1973), pp. 43–72; Martin D'Arcy, "The Immutability of God," *Proceedings of the American Catholic Philosophical Association* 41 (1967): 19–26; Joseph Donceel, "Second Thoughts on the Nature of God," *Thought* 46 (1971):346–370; James Felt, "Invitation to a Philosophic Revolution," *The New Scholasticism* 45 (1971):87–109; William Hill, "Does the World Make a Difference to God?" *Thomist* 38

(1974):146–164; Anthony Kelly, "God: How Near a Relation?" *Thomist* 34 (1970):191–229; Walter Stokes, "Freedom as Perfection: Whitehead, Thomas and Augustine," *Proceedings of the American Catholic Philosophical Association* 36 (1962):134–142; "Is God Really Related to the World?" *Proceedings of the American Catholic Philosophical Association* 39 (1965):145–151; "Whitehead's Challenge to Theistic Realism," *The New Scholasticism* 38 (1964):1–21; John Wright, "Divine Knowledge and Human Freedom: The God who Dialogues," *Theological Studies* 38 (1977):450–477. For a helpful discussion of this Catholic response to process thought, see Barry Whitney, "Divine Immutability in Process Philosophy and Contemporary Thomism," *Horizons* 7 (1980):49–68.

38 "Does the World Make a Difference to God?" p. 163.

39 Ibid., p. 164.

40 "God: How Near a Relation?" p. 228.

41 "A New Look at the Immutability of God," p. 56.

42 Ibid., pp. 68–69.

43 "Is God Really Related to the World?" p. 151. Of course, a process thinker such as Charles Hartshorne himself holds that while there are reciprocal real relations between God and the world, these relations are nevertheless asymmetrical.

44 "The Immutability of God," p. 19.

45 "Um das Geheimnis der Dreifaltigkeit," *ST*, 12:323 (ET: *TI*, 16:258).

46 "Zur Theologie des Symbols," *ST*, 4:293–294 (ET: *TI*, 4:237), my emphasis.

47 "Probleme der Christologie von heute," *ST*, 1:202, n. 2 (ET: *TI*, 1:181, n. 3).

48 "Zur Theologie der Menschwerdung," *ST*, 4:147, n. 3 (ET: *TI*, 4:113–114, n. 3).

49 Ibid., p. 146 (ET: ibid., p. 112).

50 It is important to keep this usage of the term "include" in mind throughout the remainder of this section. To say that *a* includes *b*, is nothing more than a shorthand way of saying that *a* is the inclusive term of the relation that obtains between *a* and *b*.

51 Cf. "Zur Theologie des Symbols," *ST*, 4:282–283 (ET: *TI*, 4:227–228).

52 Although, as I will show later, this contradicts the way in which Rahner speaks of the nonrelative (the abstract) and the relative (the concrete) in nondivine cases, and even in some divine cases, e.g., when he says that the self-communication of God (grace) is more determinate, more concrete than the abstract metaphysical "love" of God as the aloof *Woraufhin* of all creaturely becoming.

53 "Zur Theologie des Symbols," *ST*, 4:282 (ET: *TI*, 4:227).

54 "Zur Theologie der Menschwerdung," *ST*, 4:147, n. 3 (ET: *TI*, 4:113, n. 3).

55 Ibid., p. 148 (ET: ibid., p. 114).

56 *The Divine Relativity: A Social Conception of God* (New Haven: Yale University Press, 1948), p. 143.

57 In the sense in which I am using "personality" here, every human person has a personality, that is, every human person is characterized by a set of distinguishing qualities.

58 "Philosophie," *KtW*, p. 288.

59 "Gotteslehre," *LTK*, vol. 4, col. 1123.

60 "*Theos* im Neuen Testament," *ST*, 1:130 (ET: *TI*, 1:114).

61 *The Doctrine of the Trinity* (New York: Abingdon Press, 1958), p. 65. Unfortunately Richardson draws the following conclusion from this paradox: "We have reached the confines of human thought; and in our need to do justice both to God's absolute transcendence and to his being in relation, we can say no more than that we hold both these things to be true" (ibid.). This is similar, finally, to Rahner's own position concerning the relativity and nonrelativity of God.

62 This discussion took place in La Tourette-L'Abresle in 1961 at a colloquy on christology. The papers read at this colloquy and the discussions of these papers have been published as *Problèmes actuels de christologie*. Rahner read a French translation of "Zur Theologie der Menschwerdung" at the colloquy and it is the argument of this essay that Malevez is concerned to criticize.

63 *Problèmes actuels de christologie*, p. 402.

64 Ibid., pp. 402–403.

65 Ibid., p. 403.

66 Ibid., p. 408.

67 "Über den Begriff des Geheimnisses in der katholischen Theologie," *ST*, 4:90 (ET: *TI*, 4:65–66); *GG*, p. 127 (ET: *FCF*, p. 121).

68 "The Immutability of God," p. 51.

69 "Zur Theologie der Menschwerdung," *ST*, 4:146 (ET: *TI*, 4:113).

70 *GG*, pp. 71–72 (ET: *FCF*, pp. 62–63).

71 Ibid., pp. 85–86 (ET: ibid., pp. 77–78).

72 Thomas Pearl, "Dialectical Panentheism: On the Hegelian Character of Rahner's Key Christological Writings," *Irish Theological Quarterly* 42 (1975):126.

73 "Über die Möglichkeit des Glaubens heute," *ST*, 5:30 (ET: *TI*, 5:21).

74 "Panentheismus," *KtW*, p. 275.

75 "Some Second Thoughts on the Nature of God," *Thought* 46 (1971):352.

76 "Die ewige Bedeutung der Menschheit Jesu für unser Gottesverhältnis," *ST*, 3:53 (ET: *TI*, 3:40).

77 "Die Einheit von Geist und Materie im christlichen Glaubensverständnis," *ST*, 6:189 (ET: *TI*, 6:156–157).

78 "Christologie im Rahmen des modernen Selbst- und Weltverständnisses," *ST*, 9:236 (ET: *TI*, 11:224), my emphasis.

CHAPTER VIII
LOVE AND THE FREEDOM OF GOD

In the preceding chapter of this study I tried to indicate several basic inconsistencies in Rahner's view of the God-world relationship he holds is implied by the assertion "God is love." Now I would like to consider the adequacy of his understanding of the meaning and truth of the assertion "God is love." I have shown that "God is love" means, for Rahner, that: (1) the most fundamental and primordial divine act, which encompasses all divine activity, is the act in which God communicates Godself to the creatures, gives Godself away ecstatically to the nondivine world; this divine self-giving has both a transcendental mode, grace, in which God becomes an intrinsic principle of the self-realization of the human person, and a historical or categorial mode, incarnation, in which God takes finite reality as God's own reality; and (2) this fundamental act of divine self-communication is nevertheless a wholly free and gratuitous act on God's part, one that is necessitated neither by human existence nor by God's own essential nature.

Both of these aspects of Rahner's understanding of the assertion "God is love" must be evaluated critically. In this chapter I want to evaluate his understanding of the freedom or strict gratuity of the divine love for others, while in the next chapter I will consider the adequacy of his view that "love," in both the divine and human case, refers to an ecstatic giving away of oneself to another person.

Is Love the Fundamental Divine Act?

Without a doubt, one of the areas in which Rahner's thought has been most influential in contemporary Roman Catholic theology is the discussion of the relationship between nature and grace. As I have shown in Chapter V above, for him the problem of nature and grace involves the question of how the grace or self-communication of God can be conceived to be both intrinsic to human existence and yet wholly unexacted by, or gratuitous with respect to, human persons. Over against Thomist extrinsicism, he argues that grace is not an additional superstructure imposed upon a human nature that could function perfectly well without grace. Grace is a supernatural existential within the human being, a divinization or elevation of the basic transcendentality of the human person. Wherever human being is actually present, the grace of God is also present as an intrinsic moment within human spirit. Thus, no clear distinction between nature and grace can be made in concrete human existence, for "factual [human] nature *never* is a 'pure' nature, but is always nature within a supernatural order from which man cannot extricate himself."[1]

Yet this factual condition of human being, in which the grace of God is a co-determinant of all moments of human self-realization, is not the only condition that is conceivable. Human being could exist without grace as intrinsic to it. It is to such a conceivable state of human being that the theological concept "nature" refers. "Nature," for Rahner, does not indicate an actual mode of human existence. "Nature" is a remainder concept. It refers to the remainder that is left when the supernatural existential (grace) has been conceptually bracketed from concrete human being. Nature is never experienced as such, but if it is not retained as a concept within theology, according to Rahner, grace will be viewed as a constitutive, essential aspect of human being and not a gratuitous gift of God to the spiritual creature. He employs the nature-grace distinction in order to defend the wholly gratuitous character of the divine love of others.

One interpreter of Rahner, Karl-Heinz Weger, makes the following claim concerning Rahner's solution to the problem of nature and grace.

> Rahner is very well acquainted with the problem, but nevertheless discovers a solution that is so simple and so ingenious that it is hardly disputed today. In order to overcome the extrinsicism of grace, Rahner maintains, on the one hand, the *possibility* of a pure, human nature that has not been finalized supernaturally, and thus preserves the free gratuity of the grace of God. However, at the same time, he holds that this possibility was never an actuality. This means, concretely, that man, as he actually

exists and finds himself, neither is nor experiences himself as pure nature. Rather, grace, in the sense of the supernatural existential, is always already given to every man as an a priori and transcendental awareness, as the offer of God that precedes every act, decision, and cognition of man.[2]

While I would not want to question the fact that Rahner's solution to the problem of nature and grace has been most influential, it seems clear that his solution has been disputed and still is disputed by persons both to the "right" and to the "left" of Rahner.[3] Further, it seems to me, contrary to Weger's claim, that Rahner's solution to the problem of nature and grace is neither that simple, for it is not free of internal incoherence, nor that ingenious, for it is not so much a solution to the classical Roman Catholic problem of nature and grace, as a reformulation of the same problem in a more nuanced way.

The basic incoherence in Rahner's view of nature and grace seems to lie in the fact that the nature-grace distinction is made superfluous by his understanding that the divine love for others is the primordial divine act, although he resolutely maintains the importance of this distinction. In other words, Rahner's view that the self-communication of God to the nondivine realm is God's one final goal in relation to the world and that this self-communication is given universally as an intrinsic moment within all human experience would seem to make the classical nature-grace distinction unnecessary.

Anne Carr makes the following suggestive remark at the end of her study of Rahner's theology:

> The Christocentrism implicit in the notion of a supernatural existential is open to question. It must be argued that an existential, in Heidegger's sense, refers to an *ontological* or *essential* characteristic of the person in the world. Hence, the grace which Rahner insists is a gratuitous expansion of the human horizon is universally present (by offer at least) whether there is an explicit relation to Christianity or not. Rahner's theory of anonymous Christianity lends support to this. Since transcendental revelation (and salvation) are universally available, and operative wherever a person lives authentically and morally, Rahner's distinction between nature and grace and his insistence on the necessity of explicit Christianity seem superfluous. . . . With regard to anonymous Christianity, he dismisses arguments that this doctrine would lessen the importance of mission, preaching

the Word of God, baptizing, and so on, as failing in adequate comprehension of his thought. It remains a serious question, however, whether the thrust of his concepts of the supernatural existential and transcendental revelation does not lead to the destruction of the nature-grace distinction, and possibly to the diminished importance of explicit Christianity.[4]

What Carr is pointing to here is an apparent tension within the concept "supernatural existential." If the divine love or self-communication is an existential in human existence, then this means, if the term "existential" is used in its characteristic Heideggerian sense, that the divine love is an integral moment of human being, one that must be present if there is to be human being at all. To conceive human being at all is to conceive it as graced by God. And yet Rahner qualifies this existential by calling it a "supernatural" existential, by which he means, the intrinsic quality of divine love in concrete human being notwithstanding, that human being is conceivable without this existential. Rahner indicates that this line of thought, for him, is not merely idle speculation concerning the hypothetical, but indicates a mode of human being that genuinely could have existed.

> A reality in man must be postulated that remains if the supernatural existential, as something unexacted, is subtracted, and that must have a meaning and a possibility of existence [eine Daseinsmöglichkeit] even if the supernatural existential is conceived as being absent (for, otherwise, . . . this existential would be necessarily demanded after all).[5]

This is a clear indication that Rahner is using the term "existential," in the phrase "supernatural existential," in a sense that is significantly different from the sense in which Heidegger uses the term. That is, the supernatural existential, precisely because it is supernatural or strictly gratuitous, is an ontological or essential characteristic of *concrete* human being, but not of human being as such. While Rahner certainly has the right to qualify the concept "existential" in this distinctive way, so long as he employs the concept consistently, this qualification may imply notions that are incoherent. In particular, the view of nature and grace that is implied by the concept of the supernatural existential raises the question concerning the coherence of Rahner's understanding of the relationship between the acts of divine creation and divine self-communication.

It is William Shepherd, in his book on Rahner's view of the relation between nature and grace, who provides the clearest and most detailed demonstration that Rahner's thought is incoherent at this point.[6] He argues that there is a basic tension between the principle Rahner uses to distinguish nature and grace and the terminology he often employs in making this distinction.

Shepherd is correct, I think, when he remarks that:

> If one has to account for two distinct gifts from God, that of creation and that of elevation, then it appears that it is impossible to avoid some distinction between either man as he "once was" or man as he "could have been" and, on the other hand, man as he really is. A concept of double gratuity requires that there be some lapse, whether historical or only logical, between created and elevated nature.[7]

Rahner certainly holds to a view of double gratuity. Therefore, the question can be raised concerning the exact character of the "lapse" between natural and elevated human being in his thought.

Shepherd distinguishes Rahner's "technical doctrine of nature and grace" from his "entire theological system," which is characterized as a "theology of nature and grace." In Rahner's theology of nature and grace, according to Shepherd, creation represents merely the first step on the part of God in carrying out God's project: the communication of Godself in love to the nondivine. But, "God's decision to communicate himself to something outside himself both logically and chronologically precedes the actual creation of that something as the order embodying God's whole strategy."[8] Creation is encompassed by self-communication and does not precede self-communication in a temporal sense. Put differently, Rahner holds that nature is a remainder concept. It indicates a possible mode of human being that neither is, nor ever was, actually experienced, and that can only be arrived at by conceptually removing the supernatural existential from concrete human being. This would seem to indicate that Rahner understands the distinction between human "nature" and concrete human existence, which includes the presence of grace, to be a purely logical distinction.

However, in Rahner's technical solution to the problem of nature and grace, according to Shepherd, a somewhat different view of the relation between creation (or nature) and self-communication (or grace) is offered, namely, the traditional one grounded in the affirmation of double gratuity.[9] Here, for Rahner, creation is a wholly neutral act. That which is created could either be subsequently elevated by grace or not, depending on God's free decision. Thus, Rahner uses language that implies a temporal priority of creation with respect to self-communication. He refers to human nature as the addressee of divine self-communication. God creates human nature in order to have a creature that is not already owed grace to which God can freely communicate Godself. Therefore, although God has a single plan: to communicate Godself to the world, two distinct gratuitous acts of God are required if this plan is to be accomplished: the creation of the addressee of the self-communication, precisely as one who is conceivable without divine self-communication, and the self-communication of God itself. "God has created the servant [human nature] solely in order to make him a child. But he was able to create the child through grace . . . only by creating the servant, the addressee who has no claim to sonship."[10]

Rahner says that human being must already have a "natural" point of contact with God, namely, the human orientation toward God as the *Woraufhin* of transcendence, if grace is to be experienced as a free gift surpassing what humans might "naturally" expect and require of God. He frequently contrasts the human experience of God as radically near in self-communication with the "natural" experience of God as the distant, silent *Woraufhin* of human transcendence. Such formulations imply that human beings exist, or have existed, in some fashion independent of the grace of God, even though Rahner's stated principle is that such a "natural" state is never actually given in human experience.

Shepherd argues, rightly I think, that these two views of the relation between nature and grace, or creation and self-communication, are self-contradictory.

> It is one thing to say that there is a logical sense in which nature can be thought of apart from its inextricable conjunction with grace (supernatural existential, general revelation, uncreated grace, objective justification, indwelling of the Holy Spirit). But it is quite another to move from such an assertion, which is necessary to maintain gratuity of grace, to the temporal implications of the assertion that God created man a servant in order to make him a child through grace. "Recipient" ("ad-

dressee") language in general is specious in this context, for it implies temporal distinction among ontologically different "epochs." This sort of language and implication is expressly denied in Rahner's rejection of any historical state of pure nature prior to grace.[11]

In terms of the specific problem addressed in this study, the problem of the concept of God, this self-contradiction identified by Shepherd could be restated as follows: Rahner's thought is incoherent in that Rahner maintains, on the one hand, that God's love of others is the fundamental divine act that encompasses, and provides the *telos* for, the divine act of creation of the nondivine, while, on the other hand, he asserts that the divine act of creation is conceivable without the fully personal love of God for the nondivine.[12] Clearly, the main thrust of Rahner's thought is that the self-communication of God, God's love of others, is the one fundamental divine act. Yet he maintains that for this one act to be realized precisely as the free gift of Godself in love to others, God must engage in two distinct acts: the creation of the nondivine other *ex nihilo* through efficient causality and the communication of Godself to the other through quasi-formal causality.

This positing of two distinct gratuitous divine acts would seem to be not so much a defense of the sheer gratuity of the divine love of others, as a denial that the divine love of others is God's fundamental act. For Rahner clearly states that creation is possible without divine self-communication, even though creation is supposedly encompassed by divine self-communication. Once again, Rahner's thought seems to involve a dilemma: either the traditional scheme of double gratuity, in which the divine love of the creatures is a *donum superadditum* not entailed at all by the creation of the world *ex nihilo,* is superfluous precisely because the one, all-encompassing, primordial divine activity *is* the love of others, or God's primordial activity is not that of the bestowing of Godself in love upon others, for the creation of the nondivine is conceivable without this alleged fundamental activity. As it stands, Rahner's position includes, in a self-contradictory fashion, both of these views, namely, that God's love of others is God's primordial act and that the divine act of creation could have been realized without the loving self-communication of God to the world.

Rahner gives a clear reason for wanting to retain the traditional understanding of the double gratuity of divine creation and divine self-communication or grace. This reason is, of course, his belief that only in such a way can the divine act of love of others be the wholly gratuitous act of personal love that it must be. Rahner states that his whole scheme of nature and grace is nothing but a reflective, theological "translation" or "transposition" of the "kerygmatic" affirmation that "God wills to communicate himself, to lavish his love, which he himself is."[13] If human being were not conceivable without grace (the supernatural existential), then, simply by existing, human being would demand or exact the love of God. In this case, God would no longer be strictly independent of the world and thus would no longer be God. Likewise, the divine reality must be conceivable without the act of divine self-communication. Rahner argues that God, while creating the human person precisely as spirit that is unfailingly oriented to God, can refuse a loving, personal relationship to human persons without contradicting God's creative act. God would not be God if God could not act freely in relation to God's actual creation.

It is interesting to note that despite William Shepherd's searching criticism of Rahner's understanding of nature and grace, at this point, he agrees with Rahner completely. Shepherd proposes replacing Rahner's two gratuitous divine acts (creation and self-communication) with a single divine act, one in which God creates the world *as* elevated through grace. But Shepherd, like Rahner, holds that God need not have created human being as elevated through grace. He says, for example, that in his view, as well as in Rahner's:

> Obviously, it continues to be possible to envisage an entirely distinct world order, without grace and without ordination to glory. Other alternatives for God are sufficient to safeguard the gratuity of God's action toward *this* world order. As it happened, God acted gratuitously to create a nature graced by his presence. Rejecting the possibility of other options open to him, one perhaps in which grace would not be given with creation but would perhaps come later, and one perhaps with no grace at all, appears to lack theological warrant.[14]

It is precisely this claim that God could create a world and yet not enter into a fully personal relation of love with that world of creatures that I want to examine. My thesis is that if one decides to defend the freedom of the divine love by arguing that God could create a world and yet not love that world in the full personal sense implied in the notion of divine self-communication, then one must also accept a necessary consequence of this view, namely, that God is only accidentally, and not essentially, love of others. I will argue that the view that God is accidentally love of others is fundamentally inadequate in Christian theology, for it neither faithfully interprets the apostolic witness of scripture, nor adequately interprets our common human experience.

Lest the following argument be fundamentally misunderstood, let me point out several things that can only be argued fully in Part III of this study. First, my criticism of Rahner's defense of the gratuity of the divine love should not be taken to mean that the divine freedom and sovereignty relative to the world is not crucial to an adequate Christian concept of God. *That* God must be free and sovereign is made clear both by the Jewish and Christian scriptures and transcendental reflection on our own experience. The only question is *how* God's freedom is to be understood. My claim is that Rahner's way of defending God's freedom is bought at too high a price in that it entails a denial that God is essentially love of others. Second, I would not want to deny the need to distinguish between the creative and redemptive activities of God, both of which are gratuitous on God's part. Again, though, the problem with Rahner's understanding of the double gratuity of creation and redemption is that God, finally, is held to be conceivable as the creator of a world, without being the redeemer of that world, or conceivable as existing as God without any creaturely world at all. It seems to me that if God is love, then God cannot be conceived other than as creator and redeemer of some world of creatures. Third, note that saying that God is essentially love of others and thus the loving creator and redeemer of some world, does not imply that this world, or any other world, is in any sense necessary to God. God could be God without this or any particular world of creatures. I believe, however, that it is self-contradictory to say that the God proclaimed by Christian faith could be Godself without some world to which God relates Godself in love.

Is Rahner's View Logically Coherent?

The first step here must be to show, rather than merely to assert, that Rahner's understanding of the divine freedom necessarily implies that God is not essentially love of others.

Rahner argues that the traditional affirmation of a double

gratuity of creation and grace is not just an abstract and hypothetical affirmation with no relevance to us, but rather "reveals something theologically important and meaningful for the religious understanding of our own actual situation."[15] The notion of double gratuity ensures that God's act of self-communication is understood as a radically free act on God's part. Human being as such "demands" the existence of God as the *Woraufhin* of human transcendence. But, according to Rahner, any further activity of God toward human persons is strictly gratuitous. He says:

> Precisely because the God who is known from the world by the natural reason of man is a free transcendent person, . . . the concrete way in which God relates himself to man and wishes to act toward him cannot be calculated from human nature, from below. . . . This question cannot be answered by way of a metaphysical projection of the essence of God on the part of man, but can only be answered by God, in the event of his own free decision.[16]

Human being, according to Rahner, must reckon with either a speech or a silence of God, a self-bestowal or a self-refusal of God. The proclamation of the Christian faith is that God has in fact bestowed Godself in love. But human being is conceivable without this self-bestowal or self-communication of God. Human being could exist as oriented solely to God as the aloof horizon of human transcendence. Human being is conceivable as a *potentia oboedientialis* for the self-giving love of God, even if this final fulfillment toward which human beings strive were refused.

The love of God for the spiritual creature is not gratuitous or unexacted, for Rahner, simply because all human persons have sinned, nor because grace must be freely appropriated by the human person. Nor does the gratuity of divine self-communication reduce to the gratuity of God's creative act. That is, God's love is gratuitous not just because we might not have existed at all as addressees of the divine self-communication. Rather, God could have refused divine self-communication even to existing human persons. The gratuity of grace is a function of God's freedom and sovereignty, not simply of the freedom of contingent human persons. God's love is gratuitous because God can either bestow Godself upon the creatures or refuse Godself.

Rahner holds that "the one who *himself creates* the orientation toward the intimate, personal communion of love between two persons (in our case man and God) [can] at the same time refuse this communication without contradicting the meaning of this creation and his creative act itself."[17]

Human beings necessarily have an awareness of God. There could be no human being without the "natural," necessary relation to God. But, for Rahner, only if the character of God's activity beyond this natural relation to human being as the *Woraufhin* of transcendence is fundamentally unknown and unknowable prior to the event of God's self-disclosure can God's further act be an act of free, personal love.

> Only when we know not only that God is more than we have conceived him to be in our human knowledge, as we have established it in an anthropology, but also that he can speak or remain silent, only then can a real speech of God, if it actually occurs, be conceived as that which it is: the uncalculable act of free personal love before which man sinks to his knee in prayer.[18]

As spirit, human beings are open to God necessarily. But God's openness to human beings can be a free act of love only if spirit has no "natural" certainty that God is in fact self-bestowing love.

> The one who stands over against another as free always shows himself. He shows himself precisely as the person he wishes to be in relation to the other: either the one who is concealed or the one who is disclosed. In this sense revelation occurs necessarily. And because revelation occurs necessarily in this sense (not just could occur), man must reckon with revelation in the usual theological sense: a possible speech of God that breaks his silence and manifests the divine depths to finite spirit. And precisely because revelation is necessary in the indicated metaphysical sense, because man is always confronted with it, revelation in the theological sense is free.[19]

But notice what this position implies. If the only God-world relationship that is necessary is that between the world and God as the free, transcendent source and *Woraufhin* of the creatures, that is, if both God and human being are conceivable without the self-bestowing love of God for the creatures, then love of others cannot be essential to God. According to Rahner, both love and self-refusal are real possibilities for God, even if, in fact, God has disclosed Godself to be love within this particular world order. God's essential nature or God's primordial possibility of being must be, in a literal sense, a neutral state prior both to self-giving love and self-refusal. The decision of God to bestow Godself rather than to refuse Godself and remain solely the aloof *Woraufhin* of human transcendence is a wholly contingent decision. God is free to reveal Godself as love or not to do so. While God is essentially the creative ground and transcendental *Woraufhin* of the nondivine individuals, God is not essentially love of these others. In the strictest sense of the word, God's love for others is accidental to God, for God could be God without bestowing Godself in love upon God's creatures.

The question, now, is whether such a view is adequate when judged by the very criteria of meaning and truth Rahner proposes for theological statements, namely, does this view faithfully interpret the apostolic witness expressed in scripture in such a way as to be credible to contemporary persons.

First, I would like to suggest that this view that God is not essentially love of others, which is implied necessarily by Rahner's understanding of the sheer gratuity of the divine love of others, displays a certain internal logical incoherence. Rahner makes many explicit statements to the effect that the divine love of others is strictly gratuitous and cannot be derived from, or anticipated by, transcendental reflection on human existence. But one also finds the apparently contradictory statement that

> The faithfulness, the merciful kindness, the love, etc., that we factically experience and express are not merely the (theologically attested) necessary "attributes" of the metaphysical essence of God, but are really much more than this. For God could refuse *this* faithfulness, love, etc., which he in fact demonstrates to us without thereby ceasing to be faithful, loving, etc., in a metaphysical sense.[20]

Here Rahner claims that God can be said to be love in a metaphysical sense, that is, love can be attributed to God on wholly natural grounds, in abstraction from God's self-communication. This would mean that God in God's essence, God as the *Woraufhin* of human transcendence, is already love, in some sense.

There is another context in which Rahner speaks of an essential or necessary love of God for others, namely, the discussion of the meaning of the claim that God is *holy* mystery. Indeed, as I have shown, Rahner claims that "it can only be known through revelation that this holy mystery is also given as mystery in absolute nearness."[21] But we do know, prior to revelation, prior to divine self-communication, that the *Woraufhin* of transcendence is holy mystery. God as holy mystery can be derived, for Rahner, from a wholly secular, metaphysical analysis of human being.

As holy mystery, God is the *Woraufhin* not only of human knowledge but also of human freedom and love. This means, for Rahner, that God strictly as the *Woraufhin* of human love must be, in a certain sense, Godself love. He argues as follows:

> Therefore, when we reflect here upon transcendence as will and freedom, we must take into consideration a loving *Woraufhin* and source of this transcendence. It is the *Woraufhin* that is absolute freedom, that is active in loving freedom as that which is not at our disposal, that which is nameless, and that which disposes absolutely. It is the opening of my own transcendence as freedom and love. . . . If free, loving transcendence is oriented toward a *Woraufhin* that itself opens up this transcendence, then we can say that the one that disposes absolutely, that is not at our disposal, and that is nameless, itself acts in loving freedom. This is precisely what we mean when we say "holy mystery."[22]

Rahner explains further the sense in which the divine *Woraufhin* of human freedom and love must itself be in some sense free and loving in his discussion of the use of analogical language with respect to God. He remarks, prescinding from the special issue of the personal relationship of God to the world affirmed by Christian faith, that the assertion that God is the absolute person is as metaphysically self-evident as are the assertions that God is absolute being, the absolute ground, the absolute good, the absolute horizon of human knowing and acting.

> It is immediately self-evident that the ground of a reality that exists must beforehand possess in itself in absolute fullness and purity this reality that it grounds. For, otherwise, this ground could not be the ground of that which is grounded at all; for, otherwise it would finally be the empty nothingness that—if one takes the term really seriously—would express nothing and could ground nothing.[23]

Therefore, we can affirm God to be love solely on the basis of our natural knowledge of God, for God is the *Woraufhin* of human love. But this admission would seem to contradict Rahner's view that the love of God is known only supernaturally through revelation. It seems that Rahner must assert both that God is essentially love of others and that God is only contingently or accidentally love of others. For, on the one hand, if the self-communication of God is to be the unexpected, gratuitous wonder that Rahner claims it to be, then God cannot be understood, on the basis of a metaphysical analysis of the necessary conditions of human experience, to be essentially love of others. Yet, on the other hand, if God is to be the *Woraufhin* of human existence as a whole (including freedom and love) that Rahner claims God is, then God must already be love prior to the establishment of any personal, "gratuitous" relationships to human beings. Both of these claims, namely that God is the loving *Woraufhin* of human love, and that God's love is a wholly gratuitous act, are central to Rahner's thought. Rahner surely would be unwilling to give up either of them. And, yet, *prima facie*, they would seem to contradict one another.

This apparent self-contradiction is mitigated somewhat when it is realized that Rahner is using the term "love" in significantly different senses in these two assertions. That the love of God for others that is affirmed when Rahner says that God is the loving *Woraufhin* of human love is not to be understood as the same type of divine love for others expressed in the Christian doctrine of grace is implied when Rahner remarks that all analogical predications concerning the personhood of God are characterized by an "empty formality" or a "formal emptiness." The formal emptiness of the analogical, a priori assertions that God is a person, or that God is love, must be given a content "through our historical experience," such that "God is allowed to be a person in the way in which he factually wishes to be encountered and is encountered in individual history, in the depths of our conscience, and in the total history of mankind.[24] Elsewhere, Rahner contrasts a "metaphysical contemplation of that which is absolute and necessary and, thereby, impersonal and abstract" in God, with the biblical view of "the *personal* God in the *concreteness* of his free activity."[25] Thus, it seems that the love of God that can be conceived solely on the basis of a metaphysical view of God as the *Woraufhin* of human love, would have to be understood as a necessary, yet impersonal and abstract "love," radically distinct from love in "the full, personal sense," which Rahner defines as "the abandoning and opening of one's innermost self to and for the other, who is loved."[26]

In fact, as the following passage indicates, this is precisely how Rahner understands what might be called the essential or natural love of God for others.

> God seems to turn out to be the loving one already in the period of salvation [*die Heilszeit*] before Christ. . . . There are [in the Old Testament] patterns of thought that describe, if one can say such a thing, a metaphysical love of God. . . . The goodness (the value) of reality is traced back to its origin in the primordial ground of all being, which is thus also conceived as benevolent. That which has already been said of natural theology in general applies, of course, to this metaphysical goodness of God: it is knowable and in some sense already perceived, it is concealed by original sin, and is revealed clearly only in the experience man has of God in the supernatural history of salvation. But such "love" by itself does not really create a personal I-Thou relationship between man and God. Man knows himself to be borne by a will that, somehow, is oriented toward value and the good. But on this basis alone, he cannot, as it were, turn himself around in order to enter into a personal relationship of community and mutual love with this primordial ground of his being and value.[27]

The metaphysical or essential love of God is of such an impersonal or indeterminate nature, that the necessary presence of this divine love in no way prejudges the issue of whether God will reveal Godself as fully personal love. God, as the *Woraufhin* of human transcendence, must be love in the sense of willing the general good of the creatures. But this metaphysical type of love implies no self-giving on God's part. Therefore, the fully personal love of God proclaimed by Christian faith, in which God bestows Godself as the most immanent fulfillment of the creatures, remains a wholly gratuitous act, one that is not demanded even by the metaphysical love of God. The metaphysical love of God is a necessary aspect of God, conceived as the ground and goal of finite being. But God could be God, and could be love in this metaphysical sense, even if God were not to enter into a fully personal I-Thou relationship with human persons.

While this distinction between two senses of the term "love" allows Rahner to avoid sheer self-contradiction when he affirms both that God is essentially love of others (in the metaphysical sense of "love") and yet that God cannot be essentially love of others (in the personal sense of "love"), one could raise the question why the metaphysical sense of "love" deserves to be called love at all. It seems to me that by defining the metaphysical love of God in such a formal and abstract way, Rahner has evacuated the term "love" of its essential meaning, which, as he himself points out, is precisely the opening of oneself for, and the abandoning of oneself to, another person. I do not see how "love" as it is used by Rahner in relation to God's metaphysical love differs from the concept of benevolence. God as the *Woraufhin* of human transcendence or as holy mystery, therefore, would seem no longer to possess in absolute purity and *fullness* that which God grounds, in this case the transcendentality of human love. God as holy mystery affirms the creature as valuable, but does not communicate Godself to it. Of course, once again, the metaphysical love of God, which is necessary if God is to be the *Woraufhin* of human love, must be significantly different from the fully personal love of God disclosed in divine self-communication if the divine self-communication is to be a gratuitous act of God as a free person, one that is not demanded by God's essential nature. Rahner succeeds in showing that God satisfies the demand that a ground must possess in purity and fullness that which it grounds, only by evacuating the term "love" of its distinctive meaning.

Yet there is a further problem in Rahner's understanding of the metaphysical love of God and the fully personal love of God, one that was indicated under a different guise in the previous chapter. Once again, Rahner holds that the abstract aspect of the divine being is inclusive of the concrete aspect of God. That is to say, the ground of the unity of God as metaphysically love of others and God as fully personal love of others is precisely God as metaphysically love of others. This abstract, impersonal love of God for others is conceivable without the fully personal love of God. Because the metaphysical love of God for others is necessary or essential to the divine being and the fully personal love of God for others is wholly gratuitous, thus nonessential, Rahner implies that God as metaphysically love of others can include God as fully personal love of others, while the converse of this cannot be the case. The fully personal love of God for others is a free self-expression of the abstract, indeterminate metaphysical love of God for others. As I showed in the previous chapter, this argument that the concrete can be included within the abstract is fallacious. The abstract aspect of an individual can be coherently conceived only as the set of qualities that are exemplified by the concrete individual in its actual existence.

These considerations reveal a rather serious incoherence in Rahner's understanding of the divine love. If God's fully personal love for others cannot be included within God's metaphysical love as Rahner proposes, then either Rahner's claim that God's fundamental act is fully personal, self-giving love is merely a verbal assertion, for this fully personal love is strictly nonessential to God, or Rahner's view entails that God in Godself is not merely benevolent (love in a most abstract fashion) but is already fully personal love of others. But if God, in essence, is fully personal love of others, then it is specious to say that human being must reckon with a self-bestowal *or* a self-refusal of God. Rather, the only mode of divine activity that human beings could experience, however this activity takes shape in particular, concrete situations, would be precisely the personal love of God for God's creatures. Thus, Rahner's thought is internally incoherent: the claim that the self-communication of God, the fully personal, ecstatic love of God for the creatures, is God's primordial possibility and fundamental act can be more than a verbal assertion only if Rahner, contrary to his stated position, allows that God is essentially, and not merely accidentally, love of others.

Indeed, there are a few passages in Rahner's works where he seems to indicate that the fully personal love of God for others, while not essential to God, is nevertheless a communication of God's very essence. He says, for instance, that the metaphysical love of God for others provides no answer to the question "whether God already loves man in the sense of willing to bestow himself, as the fully personal one, *in his own essence* upon man."[28] In the following passage, Rahner states quite sharply this seemingly contradictory view that the personal love of God is both an expression of God's essence and yet not essential to God.

> "God is love" is not, therefore, primarily an assertion concerning God's essence that is enlightening in itself, but is rather the expression of the unique, undeniable,

and unsurpassable experience of God that man has only in Christ; it is the expression of the experience that God has bestowed his entire self upon man. Of course, insofar as this free behavior of God in Christ is the unsurpassable communication of all that God in essence and in freedom is and can be, it is also the communication of the divine nature. But this depends inextricably upon the fact that God, the personal one, freely wished to love us.[29]

Here, Rahner shows a certain sensitivity to the fact that God's fully personal love of others must be an expression of God's essence or nature, if it is to be God's fundamental act. And yet, at the same time, he still maintains that this fully personal love of God for others is a wholly free and gratuitous act, which means that God could have been God without entering into a fully personal relationship of love with the creatures. A self-bestowal of love or an absolute self-refusal could equally well express the essence of God, thus implying that personal love of others is not essential to the being of God.

Here again, Rahner's thought leads us to an impasse. He seems to claim, on the one hand, that fully personal love of others is God's fundamental act. This implies that God is essentially love of others, that is, that God cannot even be conceived apart from this fundamental act. But, on the other hand, he denies explicitly that God is essentially love of others. He holds that if grace is to be received by human beings as a free gift, then both God and human being must, in principle, if not in fact, be able to exist as themselves without the bestowal of the fully personal love of God. The next step in this critical appraisal is to consider whether an adequate Christian theology can affirm that God is not essentially love of others. In the following section, I will attempt to show that the view that God is not essentially love of others does not provide a faithful interpretation of the apostolic witness found in scripture, and thus cannot be adequate Christian theology.

Is Rahner's View Justified by the Apostolic Witness of Scripture?

It should be obvious that an adequate exegetical and theological analysis of the New Testament concept of God, and particularly the New Testament understanding of the gratuity of the divine love for others, cannot be provided in a study such as this, even if I were competent to undertake such an analysis. Happily, Rahner himself does not pretend to be a New Testament specialist. Thus, in this section, only the most basic elements of the New Testament understanding of God will be discussed. My analysis will be dependent largely on the work of New Testament scholars.[30] It should be noted, however, that the New Testament understanding of God, in and of itself, has not received a lot of attention in the field of New Testament studies. In fact, one prominent New Testament scholar has called the analysis of the understanding of God "the neglected factor in New Testament theology."[31] So, for this additional reason, all I can hope to do in this section is to analyze Rahner's view that God is not essentially love of others in terms of a very general picture of the New Testament understanding of God.

Rahner states or implies a number of times in his works that his understanding of the gratuity of the divine love is a faithful interpretation of the proclamation of the New Testament. But I know of only one essay, namely, "*Theos* im Neuen Testament," where Rahner deals explicitly with New Testament texts in order to defend his interpretation of the New Testament message.[32] Therefore, this essay will be the focus of my remarks here.

As Rahner himself acknowledges, the essay "*Theos* im Neuen Testament" is heavily dependent on the article on "God" in the *Theologisches Wörterbuch zum Neuen Testament*.[33] Rahner's basic point in the essay (excluding the final section, which deals with the special problem of "*theos*" as the first trinitarian person in the New Testament) is that the New Testament writers are not concerned to develop a metaphysical doctrine of God's essence, but rather seek to proclaim the concrete, personal behavior of the God who is experienced in the historical event of Jesus Christ. The starting point for the New Testament conception of God, according to Rahner, is the self-evidence of the presence of God. The New Testament does not attempt to prove God's existence, and, in fact, would not even understand the question concerning the existence of God to be meaningful. For the New Testament writers, "God is simply there."[34] The New Testament acknowledges that all persons have a certain awareness of God. However, true knowledge of God is a matter of personal decision. Not knowing God is a sinful not *wanting* to know God. This not wanting to know God is compatible with "natural" awareness of God (Rom. 1:18ff.). With the sending of God's Son Jesus

Christ, the human decision over against God now takes the form
of whether human persons will know and believe in the God
who acts concretely and historically in Jesus Christ.

Rahner goes on to indicate something of the content of the
New Testament concept of God. God is one, or rather, again
focusing on the interest of the New Testament in God's historical
activity rather than the abstract divinity of God, the God who is
encountered in Jesus Christ is the only God there is. God is
experienced as a living person who acts in the world, but whose
activity is a wholly free and sovereign activity. There is a genuine
historical dialogue between human beings and God, in which
both partners, as persons, act on, and are acted upon, by the
other. Because God is conceived as a free person, says Rahner,
the New Testament does not really understand God to have
attributes. Rather, God has freely chosen relationships to others.
God's omniscience, for example, is conceived in personal terms
as God's caring and judging regard for human beings. Likewise,
for the New Testament, God's omnipotence is not viewed in
abstract categories, but is presented as the power that raises
Jesus Christ from the dead. Finally, Rahner focuses on the love
of God and argues that, for the New Testament, God is revealed
to be definitively and irrevocably love in the event of Jesus
Christ.

But now let us turn to the real issue at hand: Rahner's
understanding of the New Testament view of the gratuity of the
divine love. At the beginning of the essay, Rahner states his own
characteristic view of the gratuitous character of the divine love,
which entails the possibility that God could have refused to
bestow God's love upon others. He implies that this is also the
biblical view.

> Precisely in order to be able to experience the personal
> self-disclosure of God as *grace*, i.e., precisely in order to
> be able to conceive grace as not being self-evident and
> not being immanent (as a part of his constitutive es-
> sence), man must be a subject that must reckon with a
> self-disclosure or a self-concealment of God. . . . If
> [human being] is to experience this personal self-dis-
> closure of God not just as the free act of God but also as
> free grace to him, the one who is already constituted
> (and this is the biblical and Christian meaning of revela-
> tion), then he must be, from the outset ("by nature"), that
> particular being that must reckon with a speech or a

silence of God, with a self-bestowal or a self-refusal of God.[35]

While the New Testament writers simply presuppose the existence of God, according to Rahner, they do raise the following question: "how does this self-evident God, who is always already given, act, so that man might thereby know, for the first time, how things stand with himself and the world?"[36]

Because God is a free, personal agent, an answer to this question can only be provided by God's own self-disclosure. Thus, says Rahner:

> That this activity of God in Christ occurs precisely now and not at some other time (Heb. 1:2: in these last days; Col. 1:26: but now; Rom. 16:25 [sic. Rom. 16:26]: but now manifested) and that it occurs with respect to sinful, lost man; that it, contrary to all human standards, is oriented precisely toward the poor, the weak, the foolish among men (Mt. 11:25; Lk. 1:51ff.; 1 Cor. 1:25ff.), toward the man who can make absolutely no valid, legal claim to it; that it, therefore, is pure grace—from this man learns that this activity of God is really a new initiative of God, an act of his freedom: will (Rom. 9:19; Jas. 1:18), counsel of his will (Eph. 1:11; Acts 20:27), purpose (Eph. 1:5,9; 1 Cor. 1:21; Gal. 1:15), predestination (Rom. 8:29f.; 1 Cor. 2:7; Eph. 1:5,11), election (Rom. 9:11, 11:5,28; 1 Thess. 1:4; 2 Pet. 1:10).[37]

Human beings, according to him, cannot calculate ahead of time how God will act toward them, for God remains the free Lord.

> Because God is the one who acts freely with respect to man, because he has mercy on whom he will and hardens whom he will (Rom. 9:15,16,18), the free, sovereign disposition of God is the first and last factor of our existence (in the modern sense of the word). With respect to God's free election to grace, *Paul*, from the outset, attempts no theodicy at all: "O man, who art Thou that repliest against God?" (Rom. 9:20). The justice and holiness of the decision of God is based upon itself, precisely because it is free, and it may not be traced back to another necessity that is wholly understandable in its necessity.[38]

Rahner remarks that, for the New Testament, this "free activity of God in relation to the world does have a metaphysical structure, if we can say such a thing, one that arises from the necessary essence of God. But through this structure, nevertheless, the concrete behavior of God is not unambiguously determined."³⁹ He then refers, once again, to Romans 9, saying that God can show mercy toward human persons or harden their hearts. God can enlighten or God can send the powerful delusion (2 Thess. 2:11), the spirit of stupor (Rom. 11:8), without ceasing to be the Holy One. I take this to be one way in which Rahner would seek to give New Testament support for his view that both God and human being are conceivable as existing whether or not God bestows God's love upon the creatures.

Rahner then lists a large number of New Testament passages that refer to God as good, merciful, loving, the God of all grace, the God of peace, the God of hope, the God of compassion, the God who desires the salvation of all persons. But, he says, this divine love is radically gratuitous.

> This merciful and benevolent love of God is, for the New Testament, in its innermost core precisely grace, which cannot be demanded, which, contrary to all expectation, encounters the "atheistic" sinner who has fallen away from God (Eph. 2:12). That God loves us, that he is "dear God," is not a self-evident truth of metaphysics, but is rather the incomprehensible wonder that the New Testament must continually proclaim and that requires the highest effort of man's power of faith to be believed.⁴⁰

Rahner goes on to elucidate the meaning of the gratuity of the divine love in the New Testament, at least as he understands it. He argues that grace is gratuitous not just because it can be faithfully accepted by human beings or rejected in unbelief. The gratuitous character of grace is not constituted by the freedom of the human response to grace. Rather, grace is gratuitous because "God himself, on his own part, sovereignly bestows or refuses his merciful love (Rom. 9:9–11). The loving call of God is always a call of his *prothesis,* an election (Rom. 8:28–33; 2 Tim. 1:9; 2 Pet. 1:10)."⁴¹

Rahner concludes that the New Testament claim that God is love (1 Jn. 4:8) is "not primarily an assertion concerning God's essence that is enlightening in itself, but is rather the expression of the unique, undeniable, and unsurpassible experience of God that man has only in Christ."⁴² God is indeed conceived to be love in the weak, impersonal sense of benevolence in the Old Testament (Ps. 145:9; 136:1–9), but no fully personal I-Thou relationship between God and human beings is affirmed in the Old Testament. What the Old Testament calls the love of God, especially for the people of the covenant, could also characterize the relationship between a master and a slave.

> Goodness, forbearance, mercy, solicitude, are attributes that can also characterize the master in relation to his slave. Such a relationship does not yet indicate that this caring, just, and forbearing master, in his own personal life, wants to have anything to do with this slave. Hence, he can remain distant and unapproachable.[43]

Only in Jesus Christ, according to Rahner, is such a personal self-giving love of God revealed (Rom. 5:8: "But God shows his love for us in that while we were yet sinners Christ died for us"; 1 Jn. 4:9: "In this the love of God was made manifest among us, that God sent his only Son into the world"; Tit. 3:4: "The goodness and the loving kindness of God our savior appeared").

> In this reality of Christ the love of God is actually and genuinely present for the first time. It has appeared (*epephane*) in the world only in the reality of Christ, it has for the first time, made itself objective (*synistesin:* Rom. 5:8), and through this real presence in the world it has been revealed.[44]

God's self-communication in Jesus Christ, while being a genuine self-communication of God, is nevertheless a unique and unexpected event, one that is wholly dependent upon God's free decision to love us.

Clearly, the main lines of Rahner's interpretation of the New Testament are correct. The New Testament authors do not engage in metaphysical speculation concerning the essence of God. Further, the only God the New Testament authors know is one who is sovereign and free, and whose love for human persons is always experienced as grace, a free gift. But, it seems to me, Rahner's interpretation of the New Testament view of the gratuity of the divine love for others is inadequate at two points. First, Rahner goes beyond the New Testament itself in speculating on an aspect of the divine essence, namely, the possibility that God could have refused absolutely to bestow God's love upon human beings. The New Testament simply proclaims that love is the very essence of God's actual dealings with the world. Second, in fact, it is only on the basis of the view that God is nothing but love that the themes of election, divine judgment, and the hardening of Israel (precisely the New Testament themes Rahner adduces to prove that God is free not to bestow Godself in love upon others) are understandable. Far from being a denial that God is essentially love, the electing, judging, and hardening activity of God is understood in the New Testament to be included within the divine love.

Although Rahner is right that the New Testament does not make metaphysical claims concerning God's essence, it seems to me to be fair to the New Testament to say that God is essentially love, that is, that all divine activity toward others can be characterized by love, however else the divine activity is to be characterized. It is interesting to note that although Rahner follows the argument of the article on the concept of God in the New Testament found in the *Theologisches Wörterbuch zum Neuen Testament*, there is no mention at all, in that article, of the possibility that God is free not to bestow God's love. That view of the gratuity of the divine love is Rahner's own. On the contrary, the authors of the article argue:

> 1 Jn. 4:8 ventures the bold equation: God is love. This does not mean that God is thought of in terms of an impersonal force. He is rather declared to be the origin and norm of all that can or should be called love. It is not that love is a deity. On the contrary, *the personal God is love in all his will and work*, and decisively in the work of Christ (Jn. 3:16).[45]

In another dictionary of the New Testament, this point is formulated even more sharply: "God is essentially love (1 Jn. 4:8), and his intention from the very beginning was love."[46] Contrary to what Rahner implies, the New Testament does not and cannot conceive God as acting in any fashion other than a supremely loving one. But even if love is "essential" to God in this sense, that is, as a characteristic of all divine activity, this still does not, for the New Testament, determine how God will act in any given concrete situation, other than to say that, somehow, God's loving purpose will be furthered in all that God does.

When Rahner argues that human beings must reckon with a speech or a silence of God, a self-bestowal or a self-refusal of God, he seems to be speculating on matters the New Testament never considers. The New Testament does not view the God-human relationship, from God's perspective, to be essentially ambiguous or bivalent. Nor do the New Testament authors ask the question "how does this self-evident God, who is always already given . . . act."[47] The New Testament proclaims, on the basis of God's historical activity, that God is love. But the New Testament never raises the question whether the situation could have been otherwise, that is, whether God could have refused to give Godself in love to human beings.

A number of New Testament texts, which Rahner does not seem to take into account sufficiently in "*Theos* im Neuen Testament," make this clear. Although he cites texts from the synoptic gospels to show that God is conceived to be merciful and loving, these texts do not seem to inform his understanding of the gratuity of the divine love. Precisely because God is not conceived to be anything other than a loving father, a central element of the proclamation of Jesus in the synoptic gospels is that persons should not fear or be anxious about their lives. God can be addressed as father. Even the more familiar form "abba" is appropriate. God cares for us and we can trust God completely with our lives. God feeds the birds and clothes the wild flowers. Likewise, God is aware of our needs, especially since we are much more valuable than birds or wildflowers (Mt. 6:25–31). God is aware of the falling of the tiniest sparrow, and the hairs of our heads are numbered (Mt. 10:29–31). Since even sinful human parents care and provide for their children, God, Jesus says, will certainly provide for God's human children (Mt. 7:9–11). Because God is aware of our needs and will care for us, we can turn to God when we are anxious and weary (Mt. 11:28–30). All of these passages show that the love of God for others is presupposed in the proclamation of Jesus.

Of course it is the Johannine literature that explicitly claims that God cannot be conceived without the divine love. This is emphasized in the Gospel of John by Jesus' references to the relationship of love that exists between God and the eternal Logos (3:35, 10:17, 15:9, 17:23–26). Even before the foundations of the world, God in Godself is love (17:24). Love is not simply one of God's possibilities, but is characteristic of all that God is and does. Because God loves the world, the Logos is made flesh so that the world might be redeemed (3:16). God's love for human persons then becomes the pattern for the new community of the redeemed (1 Jn. 4:16–21).

The christological hymn fragments found in the Pauline literature are important in this context. In Colossians 2:15–20 creation itself is viewed as being an event of the divine love since it is precisely the preexistent Christ who is the agent of creation.

Thus creation itself is already a moment within the redemptive plan of God's love, for it is this cosmic Christ who is humbled and humiliated for the sake of the redemption of human beings (Phil. 2:6–11).

All of these passages indicate that the New Testament views love to be characteristic of the divine activity as such. It is not viewed simply as one of God's possibilities, one that, in fact, was actualized, as Rahner claims.

However, Rahner is right that the New Testament understands the divine love of others to be grace, a free, unmerited gift, even if this redeeming love is that which is longed for by the whole creation (Rom. 8:22). But, once again, the New Testament nowhere defends the gratuitous character of the divine love by arguing that God's love for human beings might not have been bestowed at all.

Rahner writes that God's love, according to the authors of the synoptic gospels, is addressed to the poor, the weak, the sinful, and the outcast. But he does not seem to recognize that this is precisely the reason the divine love or mercy is a free gift. God's love is a gift, in this literature, because there are no preconditions that determine who is eligible to receive God's favor. In fact, the forgiving love of God is addressed, first of all, to those who, in the eyes of the religious establishment, have no claim to God's favor: the poor, the sinners, the outcasts. For the writers of the synoptic gospels, the divine love is gratuitous not because God need not have bestowed God's love at all, but because it comes so unexpectedly without taking into account common human standards of merit. This is the point of a number of Jesus' parables. The reign of God, which is a reign of forgiving love, is like a vineyard owner who pays all laborers the same wage even though some worked all day, while others worked nine hours, six hours, three hours, or only one hour (Mt. 20:1–16). The same gift or reward is given freely to all, regardless of what each worker seems to have earned. God is like a noble who goes out to the outcasts to bring them into a great banquet when the invited guests fail to appear (Lk. 14:16–24). These persons who were brought in had no right to be at the banquet. Their inclusion was an unexpected event arising from the love and mercy of the host of the banquet. Likewise, in the parables of the lost sheep, the lost coin, and the lost son in Luke

15, God is portrayed as one who rejoices more over the redemption of the lost than the piety of the righteous, whose love is active and seeks the lost and is not discouraged by the rebellion of the beloved.

Jesus' own activity enacts this redemptive love of God. Jesus seeks out the sinners, the poor, the outcast, the women. He dines with Zacchaeus, a man shunned by the religious establishment (Lk. 19:1–9). He allows a sinful woman to bathe his feet, much to the consternation of his Pharisee host (Lk. 7:36–50).

This would seem to indicate that the writers of the synoptic gospels never ask the question whether God could refuse to bestow God's love, let alone understand the gratuitous character of God's love to be grounded in such a possibility. Jesus proclaims and inaugurates, with his healings and exorcisms, the presence of the reign of God in which God's forgiving love is offered to those who would seem to have no claim to the divine favor. God's love is "grace" (the word, of course, is hardly used at all in the synoptic gospels), a free gift, because it is wholly unanticipated by its recipients. The question here is not: how does God act toward me (i.e., in self-bestowal or self-refusal), but is rather: since the reign of God is here, will I open myself to God's reign by acting graciously and lovingly toward others in their concrete situation (Mt. 25:31–46), or will I deal more harshly with others than God has dealt with me and thus experience the coming of God's reign as the most radical condemnation possible (Mt. 18:23–35)?

Likewise, in Paul, the gratuitous character of God's love lies not in the fact that God might not have bestowed God's love, but rather in the fact that no one deserves God's love: neither the Gentile who lives outside of the Law, nor the Pharisee who has scrupulously obeyed the Law (Rom. 7). This is the meaning of "grace" operative in Romans 3:22b–26:

> For there is no distinction [between Gentile and Jew]; since all have sinned and fallen short of the glory of God, they are justified by his grace as a gift, through the redemption which is in Christ Jesus; whom God put forward as an expiation by his blood, to be received by faith. This was to show God's righteousness, because in his divine forbearance he had passed over former sins; it was to prove at the present time that he himself is righteous and that he justifies him who has faith in Jesus.

The reason, it seems to me, the human person cannot question the justice of God's election is not, as Rahner implies, that God could refuse to love any persons at all, but rather, is because no one is worthy of God's love. We have all sinned and deserve only death as our wages. Eternal life is a free gift of God's love (Rom. 6:23). Paul does not conclude from this that God might not have bestowed God's love at all.

The gratuity of God's love, for Paul, consists in the fact that there are no preconditions that need to be met before a person can be justified, not even obedience to the Law. We are justified by grace, not by works. Justification is an expression of God's righteousness, not a reward for our own righteousness. It is in this sense that God's love is sovereign, for it is not merited, but is received only in faith. For Paul, grace would cease to be grace not if, as Rahner's view entails, God cannot be conceived other than as self-bestowing love, but only if grace is conceived as the result of human effort, attained "on the basis of works" (Rom. 1:6).

Thus, contrary to Rahner's claim that God's love is gratuitous in the New Testament because "God himself, on his own part, sovereignly bestows or refuses his merciful love," grace is gratuitous, in the New Testament, because it is God's free gift to those who do not deserve God's favor due to their sin. Whether God is love or not is not a question the New Testament raises. The "essential" love of God is presupposed. This love is gratuitous because the reason I, in my present sinful state, am addressed by God's justifying love depends not on my works, but solely on the righteousness of God. The love of God for human beings does not thereby lose its quality as a gift and become a self-evident, timeless truth. God's love is always an event, a free gift, because it demands that I decide whether or not I will accept this gift in faith, renouncing any righteousness or merit I might seem to have. As Bultmann says in relation to Paul, "God's grace is not His hitherto unknown or misconceived graciousness, but is His now occurring act of grace."[48] For Rahner, there is a sense in which grace is more than this. The bestowal of grace, in his view, also represents the settling of the question as to whether the God who would be God whether God bestowed or refused Godself actually has chosen to love human beings or not.

The New Testament writers seek to defend the sheer gratuity and sovereignty of God's love. But they are unwilling to do this at the cost of affirming that God might not have loved human beings at all. The only silence of God the New Testament knows anything about is the apparent divine silence caused by human unwillingness to attend to God's speech (Rom. 10:21). When Rahner speaks of the silence or self-refusal of God as if it were a genuine possibility for God, he has entered into an area of reflection that is foreign to the New Testament.

At times, in *"Theos* im Neuen Testament," Rahner seeks to defend his view of the gratuity of the divine love by appealing to a distinction between the experience of God portrayed in the Old Testament and the experience of God that is to be had in Jesus Christ. He implies that God is known to be fully personal love only in the New Testament. In the Old Testament, God is, at best, a benevolent master.

Such a view, first of all, would not seem to interpret the Old Testament witness of faith adequately. One clear result of recent biblical scholarship is that the facile distinction between the loving God of the New Testament and the judging (or merely benevolent) God of the Old Testament cannot be defended. God, for the Old Testament, as well as for the rabbinic Judaism of Jesus' time, is a God of fully personal love.[49]

Further, the New Testament writers do not understand themselves to be proclaiming something absolutely new when they say that God is love, that God draws near to human beings in forgiveness and mercy. Rather, the New Testament writers understand themselves to be proclaiming the decisive, eschatological re-presentation of God's one, eternal plan for the world, a plan that has been presented clearly since the creation of the world itself.

Rahner cites the passage in Hebrews in which it is said that God has spoken to us in these last days through God's own Son. But he does not indicate that the loving God who speaks eschatologically through the Son is the same God who spoke in various ways to Israel through the prophets, and who spoke protologically through the Son in creating the world. For the Son is the very image of God, the one through whom God created all things (Heb. 1:1–3). The question whether or not God is love is not settled for the first time by the eschatological coming of the Son. Instead, this question was already settled in the creation of the world itself. God's one redemptive plan is as old as creation, and is not proclaimed for the first time by the Son in these last days.

Likewise, in the prologue to the Gospel of John, the Logos that becomes flesh is none other than the Logos who was with God at the beginning, who was God, and through whom God created the world. The incarnation of the Logos does not inaugurate a new speech of God, nor does it break God's silence. Rather, to mix the metaphor in the same way that the author of the Gospel of John does, this word or Logos is the light that has enlightened every human person that has ever come into the world.

Thus, the New Testament writers do not view their proclamation of Christ to be a wholly new message. It is rather the final and decisive utterance of the God who has always been love, who has always desired just one thing: the establishment of a loving communion between Godself and the creatures.

Rahner not only seems to speculate about a possibility of God that the New Testament knows nothing about, namely, that God could have utterly refused Godself, but, in fact, the passages that would seem to support Rahner's view of the gratuity of the divine love most strongly can only be understood properly if God is conceived to be essentially love. The passages I am referring to, of course, are those that portray God as a God of judgment and of election, who hardens the heart of Israel, God's own chosen people. It seems to me that Rahner views the love of God and the judging, electing, and hardening activity of God as being, in a certain sense, equiprimordial in God, while the New Testament understands the latter to be included within the divine love and not to be a contrary possibility set over against God's love.

Bultmann has shown convincingly, I think, that, in the synoptic gospels, the judgment of God proclaimed by Jesus is not a denial of God's forgiving love.[50] Rather, it is precisely the nearness of God in forgiving love that demands of me that I make the radical decision whether I will open myself to God's forgiving love or not. It is my own unwillingness to put away all of my pretensions and accept God's reign as a child that transforms God's nearness in mercy into judgment and condemnation.

> Thus it is clear that Jesus in this connection too does not preach a new idea of God—as if God had hitherto been represented as too arbitrary and hard, vindictive and angry, and was rather to be thought of as benevolent and gracious. On the contrary. . . . No one has spoken more

> forcefully of the wrath of God (although without using the word) than Jesus, precisely because he proclaims God's grace. . . . God is a God of the present, because His claim confronts man in the present moment, and He is at the same time God of the future, because He gives man freedom for the present instant of decision, and sets before him as the future which is opened to him by his decision, condemnation or mercy. God is God of the present for the sinner precisely because he casts him into remoteness from Himself and He is at the same time God of the future because He never relinquishes His claim on the sinner and opens to him by forgiveness a new future for new obedience.[51]

Rahner's strongest evidence for his claim that the New Testament holds that God is free to bestow or refuse God's love is to be found in Romans 8–11, where Paul discusses God's election and the hardening of the Jews. Rahner rightly claims that, for Paul, "the loving call of God is always a call of his *prothesis*, an election." But Paul does not infer from the fact that God elects some to justification and glorification that God could have refused lovingly to elect any persons. This negative possibility is not even considered in the affirmation of the electing or predestining activity of God in Romans 8:28–39. Indeed, the point of this passage would seem to be found in the positive assertion of verses 35–39 that we cannot be separated from the love of God precisely because that love is sovereign and unthreatened by any created power.

Rahner infers from Romans 9–11 that God can be conceived as one who need not have bestowed God's love upon human beings at all, that is, that in principle there is a certain bivalence that characterizes the human relation to God. It seems to me, on the contrary, that the issue of whether God is love or not is not raised in Romans 9:6–18 at all. What the discussion of the loving of Jacob and the "hating" of Esau shows is that, once again, God's love is gratuitous because it has no reference to human merit. The reason Esau, the elder, must serve Jacob, the younger, has nothing to do with their relative merits, for neither had yet been born or had done anything good or evil. God's mercy is not exacted by human beings on the basis of works, but results solely from God's own righteousness (Rom. 9:11).

Further, far from being a denial that God is love, the phenomenon of the hardening of Israel is for Paul a manifestation of the divine love. Paul argues, in Romans 9:14–33 and 11:1–36, that, contrary to appearances, the hardening of Israel neither represents a denial of God's love, nor a failure of God to remain faithful to God's own promises and historical initiatives. Paul affirms that God's gifts and call, that is, God's mercy and love, are irrevocable (Rom 11:29). He does not draw the conclusion from the hardening of Israel that God has as a real possibility ultimate self-refusal or silence. Rather, the hardening of Israel furthers God's own loving plan of redemption. The hardening of Israel allows for the inclusion of the Gentiles, the wild olive branches that are grafted in. The offer of salvation addressed to the Gentiles will make the Jews jealous (11:11). The final inclusion of the Jews in God's redemption will be all the more meaningful precisely because the temporary exclusion of the Jews made it possible for God's love to be bestowed upon all persons (11:12). The hardening of the Jews does not represent a denial of God's redemptive plan but rather is the means by which all Israel, that is, the whole of humanity as recipients of the promise of God, will be saved (11:25–26). Thus, God remains a God of love even in hardening Israel, even in sending the spirit of stupor (11:8), for the sole purpose of these acts is to bring the greatest possible number of persons into communion with the God who is love.

God, for Paul in Romans 9–11, is indeed sovereign and can have mercy upon whom God will and harden whom God will (9:15, 18). However, the sovereignty of God is not a denial, but an expression, of God's love and mercy. God's act of hardening or of condemnation is not viewed by Paul to be an equiprimordial possibility along with the act of divine love of others. Rather, "God has consigned all men to disobedience, that he may have mercy upon all" (11:32). God's condemning of human sin does not negate God's love, but points out that God's love is wholly unmerited by human beings since all have sinned. The concluding passage of Romans 9–11, which begins "O the depth of the riches and wisdom and knowledge of God! How unsearchable are his judgments and how inscrutable his ways!" (11:33), draws our attention not to the possibility that God could have refused God's love absolutely, but to the fact that God's love is manifested even in the hardening of the Jews. God's judgments are unsearchable and God's ways inscrutable not, as Rahner's view implies, because God in fact loves us even though God might just as well have not loved us, but rather because all that

God does, even the hardening of Israel (an act that seems to call God's love into question), is an expression of God's free love for those who do not merit the divine favor.

Rahner's view that God could be God without bestowing God's love upon the world, which implies that God is not essentially love of others, is inadequate, therefore, because it is not fully faithful to the apostolic witness of scripture. Rahner conceives a divine possibility (that God could act in a nonloving fashion relative to the world) that is unknown to the authors of the New Testament, and does not seem fully to realize that the New Testament view of the divine love is broad enough to include the divine judgment, election, and hardening of human persons as a moment within itself.

Is Rahner's View Justified by Human Experience?

It seems to me that Rahner's view that God is not essentially love of others is also inadequate when judged by the ability of such a view to illuminate our common human experience. I would argue that a condition of the possibility of our most fundamental experience of ourselves as free agents related to other free agents is precisely the love of God for other individuals. That is, if God were not essentially love of others, then our own experience of ourselves would not be possible. And if God is not conceived within Christian theology to be essentially love, then that theology does not adequately reflect upon our basic experience of ourselves as it must to be a fully adequate Christian theology.

Rahner would affirm that the love or grace of God is a necessary ingredient in concrete human experience. But he holds, in principle, that human being is conceivable without the personal love of God for human being. For him, human being is conceivable as oriented solely toward God as holy mystery. What I want to argue here is that human being is not even conceivable unless God is related to human persons in fully personal love (as opposed to a metaphysical sense of love that reduces to benevolence). Not only would human being be different if grace were not an element of the concrete world order, as Rahner claims, in fact, *no* world order would be possible if God were not essentially love of others. This is to say, in my view, that God can be affirmed to be love on strictly secular or "natural" grounds, while, for Rahner, the love of God for others is a revealed or a supernatural datum.[52]

It is important, however, to recognize the important truth that is expressed in Rahner's claim that the assertion that God is love is much more than a self-evident metaphysical proposition. According to Rahner, metaphysical reflection, including reflection on the divine reality, expresses literal, formal truths that are strictly necessary, but abstract and even empty.[53] Metaphysics, which, for Rahner, always means *transcendental* metaphysics, uncovers the necessary conditions of human experience as such. Metaphysics reveals the logical structure of existence, but is in a certain sense neutral with respect to the concrete details of existence. Rahner argues:

> If philosophy, relative to its entire tradition, understands itself to be transcendental reflection, then it must be said that such reflection does not adequately retrieve materially the concreteness of human existence, although that which is concrete itself is experienced as grounding existence and not as an indifferent remainder. Historicity is something less than actual history; concrete love is something more (not less) than formally analyzed subjectivity (ability and need to love); experienced dread is more (not less!) than the concept of the basic situation of man.[54]

Obviously, for Rahner, in our actual existence as persons we are more than metaphysicians, we are concerned with the concrete details of our existence. Thus, persons must express the meaning of their existence in ways that are not strictly metaphysical. This applies also to talk about God. Rahner is clear that the real interest of the Christian faith is not in the metaphysical essence of God, but in God's concrete activity toward us (although he never denies that talk about God's concrete activity implies certain metaphysical truths about God[55]). Persons use nonliteral or figurative language to speak of God's concrete activity, language derived from our concrete experience and its details, rather than from the strictly formal and abstract conditions of that experience.

Rahner argues that the claim "God is love" is just such a nonliteral use of language relative to God.[56] However, to say that the assertion "God is love" is not a formal truth of metaphysics, but is instead a figurative or symbolic utterance, does not mean that "God is love" is to be taken less seriously, or is less important, than such metaphysical assertions as "God exists" or "God is the ground of being." Rahner would agree with Paul Tillich's classic statement that the phrase "only a symbol" should be avoided since it implies that nonliteral language is less true than the literal or formal language of metaphysics.[57] Indeed, for Rahner, if love is the fundamental act of human being, the act in which our whole being is gathered together and fully expressed, and if we are to conceive God not in terms of categories derived from our experience of external things, but rather in terms of categories derived from our immediate, existentiell experience of ourselves, then there could be no more appropriate or important way of speaking of God than by using the symbolic phrase "God is love."

As I will show more fully in Chapters IX and XI of this study, all of this seems to me to be entirely correct. If this were all Rahner affirmed in his claim that "God is love" is not a metaphysical assertion concerning the divine essence, then I would have no criticism to make of his position. However, as I have shown, this claim also means for him that God need not bestow Godself in fully personal love upon others in order to be God and that human being need not be the object of God's fully personal love in order to be human being. This means that "God is love" is not only a nonliteral assertion concerning the divine being, but is also an assertion concerning the divine being that can only be true contingently or accidentally. God's love of others, for Rahner, is strictly nonessential. It is this claim that I want to question on the basis of human experience itself. It seems to me that "God is love," while not a literal, formal assertion of metaphysics, is nevertheless an assertion that must be true necessarily. That is to say, neither the divine being nor human being is even conceivable unless God is a God who in some appropriate fashion loves all other individuals and unless human being is grounded essentially in the divine love.

It is Rahner himself who provides the foundations for an argument that God is essentially love, that is, that neither God nor human being can be conceived unless God is love. He shows most perceptively and persuasively that the divine love, the divine self-communication, is a necessary condition of the possibility of the distinctive spiritual activity of concrete human beings. For him, the loving God who communicates Godself to

us is the ground of the trust in the fundamental meaning and
worth of our existence that is a condition of the possibility of our
activity as free persons. God is both the transcendental *Wor-aufhin* of human freedom and an immanent principle within the
free human person. Implicit in all human activity is a drive or a
striving toward self-realization. This striving is both a striving
toward God, in that all human activity is made possible through
a *Vorgriff* of the absolute being of God as the horizon within
which such activity takes place, and a striving that is grounded in
God. Rahner says that God is not the guarantee and fulfillment
of the meaning of human existence simply by virtue of being the
creator of that which fulfills our existentiell striving. Rather, the
divine being itself, through the self-communication of God,
through grace, is the goal and fulfillment of human being.[58]
The goal of human striving is immediately imparted to human
persons, thus energizing the striving by providing the confidence that it is not in vain.

> God in absolute immediacy is, in the concrete order of
> reality, not only the fulfillment, the goal *("beatitudo objec-
> tiva")* of the spiritual creature, but is the most proper, the
> necessary, and the only truly co-natural principle of the
> movement toward the fulfillment of this goal. The final
> true movement toward fulfillment, toward the goal, oc-
> curs "in the goal."[59]

What does it mean when Rahner says that the goal of our
striving itself is a co-natural principle of the striving? Chiefly, it
seems to me, it means that the transcendental awareness that all
persons have of the love of God (given in divine self-communication) provides the confidence that our striving for self-realization and self-fulfillment is worthwhile and not futile. God is
experienced as the love that shelters us, affirms us as having final
value, and accepts us. God is that final reality, that ultimate
person, to whom we "can flee from the uncanniness of the empty
and threatened character of [our] own life."[60] God's love is our
final home, our final refuge in which we find shelter, comfort,
and forgiveness.

The God who communicates Godself to us in love is experienced to be our absolute future. God is the encompassing love
into which all human paths lead. It is the reality of God, as the
absolute future, that guarantees that our activity as persons is
finally valid and meaningful. All persons, at a transcendental

level, realize that their free acts as persons are not simply mo-
mentary occurrences that pass away into insignificance as they
are surpassed by further free acts. Rather, for Rahner, the
essential meaning of freedom is that persons, in their finitude
and history, nevertheless accomplish something of permanent
validity and meaning. He writes that in a free moral decision:

> The subject posits itself as finally valid [*end-gültig*]. In this
> decision, the subject is immediately given, in its essence
> and realization, as that which is incommensurable with
> passing time. . . . [W]here such an act of lonely decision
> is done, in absolute obedience to the higher law or in the
> radical yes of love to another person, something eternal
> occurs, and man becomes immediately aware of his va-
> lidity as something that arises in time but that occurs
> beyond its mere onward flow.[61]

But the human subject does not attain such an "eternity" strictly
on its own accord. Rather, this final validity of the human person
lies in the reality of God Godself, for it is the divine being that is
the absolute future of the world. The self-communicative activity of the absolute future makes concrete acts of existentiell
decision possible.

Because of the divine love, which is communicated immediately to all persons, radical cynicism or nihilism can only be,
according to Rahner, self-contradictory attitudes. That is to say,
all human activity, including acts of radical doubt, self-denial, or
suicide, are made possible by a prior affirmation of God as the
horizon, ground, absolute future, and inner dynamic of human
freedom. God's love for us gives persons the courage to act
morally, to create the eternal in obedience and love, even though
we know ourselves to be mortal. It is the divine love that gives us
a trust in the meaning of life that does not capitulate in the face
of death.[62] The radical hope that characterizes human being is a
hope "in the spirit of God."[63] For it is a hope based upon our
experience that the final mystery of our existence, God, does not
remain indifferent to us, but communicates itself in love to us as
the final meaning of our existence.

According to Rahner, the problem of confidence or trust in
the meaning of life is especially acute in the modern world
because of a new sense of our own radical freedom.[64] We no
longer experience ourselves to be subject to the powers of fate or
nature. Indeed, modern persons understand themselves to be

condemned to be free. We must make of ourselves whatever we are to be. There are two results of this heightened sense of human freedom. On the one hand, persons have a stronger sense of their own responsibility for all other persons and of the seriousness of existence. On the other hand, it is our own freedom (rather than nature) that appears to be dark, uncontrollable, and threatening. Persons come to dread their own freedom. Rahner argues that it is the reality of God, precisely as the God who loves us and communicates Godself to us in grace, that gives us the courage to act responsibly and humanely toward others.

> For the final, absolute ground of all responsibility of freedom and power . . . is called God. And when we speak of God, even if we give him no name and timidly look away from him, we mean precisely the one whom we encounter when we experience the power and breadth of our freedom falling down upon us as an immense burden and yet do not cowardly avoid this truth of our existence.[65]

Likewise, it is the God who is love to whom we can entrust our uncontrollable freedom, for God is experienced as the reality that shelters the mystery of our freedom. Because of the reality of God, human persons have the confidence to risk exercising their freedom.

For Rahner, it is the God of love who communicates Godself to human persons, who is the ground of the free, moral decision and action that is characteristic of human being. Put differently, the reality of the divine love for us is a condition of the possibility of the spiritual activity that characterizes the essence of human being. It is the reality of God's love that is the ground of our confidence in the meaning and value of our own lives and actions that is a necessary condition of our free action as persons. Rahner argues that human existence is characterized by a necessary, transcendental courage.[66] This courage is not a particular aspect of human existence among others, it is not "the courage to be able to do this or that, but is rather the courage that is directed towards oneself in the one totality of [one's] human reality."[67] It is the "courage to have total hope in the well being of our existence as a whole."[68] It is the courage to act, to be a person, to be ourselves as such. This radical courage or hope is grounded upon the reality of God. It is a courageous hope in God Godself as that which fulfills human existence. But this courageous hope in the final meaning of our lives is, for Rahner, a response to God's free act of self-communication. This transcendental courage or hope that characterizes concrete human being is precisely what is meant, in the Christian tradition, by faith. It is courage or hope based upon the immediate presence of the Holy Spirit, that is, God as one who in love redeems human persons from meaninglessness. One of the functions of explicit religious language concerning God is to allow persons to re-cognize (wiedererkennen) on a thematic level the transcendental, unthematic confidence in the meaning and value of life they always already have.[69]

All of this, however, is true only of concrete human being for Rahner. Human being is conceivable without the self-bestowal of the divine love. God as love, for him is indeed "the one, encompassing answer to the one, total question that man is, . . . the goal and the fulfillment of the meaning of man," but only in "pure grace."[70] Likewise, Rahner argues that the radical, courageous hope that characterizes concrete human being is grounded in the strictly gratuitous event of divine love or self-communication. He says:

> That God in himself is the object of hope; that the movement of spirit and of freedom beyond all individual things, which can be grasped one after the other, does not finally lead into emptiness; that this movement does not finally stop with an individual reality, a "creaturely" good, however important, as its only real possible fulfillment, but rather arrives at God himself, the primordial fullness and creative ground of all individual realities; that God himself is the absolute future of our hope: all this is not simply our own self-evident possibility, but is rather a gift that also could have been denied to us. It is already grace.[71]

Human being is conceivable solely as a *potentia oboedientialis* for the love of God. Human being is indeed fulfilled by the personal love of God for human being, but human being is conceivable without this final, supernatural fulfillment.[72] In fact, if the divine love were given necessarily with human existence as such, according to Rahner, this love would not be the fulfillment of human being. The essence of human being, for him, is precisely openness to the free, unexacted love of God. Human being would still be oriented toward the divine love as its goal, even if this love were refused. But persons could only hope that such a

goal, personal intimacy to God, could be obtained. There would
be no firm confidence that human being would be fulfilled in the
divine love, for God would remain solely the asymptotic goal of
human striving, refusing to give Godself as the co-natural, immanent, energizing principle of that striving. Rahner writes that
God's

> . . . final, definitive relationship to the spiritual creature
> cannot be known [naturally], because the question re-
> mains unanswered, in this kind of natural, transcenden-
> tal relationship to God, whether God intends to be for us
> the infinity that holds us, in our finitude, at a distance
> and that, remaining silent, closes itself up within itself, or
> intends to be the radical nearness of self-communica-
> tion.[73]

In the hypothetical situation in which God refuses God's
love or self-communication to human beings, a situation that has
never actually been given, but that Rahner holds must be conceivable if the love of God is to be strictly gratuitous, God would
be given to human spirit as a question but not as an answer.
While Rahner argues that human being still would have a genuine meaning and a real possibility of existing as spirit under
such conditions, talk of a radical fulfillment of such a human
person oriented solely to a self-refusing God would have to be
abandoned.

> It is to be noticed that even with respect to the pre-
> destination to salvation and to the efficacious grace of
> God, Catholic theology teaches the same gratuity, al-
> though, of course, without these realities a "natural
> fulfillment" is not even conceivable. One can indeed
> construe a "natural" positive final validity of the decision
> of freedom to be, in itself, a meaningful reality and a
> limit concept [ein Grenzbegriff] under the hypothesis of a
> refusal of the supernatural elevation of man (in order to
> clarify the gratuity of the love that God himself commu-
> nicates), but one should not call this positive, moral final-
> ity full-fillment [Voll-endung]. From this an image unfolds
> of a purely immanent fulfillment in the sense that this
> would be merely the finality of man through his own
> essential powers alone.[74]

I think Paul Wess is closer to the truth when he argues that
"a standing before the God who remains silent would mean
precisely the greatest unhappiness of man who is oriented to this

God; it would mean his ultimate and total solitude."[75] It seems to me, in the final analysis, that human being oriented to an absolutely self-refusing God not only would not be fulfilled or would be supremely unhappy and unfortunate, but could not exist at all. That is to say, for reasons Rahner himself gives, human being oriented solely toward God as question, and not as the self-communicating answer to the human question concerning meaning, is impossible, inconceivable. Rahner seems to say, on the one hand, that the divine love for us is that reality that grounds our fundamental existentiell confidence in the meaning and worth of existence. It is this confidence that allows human persons to act in freedom, to dare to act responsibly and lovingly. This confidence, according to Rahner, is affirmed in all human spiritual activity, for it is indeed a condition of the possibility of free, personal, moral action. However, on the other hand, Rahner asserts that human being must be conceivable as *spirit* without the bestowal of God's love, for, otherwise, the divine love would not be strictly gratuitous.

It is not clear to me what meaning, beyond a merely verbal meaning, human spirit can have if the ground of the existentiell confidence that makes the most characteristic activity of human spirit possible (the divine love) is to be conceived as nonessential to human being. For Rahner consistently maintains that free, moral action is an aspect of the essential meaning of human spirit. He also holds that moral activity is possible for human being that is not supernaturally elevated by the divine love. But, as I have tried to show in this section, he claims that it is precisely our implicit awareness of God's love for us that gives us the confidence and courageous hope necessary to undertake such free, moral activity. Once again, Rahner's thought seems to be impaled upon the horns of a dilemma. Either he maintains that the divine love is nonessential to human being, implying that human spirit is conceivable without the free moral activity made possible by our confidence in the meaning and worth of existence that is grounded in the divine love (thus contradicting a central tenet of his theological anthropology); or, if free moral action, and thus a basic existentiell confidence in the meaning and worth of existence, is viewed as being essential to the meaning of human spirit, then he is forced to maintain that the divine love, as a condition of the possibility of this essential aspect of human being, is itself essential, rather than nonessential, to human being (thus contradicting a central tenet of his view of God).

Although he never explicitly says so, Rahner would probably respond to this charge by saying that there is a sense in which God, solely as holy mystery, as the aloof *Woraufhin* of human transcendence, can provide the existentiell confidence presupposed by the free, moral activity of human persons. He does argue, for instance, that God, "prior" to the communication of the divine love in grace, is the absolute value or worth that is affirmed in all particular value judgments, even in a decision, such as suicide, that seems to be a denial of any final value.[76] I think it can be shown, however, that only a God of personal love can adequately ground the confidence we all implicitly have concerning the meaning and worth of existence. A God who is not essentially love of others, that is, a God who could remain totally aloof from God's creatures as their asymptotic *Woraufhin*, cannot be the ground of the confidence in the meaning of existence that human persons affirm in all their acts, even in self-contradictory acts of radical doubt, cynicism, or suicide.[77] It makes little sense to say that I trust someone who remains indifferent to my plight, for to put trust in someone presupposes, at the very least, that that person is aware of my situation and will act appropriately toward me. It makes even less sense to say that I can put my *ultimate* trust in a God who can remain silent toward me, who is unaffected by, and indifferent to, my situation. The only reality that can ground my absolutely fundamental trust in the meaning of existence is a God who is essentially love, whose very nature is to be eminently sympathetic to God's creatures. If God could genuinely and finally remain silent toward me, could refuse to give Godself to me in a personal, loving sense (even if only in principle), then God would not be the final ground of the existentiell confidence in the meaning and value of existence I evince in my every act, but would be the aloof, uncaring judge who damns me finally to my own fears and doubts. If God is not essentially love, then the human striving for self-realization, which presupposes a fundamental confidence in the meaning and value of existence, would be futile.

The only sufficient ground of the ultimate human confidence in the meaning and worth of existence is a God who is intimately related to human persons in love, and not a God who can also remain simply the asymptotic horizon of human transcendence. Human existence is not sufficiently illuminated conceptually if our confidence or hope in the meaning and worth of existence is not grounded in ultimate reality. For the reasons that Rahner himself gives, it seems that human activity is explicable only if all persons are aware necessarily, if only implicitly, that they are accepted and loved by the final mystery that encompasses them, God. Without such a confidence that is grounded in ultimate reality human being is not even conceivable.

Thus, it seems to me, Rahner's account of the conditions under which the assertion "God is love" could be judged to be true is inadequate. For Rahner, "God is love" is capable only of contingent truth. It can be a true assertion if and only if the God who is given necessarily to human persons as the *Woraufhin* of transcendence has contingently bestowed Godself upon human persons in fully personal love. This is a revealed truth, one that cannot be determined by an analysis of human nature alone. But, as I have tried to show, if there are human beings at all, which, of course, is a contingent state of affairs, then "God is love" is an assertion that can only be true necessarily. This is to say that human existence as such is conceivable only if it is grounded in the divine love. Human being, with its characteristic confidence in the meaning and worth of existence, is possible only if God is a God of personal love. Now, I think Rahner is precisely right when he argues that the characteristic human courage or hope is not simply an ultimate human *self*-confidence, but is rather faith, the acceptance of God as the ground and absolute future of our courage and hope. The question is not whether this courage or hope is a faithful response to the reality of God or not. Rather, the question is whether human being is conceivable without such a courageous hope that is grounded in the personal love of God. According to Rahner, human being is possible even if the personal love of God were not to be bestowed. I have tried to show the inadequacy of such a view on the basis of an analysis of our common human experience.

Is God Free Not to Love Others?

Rahner would probably respond to the claim that human being is not even conceivable without the love of God for human persons by saying that, in such a view, the love or grace of God is

exacted by human beings. An initial response to this charge
might be that it is not a question of human being exacting God's
love, but is rather a question of how God is to be conceived so
that both the apostolic witness of scripture and our human
experience of our radical confidence in the meaning and worth
of existence can be taken with full seriousness. Similarly, it is not
a question, for Rahner, of human being exacting or demanding
the existence of God as the *Woraufhin* of human transcendence.
Rather, God is affirmed to be the *Woraufhin* of the *Vorgriff*,
because only in this way are the conditions of the possibility of
human knowledge and freedom fully illuminated.

But the more crucial question Rahner would surely want to
press is not addressed by such a response. The question might
be raised concerning the sense in which the divine love for
others, when understood to be essential to God, is still the free
gift the New Testament so clearly proclaims it to be. It might be
objected that in such a view the divine love for others is nothing
more than a natural outpouring of the divine essence, and not
the free self-bestowal of the divine person, to employ Rahner's
distinction. Thus, it might be objected that it is not Rahner's
view, but rather the view that love of others is essential to God
that fails adequately to conceive the divine reality as fully personal love.

An adequate response to this important objection cannot be
made until Chapter XI of this study where I seek to outline an
alternative understanding of the divine freedom. I will also
suggest, in Chapter X, that Rahner's own view of the divine
freedom is internally inconsistent in that he understands the
divine freedom in a way that contradicts our fundamental experience of our own freedom. But in this present context, I will try
to show that Rahner's view of the divine freedom is inadequate
in that he applies to God a mode of existence in relation to other
persons, namely, one of final and complete refusal to give
oneself in love to other persons, that, if actualized in a human
person, would be judged to be an inauthentic mode of existence.

Rahner is right to point out that the love of one human
person for an other is a free gift precisely because the other
person could refuse to open and abandon her- or himself to me
in love. There is no necessity that I love any particular human
person. I could exist even if I had not entered into a special,
unique relationship with the particular person who is my wife,

although the actuality of my life would have been very different if I had not come to love her. My loving some particular person or persons is not necessary to my being. It is a wonder or a gift of grace that my wife and I love each other precisely because we could have had a special relationship of love with other persons instead.

But to say that I, as a human person, am free to love person *a* rather than person *b*, or to love person *a* in a much more intense and intimate way than person *b*, is not to say that I am free, in the same sense, to love no other human person at all. As I have shown a number of times, love, according to Rahner, is the fundamental act of human being, the one single act in which the essence of the human person as a whole is authentically realized. This does not mean that human persons cannot refuse to love other persons, but it does mean that the person who does not open and abandon her- or himself to any other persons exists in a state of radical nonfulfillment or nonrealization of self. The possibility of loving others and the possibilities of hating or remaining indifferent to other persons are not equi-primordial. Human beings exist only as they constitute themselves in relation to other persons. Hate and indifference are not denials of the essential relatedness of human persons to other persons, but, along with love, are concrete modes of this free self-constitution in relation to other persons.[78] Johannes Heinrichs has argued, convincingly I think, that love, hate, and indifference are three qualities of the essentially dialogical nature of human being.[79] That love is a quality of relatedness to other persons is clear. But with respect to hate, and above all, indifference, Heinrichs argues:

> While hate represents a fully interpersonal relation, of a negative type to be sure (which, as such, is only to be "conceived" as the perversion of the positive relation), indifference corresponds exactly to that which Kant called "infinite judgement": the other person is encountered as not-loved, which does not mean refused, but which rather leaves undetermined an infinite realm of neutral possibilities. Insofar as no decision with respect to the other as a free and intrinsically valuable subject is made, the encounter is pre-personal. It is evident that such a relationship can only be temporary or can only last as long as a relationship of usefulness or a merely abstract legal relationship stands in the foreground.[80]

Hate and indifference are self-contradictory modes of relating oneself to others, for in hate and indifference our essential relatedness to others precisely as free persons is explicitly denied and, at the same time, transcendentally affirmed.

Therefore, hate and indifference do not represent a lack of personal relatedness to others, but are perverted forms of personal relatedness or love. Hate and indifference are related to love as -1 is related to $+1$. Human persons are free to love other persons, or to hate others, or to remain indifferent to the others to whom they are essentially related. But hate and indifference are inauthentic modes of realizing or actualizing one's essential relatedness to others. Indeed, I am free to refuse to give myself in fully personal love to any other human person, but such an act is a self-contradictory one, a perversion of love, not an absolute denial that I am a person who is realized only in love for another human person.

But Rahner understands God to be free in precisely this sense of being able to bestow Godself upon others in fully personal love, or to remain indifferent, or, at best, passively benevolent, toward the creatures. Hate, in an absolute sense, for Rahner, can have no analogue in the divine being, for God as holy mystery, God as the asymptotic ground and *Woraufhin* of all reality, already wills the good of the creatures, even if God does not enter into any personal relationship with the creatures. God could be God without loving the creatures at all. This view, it seems to me, is fundamentally inadequate. If God is in some sense the full, pure actualization of all positive perfections, and if our human experience of ourselves must provide the concepts for an understanding of these perfections, then it would seem fallacious to attribute to God a mode of existence that in our experience of ourselves could only be judged to be inauthentic, namely, the mode of existing in pre-personal indifference to other persons.

The reason hate and indifference are real, although ultimately self-stultifying, possibilities for human persons, is that human beings are finite individuals within the totality of reality. As an individual human person, I lack a comprehensive view and understanding of the situation of myself and my fellow creatures. It is not at all surprising that my decisions are characterized by an intrinsic partiality. Since I do not and cannot take into account all of the relevant conditions and consequences of my acts, since I have an imperfect understanding of the other individuals to whom I am related, I act in ways that show a partiality to my own desires and rights and to the desires and rights of those with whom I am most closely associated.

But God, by definition for Rahner, as for the Christian tradition in general, is not subject to such limitation and partiality. God is not another finite individual agent within the totality of reality, but is the totality of reality.[81] God has no external environment, but is the universal individual, the final horizon and ground of all reality. Therefore, God does have, to speak symbolically, a perfect view and understanding of the situation of Godself and of all the nondivine individuals. God takes into account all other individuals, acts for the common good of all, and thus relates Godself to others impartially. As the universal individual, that than which nothing greater can be conceived, God cannot plausibly be supposed to exist inauthentically. Charles Hartshorne has argued that a malevolent or demonic supreme being would not be that than which nothing greater can be conceived, precisely because such a supreme being would not fully exemplify all positive perfections.[82] However God in fact constitutes Godself, it must be in a fully authentic fashion, sympathetic to the needs of all other individuals.

I would argue that while God may be free to love individual *a* more intensely than individual *b* (see Chapter XI below), God is not free not to love others at all. Yet crucial to Rahner's understanding of God is the claim that human beings, in principle, although not in fact, must reckon with a speech or a silence of God, a loving self-bestowal of God or an indifference or self-refusal of God. This, it seems to me, is to affirm of the divine, universal individual a possibility of existence that we as human persons can only understand to be inauthentic, in that it is a self-contradictory, or even perverted, form of love of others. As the universal individual, the totality of reality in some sense, God cannot exist inauthentically. God's freedom cannot plausibly be conceived to imply that God could refuse absolutely to love other persons. But this is precisely what Rahner's view implies. His understanding that the assertion "God is love" implies such a negative, even inauthentic, freedom of God would seem to be finally inadequate for Christian theology. Some alternative to Rahner's concept of God is called for, precisely so that the biblical and experiential truth that God is both sovereignly free and essentially love of others can be expressed in a way that does not characterize the divine being in terms of an inauthentic mode of human existence.

NOTES

1 "Natur und Gnade," *ST*, 4:230 (ET: *TI*, 4:183).

2 *Karl Rahner: Eine Einführung in sein theologisches Denken* (Freiburg: Verlag Herder, 1978), p. 95 (ET: *Karl Rahner: An Introduction to His Theology* (New York: Seabury Press, 1980), pp. 106–107).

3 For a scheme for organizing the set of crucial objections that have been raised against Rahner's theology, see James Bacik, *Apologetics and the Eclipse of Mystery: Mystagogy According to Karl Rahner* (Notre Dame, Ind.: University of Notre Dame Press, 1980), pp. 48–62.

4 *The Theological Method of Karl Rahner*, pp. 260–261.

5 "Über das Verhältnis von Natur und Gnade," *ST*, 1:340 (ET: *TI*, 1:313–314).

6 *Man's Condition: God and the World Process.*

7 Ibid., p. 79.

8 Ibid., p. 240.

9 Ibid., pp. 240–251.

10 "Philosophie und Theologie," *ST*, 6:96 (ET: *TI*, 6:75).

11 *Man's Condition*, p. 250.

12 As I have indicated above, the act of creation is itself an act of love on God's part, but an act of self-love, not the fully personal divine love of others. See *HW*, pp. 125–126.

13 "Über das Verhältnis von Natur und Gnade," *ST*, 1:336–337 (ET: *TI*, 1:310–311).

14 *Man's Condition*, p. 258.

15 "Fragen der Kontroverstheologie der Rechtfertigung," *ST*, 4:264 (ET: *TI*, 4:212).

16 "*Theos* im Neuen Testament," *ST*, 1:99 (ET: *TI*, 1:86).

17 "Über das Verhältnis von Natur und Gnade," *ST*, 1:332 (ET: *TI*, 1:306).

18 *HW*, p. 102.

19 Ibid., p. 115.

20 "Gotteslehre," *LTK*, vol. 4, col. 1123.

21 "Über den Begriff des Geheimnisses in der katholischen Theologie," *ST*, 4:98 (ET: *TI*, 4:72).

22 *GG*, p. 74 (ET: *FCF*, pp. 65–66).

23 Ibid., pp. 81–82 (ET: ibid., pp. 73–74).

24 Ibid., p. 82 (ET: ibid., p. 74).

25 "*Theos* im Neuen Testament," *ST*, 1:130 (ET: *TI*, 1:114).

26 Ibid., p. 141 (ET: ibid., p. 123).

27 Ibid., p. 137 (ET: ibid., p. 120).

28 Ibid., p. 138 (ET: ibid., p. 121), my emphasis.

29 Ibid., p. 143 (ET: ibid., p. 125).

30 See Jürgen Becker, "Das Gottesbild Jesu und die älteste Auslegung von Ostern," in *Jesus Christus in Historie und Theologie*, ed. Georg Strecker (Tübingen: J. C. B. Mohr, 1975), pp. 105–126; Herbert Braun, *Jesus of Nazareth: The Man and His Time*, trans. Everett Kalin (Philadelphia: Fortress Press, 1979); Rudolf Bultmann, *Jesus and the Word*, trans. Louise Pettibone Smith and Ermine Huntress Latero (New York: Charles Scribner's Sons, 1958), pp. 133–219; *Theology of the New Testament*, 2 volumes, trans. Kendrick Grobel (New York: Charles Scribner's Sons, 1951), 1:22–26, 270–291; Gerhard Delling, "Partizipiale Gottesprädikationen in den Briefen des Neuen Testaments," *Studia Theologica* 17 (1963):1–59; Christoph Demke, " 'Ein Gott und viele Herren':Die Verkündigung des einen Gottes in den Briefen des Paulus," *Evangelische Theologie* 36 (1976):473–484; Hubert Frankenmölle, "Das Gottesbild Jesu: Ein Beitrag zum Sprechen über Gott," *Katechetische Blätter* 9 (1972):65–71; Günther Hanfe, "Gott in der ältesten Jesustradition," *Die Zeichen der Zeit* 24 (1970):201–206; W. G. Kümmel, "Die Gottesverkündigung Jesus und der Gottesgedanke des Spätjudentums," *Judaica* 1 (1945):40–68; Halver Moxnes, *Theology in Conflict: Studies in Paul's Understanding of God in Romans* (Leiden: E. J. Brill, 1980); Wolfgang Schrage, "Theologie und Christologie bei Paulus und Jesus auf dem Hintergrund der modernen Gottesfrage," *Evangelische Theologie* 36 (1976): 121–154.

31 Nils Dahl, "The Neglected Factor in New Testament Theology," *Reflection* 73 (1975):5–8.

32 *ST*, 1:91–167 (ET: *TI*, 1:79–148).

33 Ibid., p. 91, n. 2 (ET: ibid., p. 79, n. 2). See *Theologisches Wörterbuch zum Neuen Testament*, ed. G. Kittel, 10 volumes (Stuttgart: W. Kohlhammer Verlag, 1938), 3:65–123 (ET: *Theological Dictionary of the New Testament*, trans. and ed. Geoffrey Bromiley, 10 volumes (Grand Rapids, Mich.: Eerdmans, 1965), 3:65–119).

34 "*Theos* im Neuen Testament," *ST*, 1:108 (ET: *TI*, 1:94).

35 Ibid., pp. 96–97 (ET: ibid., pp. 83–84).

36 Ibid., p. 108 (ET: ibid., p. 94).

37 Ibid., p. 124 (ET: ibid., pp. 108–109).

38 Ibid., p. 125 (ET: ibid., pp. 109–110).

39 Ibid., p. 128 (ET: ibid., p. 112).

40 Ibid., p. 131 (ET: ibid., p. 115).

41 Ibid., p. 132 (ET: ibid.).

42 Ibid., p. 143 (ET: ibid., p. 125).

43 Ibid., p. 138 (ET: ibid., p. 121).

44 Ibid., p. 142 (ET: ibid., p. 124).

45 From the English translation, 3:112, my emphasis.

46 "Liebe," in *Begriffslexikon zum Neuen Testament*, ed. Lothar Co-
enen, et. al., 2 volumes (Wuppertal: Brockhaus, 1970), 2:900.

47 "*Theos* im Neuen Testament," *ST*, 1:108 (ET: *TI*, 1:94).

48 *Theology of the New Testament*, 1:389.

49 See W. D. Davies, *Paul and Rabbinic Judaism: Some Rabbinic Elements in Pauline Theology* (London: SPCK, 1948); and E. P. Sanders, *Paul
and Palestinian Judaism: A Comparison of Patterns of Religion* (Philadelphia:
Fortress Press, 1977).

50 *Jesus and the Word*, pp. 194–219.

51 Ibid., pp. 203, 211.

52 "Über den Begriff des Geheimnisses in der katholischen Theologie," *ST*, 4:84 (ET: *TI*, 4:61).

53 See *GG*, p. 82 (ET: *FCF*, p. 74) and "*Theos* im Neuen Testament,"
ST, 1:130 (ET: *TI*, 1:114).

54 "Philosophie" in *KtW*, p. 288.

55 "*Theos* im Neuen Testament," *ST*, 1:129–130 (ET: *TI*, 1:112–113).

56 Ibid., pp. 131, 143 (ET: ibid., pp. 114–115, 125).

57 *Systematic Theology*, 1:131.

58 "Die menschliche Sinnfrage vor dem absoluten Geheimnis
Gottes," *ST*, 13:117.

59 "Immanente und transzendente Vollendung der Welt," *ST*, 8:601
(ET: *TI*, 10:282).

60 *GG*, p. 137 (ET: *FCF*, p. 131).

61 "Das Leben der Toten," *ST*, 4:432–433 (ET: *TI*, 4:349–350).

62 Ibid., p. 430 (ET: ibid., p. 349).

63 "Über die Verborgenheit Gottes," *ST*, 12:295 (ET: *TI*, 16:235).

64 See "Der Mensch von heute und die Religion," *ST*, 6:13–33 (ET:
TI; 6:3–20).

65 Ibid., p. 27 (ET: ibid., p. 15).

66 See "Glaube als Mut," *ST*, 13:252–268.

67 Ibid., p. 256.

68 Ibid., p. 268.

69 *GG*, pp. 136–137 (ET: *FCF*, p. 131). For a similar account of the
role the divine reality plays as the ground of our basic existentiell faith
or trust in the meaning and value of existence, and the role of religion
in reassuring us of this basic faith, see Schubert Ogden's essay, "The
Reality of God," in *The Reality of God and Other Essays* (New York: Harper
& Row, 1966), pp. 1–70, esp. pp. 21–44. John C. Robertson, Jr., in
"Rahner and Ogden: Man's Knowledge of God," *Harvard Theological
Review* 63 (1970): 377–407, illustrates the basic similarity between the
views of Rahner and Ogden concerning the necessary human faith in,
and affirmation of, the meaningfulness of existence that is based upon
the reality of God (pp. 393–396). Still another account of the funda-

mental trust characteristic of human being, an account that is apparently independent of Ogden's, is to be found in Hans Küng's book *Does God Exist? An Answer for Today*, trans. Edward Quinn (Garden City, N.Y.: Doubleday, 1980), pp. 460–477.

70 "Die menschliche Sinnfrage vor dem absoluten Geheimnis Gottes," *ST*, 13:116–117.

71 "Glaube als Mut," *ST*, 13:262.

72 "Immanente und transzendente Vollendung der Welt," *ST*, 8:602–603 (ET: *TI*, 10:283).

73 *GG*, p. 173 (ET: *FCF*, p. 170).

74 "Immanente und transzendente Vollendung der Welt," *ST*, 8:603 (ET: *TI*, 10:283–284).

75 *Wie von Gott sprechen?*, p. 89.

76 *HW*, p. 130–131.

77 Such acts are self-contradictory in that in the very act of killing myself, for example, I affirm implicitly that it is better to die than to go on living in such a "meaningless" fashion. Likewise, to say that existence is meaningless, presumably, is itself intended to assert something meaningful. Thus, in advancing the claim that existence is meaningless one has implicitly affirmed what the claim itself denies.

78 "Über die Einheit von Nächsten- und Gottesliebe," *ST*, 6:288 (ET: *TI*, 6:240–241).

79 "Sinn und Intersubjektivität: Zur Vermittlung von transzendentalphilosophischem und dialogischem Denken in einer 'transzendentalen Dialogik,'" *Theologie und Philosophie* 2 (1970): 161–191.

80 Ibid., p. 185. Obviously, Heinrichs is concerned to distinguish quite sharply between hate and indifference. For my purposes here, it is enough to show that neither hate nor indifference, however they are to be distinguished from one another, constitutes a denial of the relatedness to others that is essential to human being.

81 *GG*, pp. 71–73, 85–86 (ET: *FCF*, p. 62–65, 78–79).

82 *Man's Vision of God and the Logic of Theism* (Hamden, Conn.: Archon Books, 1964), p. 303: "The old objection that if a perfect being must exist then . . . a perfect devil must exist is not perhaps very profound. For it is answered simply by denying that anyone can conceive perfection, in the strict sense employed by the argument, to be possessed by . . . a devil. A perfect devil would have at the same time to be infinitely responsible for all that exists besides itself, and yet infinitely averse to all that exists. It would have to attend with unrivaled care and patience and fullness of realization to the lives of all other beings (which must depend for existence upon this care), and yet it must hate all these with matchless bitterness. It must savagely torture a cosmos every item of which is integral with its own being, united to it with a vivid intimacy such as we can only dimly imagine. In short, . . . a perfect devil is unequivocally nonsense."

CHAPTER IX
LOVE AND THE SELF-COMMUNICATION OF GOD

Rahner understands the assertion "God is love" to mean that God bestows Godself upon the creatures in a free act of ecstatic self-giving or self-communication. So far in this critical appraisal of Rahner's view, I have tried to make two basic points. I tried to show, in Chapter VII, that Rahner's understanding of the God-world relationship, which he holds to be necessarily implied by the fact that God is love, is self-contradictory. I argued that Rahner's key assertion that God is relative to the world in God's other while remaining strictly nonrelative to the world in Godself, is either merely a verbal solution to the problem of the relativity and nonrelativity of God, one that does not represent an advance beyond the dualism of traditional scholastic thought, or else entails a real relatedness of God in Godself after all. Then, in Chapter VIII, I showed that Rahner's understanding of the freedom or gratuity of the divine love implies that God is not essentially love of others. I argued that this position is inadequate in Christian theology. It is not free of internal contradiction, it does not faithfully interpret the apostolic witness found in scripture, and it does not credibly interpret our common human experience.

Now I want to turn to an evaluation of the other aspect of Rahner's understanding of the meaning of the asertion "God is love," namely, that God's love for others is an ecstatic act of self-communication. To do this, the largely immanent criticism of Rahner's view of the divine love carried out in the two preceding chapters will have to be augmented. I want to make use of the results of two contemporary theological discussions of love in my evaluation of the adequacy of Rahner's understanding of the divine love. In these contemporary discussions, the essence of love is understood to be a relationship between persons that is intended to facilitate the full self-realization of the beloved as a

288 God is Love

person. Love is seen as having both an active and a passive moment. I will argue that, although Rahner understands human love in this way, his view of the divine love is inadequate in that no passive moment of love is allowed in the divine case. I will try to show that the inadequacy of Rahner's understanding of the divine love is particularly evident when one considers his concept of God as the absolute future.

What Is the Essence of Love?

The parameters and the basic issues of the contemporary discussion of love in Christian theology and ethics have been established, to a large degree, by Anders Nygren in his book *Agape and Eros*.[1] One ethicist has made the following claim concerning Nygren and his argument in this book:

> He so effectively posed issues about love that they have had a prominence in theology and ethics they never had before. His critics have been legion, but few have ignored or been unaffected by his thesis. Thus, whatever the reader may think of it, one may justifiably regard his work as the beginning of the modern treatment of the subject.[2]

Nygren's famous thesis is that there are two opposed fundamental motifs concerning love in the West: *agape* and *eros*. The *eros* motif, according to Nygren, is a product of Greek culture, while *agape* is "the Christian motif par excellence. . . . It sets its mark on everything in Christianity. Without it nothing that is Christian would be Christian. Agape is Christianity's own original basic conception."[3] Nygren believes that *eros* and *agape* have been intimately, if erroneously, intertwined in Christian thought. His own project is to recover the *agape* motif in its distinctiveness as Luther did during the Protestant Reformation. Nygren contrasts *eros* and *agape* as follows:

> Eros is acquisitive desire and longing. Agape is sacrificial giving. Eros is an upward movement. Agape comes down. Eros is man's way to God. Agape is God's way to man. Eros is man's effort: it assumes that man's salvation is his own work. Agape is God's grace: salvation is the work of divine love. Eros is egocentric love, a form of self-assertion of the highest, noblest, sublimest kind. Agape is unselfish love, it "seeketh not its own," it gives itself away. Eros seeks to gain its life, a life divine, immor-

talised. Agape lives the life of God, therefore dares to
"lose it." Eros is the will to get and possess, which depends on want and need. Agape is freedom in giving,
which depends on wealth and plenty. Eros is primarily
man's love; God is the object of Eros. Even when it is
attributed to God, Eros is patterned on human love.
Agape is primarily God's love; "God is Agape." Even
when it is attributed to man, Agape is patterned on
Divine love. Eros is determined by the quality, the
beauty, the worth, of its object; it is not spontaneous, but
"evoked," "motivated." Agape is sovereign in relation to
its object and is directed to both "the evil and the good";
it is spontaneous, "overflowing," "unmotivated." Eros
recognizes value in its object—and loves it. Agape
loves—and creates value in its object.[4]

Nygren's claim that there are these two opposed fundamental forms of love, *agape* and *eros,* has sparked a lively debate.
What is significant is that most of Nygren's critics have accepted
the fundamental distinction between *agape* and *eros,* and have
tried to present a more adequate account of their interrelationship or a more nuanced understanding of the nature of
agape and *eros.*[5]

John Burnaby argues against Nygren that Augustine's concept of *caritas* is not a mere synthesis of Greek *eros* and Christian
agape. Rather, he says, for Augustine, *caritas* is the Holy Spirit,
the *amor dei,* which unites the human person with God.[6] Martin
D'Arcy agrees with Nygren that there are two basic types of love,
eros and *agape,* or, in D'Arcy's own scheme, *animus* and *anima.*[7]
But D'Arcy argues that these two types of love cannot be completely separated as they are in Nygren's thought. Rather, both
are forms of human love, and as such, are good. They require
one another. They should serve and complement one another.

> One love takes and possesses; the other love likes to be
> beside itself and give. One is masculine, the other is
> feminine. The two are necessary for one another, and
> together they tell us what we are and where we are
> going. To neglect either is to court death.[8]

Paul Tillich writes that Nygren's analysis is helpful in that it
points out various qualities of love. However, Tillich argues that
Nygren goes too far in speaking of distinct *types* of love.[9] Tillich
holds that there is one love, the essence of which is "the drive
towards the unity of the separated." But this one love has various
qualities that are present in all love relationships: *epithymia* or

libido, the drive to self-fulfillment; *eros,* the drive toward union with that which is a bearer of values because of the values it bears; *philia,* the personal quality of love that allows an I to relate to a Thou; and *agape,* the depth of love, love in relation to the ground of life, the manifestation of ultimate reality that transforms life and love.[10] Gene Outka attempts to provide solutions to a number of specific ethical and metaethical problems raised by the distinctively Christian form of love, *agape.*[11] Outka discusses the relation of *agape* to self-love, justice, ethical rules, virtue, and self-sacrifice. Outka argues that *agape* is to be understood primarily as equal regard of others.

What is common in all of these critical treatments of Nygren's thesis, and thus what is characteristic of the Christian theological and ethical discussion of love from 1930 until the mid-1960s, is the fundamental concern with properly elucidating and relating various forms of love. It seems to me, however, that this approach to the problem of love in Christian theology and ethics has recently been called into question from two different perspectives: on the one hand, an ontological or metaphysical analysis of the essence of love, and, on the other hand, a feminist criticism of the one-sided orientation of much of Christian ethical theory toward male experience. As a result of these two new approaches to the topic of love, a much more adequate understanding of love is now available. This understanding of love is directly relevant to the issue of the meaning and truth of the assertion "God is love," which is under examination in this study.

A number of thinkers have raised the question concerning "the nature of love at the heart of all loves."[12] This is the question of the one spirit that is active in all the various forms of love, to paraphrase the title of Daniel Day William's book.[13] Jules Toner formulates this problem as follows: "My aim is to uncover within these differently qualified forms of human love that by reason of which every one of them can without equivocation be called love—if, indeed, there is any such thing to uncover."[14] According to Toner, this question concerning that which constitutes all the forms of love precisely as love, has been largely overlooked in the literature concerning love in Christian thought since the publication of Nygren's *Agape and Eros,* as being of only secondary importance.[15]

Daniel Day Williams proposes that there are five "categories" or "conditions of being" that are necessary to love: (1) "individuality and taking account of the other"; (2) "freedom"; (3) "action and suffering"; (4) "causality"; and (5) "impartial judgment in loving concern for the other."[16] Love requires real individuals, unique beings, who have their own unique lives and experiences, and who take other persons into account precisely as unique individuals. Love is a relationship of concern for the other, one that "does not negate the selfhood of the lover or destroy the uniqueness of the one who is loved."[17] Freedom is also a necessary condition for love. That is to say, love is a matter of decision and commitment, not of fate. "To love is to affirm and accept the freedom of the other."[18] To love is to make the history of another free person one's own history. It is a risking of our very being in relationship to another person. Love requires action or movement toward the beloved. In love, we actively give of our own unique, personal being. But, says Williams, to love is also to be acted upon, for the act of giving oneself to another is

> . . . to respond, to have one's actions shaped by the other. It is this side of love which is often overlooked or misinterpreted, and it is of especial importance. It is the other side of the category of individuality. In love we give of our personal being and uniqueness. But we do not love unless our personal being is transformed through the relation to the other.[19]

Love, therefore, is also suffering; it is "the capacity to be acted upon, to be changed, moved, transformed by the action of or in relation to another."[20] Love involves a causal relation between persons that is compatible, nevertheless, with their essential freedom. Love has an efficacious power whereby a person is transformed by another and transforms that other.[21] Finally, "there can be no real love without the rational function which aims to transcend personal bias, and which assesses objectively the human situation, including that of the lover, the beloved, and their relationship."[22] Love is a realistic concern for the other, one that is not opposed to justice.

Jules Toner presents a view of the essence of love that is similar to that of Williams.[23] Toner argues that radical love (the essential nature of love found in all the forms of love) has three aspects. Radical love is response, union, and affirmation.[24] Love, for Toner, involves both activity and passivity. As a spontaneous act, love is an actuation of one's own personal being. But this act of self-actuation occurs in response to the beloved's own act of self-actuation. Thus, "love is an act immanent to the lover, a response made possible by the object of love, which in some way influences the subject of love."[25] Second, for Toner, love is a mutual, affective "being-in" another person. The lover, in a real sense, is in the beloved, and vice versa. Love is an "ecstatic being out of self in the beloved," and also a "having of the beloved in the lover."[26] Love is a "consonant" mutual being-in each other of two persons (for mutual being-in also characterizes hate). It is the act in which human beings exist most fully as persons.[27] Love is the full participation of two persons in each other's lives, which involves both self-giving and accepting the other. There is no loss of self associated with giving oneself to another person, or accepting the other person into oneself.

> In this experience [of love] I am neither projecting my life into the other and so at root loving myself in him, nor am I introjecting his life into me as to lose hold on my distinct and unique self-identity. . . . Not only is participation in the beloved's life . . . in direct ratio to the intensity and purity of radical love, but so also is the realization of the distinct and unique personal reality of both the loved and the lover.[28]

Finally, in love, one co-affirms or co-declares the being of the beloved. Love is an affirmation of oneself and of the other person. The beloved is not affirmed *as* myself, but as the unique individual she or he is. However, the beloved is affirmed with the same radical affirmation with which I affirm myself. In love, I am related to the one I love as she or he is related to her or his own self.[29]

The view that love necessarily includes both an active and a passive moment, expressed by both Williams and Toner, seems to me to be essential to an adequate understanding of love. However, as Williams and Toner remark, the passive moment in the one act of love is easy to overlook.[30] It is precisely this passive moment of love that has been overlooked in most discussions of love written since Nygren's *Agape and Eros. Agape* has been presented as a wholly active, self-giving love that is not motivated by the beloved one. Williams argues that this is an incomplete and inadequate view of love.

> [T]here can be no love without suffering. Suffering in its widest sense means the capacity to be acted upon, to be

changed, moved, transformed by the action of or in relation to another. The active side of love requires that we allow the field of our action and its meaning to be defined by what the other requires. To be completed in and by another is to be acted upon by that other. To be fulfilled in human love is to have one's freedom circumscribed (not destroyed) by the other's freedom. . . . Suffering therefore is not something incidental or external to love; but it enters into the new life which love creates between persons. It is not only that in committing oneself to another we take the risks of certain kinds of suffering. It is that we accept the inevitability of being conformed to the other. When we love, we enter a history in which suffering is one condition of the relationship. The sacraments of loving, the giving and receiving, the shattering of self-centeredness in authentic love, the refusal to possess without the free acceptance of the other, all disclose the significance of suffering as a constituent aspect of love.[31]

Further, as Williams suggests, the active and passive moments of the one act of love are not simply coordinate with one another. While both are essential to love, there is a certain sense in which the passive moment of love is a necessary condition of the possibility of the active moment of love. For me to act lovingly toward another person by giving myself to that person, presupposes that the other person simply in her or his personal being has addressed me and made a claim upon me. I must accept the other person as the individual she or he is, before I can give myself in love to that person. Jean Mouroux argues:

Love is passivity and activity. It is in virtue of his deepest aspiration that man lies open to love but the act of love is an impossibility unless he falls in with something capable of attracting it. Hence the essential passivity of love; if it is to exist at all another must first find entrance into the soul and awaken it to itself. The loved one acts always as a nourishment that comes to satisfy a hunger, as the beauty that comes to set the longing at rest, as the plenitude that comes to fill a void; and love is always the offspring of riches and poverty. It supposes therefore a hold established by the other on the will, a transforming presence in the will of the lover; and since the beloved can neither enrich nor transform save only by communicating himself, he brings the will into tune with his own, he makes it vibrate to his own rhythm, and thus sets up a harmony and fraternity between these two which are love's first trait. They were two, and now are one, in

this divine connaturality that henceforth links them together, in this gladdening presence which is now about
to awaken the lover to action.[32]

If such a passive moment of receiving or accepting the
beloved were not given, then the "gift" of myself in love would
not be a gift at all, but would be something imposed imperi-
alistically upon another person of whom I would have no real
understanding. Margaret Farley, in a discussion of Toner's view
of love, writes:

> For love to arise, it is necessary *first* that an object in some
> way touch our affectivity, break through our con-
> sciousness to call forth a response to the object as lovable,
> as liberating, specifying the capacity for love within
> us. . . . Human love essentially implies receiving the be-
> loved, being awakened by the lovableness of the beloved,
> and hence responding. Because human love is a re-
> sponse, it can arise only when the beloved is somehow
> allowed to enter, is received into one's own being in such
> a way as to touch the power of affective response. One
> who is impenetrable to the beauty of the beloved cannot
> love.[33]

It is my receptivity of, or passivity to, the beloved that activates
the act in which I actuate or constitute myself in relation to that
person. It is the gift of the other person's being that allows me to
break out of my self-centered concern with myself. The passive
moment of love is not, therefore, enslavement or a denial of my
freedom, but is rather liberation. The beloved liberates me to
love, to constitute myself in intimate relations to other persons. I
can give myself ecstatically, even sacrificially, to others, only if I
have been freed from my sinful egoism or solipsism.

The Dutch phenomenologist William Luijpen provides a
helpful analysis of the necessary, liberating nature of the passive,
receptive moment of the act of love.

> The loving encounter always presupposes the appeal of
> the other to my subjectivity. A call goes out from him,
> embodied in a word, a gesture, a glance, a request. His
> word, gesture, glance, or request means an invitation to
> me whose true meaning is difficult to express in words.
> No matter, however, in what form the appeal of the
> other is embodied, it always implies an invitation to tran-
> scend myself, to break away from my preoccupation with
> myself and my fascinated interest in myself. . . . Accord-

ingly, understanding the other's appeal to me ties in not
with his facticity but rather with what the other is over
and above his facticity—namely, a subjectivity. His subjectivity itself is the appeal that is addressed to me. It is a
plea that I participate in his subjectivity. Marcel endeav-
ors to express this plea in words: "Be with me." It is the
call of the other to go out beyond the confines of myself,
to support, strengthen and, as it were, increase his subjectivity by participating in it. . . . It is precisely the appeal of the other which makes it possible for me to
liberate myself from myself. The other's appeal reveals
to me an entirely new, perhaps wholly unsuspected dimension of my existence. Who am I? Am I not more
than the sum total of my objective qualities? Am I not
more than a file card full of predicates? Am I not more
than the role I play? Certainly, my being-human is
richer. I am not identical with my facticity, I am a subjectivity, called to give again and again meaning to my
facticity in free self-realization. I am not a thing-in-the-
world, but I am a project-in-the-world, called to realize
myself in the world and to make the world a human
world. . . . I am called to realize myself in the world, but
for you. The encounter with you reveals to me my destiny
as destiny-for-you. Through you I understand the
meaninglessness of my egoism and self-centeredness,
which would fatally tempt me to lock myself up in myself
and in my world. Yielding to this temptation would
mean that I would miss my destiny.[34]

Thus, the passive moment of love is a necessary condition of the
possibility of the active, self-giving moment of love, for the act of
constituting myself in loving relations to other persons presupposes that those other persons have addressed me, made a claim
upon me, and liberated me from my self-centeredness.

It is also important to note that, in the understanding of
love proposed by Williams, Toner, and others, "love" is understood to refer to a relationship in which the lover (the subject of
love) acts to facilitate the full, authentic self-realization of the
beloved (the object of love) as a person. At the same time,
precisely in acting on behalf of the authentic self-realization of
the beloved, the lover her- or himself is realized as a person. It is
not enough to say that love involves taking account of another
individual and acting toward that individual, for this would also
be true of hate. Rather, love is a receiving of the other person
and a giving of oneself to that other person that has as its

immediate goal nothing other than the full self-realization of the other person. In acting to accomplish this goal, the lover is also realized or constituted as a person.

This does not mean that the lover enters into the love relationship simply, or even primarily, in order to realize or fulfill her- or himself. That is, the beloved is not an instrument that serves the lover in her or his search for self-fulfillment. But since human persons constitute themselves in their relationships to other persons, the lover's project of self-constitution is furthered in a love relationship, just as it would be furthered, although in an inauthentic way, in a relationship of hate for another person. The difference is that, in love, in the servicing of the beloved's authentic self-realization, the lover her- or himself comes to be most authentically realized as a person.

This is true of love as such, even "unrequited love." That is to say, the definition of love in terms of passivity, activity, and the facilitation of the beloved's authentic self-realization, does not require that the beloved reciprocate by acting so as to facilitate the authentic self-realization of the lover. The beloved may remain indifferent to, or even may seek to evade, the lover's gift of her- or himself. In the case of unrequited love, nonetheless, the lover is somehow constituted as a person in this relationship. However, the lover is not fully actualized as a person since the beloved does not respond in like manner by giving her- or himself freely and fully to the lover. Although, it must be said, the beloved has offered enough of her- or himself to claim the lover's love and to make a difference in the life of the lover. In a fully mutual relationship of love, both the lover and the beloved act to facilitate the other's authentic self-realization. Both persons, in requited love, make the other a constitutive element of their own existentiell project of self-creation, and both act toward the other person so as to maximize the free self-creation of the beloved. As Maurice Nédoncelle says, using the *agape/eros* terminology of Nygren, "in the gift of self the *I* enhances the Thou and this constitutes an *agape;* and the I is enhanced by the *Thou,* which constitutes an *eros.* The circle is inevitable."[35]

These same topics of love as activity and passivity, and love as the facilitation of the self-realization of the beloved appear in connection with the attempt to reconceive love from a feminist perspective. A number of thinkers have raised the objection that the usual concept of love in Christian theology and ethics is inadequate or one-sided in that it is uncritically derived from the experience of men.

Barbara Hilkert Andolsen writes that

> . . . the contemporary Protestant discussion of agape has stressed the concept of other-regard often epitomized by self-sacrifice. . . . In Nygren's work, sacrifice of self for the sake of others is the paradigm of Christian love. Agape is "a love that gives itself away, that sacrifices itself, even to the uttermost." Agape is utterly heedless of the self's own interests.[36]

Andolsen charges that this view of love as self-sacrifice reflects male experience and ignores the experience of women, who, in sexist society, "have a tendency to give themselves over to others to such an extent that they lose themselves. They squander their distinctive personal abilities."[37] Love, understood exclusively as self-sacrifice, "is not an appropriate virtue for women who are prone to excessive selflessness."[38] In fact, says Andolsen, this view of the chief Christian virtue of love as self-sacrifice has reinforced women's sin, that is, the sin of failing to realize oneself as a person. More appropriate virtues for women are autonomy and self-realization.[39] Thus, Andolsen argues, love is to be conceived not simply as self-sacrifice, as active giving of oneself to another person, but as mutuality, in which both parties are affirmed and enriched, in which both parties are active and passive in relation to the other person.[40] Andolsen says that receptivity to, and dependence on, others are just as difficult personal tasks as is the sacrificial giving of oneself to others.[41]

In making her claim that love is most appropriately understood as mutuality, and not simply as self-giving or self-sacrifice, Andolsen refers to the work of Margaret Farley.[42] Farley writes that the theme of self-sacrificial love in Christianity has too often been linked to the submission of women to men. That is to say, love as self-giving or self-sacrifice has meant the self-sacrifice of women for the sake of the advancement or self-realization of men.[43] Farley argues:

> . . . there is, I suggest, an implicit but direct connection between historical theological interpretations of woman as passive and historical difficulties in interpreting agape as active. In both cases receptivity constitutes a stumbling block.[44]

Woman has traditionally been understood to be passive in social relationships, while man has been understood to be active. At the same time, human persons have been understood to receive the divine *agape* passively, while human *agape* for one's neighbor has been viewed as wholly active, and not as a response motivated by the intrinsic lovableness of the neighbor. These forms of passivity or receptivity, according to Farley, are inappropriate, even oppressive. Yet this is not the only way to understand the activity and passivity of love.

> Theologians who worry that if agape is active in relation to God, God's power will not be preserved, or theologians who worry that if agape is receptive of neighbor it will inevitably be a self-centered love, fail to understand that receiving can be self-emptying, and that giving can be self-fulfilling. They fail to see the meeting between lover and beloved, . . . which is utterly receptive and utterly active, a communion in which the beloved is received and affirmed, in which receiving and giving are but two sides of one reality which is other-centered love.[45]

Love, for Farley, is a relationship between two individuals that affirms both parties as persons, and in which both persons are active and passive in relation to the other.

I would formulate the understanding of the essence of love that arises from these two recent approaches to the topic of love in Christian theology and ethics as follows. "Love" refers to an affective and active relationship between persons that has as its immediate goal the full, authentic self-realization of each of the persons involved as persons. There are two essential aspects of love that can and must be distinguished. First, in love, one allows another person or persons to make a real difference in one's life; one is open to the beloved or beloved ones to such an extent that this person or these persons have a determinative influence upon one's own experience and personal being. This is the passive moment of love in which one is receptive to, and determined by, the other person or persons who are loved.

But there is also an active moment of love. On the basis of the difference the other person or persons make in one's life, one acts appropriately toward the beloved or beloved ones in order that the beloved or beloved ones may share one's own experience and personal being and be determinatively influenced by them. In this moment of love, the lover gives, or, more accurately, offers her- or himself to the person or persons who are loved, so as to facilitate the beloved's or beloved ones' existentiell project of self-constitution.

Both the passive and the active aspects of love involve risk. In the passive aspect of love I risk opening myself to another person, I risk allowing that person to determine me. But, then, in the active aspect of love, I risk giving of myself to another person, I risk allowing that person to share my own being. Without both the passive and the active moments, there can be no love. Indeed, the active self-offering or self-giving that is a part of the one act of love is itself a response to the offering of the beloved as a person. The passive moment of love is a necessary condition of the possibility of the active, self-giving moment of love. It is only because the beloved or beloved ones make a claim upon me, and liberate me from my self-centeredness and self-reliance that I can offer myself as a gift to them. It is the act of receiving the gift of the being of another person or persons that enables me to make a gift of my own being for someone else.

It seems to me that this characterization of love as the passive letting another person make a determinative difference in one's life and the active acting appropriately toward the other person on the basis of the difference she or he makes to one, applies not just to the more private, intimate relationship between two friends or "lovers," but also to the love a person can have for a person or persons much farther removed from one in a physical, economic, or social sense. For instance, I would argue that one could talk of my love for the peasants of El Salvador or Guatemala in terms of passivity, activity, and the facilitation of the self-realization of the beloved. The being, the situation of the people of El Salvador and Guatemala addresses me and makes a claim upon me as a human being. Their oppression decisively qualifies my existence and my understanding of myself, the world, and God. On the basis of the difference these persons make in my life, if I love them, I will take some appropriate action aimed at facilitating their full self-realization as human persons. In this particular case, my active self-giving on behalf of the people of El Salvador and Guatemala perhaps may not involve any individual, person-to-person contact. Instead, the active moment of my love for these oppressed persons likely will involve an attempt, as a citizen of the First World, to effect some change in the structures and policies of my own affluent society that are the chief causes of the oppression of the people of El Salvador and Guatemala. It would be a mistake to view the characterization of love as passivity and activity as applying solely to the love between two individuals.[46]

Is Rahner's View of Love as Ecstatic Self-Communication Adequate?

It would appear, at first glance, that Rahner also understands human love to be a relationship of affective and active mutuality between persons, the purpose of which is the full self-realization of lover and beloved as persons. Love is the fundamental or primordial human act for Rahner, which means that

> . . . in the act of love for the other, and in this act alone and before all else, the primordial unity of what man is and what the totality of his experience is, is gathered together and fully realized. The love for the other concrete Thou is not something that exists in man alongside many other things, but is man himself in his total realization.[47]

In love, for Rahner, through the mediation of the beloved, human persons realize themselves fully and constitute themselves most authentically, while facilitating the fully authentic self-realization of the beloved. "Love is inseparable from the desire to bring the beloved, in himself, to the fulfillment of his essence; in attempting this, the lover takes up the unending task of realizing himself."[48]

Rahner also seems to acknowledge that this primordial act of love includes both a passive and an active moment. Recall the definition Rahner gives of love: "love is the *abandoning* and *opening* of one's innermost self *to* and *for* the other, who is loved."[49] Elsewhere, Rahner seems to indicate that love involves both a receiving of the beloved as an autonomous person and a giving of oneself to the beloved. He asks rhetorically:

> Is it not the case, where a man encounters another in genuine personal love, that there is an acceptance of one who cannot be fully understood, an acceptance of that in the person of the beloved that one does not know and, thus, has not forcefully made subservient to oneself? Is not personal love the trusting giving away of oneself to the other person without any guarantee [of reciprocation] precisely because the other person is and remains free and incalculable?[50]

It is true, despite formulations such as these, that Rahner tends to speak of love not as activity and passivity, but solely as activity. As I showed in Chapter III, the primary meaning of love, for Rahner, is *ecstatis,* that is, the active being away from oneself *(das Von-sich-weg),* the letting oneself go *(das Sich-selbst-Loslassen).*[51] Although Rahner defines love as both the abandoning of oneself and the opening of oneself to another person, he more characteristically refers to love simply as the active communication or bestowal of a free person upon another person. In fact, at times Rahner uses the term "opening," found in the phrase, "the opening of one's innermost self for the other" *(das Eröffnen seines innersten Selbst für den andern),* a term that seems to indicate a passive moment of the act of love, to refer precisely to the active, ecstatic giving of oneself to another.[52] Yet, even if Rahner does not consistently speak of love as having an active and a passive moment in the way that Williams, Toner, Andolsen, Farley, and others do, it is clear that the essential passivity or receptivity of the human being is a condition of the possibility of the ecstatic, self-giving act of human love. Human beings, for Rahner, realize or constitute themselves as persons only in relation to other persons, for human beings are essentially receptive. "The personal Thou [is] the mediation of the *Beisichsein* of the subject."[53] Thus, it seems to me, Rahner's understanding of human love is largely adequate, for he recognizes that the lover strives to facilitate the authentic self-realization of the beloved and that the active self-giving aspect of love presupposes an essential passivity or receptivity of the lover in which the beloved acts determinatively upon the lover, even if this passivity is not understood by Rahner to be a moment of the act of love itself.

Of course, the real issue here is not the adequacy of Rahner's view of human love, but rather the adequacy of his view of divine love. As I have said before, the assertion "God is love," for Rahner, is an analogical statement. He defines analogy as follows:

> "Analogy" means that a concept, without losing the unity of its content, undergoes a real variation of meaning as it is applied to different individual beings or to different realms of being. (In distinction from: equivocation—a single word has completely different meanings; univocation—a concept always has strictly the same meaning and, in its employment, is differentiated only through external characteristics.) In the content of the analogical

> concept, that which is similar and that which is different,
> that which is like and that which is unlike in that which is
> meant are comprised in a unity that cannot logically be
> divided. The analogy of being is grounded in the analo-
> gical commonality and differentiation of each particular
> being with its being. . . . The human spirit, in its actual
> knowledge, can attain being as such only through par-
> ticular beings; this, however, through its transcendence,
> such that the analogical understanding of being is the
> primordial, supporting ground for all (univocal) con-
> cepts of individual realities. . . . Analogy, as a form of
> speech and thought about God and his relationship to us
> and to the world, is not a logical trick by which human
> knowledge takes possession of God, but is rather the
> transcription of the fundamental actuality of human
> knowledge: that it always and from the outset is oriented
> to the absolute mystery that is given nonobjectively to
> human knowledge, without negating the mysterious
> character of this fundamental actuality or of the in-
> comprehensibility of God.[54]

There are several aspects of this understanding of analogy that
are crucial to an adequate appraisal of Rahner's view of the
divine love for others.

First of all, "God is love" is not, for Rahner, a literal, formal
(i.e., univocal) statement of metaphysics. That is to say, "love" is
not a transcendental characteristic that could be attributed to
any and every particular being simply because that particular
being exists or participates in being. For if love is to be understood in a personal sense, that is, as "the free bestowal of a
person who possesses himself," rather than as "a natural flowing
out of the self," then subpersonal realities could not plausibly be
said to be love.[55] So, for Rahner, as I argued in the previous
chapter, to attribute love to God is to select a particular, material
aspect of our experience and to apply it to God. It is not to
attribute to God a purely formal, metaphysical characteristic that
applies as equally to God as to the tiniest bit of matter.

At the same time, however, to assert that God is love is not
logical sleight of hand, for Rahner. Because of the ontological
commonality of finite and infinite being, the world and God,
concepts such as love, will, and knowledge can meaningfully be
used in relation to the divine reality. The alternative to such
analogical speech about God would be the absolute refusal to say
anything about God at all.

> It is impossible, given a Christian doctrine of creation, to refuse to assert that that which is created, because it is caused by God, is *like* the cause. Each creature, to a different degree, "participates" in the perfection of God according to the degree of its own ontological intensity of being. Otherwise, all positive statements concerning God would be absolutely impossible from the outset. The consequence of this would be a negative theology that would be identical to atheism.[56]

Further, although Rahner holds that analogy is distinct from equivocation and univocation, he argues that analogy is not simply a "midpoint" between these two modes of predication. Analogy is not a "hybrid" between a univocal affirmation and an equivocal negation concerning God, "as if one had to say something about God and then were to see that one could not really say such a thing because the original understanding of the content of the expression comes from elsewhere, from something that does not have much to do with God."[57] Rahner says that analogy is much more deeply grounded in human transcendental experience than is implied in the traditional view of analogy as an inexact midpoint between univocation and equivocation. Analogy arises from the difference between the human experience of particular objects and the transcendental experience of absolute being that is a condition of the possibility of all acts of experience of particular beings. Human beings exist in the difference or tension between the categorial and the transcendental. We know being as such only through particular, finite beings, and yet, particular beings are known thematically only because of a prior, unthematic awareness of being.

> One could say that we ourselves exist analogically through our being grounded in the holy mystery that always withdraws from us, in that it constitutes us by withdrawing and by pointing us to the individual, concrete, categorial realities that encounter us within the realm of our experience. Conversely, these individual, concrete, categorial realities are once again the mediation and the point of departure for our knowledge of God.[58]

If we must speak of God in terms of categories derived from our most fundamental experience of ourselves, then one of the most appropriate analogies for the divine being, according to

Rahner, is provided by the experience of love, since in this act
the human person is presented and realized as a whole.

But how, for Rahner, is one to determine whether one has
appropriately or truthfully attributed an analogical predicate, in
this case, "love," to God? Rahner is clear that the analogical
statement that God is love is not intended to dissolve, but to lead
us into, the holy mystery that is God. That is to say, we must
realize, when we say "God is love," that the divine love is very
different from human love. In this analogical predication, the
concept "love" "undergoes a real variation of meaning."[59]
Rahner cites the affirmation of the Fourth Lateran Council that,
"no similarity between creator and creature can be affirmed
unless it includes a greater dissimilarity between the two."[60] And
yet, at the same time, he asserts that a concept applied analogically to God does not "lose the unity of its content."[61] I take this
to mean that a requirement of an appropriate analogical predication of term x to God, notwithstanding the radical difference
between the divine and the human referents of x, is that the
essential, positive meaning of x, the integrity or unity of content
of x, in its original, literal application to human being, cannot be
negated when x is applied analogically to God.

If this is the case, then it would seem that for "God is love" to
be true, analogically to be sure, the divine love must exemplify,
however eminently, the essential elements of human love. Given
the discussion of the essence of love in the first section of this
chapter and the review of Rahner's understanding of human
love, this means that the divine love of others, like human love,
must involve a relationship between the divine person and
human persons in which God both acts toward the object of the
divine love, by giving of Godself to the creatures, so as to facilitate the self-realization of God's beloved and is acted upon by the
beloved. In other words, if "God is love" is to be a true analogical
assertion, the divine love must be characterized by passivity and
activity, for these two aspects are essential to the concept of
human love. They constitute the integral essence of love. However else the divine love may differ from human love, for instance, in being an absolutely steadfast love, this essential
meaning of love must apply to the divine love. Otherwise, there
would be no justification for speaking of God as love at all. This
is simply a reformulation of the demand that the most primordial human experience of self in relation to others and God, as

Rahner understands it, must provide the starting point for, and the essential categories of, a concept of God.

Given this criterion for the truth of analogical predications with respect to God, and given his view of human love, Rahner's account of the divine love would seem to be inadequate. Although he understands human love to be an act in which a person actively bestows her- or himself upon another in order to facilitate the full self-realization of the beloved and, thereby, realizes her- or himself in relation to the beloved, and although he understands this act of self-giving or self-bestowal to be made possible by an acceptance of the beloved into one's own personal being, his view of the divine love seems to suffer from a certain one-sidedness. It is oriented solely toward the active moment of love, the divine self-giving or self-communication. At best, as I argued in Chapter VII, Rahner only incoherently affirms a passivity or a receptivity of the divine being. Often he explicitly denies that the divine love or the divine being is in any sense passive or receptive to other individuals. There is no clear sense in which the nondivine creatures, as the objects of the divine love, are passively accepted or received by God, so as to qualify or to influence determinatively the personal being of God. But I have shown that this passive moment of love (or a more general passivity of personal being) is a necessary condition of the possibility of the active moment of love. Thus, the divine self-giving is not fully illuminated in Rahner's thought. Rahner's analogical assertion that "God is love," finally, cannot be justified, for in applying love to God analogically, an aspect of the essence of the concept of love, as it is disclosed in human experience, has not coherently been applied to the divine reality, and often is explicitly denied in the divine case.

Rahner does understand the divine love for others to be a relationship of mutuality in which God is fully actuated or realized. (More correctly, one should say, according to Rahner, that in the divine love the pure, eternal actuality of the God who is always fully self-realized is most clearly revealed.) As I argued in Chapter IV, the divine love for the creatures is the fundamental, all-encompassing act of God. The divine love or self-communication is the purpose behind, and the unifying goal of, the divine activity as such, in the same way that human love is the one act in which the being of the human person is fully and authentically actuated.

Likewise, Rahner holds that the divine love of others is similar to human love in that it involves an ecstatic self-giving on the part of the lover, in this case, God. In Chapter IV I showed that the divine self-communication, for him, both in its transcendental mode (grace) and in its historical mode (incarnation), is the act in which "God himself goes out from himself as the fullness that lavishes itself."[62] In the divine love, God goes out from Godself to the creature, and communicates not some created quality to the creature, but the divine being itself. The love of God for other individuals is the act in which the ultimate giver, God, is Godself the gift that is freely bestowed.

But Rahner seems to understand the divine love *solely* in terms of this ecstatic self-giving. There is no indication that there is a logically prior passive moment of the divine love, in which God receives and is qualified by God's beloved. The term self-communication suggests the image of a wholly active love, one in which God, as lover, is outside of Godself ecstatically, and gives Godself to the beloved. The other terms that Rahner employs as synonyms for "self-communication" also indicate that the divine love is wholly active: "the self-expression of God," "the self-manifestation of God," "the self-externalization of God," even "the self-emptying" or "self-alienation of God."

Further, the model of quasi-formal causality, which Rahner introduces in order to explicate the self-communication of God, implies that the divine love is to be viewed solely in active terms. In love, God gives Godself to the spiritual creatures in a mode of radical nearness. God becomes an immanent principle, a supernatural existential, within human being. This act in which the giver is itself the gift can only be understood in terms of quasi-formal causality, whereby "a particular being, a principle of being is a constitutive moment in another subject, such that it communicates itself to this subject and does not only effect something different from itself."[63] In this act of self-communication, Rahner conceives God solely as a causal agent. As I argued in Chapter VII, a causal agent as such, even in the case of quasi-formal, as opposed to efficient, causality, is wholly active. The passivity or receptivity of a being, in this case God, is not uncovered when that being is viewed strictly as a causal agent. Yet, Rahner orients his entire discussion of the love or self-communication of God precisely to God as an agent who acts by way of quasi-formal causality.

It might be objected that it is unfair to criticize Rahner's view of the divine love for not including a passive moment since he does not really conceive human love as such to have a passive moment. This is true enough. But I think it can easily be shown that Rahner never coherently explicates a notion of the passivity or receptivity of the divine being as a condition of the possibility of the self-giving act of divine love in the way that he shows that human self-giving love presupposes an essential passive moment of human being.

As I have shown, human being, for Rahner, is essentially intercommunicative or interpersonal. That is to say, human being is *beisich* only as it is with another, whether this other is an object of human knowledge or another human person. The human person is constituted by real or internal relatedness to others. This essential relatedness, according to Rahner, is a function of the materiality of the human person. He says, for instance, that

> . . . all creaturely spirituality has an essential relation to matter, because, finally, . . . creaturely spirituality is receptive and intercommunicative spirituality. . . . Matter, in the metaphysical sense, is the condition of the interpersonal influence of finite spiritual beings upon one another.[64]

In another passage, Rahner equates the essential interpersonal nature of human being, the creatureliness of human being, and the materiality of human being.[65]

But since God, for Rahner, is not a creature and is not material, God is not essentially receptive or related to others. As I argued in Chapter VII, the relativity of God that Rahner affirms on the basis of the incarnation is not an essential relativity, but is a relativity of God in God's other, a notion I suggested is incoherent. The divine *Beisichsein* is not being with another *(das Bei-einem-anderen-sein)*.[66] In essence, God knows and loves others by knowing and loving God's own creative act. The divine love is wholly active. It is a love that creatively posits the world of nondivine individuals and graciously bestows the divine being upon that world in the spiritual creature. The divine love for Rahner is an ecstatic love that does not depend upon any prior receptivity of God to the object of the divine love. God loves because God is the overflowing fullness of absolute being, not because the creatures make a claim upon God,

qualify the personal being of God, and thus elicit a loving response of God. The divine being, and thus the divine love, for
Rahner, do not and cannot have a passive moment.

But if love necessarily includes a passive moment, as Rahner
himself would agree in the case of human love, such a view of
the divine love is inadequate. A necessary condition of the possibility of divine self-giving, namely, divine passivity or divine
receptivity, is not clearly provided for in Rahner's thought. The
self-communication of God would not seem to be possible unless
God is really or internally related to those whom God loves. That
is to say, if person a were not really or internally related to
person b, if person b's actual situation, experience, and being
made no difference to person a, then any activity of person a
toward person b would be self-imposition (even if benevolent
self-imposition) and not loving self-communication. True personal self-communication would seem to be possible only if the
person who communicates her- or himself is able to be qualified
by, and to take account of, the persons to whom the self-communication is addressed. Yet such a qualification by, or taking
account of, other individuals cannot apply to God in Rahner's
view.

Put differently, Rahner's view of the divine love seems to me
to be inadequate in that he does not apply one essential aspect of
human love, namely, passivity, to God, although he does apply to
God the other necessary aspect of human love: love as a free act
of self-giving aimed at facilitating the self-realization of the beloved. Given Rahner's own understanding of the criteria for
appropriate analogical predications concerning God, his account
of the divine love is inadequate for this aspect of the essence of
human love is not applied to the divine love. He conceives the
divine love, like human love, to be an act of self-giving intended
to facilitate the full self-realization of the beloved and the lover.
But he fails to apply to God the essential intersubjectivity and
receptivity of human personal being that is a necessary condition
of the possibility of the self-giving act of love. Now, of course, the
divine love differs radically from human love.[67] But while God
eminently exemplifies love, it would seem that if "God is love" is
not to be, in Rahner's words, a logical trick, then God must
eminently *exemplify* the essence of the human experience of love.
And the passivity of love, or at least of human being in general,
is recognized by Rahner himself to be an essential, positive

aspect of the reality of human love. Thus, Rahner's view of the divine love involves a negation or a denial of a positive aspect of the essence of that most fundamental human experience of love on the basis of which the divine being is to be conceived.

The work of Daniel Day Williams is extremely helpful at this point, for he extends his reflections on the essence of human love to the divine love. He writes, for instance, that:

> If individuality, freedom, action and suffering, causality, and impartiality are categorical conditions of human love, then there is an initial presumption for Christian thought that the being of God, who is love, is in some way reflected in these structures of our existence. There is no good reason for taking away from love all that constitutes its distinctively human aspects and using the remainder to construct a doctrine of love in God.[68]

Williams argues that the traditional theological view that denies to the divine being, and thus to the divine love, the characteristic of suffering (the passive moment of love) makes "nonsense out of the profoundest aspects of love in human experience."[69] For Williams (as for Rahner in the case of human love) "to love is to be in a relationship where the action of the other alters one's own experience."[70] The traditional understanding of the non-relativity or impassibility of God makes love, in this sense, meaningless, and thus ought to be modified. According to Williams, "the love God offers is responsive love, in which he takes into himself the consequences of human actions, bears with the world, and urges all things toward a society of real freedom in communion."[71]

The inadequacy of Rahner's account of the divine love, which lies in his failure coherently to conceive a genuine passivity or receptivity of God in relation to the creatures, is even more clearly revealed in his claim that the God of love is the absolute future of the world and its historical development. As I showed in Chapter IV, Rahner argues that the final horizon or goal of human existence is not a finite, innerworldly future in which the free spiritual acts of the human person are simply succeeded endlessly by other free acts and thus vanish into insignificance. Such a future would deny, rather than ratify, the validity of the decisions and actions of the present.[72] Rahner holds that:

> Christianity understands itself in terms of salvation his-
> tory. That means, however, that Christianity is not, fi-
> nally and fundamentally, a doctrine of a static nature of
> the world and man, which, always remaining the same,
> repeats itself in an empty time-space without really pro-
> gressing further. Rather, Christianity is the proclama-
> tion of an absolute becoming, one that does not continue
> into emptiness, but really attains the absolute future,
> indeed already moves *in* the absolute future. . . . The
> infinite reality of this future is active as an inner, if
> independent, constituent of this becoming that supports
> this becoming.[73]

It is the divine being, and in particular the loving self-
communication of God, that provides the lasting significance of
personal decision and activity. The final, definitive validity of
human activity and history is attained in God, for God is the
absolute future of the world.

> History builds its own final validity. That which is perma-
> nent is the *work* of concrete love in history. This final
> validity remains as that which is achieved by man; it is
> not merely a moral distillate that history leaves behind as
> the grape skins from which the wine has been pressed.
> History itself enters into the final validity of God.[74]

It seems to me that Rahner is right that the free moral
activity of human persons is made possible by the reality of the
divine love. The divine love is the ground and absolute future of
the existentiell confidence in the meaning and value of existence
exhibited in all human activity. In the previous chapter I argued
that although Rahner holds this to be true of concrete human
being, his view that God is not essentially love of others, which is
implied by his understanding of the sheer gratuity of the divine
love, is inadequate in that it entails that human being is conceivable without God as loving absolute future. It seems to me that in
this present context a further charge could be made with respect
to Rahner's understanding of the absolute future, namely, that
his claim that the God of loving self-communication is the absolute future is either merely a verbal claim, or else entails that
God, precisely in God's love for the creatures, is really or internally related to the world of which God is the absolute future.
Rahner is correct when he argues that human decision and
activity demands the love of God as its absolute future, the
ground of its final validity. But the question is: How must God be

conceived such that the claim that God is the absolute future can be justified?

There would seem to be two essential conditions for God being the absolute future or the final ground of the significance of human activity. First, God must in some genuine sense be the *absolute* future of the world. God must not be another individual within the world, but must transcend the world. God must be unthreatened by the futility of the world if God is to be the ground of the significance of all worldly activity. Otherwise, God's situation would not be different from our own, and God's own activity would pass away into insignificance. No permanent validity would be attained in the free activity of spiritual subjects.

Yet at the same time, God must be the absolute future *of the world*. That is to say, the world must make a real difference to God. God must be really or internally related to the world such that God receives the world and the deeds of its agents into Godself. If God were not intimately related to the world in this fashion, the significance of the world would find no grounding in God. For if God were not really related to event *a*, then *a* would be strictly indifferent to God, that is, *a* would make no difference to God and would be of no significance to God. Whatever significance *a* might have could not be finally grounded in God.

As I have shown a number of times, the first condition for God being the absolute future and final ground of the significance of the world, namely, that God is independent of the world and unthreatened by transience, is granted by Rahner. God, as the absolute future, is not a particular, innerworldly future, but is the transcendental horizon of all worldly situations. However, Rahner does not, it seems to me, adequately explicate the second condition, namely, that God is really related to the nondivine individuals, and receives them into the divine life. He speaks of history "entering into" God as its absolute future, but it is clear that this does not mean that the divine reality is inclusive of the reality of the world. Rather, as the absolute future, God communicates Godself to the world, enters into the world, and by becoming a finite individual in the incarnation adopts the reality of the world as God's own reality. As the absolute future, God is immanent within the world by way of quasi-formal causality. But such ecstatic acts of God are not sufficient to demonstrate that God is the final ground of the significance of the world. For in each case, for Rahner, God is solely an active, causal agent with respect to the world. According to him, "the absolute future is God himself, that is, the act of his absolute self-communication, which he alone carries out; . . . it is *the determination of the world* as a whole, which encompasses the totality of reality and establishes everything in its full realization."[75] Yet, as I argued, a necessary condition of God's being the absolute future of the world is that God be not only a causal agent, but also a receptive patient in relation to the world. The world must be of significance to God, must affect God, if God is to ground the significance of the world. It is not clear how this can be the case in Rahner's thought. The concept of the absolute future is suggestive, but finally unclear.

Is God Essentially Self-Love?

It might be objected that while the reasons for my arguments against Rahner in this chapter and in the preceding one are sound, namely, that love must have an essentially passive moment and that God, in an adequate Christian theology, must be understood to be essentially, not accidentally, love, Rahner may, in fact, provide just such an essential, and essentially passive, divine love in his view of the divine self-love. It might be suggested, for instance, that God is essentially love *of self* and that this divine self-love can be characterized in terms of passivity and activity. This would enable Rahner to affirm, after all, that God is essentially love, without also forcing him to assert that God is essentially related to some nondivine others. One might suggest that Rahner understands this essential divine love of self to be the intratrinitarian love of God the Father for God the Son. The theology of Karl Barth could be consulted to provide a concept of such an intratrinitarian love. Barth says that:

> God loves us, God loves the world in accordance with his revelation. But he loves us and the world as the one who would be the loving one even without us, even without the world. He loves as the one who has no need of any other, the existence of which would ground his being the loving one and thus God. . . . It does not belong to God's being and acting that it, as love, must have as its object another that is distinct from him. God is himself sufficient as an object and thus also as an object of love.[76]

This love of God that has Godself as its object is, for Barth, the mutual love of the Father for the Son and the Son for the Father, i.e., it is the Holy Spirit. It might be argued that this divine self-love constitutes not a denial, but rather an eminent exemplification, of the phenomenon of human love.

Rahner explictly acknowledges the influence of Barth's concept of God's "three ways of being" *(drei Seinsweisen)* upon the formulation of his own notion of the "three relative ways in which God subsists" *(drei relative Subsistenzweisen).*[77] Rahner, like Barth, holds that God as the unoriginate source (Father) does indeed posit a genuinely distinct other (Son) and accepts that other precisely as God's own other (Holy Spirit). Further, Rahner would agree with Barth that the divine self-expression *ad intra* is strictly necessary to the divine being, while the self-expression of God *ad extra* is wholly gratuitous and nonessential to God. But as far as I can tell, Rahner never speaks of a love of God the Father for God the Son, God's other, in which God is passive in relation to the (divine) object of the divine love. Rahner does say that

> . . . in God in himself exists the real difference between one and the same God as necessarily and in one the unoriginate one who communicates himself to himself (Father), the one who in truth is expressed for himself (Son), and the one who in love is received and accepted for himself (Spirit).[78]

However, this is not to say with Barth that the Holy Spirit is the love between Father and Son. It is to say only that the term "Holy Spirit" refers to that aspect of God in which God lovingly accepts God's own self-expression.

Indeed, given Rahner's principle that the economic trinity is the immanent trinity, and vice versa, Rahner cannot speak of a love of God the Father for God the Son in the way that Barth does. To speak of a love of God for God's other would be to abandon the salvation-historical starting point of all our talk about God and lapse into a misleading psychological doctrine of the trinity. Rahner argues that:

> The psychological doctrine of the trinity leaps over the experience of the trinity in the economy of salvation in favor of what seems to be an almost gnostic speculation concerning how things go on in the interior of God. In

314 God is Love

> so doing, it really forgets that the countenance of God, as
> it is turned toward us in the self-communication meant
> here, is, in the threefold character of its being turned
> toward us, precisely the in itself of God himself.[79]

Further, to affirm that God the Father loves God the Son
would seem to deny that Father and Son are simply relatively
distinct ways in which God subsists. That is, if God the Father,
Son, and Holy Spirit are, for Rahner, three relatively distinct
ways in which the one divine individual subsists and not three
"persons" in the modern sense of individual centers of consciousness and activity, and if love can only be attributed to
persons who are free to give themselves ecstatically to others or
to refuse themselves, then it would seem impossible to say of
Father, Son, and Holy Spirit that they could love each other. It
would be nonsensical to say that one relatively distinct way in
which God subsists could love another relatively distinct way in
which God subsists. The Son or Logos, for Rahner, is genuinely
distinct from the Father and is the Father's other or real symbol.
But if the Father and the Son are not separate centers of consciousness, then they cannot be said to love one another.

While Rahner may not speak of an intratrinitarian divine
love, that is, a love of God the Father for God the Son, which love
is God the Holy Spirit, there can be no doubt that he does speak
of a divine self-love. Recall the passage cited earlier in this study
in which he states that

> . . . the free, contingent being is illuminated in the free
> love of God for himself, and, thereby, for his freely
> posited work. . . . Inasmuch as God, in love, freely loves
> himself as the creative power of the finite, he lovingly
> apprehends the finite itself.[80]

So, it might be argued, even if Rahner does not go as far as
Barth in affirming an intradivine "other" as the object of the
divine self-love, he does speak of a divine self-love that makes it
possible to assert that God is essentially love (of self) without
asserting that God is internally or really related to the creatures.

The problem with this suggestion is that it leads us back into
the same impasse that was discussed earlier in this chapter. That
is to say, since Rahner defines love as the opening and abandoning of oneself to another person, it is unclear what meaning such
a divine love of self could have. It is not clear in what sense God

could be said to open or to abandon Godself to Godself once the view that it is the Logos or Son that is the object of the divine self-love has been rejected. Rahner simply does not develop a concept of self-love, divine or human. "Love," as Rahner defines it, would seem to apply only to a relationship between two (or more) persons. So, at best, to propose that God is essentially love in that God, prior to the freely bestowed love of God for the creatures, already is a lover of Godself, would seem to depend, at least with respect to Rahner's theology, upon an argument from ignorance. There is no explicit concept of self-love in Rahner. Further, such a proposal is subject to the objection raised in this chapter, namely, that such a view of the divine love cannot plausibly be derived from our own most fundamental experience of love, in which, according to Rahner himself, a person freely opens and gives her- or himself to another person. This would contradict his principle that we are to derive the categories to be used in a concept of God from our most basic experience of ourselves.

And even if one were to augment Rahner's theology with a well-developed concept of self-love, in relation to which it would make sense to say that God is essentially love of self, such a view of the divine being as a self-lover would still be inadequate in that it would not apply to God an essential category disclosed in our own experience of ourselves as persons, namely, that to be a subject at all is to be constituted by real or internal relatedness to other subjects. Even if we were to grant a divine self-love in which God can be said to be essentially, and not simply accidentally, love, without also being essentially related to the creatures, Rahner's concept of God would still not be rescued from self-contradiction. For, as I will show in the following chapter, Rahner asserts that the most basic concepts that are to be used in relation to God must be derived from our existentiell experience of ourselves as persons. Yet his view of God as an individual who requires absolutely no relatedness to others in order to exist as God cannot plausibly be held to derive from our experience of ourselves as essentially related beings.

So, it seems to me that the suggestion that Rahner's thought is not as vulnerable on the point of the essential love of God as I have portrayed it to be above, in that Rahner shows God to be essentially love (of self) prior to, and without reference to, God's free love for nondivine others, is not, finally, that illuminating.

The notion of an essential divine self-love does not provide a way around the impasse present in Rahner's thought concerning the essential love of God and the essential passive moment of love, because this notion itself leads to a conceptual impasse. On the one hand, if this alleged divine self-love is to be recognizable as *love* (as the passive opening of oneself to another person and the active abandoning of oneself to that other person), then Rahner must posit one of the "persons" of the trinity as the object of the divine self-love and another "person" of the trinity as the subject of that love. But this position is excluded from the outset by Rahner's axiom that the economic trinity is the immanent trinity, and vice versa, and his claim that the three "persons" of the trinity are three relatively distinct ways in which God subsists. On the other hand, if the persons of the trinity cannot conceivably be said to be persons in the modern sense of the term and, thus, cannot conceivably be said to be capable of love one for another, then it is no longer clear what meaning the divine self-love might have, since Rahner understands love to presuppose another person who is the object of my love, and in relation to whom I am both active and passive.

NOTES

1 This book was first published in 1930 (Part I) and 1936 (Part II) in Swedish. I will refer to the revised, one volume edition of the English translation by Philip Watson (London: SPCK, 1953).

2 Gene Outka, *Agape: An Ethical Analysis* (New Haven: Yale University, Press, 1972), p. 1.

3 *Agape and Eros*, p. 48.

4 Ibid., p. 210.

5 For an overview of both the Protestant and Roman Catholic discussions of Nygren's thesis, see Robert Hazo, *The Idea of Love* (New York: Frederick A. Praeger, 1967), pp. 100–160.

6 *Amor Dei: A Study of the Religion of St. Augustine* (London: Hodder & Stoughton, 1938).

7 *The Mind and Heart of Love: Lion and Unicorn. A Study in Eros and Agape* (New York: Henry Holt, 1947).

8 Ibid., p. 313.

9 *Love, Power, and Justice: Ontological Analyses and Ethical Applications* (London: Oxford University Press, 1954).

10 Ibid., pp. 27–34.

The Self-Communication of God 317

[11] *Agape: An Ethical Analysis.*

[12] Maurice Nédoncelle, *Love and the Person,* trans. Ruth Adelaide (New York: Sheed and Ward, 1966).

[13] *The Spirit and the Forms of Love* (New York: Harper & Row, 1968).

[14] *The Experience of Love* (Washington, D.C.: Corpus Books, 1968).

[15] Ibid., p. 8. Tillich's ontological analysis of love represents an important exception to this rule.

[16] *The Spirit and the Forms of Love,* pp. 114–122.

[17] Ibid., p. 115.

[18] Ibid., p. 116.

[19] Ibid., p. 117.

[20] Ibid.

[21] Ibid., pp. 118–120.

[22] Ibid., pp. 120–121.

[23] *The Experience of Love.*

[24] Ibid., chapters 5, 6, and 7 respectively.

[25] Ibid., p. 95.

[26] Ibid., p. 120.

[27] Ibid., p. 136.

[28] Ibid., p. 134.

[29] Ibid., pp. 141–150.

[30] *The Spirit and the Forms of Love,* p. 117; *The Experience of Love,* p. 120.

[31] *The Spirit and the Forms of Love,* p. 117.

[32] *The Meaning of Man,* trans. A. H. G. Downes (New York: Sheed & Ward, 1948), p. 202.

[33] *A Study in the Ethics of Commitment within the Context of Theories of Human Love and Temporality,* Ph.D. Dissertation, Yale University (Ann Arbor: University Microfilms, 1978), pp. 120, 148, my emphasis.

[34] *Existential Phenomenology,* trans. Henry Koren, Duquesne Studies, Philosophical Series, no. 12 (Pittsburgh: Duquesne University Press, 1960), pp. 215, 217–218. Luijpen's "phenomenology of love," (pp. 214–231) is very similar to the views of Williams and Toner.

[35] *Love and the Person,* p. 24.

[36] "Agape in Feminist Ethics," *Journal of Religious Ethics* 6 (1981):69–70.

[37] Ibid., p. 74.

[38] Ibid.

[39] Ibid.

[40] Ibid., p. 77.

[41] Ibid., p. 78.

[42] See *A Study in the Ethics of Commitment within the Context of Theories of Human Love and Temporality,* and "New Patterns of Relationship: Beginnings of a Moral Revolution," *Theological Studies* 36 (1975): 627–646.

43 "New Patterns of Relationship: Beginnings of a Moral Revolution," pp. 634–635.

44 Ibid., p. 635.

45 Ibid., p. 639.

46 Although I have no desire to enter into the debate over whether "love" applies only to relationships between human beings, it would seem that if one were to decide that one could legitimately speak of a human love for works of art, or for pets, or for the earth as a whole, the understanding of love as passivity and activity once again would be applicable. Even a nonhuman reality, if I "love" it, makes some difference in my life: perhaps Picasso's *Guernica* or Chagall's *Hommage à Apollinaire* or Handel's *Messiah* have a very important and determinative place in my total understanding of myself, the world, and God. These works of art claim me as a person. In response, I give myself to the work of art in that I continue to look at it, or to listen to it so that it might "be free" to disclose even more fully the truth about existence it contains or represents. Likewise, pets, or even the earth as a whole, lay claims upon us, and in response, if we are loving persons, we take steps to protect animals or the environment and to facilitate their development.

47 "Über die Einheit von Nächsten- und Gottesliebe," *ST*, 6:290 (ET: *TI*, 6:243).

48 "Liebe," *KtW*, pp. 227–228.

49 "*Theos* im Neuen Testament," *ST*, 1:141 (ET: *TI*, 1:123), my emphasis.

50 "Die menschliche Sinnfrage vor dem absoluten Geheimnis Gottes," *ST*, 13:124–125.

51 "Zur Theologie der Hoffnung," *ST*, 8:568–570 (ET: *TI*, 10:250–251).

52 *HW*, p. 207. Of course, the terms "opening" or "openness" are systematically ambiguous in that they can refer both to an opening of the self that allows another person to be passively received and to an opening that allows oneself to be actively given to another person. For something can either be poured into or poured out of an open container.

53 "Über die Einheit von Nächsten- und Gottesliebe," *ST*, 6:288 (ET: *TI*, 6:241).

54 "Analogie," *KtW*, pp. 17–18.

55 "*Theos* im Neuen Testament," *ST*, 1:141 (ET: *TI*, 1:123).

56 "Zum theologischen Begriff der Konkupiszenz," *ST*, 1:386, n. 1 (ET: *TI*, 1:356, n. 1).

57 *GG*, p. 80 (ET: *FCF*, p. 72).

58 Ibid., p. 80 (ET: ibid., p. 73).

59 "Analogie," *KtW*, p. 17.

60 Ibid., p. 18.

61 Ibid., p. 17.

62 "Zur Theologie der Menschwerdung," *ST*, 4:148 (ET: *TI*, 4:115).

63 *GG*, p. 127 (ET: *FCF*, p. 121).

64 "Christologie im Rahmen des modernen Selbst- und Weltver-ständnisses," *ST*, 9:230 (ET: *TI*, 11:218).

65 "Theologie der Macht," *ST*, 4:492 (ET: *TI*, 4:396).

66 *HW*, p. 151.

67 For my own view of the radical difference between divine and human love, see Chapter XI below.

68 *The Spirit and the Forms of Love*, pp. 123–124.

69 Ibid., p. 137.

70 Ibid., p. 127.

71 Ibid., p. 137.

72 Das Christentum und der 'neue Mensch,'" *ST*, 5:170 (ET: *TI*, 5:145).

73 "Marxistische Utopie und christliche Zukunft des Menschen," *ST*, 6:78 (ET: *TI*, 6:60).

74 "Über die theologische Problematik der 'neuen Erde,'" *ST*, 8:590 (ET: *TI*, 10:270).

75 "Die Frage nach der Zukunft," *ST*, 9:523 (ET: *TI*, 12:185).

76 *Die kirchliche Dogmatik*, 4 volumes (Zürich: Evangelischer Verlag, 1946), 2, part 1:314–315 (ET: *Church Dogmatics*, 4 volumes (New York: Scribner's, 1957), 2, part 1:280).

77 "Der dreifaltige Gott als transzendenter Urgrund der Heilsgeschichte," pp. 365, n. 26, 389–392 (ET: *The Trinity*, pp. 74, n. 27, 110–113).

78 Ibid., p. 384 (ET: ibid., pp. 101–102).

79 *GG*, p. 141 (ET: *FCF*, p. 135).

80 *HW*, pp. 125–126.

CHAPTER X
THE TURN TO THE SUBJECT AND RAHNER'S CONCEPT OF GOD

In the three preceding chapters I have argued that Rahner's account of the meaning and truth of the assertion "God is love" is less than fully adequate at three points. I showed that his understanding of the relativity and nonrelativity of God, which he takes to be implied by the truth of "God is love," is incoherent; that his view of the freedom or gratuity of the divine love entails that God is not essentially love of others, a view that is not justified by the apostolic witness of scripture or by our common human experience and reason; and that his understanding of the divine love is subject to a certain one-sidedness in that the divine love, as distinct from human love, does not include a passive moment in which the divine lover is open to, and determined by, the creaturely beloved.

It seems to me that all of these shortcomings betray a more fundamental inconsistency in Rahner's thought. Contrary to his own intentions, Rahner does not fully carry through the methodological turn to the subject in the formulation of his doctrine of God. With respect to the love, freedom, and relativity of God, Rahner's concept of God seems to involve categories that are not derived from what he takes to be the fundamental existentiell experience that human beings have of themselves. At these three points, his concept of God seems to be imposed upon his view of fundamental human experience rather than derived from it. In all three cases, some essential aspect of the meaning of "love," "freedom," and "relativity," as disclosed in our most fundamental experience of ourselves, is denied when these terms are attributed analogically to God. This denial violates Rahner's own criterion for the appropriate attribution of analogical predicates to the divine reality. The purpose of this chapter is to illustrate this deeper inconsistency in his thought.

What is the Origin of the Basic Categories in Rahner's Concept of God?

The charge that Rahner is inconsistent in his use of basic categories derived from the fundamental experience of human persons with respect to the concept of God has already been made in Chapter IX. There I argued that an essential aspect of the meaning of the concept of love, as it is used in relation to human being, is denied when Rahner applies "love" analogically to God. Human love is characterized as the fundamental human act in which both the lover and the beloved attain their full, authentic self-realization through their mutual interrelationship. Human love, according to Rahner, consists of the opening of oneself to another person and the ecstatic giving of oneself to that other person. His concept of the divine love, however, differs significantly from this understanding of human love. Like human love, the divine love is conceived to be an act of free ecstatic self-giving that facilitates (or reveals) the full self-realization of both God and the creature. But Rahner does not apply to the divine being and the divine love a passive moment, a moment that, in the case of human love, is necessarily presupposed by the active moment of love. An essential aspect of the human experience of love is denied in his account of the divine love. There is, therefore, initial reason to doubt that the fundamental human experience of love provides Rahner with the categories used in his concept of the divine love, for a view of love that does not include a recognition of the essential passivity of love does not make full use of the categories that derive from the human experience of love.

A similar tension exists within Rahner's view of human freedom and divine freedom. It seems to me that his understanding of the divine freedom is very different from the view of freedom that he develops as a result of transcendental reflection upon the basic experience of the human person. As I have shown above, freedom, for Rahner, is the ability of a free subject to realize or constitute itself, to choose itself, to take possession of itself.

> The free act, in its primordial essence, is not so much the positing of another, something that is alien, a work that stands over against the act in its otherness, but is the fulfilling of [the subject's] own essence, a taking posses-

sion of itself, a taking possession of the reality of its own creative power over itself.[1]

But, as I have also shown, this taking possession of oneself, this freedom, which is an essential moment of all human activity, occurs only through the mediation of other free persons. This is to say that freedom is the ability of a person to constitute her- or himself in relation to other persons. Human freedom is essentially a freedom in relation to other free persons.

> Freedom is always the freedom of a subject that stands in interpersonal communication with other subjects. Thus, it is necessarily freedom over against another subject of transcendence; ... [freedom] is the condition of the possibility of the *Bei-sich-sein* of a subject that is with itself and just as primordially with the other *subject*.[2]

This is a wholly positive conception of freedom. That is, a subject is free to constitute itself as this, as opposed to that, sort of person in relation to others (e.g., as a loving or a hating, a responsible or an irresponsible, person). But Rahner understands the divine freedom in a negative as well as a positive sense. God is independent of the world, and would be God even if God had not created the world at all. Rahner says that God "cannot need finite reality, called 'the world,' for otherwise he would not be radically different from the world, but would be part of a larger whole."[3] God is free to constitute Godself independently of all relationships to other individuals.

This is the case, for Rahner, with respect both to the creative and to the self-communicative activity of God. In the very positing of finite reality, the primary object of the divine will is God's own being.

> For he intends himself in his free creative power. . . . The finite, contingent being is illuminated in the free love of God for himself, and, thereby, for his freely posited work. . . . Inasmuch as God in love freely loves himself as the creative power of the finite, he apprehends the finite itself.[4]

Likewise, the self-communication or personal love of God for the creatures is a strictly gratuitous act. Here again, Rahner reveals a negative understanding of the divine freedom. God could have refused to bestow Godself upon the creatures. God could have remained the silent, aloof, asymptotic *Woraufhin* of human transcendence. God would still have been God in this situation of radical self-refusal.

While a human being, for Rahner, is free only in the positive sense of being able to constitute her- or himself as this, as opposed to that, particular kind of person in relation to others, God is free in the negative sense of being able to constitute Godself without reference to any other individuals. Once again, it is unclear, given Rahner's own understanding of human experience, how this negative view of freedom can be derived from the basic experience of freedom we all implicitly share as persons. There is simply no experiential basis for such a negative concept of freedom.

These views of the divine love and the divine freedom indicate that, for Rahner, relatedness to others is not essential to the divine being, while it is essential to human being. The human person is constituted by her or his relations to other persons. Human *Beisichsein* or subjectivity is always already a being with another. This is not the case with respect to God. God, in fact, has chosen to create the world, and further, to communicate Godself in love to the spiritual creature. But, for Rahner, it could have been otherwise. God could exist as God without having loved the creatures, or without having created the creatures at all.

The relativity of the human being is essential. But God is not essentially related to others. The personal relationship between God and the world is strictly gratuitous on God's part, and thus accidental. This view of the divine being would seem to involve a denial of an essential aspect of the fundamental human experience of self. In our immediate experience of ourselves we always find ourselves in relationship to other persons. As Rahner says, there is no "region" of our personal being into which we can withdraw in order to escape our necessary relatedness to other persons.[5] But he argues that the divine being is not essentially constituted by relatedness to others. The personal being of God, at this point, is radically different from our own personal being as we experience it, at least implicitly, in all moments of our existence.

So far in this chapter I have done nothing more than to suggest that Rahner's understanding of the divine love, freedom, and relativity differs significantly from his understanding of human love, freedom, and relativity. But to have indicated such a difference is, of course, not to have demonstrated an inconsistency within his thought. To demonstrate this requires the further step of showing that the formulation of Rahner's concept of God violates his own principles concerning the nature of appropriate reflection upon the divine being. I want to turn now to a demonstration of this tension in Rahner's doctrine of God.

It seems to me that Rahner's way of conceiving the divine love, freedom, and relativity is at odds with his own view of analogy. Recall the definition that he gives of "analogy": " 'Analogy' means that a concept, without losing the unity of its content, undergoes a real variation of meaning as it is applied to different individual beings or to different realms of being."[6] As Rahner indicates in this definition, there must be a real variation of the meaning of a concept that is derived from our experience of ourselves when such a concept is used in relation to the divine being. The divine love, unlike human love, is a steadfast and enduring love. God is existentially free in relation to all other individuals in a way that we as contingent beings are not. The relativity of God to the world entailed by the incarnation does not constitute a denial of God's immutability and transcendence. Thus, to say that God is love, or is free, or is related to other individuals, is not to attribute "love," "freedom," and "relativity" univocally to God. Up to this point I would agree with Rahner completely. The question, however, is whether the essential meaning, the "unity of the content" of concepts such as "love," "freedom," and "relativity," which are said to be applied analogically to God, is maintained when these concepts undergo such a real variation of meaning. If the essence of the meaning of a concept derived from our experience of ourselves is not maintained when applied to God, then, given Rahner's own view, one has not analogical predication, but sheer equivocation.

It seems to me that an essential aspect of the meaning of the concepts "love," "freedom," and "relativity" has been denied when Rahner conceives God as loving, free, and relative to others. That is to say, Rahner applies "love," "freedom," and "relativity" to God not analogically, as he claims to have done, but equivocally. In each case, an aspect of what essentially constitutes human love, freedom, and relativity, namely, real or internal relatedness to others, is not applied to the divine being. Now, of course, Rahner holds this essential real relatedness of human being to be a function of the materiality of human being. He follows the philosophical and theological tradition that refuses to admit materiality to God. But given his understanding of analogy, this refusal to apply to God an essential relatedness to others appears to be arbitrary. That is to say, when Rahner speaks of the divine love as a wholly active love that does not include a passive moment, or of the divine freedom as the negative freedom of God to constitute Godself independently of all relatedness to others, or of God as a subject who can exist without being related to any other individuals, he seems not to be *varying* the meaning of "love" or "freedom" or "relativity," but rather to be employing these concepts in very different, even equivocal, senses. To paraphrase an argument of Daniel Day Williams, Rahner seems to have removed one aspect of the distinctive meaning of "love," "freedom," and "relativity" as these terms are used in relation to our most fundamental experience of ourselves as persons, and used the remainder to construct a concept of the love, the freedom, and the relativity of God.[7]

I think it is important to note that in refusing to admit a real relatedness of God to others, Rahner is not simply, and justifiably, denying to God some human deficiency or imperfection. Of course, one would not be justified in applying analogically to God the limitations of human knowledge, for instance. God, unlike human beings, is omniscient. But real or internal relatedness to others, as Rahner himself argues, is not a limitation or an imperfection of human being, but is part of the essential, positive nature of human being. Relatedness to others is not an impediment to, or a limitation of, the realization of the human person, but is a necessary aspect or condition of human self-realization. Relatedness to others is an essential structure of human being, one that can be realized in an authentic way (love) or in deficient and inauthentic ways (indifference, or hate). Thus, it is unclear, given Rahner's own understanding of analogy, why this essential aspect of human being, relatedness to others, which is a necessary condition of the possibility of human love and freedom, should not be applied to God, in some appropriate fashion, when God is said, analogically, to be loving and free.

At this point Rahner's concept of God seems to be in conflict with the principle that he sets out in the following statement:

> The ground of a reality that exists must beforehand possess in itself in absolute fullness and purity this reality that it grounds. For, otherwise, this ground could not be the ground of that which is grounded at all; for, otherwise, it would finally be the empty nothingness that—if one takes the term seriously—would express nothing and could ground nothing.[8]

For God to be the ground of human being, and, indeed, of the finite world as such, it would seem that God must possess in absolute fullness, although also in absolute purity, the real relatedness to others that is essential to human being and finite reality. And yet, for Rahner, God must be essentially free of all relations to other individuals if God is to be God. Rahner does not apply even an appropriately "purified" form of internal relatedness to others to God. He emphatically denies that God is essentially related to others. His view of God seems to be inconsistent at this point. On the one hand, he seems to indicate that God must possess some appropriately divine form of essential relatedness to others if God is to be the final ground of the finite world, and yet, on the other hand, he denies that God is essentially related to others.

Does Rahner Fully Take the Turn to the Subject?

For the reasons just given, it seems to me that Rahner fails fully to take the turn to the subject, that is, he does not conceive God solely by using categories that derive from the basic experience human beings have of themselves as persons. Instead, he conceives God using categories that cannot be derived from our experience of ourselves. This contradicts his own call for a turn to the subject in theology.

As I showed in the Introduction to the study, Rahner holds that the distinctively modern methodological turn to the subject, whereby the most fundamental experience the human person has of her- or himself provides the starting point and paradigm for all theological and philosophical reflection, must also inform an adequate contemporary concept of God. Further, he claims that such a conception of God using categories derived from the immediate experience the human person has of her- or himself as a free subject, has not yet been provided. That Rahner attempts to provide such a revisionary concept of God is clear. His use of concepts such as love and freedom as the central concepts of his doctrine of God represents a very important contribution to this revisionary task. But it seems to me that there is an arbitrary refusal on Rahner's part fully to carry through this turn to the subject in relation to the formulation of a concept of God. He clearly identifies the basic human experience that is to provide the starting point for all theological reflection, namely, the existentiell experience the human person has of her- or himself as a free subject that must constitute itself in relation to other human persons and to God. But as I have tried to show in this chapter, at one key point Rahner's concept of the divine love, the divine freedom, and the divine relativity, seems to involve categories that are not derived from this basic human experience of self. In fact, his concept of God constitutes an explicit denial of the experience of the human self as essentially related to others.

It is my view that at this key point the categories Rahner uses to conceive the divine reality are imposed upon, rather than derived from, our basic experience of ourselves as persons. Given Rahner's own understanding of human love, human freedom, and human relativity, and taking the basic experience in which love, freedom, and relativity are disclosed as the prime datum for theological reflection, as he says must be done, there is no experiential evidence for a love that does not have a passive moment, or for a free agent who can constitute itself independently of relations to other free agents, or for an individual that could exist without real or internal relatedness to any other individuals. In his view of the divine love, the divine freedom, and the divine relativity, Rahner seems to be appealing to a traditional understanding of God as strictly nonrelative and radically *a se*, rather than developing a concept of God on the basis of our own most fundamental experience of ourselves. He gives no methodological justification for this procedure. Indeed, he argues that all theological and philosophical reflection must take as its prime datum and paradigm this fundamental experience of the human subject. Thus, his concept of God is less than adequate in that it does not fully exemplify the methodological turn to the subject that Rahner himself argues must be taken.

William Shepherd argues that Rahner's theology is "disjointed" in that his basic theological enterprise (his "theology of nature and grace") is "conceived and carried out within the context of a modern, non-static, unified, historical, evolving view of the universe," while his "technical doctrine of nature and grace" is carried out using "terms drawn from the traditional, hierarchical, static, layered view of the world."[9] It seems to me that something similar could be said of Rahner's understanding of God. On the one hand, he proposes that God is to be conceived in terms of categories that derive from the basic experience human beings have of themselves as free persons, rather than in terms of categories that derive from our experience of things. This approach leads Rahner to reconceive aspects of traditional scholastic theology in a revisionary fashion. For example, he conceives the God-world relationship in terms of a personal dialogue and the grace of God in terms of the communication of one person (God) to other persons (human beings). And yet, on the other hand, he seems finally to appeal to a traditional view of God as strictly nonrelated to others, and employs concepts of the divine love, freedom, and relativity, that could not plausibly be held to derive from our immediate experience of ourselves as free persons who must constitute ourselves in relation to other persons and God. At this point there is a tension between the revisionary theological project Rahner sets for himself and the actual formulation of his concept of God, which does not seem to be informed by the methodological turn to the subject and its revisionary implications for theology.

Several other interpreters of Rahner see a similar tension in his thought, and identify it as a tension between the subject-oriented approach of transcendental philosophy and the substance-oriented approach of Thomism.[10] Johannes Heinrichs says with respect to Rahner that

> . . . one can no longer close one's eyes to the fact that the gulf between a Thomistic philosophy of being and a transcendental-philosophical hermeneutic of meaning is of prodigious dimensions, and . . . still is not bridged in his thought.[11]

Walter Hoeres makes the even broader claim that these two philosophical approaches cannot be reconciled.[12] Similarly, Bernard Nachbar asks rhetorically whether

> . . . it is not an impracticable task and an illusory project to develop a transcendental Thomism, i.e., to bring into an harmonious and intelligible synthesis an anthropocentric and critical form of thought on the one hand and

a cosmocentric, pre-critical form of thought on the other.[13]

Schubert Ogden argues that the material axioms, and thus the conclusions, of transcendental Thomism are of pre-critical, and not post-critical origin.[14] Ogden claims, therefore, that:

> Transcendental Thomism is exactly that, adjectivally transcendental and substantivally Thomism. I say this not as a reproach, for my respect for the Thomistic tradition is unreserved, especially when it is expressed with the genius and will to truth that so obviously distinguish some of its recent exponents. But I do wish to indicate . . . where I see the limitations of this significant new philosophical movement. My conviction, which I cannot defend here, is that the characteristic positions of Thomistic metaphysics have been shown to be sufficiently problematic that they can no longer serve either as an adequate philosophy or as an appropriate conceptuality for interpreting the Christian faith. The core of the problem is that these positions all rest, finally, on the classical prejudice for the absolute and unchanging against the relativity and change, the utter sociality, of our concrete experience.[15]

In summary, it seems to me that there is a fundamental tension within Rahner's concept of God. On the one hand, he states formally that God must be conceived using categories that derive from our own fundamental experience of ourselves as free subjects who are essentially social in our being and who, therefore, constitute ourselves solely in relation to other persons. On the other hand, his actual concept of God does not seem materially to be constructed using categories derived solely from this fundamental human experience of self. For Rahner, divine being is not essentially social being. God can be God without being really related to any other individuals. God is free in the negative sense of being able to constitute Godself independently of any relatedness to other individuals. The divine love is a wholly active self-giving love that does not entail, as a condition of its possibility, a passivity of God with respect to the creature whom God loves. Thus, Rahner seems to impose an arbitrary limit upon the use of personal categories, which are derived from our basic experience of ourselves as free persons, in the formulation of his concept of God. He is careful to defend his revisionary, subject-oriented theological method. Also, many of his foundational assertions concerning God involve the use of personal categories derived from the basic human experience of self, such as self-communication, love, intimacy, and personal dialogue. But there is a point at which he abandons this anthropologically oriented approach to the doctrine of God, and imposes upon the human subject's self-experience a traditional view of God as strictly nonrelated to others that has no experiential warrant.

Here again, Rahner's thought leads us to a conceptual impasse. Rahner proposes taking the methodological turn to the subject with respect to the formulation of an understanding of God, but does not fully carry out this project. As it stands, his thought is inconsistent, allowing for two very different options. First, one might modify his claims concerning the applicability of the methodological turn to the subject to reflection upon the reality of God, in order to indicate more clearly the limits of categories derived from our common human experience of ourselves when used to conceive God. Or, second, one might try to take the turn to the subject in a fully consistent fashion with respect to the concept of God. This would entail conceiving God, in an eminent or pure sense, to be sure, as a social being, constituted by essential real relatedness to other individuals. For reasons that were stated in the Introduction, it seems to me that only this second option represents an adequate response to the task of contemporary theology. In Part III of this study, I want to sketch the outlines of a concept of God consistently using categories derived from the fundamental human experience of self as a free self-creator constituted by relations to other free self-creators.

NOTES

[1] *HW*, p. 123.
[2] *GG*, p. 74 (ET: *FCF*, p. 65).
[3] Ibid., p. 85 (ET: ibid., p. 78).
[4] *HW*, pp. 125–126.
[5] "Der eine Mittler und die Vielfalt der Vermittlungen," *ST*, 8:226 (ET: *TI*, 9:176).
[6] "Analogie," *KtW*, p. 17.
[7] See *The Spirit and the Forms of Love*, pp. 123–124.

8 *GG*, pp. 81–82 (ET: *FCF*, pp. 73–74).

9 *Man's Condition*, p. 25.

10 It seems to me that one might catalogue the various critical responses to Rahner's thought in terms of the way in which each interpreter evaluates the possibility of developing a "transcendental Thomism." There is a "right-wing" reponse to his theology, exemplified by Jacques Maritain and Hans Urs von Balthasar, in which a "transcendental Thomism" such as Rahner's is viewed as being illegitimate in that the adoption of a transcendental mode of inquiry represents the introduction of unwarranted subjectivism and anthropocentrism into philosophical thought. Then there is a middle position that is basically sympathetic to Rahner and that would recognize the promise, even necessity, of a synthesis of Thomism and modern transcendental philosophy. This position is represented by thinkers such as Bert van der Heijden, Klaus Fischer, Karl-Heinz Weger, and Anne Carr. Finally, as I seek to indicate above, there is a "left-wing" response that would argue that transcendental Thomism is impossible in that adopting the starting point and methodology of transcendental philosophy can only show the substance-oriented metaphysics of Thomas to be finally inadequate.

11 "Sinn und Intersubjektivität," pp. 189–190.

12 *Kritik der transzendentalphilosophischen Erkenntnistheorie*, p. 11.

13 "Is it Thomism?" *Continuum* 6 (1968):233. Of course, as Nachbar himself indicates, Rahner, and even more explicitly, Metz, have argued that the modern turn to the subject is already anticipated to a significant degree by Thomas. Thus, in this view, a synthesis of Thomism and critical, transcendental philosophy is not as difficult a task as it might appear at first glance.

14 "The Challenge to Protestant Thought," *Continuum* 6 (1968):239.

15 Ibid. Ogden develops this criticism much more fully in relation to the thought of Bernard Lonergan in an essay entitled "Lonergan and the Subjectivist Principle" (*Journal of Religion* 51 (1971):155–173). Ogden argues that despite Lonergan's affirmation of the subjectivist principle (what I have called, in this study, the turn to the subject), the key categories that he uses to conceptualize the divine reality are not derived from his analysis of the human subject's own experience of her- or himself. Leslie Dewart advances a similar argument against Rahner, Lonergan, and Coreth in "On Transcendental Thomism," *Continuum* 6 (1968):389–401.

PART III
THE OUTLINES OF AN ALTERNATIVE CONCEPT OF GOD

CHAPTER XI
GOD IS LOVE

The goal of the third and final part of this study is to outline one way in which Rahner's concept of God might be recast in a coherent form so as to avoid the impasse into which it presently leads. The methodological starting point for this alternative concept of God is the conviction that God must be conceived using categories that derive from our most basic experience of ourselves as persons. I argued in Chapter X that Rahner affirms, formally, the necessity of taking this turn to the subject, but does not inform his own concept of God sufficiently with such a turn. The alternative concept of God that is outlined here represents an attempt to apply to God the basic categories that Rahner derives from an analysis of our fundamental existentiell experience of ourselves as persons essentially related to other persons. Therefore, the argument of this part of the study does not constitute a denial of Rahner's concept of God, but is rather an attempt to carry out more fully and consistently what he takes to be the contemporary task of formulating an adequate concept of God.

Obviously, I cannot hope to provide a fully developed alternative to Rahner's rich and nuanced concept of God in the final two chapters of this study. My goal is much more modest. In this chapter I hope to show that by consistently applying to God categories derived from our fundamental experience of ourselves, one can avoid the threefold impasse into which Rahner's concept of God presently leads, that is, the impasse constituted by his claims that God can freely adopt a relativity to others in God's other while remaining strictly nonrelative in Godself (Chapter VII); that God cannot be essentially love of others if the divine love is to be wholly gratuitous (Chapter VIII); and that the divine love, understood as ecstatic divine self-communication, does not imply an essential passivity of the divine love or the divine being (Chapter IX). But I also hope to show that this

recasting of Rahner's concept of God does not entail denying or
slighting the concerns that led to this impasse in the first place. I
will argue that the concept of God outlined here, in which God is
affirmed to be essentially love of others, does not deny, but
reexpresses in a more coherent fashion, the crucial themes of
Rahner's understanding of God that were identified in the first
part of this study: the identity and difference, relativity and
nonrelativity of God with respect to the world, and the activity of
God "in" the world (Chapter VI); the freedom of God and the
gratuity of the divine love (Chapter V); the self-communication
of God to the world (Chapter IV); and, finally, the essentially
mysterious character of the divine being (Chapter III). Therefore, the formulation of this alternative concept of God is intended both to lead beyond the impasse in Rahner's theology
identified in the second part of this study and to lead back into
the analysis of the central themes of his concept of God carried
out in the first part of the study. Finally, in Chapter XII, I want
to discuss some of the wider theological implications of this
recasting of Rahner's concept of God.

In my recasting of Rahner's concept of God I have found
resources offered by process or neoclassical philosophy and
theology to be helpful.[1] I think it is important to state clearly, at
the outset, the role process thought plays in these two chapters,
since it has not played a critical role in the first ten chapters of
this study.

I do not believe that the resources of process thought are
needed to supplement or correct Rahner's understanding of the
fundamental experience we have of ourselves as human persons.
As the entire argument of this study implies, I find his account
of our basic existentiell experience of ourselves as free self-
creators related to other free self-creators to be largely adequate.
It seems to me that for the purposes of this study the process and
Rahnerian views of the fundamental human experience of self
do not differ significantly. Now, if one were to discuss the basic
metaphysical outlooks that lie behind these similar accounts of
human experience, one would have to point out the differences
between Rahner and process thought. The most crucial difference would seem to be that Rahner holds with the classical
Western metaphysical tradition that the world is composed of
enduring individuals or substances, which retain an essential

self-identity throughout their entire "life-span." In process thought, the final real things of which the world is composed are events or "actual occasions": thoroughly atomic happenings, moments of becoming, which exist only fleetingly and then perish as subjects becoming the objective data for other futural, actual occasions. What we ordinarily call "individuals," whether electrons, stones, or human beings, are ordered societies of actual occasions. Individuality refers not to the enduring nature of a self-identical substance, but rather to the abstract, identifying qualities of a particular series of actual occasions. I do not believe it is necessary, in this study, to criticize Rahner's account of our basic experience of ourselves in terms of this neoclassical metaphysics. What is important is the view, shared by both Rahner and the process thinkers, that an individual is constituted by real or internal relations to other individuals, which means that an individual creates itself in response to the difference other individuals make in its life and then acts toward those individuals so as to make some difference in their lives.

Nor do I believe that it is necessary to reexpress Rahner's understanding of selfhood in terms of the technical vocabulary of process thought, which involves terms such as "actual occasion," "prehension," "subjective aim," "nexus," "eternal objects," "creative advance," "primordial and consequent natures of God," and so forth. The nontechnical vocabulary already established in the preceding ten chapters of this study will suffice, e.g., "real" or "internal" and "nominal" or "external relatedness," "relativity and nonrelativity," "free self-creation" or "self-constitution," "allowing someone to make a difference in one's life and acting on the basis of that difference," "object and subject," "person and personality." The one term that does derive from the technical vocabulary of process thought that will be used sparingly in this chapter is "to synthesize." But I will employ this verb, and the related noun "synthesis," simply as a shorthand way of saying "to have one's being determined or qualified by another individual by making the reality of that other part of one's own experience and being."

So, the resources of process thought are needed neither to correct the starting point and formal paradigm of Rahner's concept of God, namely, the view that to be a human person is to be a free self-creator constituted by internal relatedness to other free self-creators, nor to reexpress this model of selfhood in more adequate terms. I believe that Rahner's basic concepts are adequate to the task of creating a contemporary concept of God that is faithful to scripture and credible in terms of our common human experience. What is lacking in his thought is a grammar or a syntax that would enable these basic concepts to be employed so as to create a coherent account of the divine reality. As it stands, in Rahner's thought, the model of selfhood derived from our most fundamental existentiell experience of ourselves is not consistently applied to God. As a result, Rahner is unable to affirm coherently both the relativity and the nonrelativity of God; both that love of others is God's fundamental act and that it is a free gift; and that the divine love, like human love, has both a passive and an active aspect. What is needed is some way of recasting Rahner's thought so that the various elements of his concept of God can be coherently related. I believe that process thought offers such a grammar or syntax whereby divine relativity and nonrelativity, essential, and yet free, love, and passive and active divine love can all be coherently affirmed. The resources of process thought will be used, therefore, to recast concepts and vocabulary already present in Rahner's concept of God. Process thought provides a model for carrying out consistently what Rahner states must be done, but is unable to do adequately himself: apply the basic categories deriving from our experience of ourselves to God as the eminent exemplification of these categories.

Now, if the resources of process thought are utilized simply as a model for a way in which Rahner's concept of God might be recast, then it would be irrelevant to attempt to explicate or even outline the process view of God. The focus of this chapter must be, rather, Rahner's own understanding of God. The process view of God will appear only indirectly as I attempt to recast Rahner's concept of God so as to avoid the threefold impasse into which it presently leads, while seeking to appropriate the chief theological concerns that lead to this impasse in the first place.

God as Essentially Love of Others

In the first three chapters of this study, using the thought of Rahner as my guide, I argued that human persons, as a condition of the possibility of all their acts, have an inner, unthematic awareness of themselves as subjects. Human beings are aware that they are not things, but subjects, who must constitute themselves through their own free decisions. Our being is an issue for us. Human existence is a task, a project that each person must take up for her- or himself.

At the same time, this free, personal mode of being is never given in isolation from other persons. Human beings are essentially related to other persons; they constitute themselves only through the mediation of others. Human being is a being with others. Presupposed in all human experience is an awareness of the social nature of human being. To exist as a human person presupposes that one is constituted by an essential relatedness to other persons.

I also have argued that Rahner is right that the fundamental activity of the human person is the activity in which the person freely constitutes her- or himself as a person. The first act of human freedom is the act of self-creation or self-constitution in which a person accomplishes her or his fundamental task of existing as a person. Once again, this primary activity of free self-creation is always an activity that is carried out in relation to other persons. It is an act in which the human person constitutes her- or himself in response to the other persons to whom she or he is related.

It is important to note what this constitution of oneself "in response to others" means. As Heinrich Ott writes, in a passage cited in Chapter II of this study,

> . . . because personal being is a being in the between, persons are not sharply marked off from one another. Rather, the spheres of their personal reality overlap and interpenetrate. A man is not merely *external* to the other (as one who is opposite), but, insofar as he has something to do with the other, is also internal to the other.[2]

To be related to another, to constitute oneself in relation to others, means to be open to the personal being of another person, to include something of the person to whom I am related within myself, to have that person within me.

Rahner, as I showed in Chapter III, holds that human being is essentially intercommunicative. Human relationships involve the communication of one's personal being to another person and the reception of the other person's being into oneself. For

him, the other human person, the Thou to whom I am unfailingly related, is the "material," the condition of the possibility
of my own self-creation as a person.[3] To create or constitute
myself as a human person means to appropriate the personal
being of another person into my own personal being. The other
person is taken into myself and thereby becomes a determinative
factor in my own free self-constitution. Likewise, my own personal being is offered to others as the material for their own
projects of self-constitution. This is to say that the relationship
between person *a* and person *b*, in which *a* constitutes her- or
himself in response to *b*, is a real or internal relationship for *a*.
Person *a* is constituted by including person *b* within her- or
himself.[4]

To be human is to actuate or constitute oneself as a person
in relation to other persons. One cannot exist independently of
relations to others. But what sort of person one constitutes
oneself as in relation to others is free, a matter of personal
decision. According to Rahner, the human person can constitute
her- or himself authentically, by responding in love to other
persons, that is, by opening oneself to other persons and by
giving or abandoning oneself to others. In love, one responds to
the other person in such a way as to facilitate her or his full, free
self-constitution. On the other hand, a person is free to constitute her- or himself inauthentically by remaining indifferent
to other persons, or even by hating them. In either case, one
does not respond to the others to whom one is essentially related, whose being mediates one's own personal being, in a way
that facilitates their full development as persons. As human
persons, we always and essentially exist in relation to others. But
we are free to ratify and enact authentically this essential relatedness to others, or to deny in our free activity, in a self-contradictory fashion, that we are essentially constituted by our relations
to other persons.

Love, for Rahner, is the most fundamental human act, in
that love represents the full, authentic realization of the human
person. (Again, indifference and hate represent not the mere
absence of love, but, rather, perverted or debased forms of love.)
Love is the particular mode of the free self-constitution of the
human person in which the other persons to whom one is
essentially related are allowed to make a real difference in one's

life and to be a determinative factor in one's own self-constitution. On the basis of the difference the other person makes in one's life, one acts toward that other person to facilitate her or his free self-constitution. One offers oneself as a determinative factor in the free self-creation of the other person. One offers oneself for inclusion within the personal being of another.

Rahner argues, formally at least, that it is this human experience of self as a free self-creator essentially related to other free self-creators and authentically realized through loving relationships to others that is to provide the basic categories for all philosophical and theological reflection, including reflection on the reality of God. But he fails to carry through fully this turn to the subject in his doctrine of God. At this point, the execution of his concept of God stands in tension with what he says Christian theology must do if it is adequately to conceive God. For Rahner to be consistent with his own principle, God ought to be understood to exemplify eminently the essential sociality of being, as disclosed in our most fundamental experience of ourselves. If this step is taken, that is, if God is conceived to be a free self-creator who constitutes Godself only in relation to other (nondivine) self-creators, then the threefold impasse into which Rahner's concept of God presently leads can be avoided.

If God is to be conceived using categories based upon our fundamental experience of ourselves, then God must be understood to be constituted by real or internal relations to other individuals. God does not create or constitute Godself in abstraction from relations to others. I argued that at this point Rahner's view of God is inconsistent. He recognizes that there must be a genuine relativity of God if the claim that God is love is to make sense. And yet his formulation "God is relative in God's other and strictly nonrelative in Godself," can represent more than a merely verbal affirmation of a relativity of God only if a relativity of God in Godself is admitted.

Rahner's concept of God must be recast in order to avoid this impasse. God in Godself must be viewed as essentially related to others, for there is no other understanding of selfhood that can legitimately by derived from our basic experience of ourselves. There simply can be no selfhood without real or internal relatedness to other selves. The view that God can constitute Godself independently of real relatedness to other

individuals represents a denial of our fundamental experience
of the social nature of reality. Relatedness to others is not simply
one of God's possibilities, one that God freely decided to actualize. Rather, sociality, relatedness to others, is essential to all
actual selves. God cannot even be conceived except as really
related to other individuals. In this connection, Schubert Ogden
writes:

> If we begin by taking the self as thus experienced as
> paradigmatic for reality as such [i.e., the self as con-
> stituted by real relatedness to others], the result is a
> complete revolution of classical metaphysics. It there-
> upon becomes clear that real internal relation to others
> and intrinsic temporality are not "mixed perfections"
> peculiar to finite beings such as ourselves, but "simple
> perfections" inherent in the meaning of "reality" in the
> most fundamental use of the word. In consequence, the
> chief category for finally interpreting anything real can
> no longer be "substance" or "being" (as traditionally un-
> derstood), but must be "process" or "creative becoming"
> construed as that which is in principle social and tem-
> poral. Whatever is, is to be conceived, in the last analysis,
> either as an instance of, or an element in, such creative
> becoming and thus as somehow analogous to our own
> existence as selves. By *this* "analogy of being," however,
> God, too, must be conceived as a genuinely temporal and
> social reality, and therefore as radically different from
> the wholly timeless and unrelated Absolute of traditional
> theism.[5]

There are several consequences of conceiving God as constituted by real relations to others that are immediately suggested. The first is that God never exists without some world of
nondivine creatures. To be God is to be God of some world. Just
as there can be no essentially isolated human self, one who
constitutes her- or himself independently of real relations to
some other individuals, so the divine self cannot be conceived
except as constituted by real relations to others. Second, the
actuality of the creatures makes a real difference to God. God
creates Godself partially in response to the world. The divine
actuality would not be the same if there were some different
world of creatures in existence. God is genuinely affected by the
creatures. For to be related or relative to others is to reflect the
actuality of other individuals in one's own self.[6] Thus, God is not

adequately conceived solely as the absolute or nonrelative one. Rather, God is also the maximally relative one, for the actual states of all other individuals are reflected in the divine actuality. God is the one individual who constitutes self in response to all other individuals.

Having taken this step, we are in a position to move beyond the second impasse in Rahner's concept of God, which results from his view that God is not essentially love of others. Just as the fundamental human activity is that of free self-constitution in relation to others, so, in this alternative view, the fundamental divine activity must be conceived to be the activity in which God creates or constitutes Godself freely in relation to others. The fully authentic mode of such active self-constitution has been shown to be love. Since, as I have argued, God cannot constitute Godself in an inauthentic fashion, the fundamental divine act must be that of love of others.

Now, of course, I have shown that Rahner, too, claims that the fundamental divine act is that of love of others. But he qualifies this claim by saying that it applies only to this actual world order. It could have been otherwise. God could just as well have refused to give Godself in personal love to others without violating God's own essential nature. I tried to show that such a view, which entails that the divine love of others is strictly accidental to the divine being, cannot be justified either as a faithful interpretation of the apostolic witness of scripture, or as an adequate interpretation of our fundamental experience (in particular, the ineradicable confidence in the meaning and worth of existence that is presupposed in all human activity).

But if God is understood to be constituted essentially by real relations to other individuals, then one can affirm, without qualification, that God's fundamental act is that of love of others, that God is essentially, not accidentally, love of others. That is to say, God could not exist as God without loving all other individuals in a supremely appropriate manner. Here, the second impasse in Rahner's concept of God is overcome and the essential love of God for others that is implied by the New Testament message and by our common human experience finds coherent expression.

This fundamental divine act of love is to be understood as exemplifying the essential characteristics of the human experience of love. This means that God constitutes Godself in sympathetic, loving response to all of the nondivine individuals. God allows the nondivine individuals to make a difference to God, to determine God in part, to influence, affect, and enrich God. Most primordially, God acts by modifying Godself in response to the being and activity of others. God includes the actuality of all other selves within the divine actuality in accordance with God's own existentiell project. In each moment, the actuality of God is constituted anew by God in free response to the ongoing self-creative projects of the nondivine individuals. God, in such a view, is genuinely self-transcendent. God is a dynamic, growing self who transcends Godself by responding anew in each moment to the other selves to whom God is essentially related. Because God responds in love, God modifies Godself and thus acts toward others so as to facilitate the full self-realization of all of the nondivine individuals. God's goal or motive in the act of divine self-constitution is the advancement of the interests of all others. But since God includes the actuality of all of the nondivine individuals within God's own actuality, God's interest in the interests of others, at the same time, serves God's own interests as the all-inclusive individual. God's project is that of the mutual, loving self-creation of Godself and the nondivine individuals.

It remains true, however, that the divine love is the *eminent* exemplification of our own fundamental experience of love. The divine love is like human love in that God allows the creatures to make a difference to God and acts appropriately toward the creatures on the basis of this difference. But the divine love is radically different from human love in that *all* of the creatures make a difference to God and in that God acts toward *all* of the creatures so as to optimize their full, authentic self-realization. Human love, by contrast, is a severely limited form of love. We are affected by, and act toward, only a tiny portion of our fellow creatures. This difference between being acted upon by, and acting toward, *all*, as opposed to *some*, creatures is truly a radical difference, a qualitative difference, not simply a quantitative difference. In logic, there simply is no greater difference than the difference between the universal and the particular, between the universal quantifier (all x) and the existential quantifier (some x). The difference between loving all individuals and loving some individuals is not just a vast difference, a difference in degree, but is a radical difference, a difference in kind.

This recasting of Rahner's concept of God so as to overcome the second impasse present in his thought also has implications for our understanding of the God-world relationship. I would argue that Rahner's attempt to understand the God-world relationship nondualistically as a dialogue of mutual love can be carried out more consistently and without qualification on the basis of the view that God is essentially love of others. Rahner holds that the dualistic view of the God-world relationship in which God and the world are seen as two particular entities that lie side by side and that are included within the larger whole of reality, is inadequate. Although he argues that God must be the totality of reality, I tried to show that this can only mean, for him, that God is the *Woraufhin* of all reality, since he refuses to admit a real relativity of God in Godself. But, in the alternative concept of God outlined here, it can be said without equivocation that God is the totality of reality in that God includes all of reality within Godself. God is the all-inclusive subject of love, for God constitutes Godself in loving relations to all other individuals. God is literally the one who "encompasses everything, in whom all ways become lost, in whom we live, move, and have our being, who is not far from any of us, who supports and surrounds all and who is comprehended and surpassed by none."[7]

Likewise, I indicated that the sense in which the God-world relationship can be a dialogue for Rahner is unclear, in that God is held to be essentially nonrelative to others. But if God is essentially love of others, then it can be said without qualification that God and the nondivine creatures are partners in a historical dialogue (i.e., history itself), in which both partners act and are acted upon by each other. It is literally true, in such a view, that

> . . . the free act of God is again and again kindled by the activity of man [and the other creatures]. History is not merely a play that God himself performs and in which the creatures are simply what is performed. Rather, the creature is a genuine co-performer in this divine-human dialogue.[8]

God and the nondivine creatures genuinely participate in the free self-creation of one another.

Given this account of the divine love, the third impasse in

Rahner's concept of God can be overcome. Recall that two aspects of the fundamental act in which a free self constitutes itself in loving relations to other selves can be distinguished. That is to say, the activity of love has two essential aspects. In Rahner's terms, love involves opening and abandoning oneself to the beloved. As a *subject,* the self acts to constitute or create itself in relation to other selves. This act of self-constitution involves an essential openness or passivity of the self. The subject creates itself in response to others, allowing those others to determine and enrich the self by including those others within oneself. But, then, on the basis of this responsive act of self-constitution, the self acts upon other selves, and, as an *object,* is influential in the free self-creation of other subjects.[9] The product of the fundamental act of self-constitution is expressed in all the other acts of the self and is thereby made available for other subjects in the process of their free self-creation. Here the self is an object for other selves, partially determines the other selves, and thus participates in their acts of self-creation.

As a subject, the self is really or internally related to others, which, in turn, as objects, are nominally or externally related to the subject. (This is the case because, as such, my act of including the actuality of my wife within my own life, for instance, affects my being, but not that of my wife. Subsequently, of course, in acting toward my wife, she is the affected party, while I am strictly nonaffected.) Then, as an object for other subjects, who are really or internally related to the self, the self is nominally or externally related to others. Here, the self that I have freely chosen to be in response to other selves, is influential with respect to other selves as they constitute themselves freely.[10]

The same must be conceived to be the case with respect to God's relationship to the world. The divine love, the fundamental divine act of self-constitution in relation to others, has both a passive and an active moment or aspect. As a subject, God constitutes Godself in response to the creatures. God is affected, determined, and acted upon, by the nondivine individuals. Here God is really or internally related to the world, which is God's object. Then, on the basis of the difference the creatures make to God, God acts toward the nondivine individuals. Here, God is the world's object. The nondivine individuals include something of the divine being within their own being. As an object, God is nominally or externally related to the nondivine individuals.

For Rahner, on the contrary, the divine love is wholly active. He does indeed seek to conceive the God-world relationship in personal terms, using the experience of love as a paradigm. He proposes understanding the intimacy of God's relationship to the world in terms of quasi-formal causality. But, even in the case of quasi-formal causality, God remains strictly an object in relation to the world. What is required in order to affirm a genuine relativity of God, is that God be conceived as a subject who is affected by others. But once this step has been taken, that is, once God has been conceived to be essentially love of others, and, therefore, really related to the creatures, there is no impediment to saying that the divine love has a passive as well as an active moment. In this way the third impasse in Rahner's concept of God is avoided.

On the one hand, in this alternative concept of God, the world makes a real difference to God. God is open to the non-divine individuals and is sympathetically receptive to them. In the process of God's own self-creation, God accepts the product of the self-creation of the creatures into God's own being. God allows the world to qualify and partially to determine God. Here God is passive with respect to the world, really or internally related to the world. Just as we grow and transcend ourselves, so God transcends Godself by including the actuality of the world within God's own actuality. This process constitutes the divine self-creation.

But then, on the other hand, the product of the divine self-creation, which is new in every moment, is included to some extent, however slight, by the nondivine individuals in the process of their own self-creation. That is to say, God acts on the world by modifying Godself as the world's object. On the basis of the difference the world makes to God in God's free self-creation, God gives or offers Godself to the creatures as they create themselves freely. In this moment or aspect of the divine love, God is active with respect to the world, nominally or externally related to the world. God is influential in the self-creation of all creaturely individuals. The creatures include some aspect of the divine reality within themselves, in that the divine reality is the final repository of all previous worldly states. In this sense God is determinative in the self-creative processes of all other selves.[11]

Here, both the passive and the active moments of love disclosed in human experience are exemplified eminently in the divine love. As lover and beloved, both God and the creatures participate in each other's being and yet retain their own distinct identities. Each is partially determined by the other, and each gives of itself partially to determine the other. Each constitutes itself through the mediation of the other and acts to facilitate the self-realization of the other by modifying itself as the other's object.

The character of the divine love can be elucidated further through a more detailed examination of its passive and active aspects. It seems to me that these two aspects of the one essential divine love for the creatures express well the traditional distinction between God as redeemer and God as creator. In other words, the essential love of God for others is both redemptive and creative.[12]

Rahner is right, it seems to me, when he argues that the self-creative and self-transcendent activity of the creatures, and especially of human beings, requires that there be some final, lasting validity attained by the process of worldly becoming. The activity of the creatures, and above all the free decisions of the spiritual creatures, would be absurd, literally meaningless, if each act were simply superseded by another act and passed away without having any lasting significance. This indicates that the real existentiell problem concerning the meaning and significance of our lives is the problem of transience. Rahner shows that the final significance of the creatures lies in the being of God, for God alone is not threatened by the futility and meaningless of perishing, of passing out of existence. It is in the everlasting being of God that the nondivine world finds its final significance and thus is redeemed. In the case of human being, it is the redemptive love of God that provides us with the fundamental confidence in the meaning and worth of existence that is presupposed in all human activity.

But I argued that it is genuinely unclear in Rahner's thought how God can provide the final significance of the world, since, finally, God is free to love or not to love others. Rahner understands the divine freedom in such a way that, in essence, the world does not make a real difference to God. I argued that, for reasons Rahner himself suggests, the love of God for the creatures must be essential, not accidental, to both God and the creatures. In other words, neither God nor the creatures can be understood except as the subject and objects of the divine love.

In the view of God outlined here, this can be affirmed coherently and without qualification.

By including the product of the self-creation of all other
selves within God's own reality, God redeems the creatures, that
is, God provides them with an everlasting significance and
meaning. The experiences and deeds of the nondivine individuals attain a lasting validity by being preserved in the everlasting
being of God. The only way for an individual to have a significance that outstrips its own finite lifetime is to be included in the
life of another individual, to be remembered by that individual.
As Augustine saw, it is in memory alone that the past exists and is
real.

> It is manifest and clear that there are neither times
> future nor times past. Thus it is not properly said that
> there are three times, past, present, and future. Perhaps
> it might be rightly said that there are three times: a time
> present of things past; a time present of things present;
> and a time present of things future. For these three do
> coexist somehow in the soul, for otherwise I could not
> see them. The time present of things past is memory.[13]

It is God's "memory," the loving inclusion of the creatures within
Godself, that, finally, enables the perishable, transient creatures
to have an everlasting presence and significance. Without this
redeeming love of God, our lives might have an impact upon,
and a meaning for, a tiny number of our fellow creatures. We
will likely be remembered by some for a short while after we die.
But, eventually, those for whom our lives have made a difference, those whose self-creations we have affected, will likewise
die. Our influence and thus our significance will cease.

However, God unfailingly receives all of the creatures and
their accomplishments (whether for good or for ill) unto Godself
and thus preserves them. Our lives do not contribute merely to
the lives of a few other finite, mortal individuals. Rather, we
contribute to the lasting wholeness of reality itself, that is, the
being of God, the one who makes its own all of creaturely
experience and reality. In a very literal sense, we exist for the
glory of God, for it is the divine being that we finally affect in our
every decision and act.

God's love is also creative in that it contributes to the free
self-creation of all of the nondivine individuals. An important
presupposition involved in speaking adequately of the creative

activity of God is that there is no basis in our fundamental experience of ourselves for the view that an individual, even God, can totally determine or create another individual. As has been shown, Rahner understands the meaning of being *(das Sein)* to be *Beisichsein*. To be actual as an individual at all, for him, is to have some degree of self-possession, some ability, however slight, to create or determine oneself. Further, for Rahner, individuals create themselves in relation to other individuals: they include the experience of other individuals within themselves in accordance with their own freely chosen existentiell projects. This self-creation requires data, or material, that is, some set of existentiell possibilities actualized by others from among which the self-creating individual can choose. Here, Rahner argues that the free individual, above all, the human person, can create her- or himself only because these past existentiell possibilities, the products of the self-creative activities of previous self-creators, are retained through *anamnesis* and are thus available as futural possibilities to be actualized. I want to suggest that, in the view of God as essentially love of others, it is the love of God that is the final, universal *anamnesis* required by our experience of ourselves as free self-creators. It is the love of God that preserves the product of the free self-creative processes of all past individuals and makes it available, in the present, for all actual self-creators, including God Godself. It is the divine love, in its active or creative aspect, that provides all individuals with the material required if they are to create themselves freely.

Once again, God's primary act is that of divine self-creation in loving relations with the creatures. In this act, God includes within Godself the product of the self-creative processes of all other individuals. It is the product of the divine self-creation that is, at any given moment, a complete repository of all past states of divine and nondivine actuality. In this way, God provides the material for the ongoing self-creative processes of all individuals. To co-create another individual, or to act creatively upon another individual, is to offer oneself as material or data for that individual's self-creation. God offers Godself in this fashion to all other individuals. The reality of God, in fact, is the ultimate source for the self-creative activity of the creatures, since it is in the divine being, and there alone, that the achievements and failures of *all* past instances of self-creation are preserved and available. It is in this sense, I would argue, that the traditional language concerning God's *creatio ex nihilo* is to be understood, as Hartshorne indicates in the following passage:

> [T]he total concrete cause of *this* world is not merely the absolute divine essence; rather, it is God as having actually created and now possessing all previous worlds. On this assumption one may in a sense say that God creates us "out of nothing." . . . True, since the present world-state involves memories of past states, to say that the present is created out of nothing is to say that our memories are memories of nothing. A memory can only be created by a cause which includes that which is to be remembered. Yet God as supremely relative is the "valuation of the world" (Whitehead), wholly containing it as datum of his valuative act. Thus the other-than-ourselves-now which creates us is God and in addition to God, nothing. Our past, which . . . is required material for our present self-creation, is already included in God's receptive valuation, just as our new present is about to be, or is in the process of being, included. God then is the *whole* creative source; but not God as First Cause, or as "absolute" source; rather, God as the ever-new ideal summation of the already created.[14]

Rahner rightly argues that the divine creation is not an isolated moment of the past (namely, the "first" moment), but is an ongoing process that occurs in every moment. Likewise, I would argue that the divine redemption is an ongoing process of the divine love. Here, then, is the fruition, it seems to me, of Rahner's suggestion that the divine love is the final ground and goal of our lives. The divine love is the final ground and source of reality, and also the final goal and horizon of the process of creaturely becoming. God is the ultimate benefactor and the ultimate beneficiary of reality, the ultimate cause and the ultimate effect of the activity of all actual individuals.[15] It is from the love of God that we come; we live, move, and have our being in the divine love; and the love of God is the final resting place of our lives. The ultimate cause that we are called to serve is nothing less than the divine self-creation itself.

The Relativity and Nonrelativity of the God Who Is Essentially Love of Others

In the preceding section I have sketched the outlines of a concept of God attained by recasting Rahner's understanding of

God so as to avoid the threefold impasse into which it presently
leads. The central claim of this alternative concept of God is that
God is essentially love of others. The time has now come to show
that this concept of God does not avoid the threefold incoherence of Rahner's thought simply by ignoring the concerns
that led him to this impasse in the first place. By doing this, I
hope to show that the alternative concept of God proposed here
does not use Rahner's understanding of God as a foil, but rather
is an attempt to address the central concerns of this powerful
understanding of God in a more coherent fashion.

It might appear that in the view that God is essentially love
of others, a view that implies that God is really related to, and
genuinely affected by, the creatures, there is a failure to take
account of the radical distinction between God and the world. It
might be objected that a God who is really related to the creatures, a God who cannot be conceived to exist without some
world of creatures, is not the God of Christian faith but a finite
or limited God. In portraying God as internally related to others,
temporal, self-surpassing, and so forth, one might appear to be
improperly identifying God with the world. Such an identification of God and the world would seem to ignore the truth
expressed by Rahner when he argues that God must be the
absolute one, the one who is existentially independent of the
world, if the basic human experience of transcendence is to be
possible. Christian theology, and, indeed, theistic philosophy as
such, he claims, must confess:

> God as the "unchangeable one," who simply *is*—*actus*
> *purus*—who in blessed security, who, in the self-suffi-
> ciency of infinite reality, from eternity to eternity in
> absolute, unmoved, serene fullness, always already pos-
> sesses what he is, without becoming, without having to
> achieve what he is. And precisely when *we* have received,
> for our part, the burden of history and becoming as
> grace and an honor, do we necessarily confess *such* a
> God. For only because he is infinite fullness can the
> becoming of spirit and nature be more than a mean-
> ingless coming to itself of absolute emptiness, which
> collapses into the void that it itself is. Thus, the con-
> fession of the unchangeable and unchanging God of
> eternal, perfect fullness is not merely a postulate of
> philosophy, but is also a dogma of faith.[16]

The first thing to notice is that while there is a certain
identity of God and the world implied by the view that God is

essentially love of others, this identity is conceived in experiential or "synthetic," not substantival terms. Unlike a classically pantheistic view, such as Spinoza's, I would not argue that God alone is real, as if there were just one substance. Rather, God includes the reality of the world within the divine reality. God "synthesizes" the lives of the creatures into the divine life. But this process of synthesis does not deny the distinction that exists between God and the creatures. As Hartshorne argues, to say x includes y within itself presupposes that x and y are different.[17]

For instance, when I say that I include something within my experience, within myself, what I mean is that in a very real sense an event becomes a part of my being. I include the objects of my experience within myself. They qualify me and determine me to a greater or a lesser degree. I am really or internally related to them. To experience a beautiful sunrise means to include within myself something of the sunrise, to have my being affected by it. As a person, I am constituted by my experiences. But, at the same time, the inclusion of some object within my experience, and, thus, within myself, does not deny, but presupposes, that the object is genuinely different from me, the experiencing subject. My inclusion of the beautiful sunrise within myself in no way entails that the sunrise and myself are the same being. In the same way, God includes all of creaturely reality within Godself, and is, in this sense, the totality of reality. The world remains worldly, distinct from God, and fully autonomous. No pantheistic identification of God and world is implied. God does include the reality of the creatures within God's own actual being, but this entails precisely the autonomy of the creatures and their distinction from God.

I would argue that the recasting of Rahner's view of God, such that God is held to be essentially love of others, meets more adequately the demand for an alternative both to dualism and pantheism than does Rahner's concept of God as it presently stands. Over against dualism, it is clear, in the view that God is essentially love of others, that God and the world cannot be conceived as existing side by side within a larger whole: the totality of reality composed of the world plus God. Rather, God Godself is the totality of reality, in the sense that God includes the reality of the world within the divine being. God is internally, and not just externally, related to the world. The creatures make a difference to God and affect the divine self-constitution. And yet, over against pantheism, God and the world are distinct.

Each is not only internally or really, but also externally or nominally, related to the other. The inclusion of the world in God, does not change the fact that the world is radically contingent, and genuinely other than God.

A real mutuality characterizes the relationship between God and the creatures. Both God and the nondivine individuals are internally and externally related to each other. Both influence and are influenced by the other. As Whitehead argues in a famous passage from his *Process and Reality:*

> It is as true to say that God is permanent and the World
> fluent, as that the World is permanent and God is fluent.
> It is as true to say that God is one and the World many, as
> that the World is one and God many. It is as true to say
> that, in comparison with the World, God is actual emi-
> nently, as that, in comparison with God, the World is
> actual eminently. It is as true to say that the World is
> immanent in God, as that God is immanent in the World.
> It is as true to say that God transcends the World, as that
> the World transcends God. It is as true to say that God
> creates the World, as that the World creates God.[18]

But, for all this, the God-world relationship is not symmetrical. God, as essentially love of others, as really related to the world, remains qualitatively different from the world. It was suggested that God cannot be conceived except as existing in relation to some world of nondivine creatures. This does not mean, however, that any particular world of creatures is necessary to God. Our own world, and any other conceivable world of creatures would, by definition, be a contingent world, one that need not exist. God could exist as God without this world, or without any other particular world of creatures. All that is entailed by the view proposed here is that God could not exist except as the God of *some* world of creatures. The class "world" cannot be empty, but no particular member of that class is necessary. There is a radical asymmetry that characterizes the God-world relationship. The existence of God does not require any particular world. All that is necessary is that there be *some* world of creatures. But, this world, or any other particular world, requires, for its very existence, precisely *the one and only* God who is externally and internally related to the creatures, maximally absolute and maximally relative.

As an actual individual, God is constituted by real relatedness to other individuals. This means that there is a real sense in which God's actuality is contingent upon the actuality of whatever creatures happen to exist. God's actual being always reflects the actuality of the creatures, for God constitutes Godself by lovingly including the reality of the creatures within God's own reality. The creatures contribute to God's self-creation and genuinely determine God. But this divine relativity or contingency does not represent a denial of the traditional theistic claim that God exists necessarily. As Rahner argues, God must be existentially independent of this (or any other) particular world. God does not depend upon the world for God's existence. That God is relative to whatever creatures exist is not itself relative. That the actual divine state in any given moment is contingent upon the actuality of the creatures is not contingent, but necessary.

Unlike the creatures, God exists necessarily. This means that God's existence will be exemplified in any contingent moment of actuality. In any state of affairs God will be actualized. This is strictly necessary. But *how* God will be actualized in any concrete state of affairs is contingent, both upon the creatures and upon God's free decision. That God will be actualized as God in any state of affairs can be determined a priori, but the nature of the concrete being of God in a given state of affairs cannot be determined a priori.

Just as Rahner implies, God must be both absolute and relative. In the alternative concept of God proposed here, it is clear that the absoluteness and the relativity of God apply to two different aspects of God. As an actual subject, God is relative to others, contingently determined by the creatures. However, abstracting from the actual being of God, one can say that God is absolute, independent of all other individuals. The absoluteness, the nonrelativity of God is not an actual divine state, but is rather an abstract quality of all divine states. That is to say, in all moments of the divine actuality, God will be characterized by certain qualities: God will be actualized in all states of affairs, God will be affected by all actual individuals, God will relate Godself in love to all of the creatures. These qualities constitute the divinity of God. The divinity of God, that is, God's abstract qualities, God's omnipotence, God's omniscience, God's omnipresence, God's existential independence (aseity), is absolute and unchanging. In God's divinity God is strictly nonrelative, immutable. The divinity of God is not enriched or affected by the creatures, but remains constant in all states of affairs. It is to the divinity of God, I would argue, that all of the classical attributes concerning the absoluteness of God apply. However, in God's actual being, God is not absolute, or nonrelative at all, but rather supremely relative, in the sense indicated above.

Although it is true, in the view of God as essentially love of others, that God is not simply the *actus purus*, but is in a process of becoming, self-actualization, or self-creation, this must not be understood to mean that such a God is a finite God, one who is in danger of being surpassed by the world. To say that God is perfectible is not to say that God is imperfect. At any given moment, the divine actuality is literally unsurpassed and unsurpassible by any other actual individual. The divine actuality, at any moment, is the one wholly appropriate or perfect synthesis of all past acts of self-creation, both divine and nondivine. The only actuality that could surpass God at any moment is a future divine state.[19] God is always the supreme being. God surpasses all other individuals simultaneously and surpasses Godself subsequently.[20]

Again, God's character, God's nature is strictly absolute and is not perfectible. As Hartshorne says, God is ethically perfect: God's love for the creatures is unfailing and undivided. God holds out constant goals for the creatures. It is the concrete state of God that is co-determined by the creatures, not God's character as God. God is only aesthetically perfectible.[21]

As was indicated earlier in this chapter, God is qualitatively different from the world in that God is perfectly or eminently relative, subjective, and passive. God is internally related to all of the creatures. All differences in the creatures are reflected in the divine being. God includes, without loss or exception, all of worldly reality within the divine reality. The material of the divine self-creation is the totality of actuality. God takes into account all nondivine individuals, past and present, in the divine self-creation. The nondivine individuals, on the other hand, are only imperfectly relative, subjective, or passive. They are related to only a few other individuals. They include within themselves imperfectly the reality of only a tiny number of their fellows. The material of the finite self-creators is very limited, for they take into account only a few other individuals in their project of self-creation. The difference between God and the creatures is nothing other than the qualitative difference between all and some.

Likewise, God is perfectly absolute, objective, or active. God acts upon all other individuals, is influential in the self-creation of all others. Something of the divine being is included within all other individuals as they freely constitute themselves. The non-divine individuals are as imperfectly absolute or objective as they are imperfectly relative or subjective. They are active upon only a tiny number of their fellows. The reality of any given finite individual is included within the reality of only a few other finite self-creators.

Thus, in the view of God I am outlining here, God is the supreme being, the one individual who eminently actualizes all perfections. But, in contrast to Rahner's view, God is not only maximally absolute, but also maximally relative. Rahner's claim that the God of Christian faith is the supreme being must be affirmed. God must be the everlasting ground of our confidence in the meaning and worth of existence. God cannot be just another finite individual. God's cause must be an eternally valid cause. God must be radically different from the finite world if God is to create and redeem the world. And yet, our concrete situation must make a real difference to God if God is to be *our* creator and redeemer. God must be genuinely relative to the creatures.

As I have shown, Rahner speaks of God as relative to the creatures as a self-expression or self-limitation of God as strictly nonrelative. I argued that, on Aristotelian and scholastic grounds, it is impossible to derive a relative, concrete aspect of an individual from a nonrelative, abstract aspect. In the view proposed here, God as relative to others is not a self-limitation of God as absolute. Rather, the divine self as actual is constituted by relatedness to others. That is to say, God as actual is a concrete individual intimately related to others. God as absolute is derived by abstracting the defining characteristics of God from the actual being of God. God's actuality at any given moment is partially determined by, or contingent upon, the creatures. But the qualities that characterize the divine being in relation to the creatures at any given moment are strictly nonrelative.

God, for instance, will be love in all moments of the divine actuality. God will sympathetically attend to the creatures, will allow them to qualify God's own project of self-creation, and will act appropriately toward the creatures so as to facilitate their full self-realization. All of this is strictly nonrelative to the actual

world of creatures to which God is related. This would be true of
God's relation to any world. But how God's love will be concretely expressed does depend on the creatures, their actual
situations, their need. God's essence, or nature, or divinity is
strictly nonrelative, but the actual expression or embodiment of
that essence is relative, contingent, new in each moment in
response to the creatures. The abstract qualities of God, the
absoluteness of God, is contained within God as an actual individual related to others in the same way that a person's personality is included within, or is a part of, that person as actual. The
concrete divine individual, God as related to others, is inclusive
of God as absolute, God as nonrelated to others, the abstract
qualities that characterize God as God. Here, both the relativity
and nonrelativity of God are taken seriously, and yet the account
of the relationship between God as relative and God as nonrelative is free of the internal incoherence of Rahner's view.

Further, it seems to me that recasting Rahner's thought so as
to conceive God to be essentially love of others does not entail
abandoning his account of the activity of God in relation to the
world. For Rahner, God is not an individual, categorial actor
within the world. He argues that "God causes the world and does
not really act causally within the world. [This] means he supports
the causal chain but, in his activity, is not interposed as a member
of the chain of causes as one cause among others."[22] The world
process is closed. Any alleged intervention of God into this
closed chain of events would involve a mythological representation of the divine activity. For these reasons, it is more appropriate to say that God "does" the world as a whole, than to say that
God does something in the world. God does not act in the world
at particular points at all. Rather, the world of creatures as such
is God's act.

In a view in which God is essentially love of others, this
Rahnerian view that the world as such is God's act might be
preserved and reexpressed in the following manner. God acts by
modifying Godself as the world's object. God acts by establishing
the conditions under which other free subjects can constitute or
create themselves. God, in the process of the divine self-creation,
includes within Godself the product of the self-creation of all
other individuals according to God's own freely chosen plans. In
general, these plans are aimed at maximizing the free self-
creation of all individuals while minimizing the hindrances to

the free self-creation of all. The product of this process of divine self-creation, then, is available to the nondivine individuals, as the material for their own self-creation. God is supremely influential upon others in that the product of the divine self-creation is offered to all other self-creators.

It would be a grave mistake, it seems to me, to view such activity as insignificant. Indeed, there could be no more significant activity that God could undertake. While God does not act as one finite agent among others, it is the divine activity that is the single, final ground of reality as such. It is the divine activity that alone makes possible the activity of the myriad finite agents. The divine activity is not in competition with the activity of the finite individuals. The divine activity is not quantitatively distinct from that of creaturely agents, but rather is infinitely, qualitatively distinct. God does what no creature could ever do: establish the conditions under which creaturely activity can take place. Such a view might seem to diminish the role of God in the world. But as Rahner points out, all that has been denied in the view that the world as such is God's act is a mythologically conceived form of divine activity in the world. This view might seem to reduce the scope of the divine activity, in that God is not invoked directly to explain the functioning of the world system. And yet, one can say, literally, that all creaturely activity is indirectly the act of God, in that it is the divine activity of self-creation that alone makes it possible for finite agents to act at all.

It should be noted that the term "world," in a phrase such as "the world as a whole is God's act," is really a shorthand way of referring to the set of all nondivine agents. That is to say, in reality, God does not act in a weak, indirect way upon some abstraction called "world," but rather acts directly upon each individual creature. God is internally related to each finite individual as an individual in every moment of its actuality. And, in every moment, each finite individual is internally related to, and thus influenced by, God. There could be no more direct or intimate action of God conceivable. God takes each individual into account as an individual, and acts upon that individual, offering to it its ownmost possibilities of existence.

As I argued in Chapter VII, the chief problem in Rahner's understanding of the divine activity involves his interpretation of the meaning of the incarnation. I showed that his view of the divine activity is inconsistent in that he proposes, as a general principle, that God cannot plausibly be held to be a categorial actor within the world, and yet holds that in the incarnation of the divine Logos in the man Jesus, God adopts as God's own a finite, creaturely reality. I find Rahner's argument against any mythological interpretation of divine "intervention" in the world, convincing. I would argue that Rahner's general principle that God does not act in the world in specific events, but acts upon the world as its final ground and goal, cannot be compromised. The question, then, is how the event of Jesus Christ is to be understood in relation to this axiom concerning the divine activity.

On the basis of this principle concerning the divine activity, it would seem that the significance of the Christ event cannot lie in the fact that in this event there is a special divine activity that differs in kind from the divine activity in each moment of the world process. The divine activity in the event of Jesus Christ is the same as in all other events: the divine love is the creative ground and redemptive goal of all creaturely events. It is not, as Rahner sometimes implies, that the divine love is first present, or fully bestowed, from God's point of view, in the Christ event. Rather, in the event of Jesus Christ the creative and redemptive love of God that is present in all events is, for Christian faith, most fully and decisively revealed or represented to us. To use Rahnerian terms, the life, death, and resurrection of Jesus Christ, and the subsequent proclamation of these events by the church, constitute a thematization or objectification of the divine love for us, a thematization that, in Christian faith, becomes the standard by which all particular thematizations of our transcendental relationship to the God of self-communicating love are to be measured. The event of Jesus Christ is the decisive thematization of the divine love for us, the decisive revelation of the divine love.

In the event of Jesus Christ, the creative and redemptive love of God, which is an existential in, or an essential constituent of, human being, is objectified and thematized for us. The proclamation of the event of Jesus Christ presents us with a gift and a demand, and calls us to make a decision. The gift is that the divine love has been bestowed upon us and offers us a new possibility of existence in which we trust God and not ourselves or our works for the final meaning of our lives. The demand is that we love ourselves, others, and God as God has loved us if this trust or faith in God is to be effectual. We are called to decide whether or not we will accept the possibility of existing as loved creatively and redemptively by God, whether or not we will constitute ourselves in loving relations to others, whether or not we will open ourselves and give ourselves to others as God has opened and given Godself to us.

The Freedom of the God Who Is Essentially Love of Others

In the preceding section I have tried to show that the proposed recasting of Rahner's thought, in which God is affirmed to be essentially love of others, does not entail a denial of Rahner's views that God must be both relative and nonrelative, that the God-world relationship must be a dialectic of identity and difference, and that God's act is the world as such. Indeed, it seems to me that these legitimate concerns come to expression more coherently in the concept of God sketched above than they do in Rahner's concept of God as it presently stands. Now I want to indicate that this alternative concept of God does not entail a denial of the divine freedom. It might appear that the view that God is essentially love of others is able to avoid the threefold impasse present in Rahner's thought only by ignoring or violating his principle that "God must have an unlimited range of free action with respect to his creatures."[23] It could be argued that, in the view proposed here, God does not act freely and spontaneously in relation to the creatures precisely because God is *essentially* love of others. And if God is not a genuinely free agent in relation to the creatures, then the biblical view of God as sovereign is lost.

In this study I have indicated two senses of freedom that do not apply to God. I argued in Chapter X that God cannot be conceived to be free in the negative sense of being able to constitute Godself in abstraction from relatedness to other individuals. To deny that God is free in this sense is not to limit the divine freedom, for such a negative concept of freedom has no basis in our fundamental experience of ourselves. The freedom to exist as a self without being related to other selves is not a coherent, meaningful concept at all. To refuse to apply a meaningless concept to God is not to limit God.

I also argued in Chapter VIII that God, as the supreme, perfect individual is not free to exist inauthentically. In other words, God cannot be conceived to close Godself off from other individuals and to refuse to give Godself in love to those others. However God constitutes Godself in relation to the creatures, it is not in a manner characterized by indifference or hate. To deny to God the possibility of constituting Godself inauthentically is not to impose an arbitrary, external limitation on the divine freedom. If God *is* essentially love of others, then it would not be accurate to say that the divine freedom is limited in that God cannot hate or remain indifferent to others. In loving others, God is simply "remaining" true to the divine nature, God is simply being God.[24]

According to the basic methodological principle adopted in this chapter, a principle derived from Rahner's thought, the divine freedom is to be understood in terms of categories derived from our basic experience of ourselves as free self-creators. This means that the divine freedom is to be understood much as Rahner understands human freedom, that is, the primordial freedom to constitute oneself, to take possession of oneself, in relation to other persons. If this turn to the subject is really taken in relation to our concept of God, and not qualified as it is in Rahner's thought, then the primary meaning of the freedom of God is the freedom God has to constitute Godself in accordance with God's own existentiell plans and purposes in response to the other individuals to whom God is related. Just as any self is free, God is free to create Godself as a subject in relation to other subjects.

This means, first of all, that the creatures partially, but really, determine God's free self-creation. The divine freedom is a freedom that takes into account the other free individuals to which God is related. The divine freedom is, in part, a freedom in response to the free actions of the creatures. Because God perfectly and wholly includes the reality of the creatures within God's own reality, God's response to the creatures is an eminently realistic response. That is, in freely constituting Godself, God cannot simply ignore the way in which the creatures have actually constituted themselves. God includes within Godself the actual product of the self-creation of the creatures, whether for good or for ill. God is not free to ignore the destructive activity of the creatures, for example, even if that activity represents a hindrance to God's own project of providing the optimal conditions for the free self-realization of all of the creatures. To this extent, the free self-creation of God is dependent upon the actual state of the creatures.

But, at the same time, God is free, just as any subject is, to constitute Godself in relation to others according to God's own free decisions. All subjects are free, to some extent, to make use of the data of their experience in different ways, as they see fit. This is the case because the self-constitution or self-creation of a subject involves decision and choice. In our own case, we are free to take certain aspects of our experience more seriously than other aspects. We are free to attach greater significance to some events or relationships than to others. We are free to allow certain experiences to have a determinative influence upon us, while other experiences are hardly attended to at all. In each case, we have not really changed the data of our experience. Rather, we have appropriated each moment of our experience in accordance with (or in opposition to) our understanding of ourselves and others and in accordance with our goals and plans.

Likewise, God might be conceived to make use of the data of the divine self-creation (all actual divine and nondivine states) in different ways (although, as I have argued, all of these ways will be expressions of the divine love for others). As God, God takes account of all reality in a supremely realistic fashion. God includes all events within the divine being and preserves them there everlastingly. But God is free to take account of, or to respond to, nondivine reality in various ways so as to further God's own plans and purposes. While God is not free to ignore an event, God is free to attach to an event whatever significance God sees fit and to hold out more prominently certain possibilities, as opposed to others, for the nondivine self-creators. God must take account of evil, destructive acts of evil, as contrary to God's plan. But God can, and does, include evil acts within Godself in such a way as to offer to the creatures ways of overcoming evil with good. God is free to emphasize good over evil, to persuade the creatures to contribute to, rather than hinder, the full, free self-realization of their fellows.

In short, God is not free to constitute Godself independently of relations to some world of creatures, nor is God free to constitute Godself in an inauthentic fashion as indifferent or hostile to others. Because God is essentially love of others, God cannot be conceived except as responding to and acting toward all other individuals in a supremely sympathetic and affirming way. God loves each individual. God allows every other individual to make a difference to God and acts toward that individual in such a way as to facilitate its full self-realization. But how, concretely, God loves each individual is free on God's part. The manner in which God evaluates and appropriates the product of the self-creation of other subjects depends upon God's own free decision and plans. In this sense, as Rahner rightly demands, God does have a perfect, unlimited range of freedom with respect to the creatures, and even with respect to past states of the divine being.

This discussion of the freedom of the God who is essentially love of others raises the further question concerning the meaning of the "grace" of God. If God is essentially love of others, if God cannot be God and the creatures cannot be the creatures without being, respectively, the subject and the objects of the divine love of others, then in what sense is God's love for us a gift, an event of grace? It might be argued that the view that God is essentially love of others cannot be finally adequate within Christian theology because it entails a denial of the gratuity of the divine love. According to Rahner, the gratuity of the divine love is essential to the message of the Christian faith. He says simply, but pointedly: "that God loves us, that he is 'dear God,' is not a self-evident truth of metaphysics, but is rather the incomprehensible wonder that the New Testament must continually proclaim and that requires the highest effort of man's power of faith to be believed."[25]

I showed, in Chapter V, that, for Rahner, God's love is a wonderful, gratuitous event in that God could finally have refused to bestow Godself upon the creatures in fully personal love. The personal love of God for the creatures is necessary neither for God to exist as God, nor for the creatures to exist. Rahner argues that the classical Roman Catholic distinction between nature and grace serves to safeguard, theologically, the gratuity of the divine love. Although human "nature" as such has never been given in actuality, it is a real possibility: human being oriented to God solely as the aloof *Woraufhin* of human transcendence, that is, human being without the loving self-communication of God to human persons. Or, expressed in another way, God has just one final goal, the intimate communion of God and creature established by the self-communication of God. But, to accomplish this goal, God must engage in two distinct activities: the positing of the creature and the bestowal of the divine love upon that creature. While, in fact, the creatures were created so that the divine love would have an addressee, God, for Rahner, could have created the creatures without also entering into a personal relationship with the creatures. The bestowal of the divine love is a second gratuitous divine act that is not required by the creation of the creature.

I tried to show, in Chapter VIII, that such view of the gratuity of the divine love is inadequate in Christian theology when judged by the very criteria Rahner proposes for the meaning and truth of theological statements. This view entails that God is not essentially love of others. I argued that while human love is indeed a gift, and a wonder of grace, as Rahner states, because there is no necessity that the other person love me, because that person might just as well refuse to give her- or himself to me in love, this sense of gratuity does not apply to the divine love. An absolute refusal to love others, in the human case, is an inauthentic, even self-contradictory, way of relating to the persons who co-constitute us as persons. I argued that God cannot plausibly be supposed to constitute Godself in such an inauthentic fashion. The New Testament does not admit the possibility that God could have refused to bestow the divine love on the creatures. The human confidence in the meaning and worth of existence that is exhibited in all human activity presupposes, as Rahner himself argues in a qualified sense, the everlasting, redeeming love of God for us. Thus, in order to interpret adequately the New Testament witness of faith and our own existence as human beings, the only relationship God can be conceived to have to creatures is one of love.

It is clear that if God is conceived to be essentially love of others, then to exist at all is to be loved by God. This means that the divine love is not gratuitous in the sense that it might not have been bestowed by God at all. Being a recipient of the divine love constitutes part of the meaning of being a creature. Even in principle, no creature is conceivable except as an object of the divine love. If this is the case, then the nature/grace distinction, as employed by Rahner, is specious. "Nature" can no longer function even as a remainder concept, derived by bracketing the supernatural existential (the self-communication of God) within concrete human existence. For not only has the state of pure "nature" (the state of existing independently of the personal love of God) never been actualized, since God decided to bestow God's grace to all, in fact, such a state is not even conceivable. As has been argued above, God would not be God unless God loved all of the creatures, and would love any conceivable world of creatures, in a supremely intimate way. Likewise, no creature could exist except as loved by God.

But if God's love cannot be held to be gratuitous in Rahner's sense, then what does it mean, if anything at all, to say that the love of God for others is gratuitous, an event of grace?

The love between two human persons is a wonder, a gratuitous event, it seems to me, because right now, in this moment, another person stands over against me, affecting me, claiming me, calling me to open myself fully to that person, to let her or him make a decisive difference in my life, and to give myself to that person, to participate in her or his self-realization. It is this relationship to another person that is a gift. I could exist without loving this particular person, and so our love is a gift, not a necessity.

Somewhat the same thing could be said of the divine love for me, or for any other creature. I am radically contingent. There is no necessity that I exist. The very fact that I do exist as an object of the divine love is a wondrous gift, an event of grace. As Rahner seeks to demonstrate, the loving communion of God and creature is the final purpose of existence. The self-communication of God to the creature is the one final goal of God, the primordial divine act in relation to others. And the final goal of the creatures (through the spiritual creature) is immediacy to God. This communion with God is the gift of grace.

The wonder is not that God does in fact love us when God could have done otherwise. The gratuity of the divine love lies in the fact that we need not have existed at all to share in the divine love. To exist as the beloved of God is the final wonder, or gift, of life. We receive our status as the beloved ones of God as a gift that comes to us from beyond ourselves. It is sheer grace that we are able to participate in the divine self-creation and, thereby, can create ourselves freely in relation to others. This gift of existing as the objects of God's love, further, is not a gift given one time only. Rather, in each moment we receive our existence anew from God, the creative ground of our lives. Thus, as Rahner argues, the divine love is an event, not a timeless principle. The divine love for us is the ever new event of God accepting us into God's own self-creative process and then acting toward us so as to facilitate our own free self-creation.

Now, the love of God, which is received as a gift on our part since there is no necessity that we exist as the objects of the divine love, has two distinct aspects: God's love as redemptive and God's love as creative, both of which are wholly gratuitous in the sense just indicated. We are the objects of the redemptive love of God. God opens Godself to us in love. God accepts us into the divine actuality and includes us within Godself everlastingly. This is an event of grace, for there is no necessity that I exist as the object of God's redemptive love. My redemption depends not on my initiative or effort but solely upon God's eminent relativity or openness to the creatures. Likewise, the creative love of God is the final ground of our existence. Our being depends, moment by moment, upon our *anamnesis* or projective memory of past possibilities of existence. But these past possibilities are preserved, finally, in the divine being and nowhere else. We are radically contingent. Our existence as objects of the divine love is finally God's responsibility not our own. We constitute ourselves freely out of God, out of the possibilities that God alone retains everlastingly. *Creatio ex nihilo* is, in this sense, *creatio ex deo*, for God is the final repository of all past actuality. It is this past actuality that is the material for our own self-creation in each new moment of existence.

The wonder is not that God is, in fact, love, when God could just as well have remained the indifferent, aloof *Woraufhin* of human transcendence. Rather, the wonder is that we exist at all as the objects of the divine love. There can be no such thing, in the view adopted here, as existing as a creature and *not* being the object of God's redemptive and creative love. But there is absolutely no necessity that any particular creature exist as the object of the divine love. The fact that we exist at all as the objects of the divine love is, finally, God's responsibility and God's alone. Existence as the object of God's redemptive and creative love is the primordial wonder, the event of grace. It is a free gift of God's love, which redeems us from transience and creates us *ex nihilo*.

Rahner's legitimate concern that the love of God be understood to be gratuitous is taken seriously precisely in the view that God is essentially love of others. Moreover, *two* gratuitous divine acts can be distinguished: redemption and creation. But in contrast to Rahner's view of double gratuity, redemption is not conceived as a *donum superadditum* beyond the gratuitous act of creation. The redemptive love and the creative love of God are the two aspects of the one divine love for others. They are two aspects of the one gift of existence, which is the gift of being the object of the divine love. Redemption and creation should not be separated. To be is to be an object of the redemptive and creative love of God. But neither should redemption and creation be confused or identified. They can and must be distinguished, for there could be nothing more different than the internal relatedness of God to the creature (implied by redemption) and the external relatedness of God to the creature (implied by creation). Both aspects of the divine love are wholly gratuitous with respect to the contingent creature.

Therefore, I do not believe that Rahner's affirmation of a (double) gratuity of the divine love is denied in the view that God is essentially love of others. Further, such a view can be understood to retain his distinction between the transcendental and categorial modes of the divine love or self-communication. That is to say, the gift of God's love is addressed to us at two different levels of our being. On the one hand, it addresses us, to use Rahner's term, at the level of immediate self-possession. The divine love is an ingredient in our primordial, unthematic appropriation and actuation of ourselves as persons. In this sense the divine love is prevenient grace. It precedes our every particular, categorial act. Even before we are aware of the divine love that love is there, creating and redeeming us. At this level, the gratuity of the divine love, as indicated above, consists in the fact that we are radically contingent and need not exist as the objects of the divine love. At this primordial level of our being all persons, simply by virtue of existing as persons, have unthematically accepted or affirmed the divine love for themselves. This acceptance of the divine love is the fundamental trust in the meaning and worth of existence exhibited in all human acts, even the self-contradictory acts of radical despair, cynicism or suicide. The human possibility of radical self-contradiction indicates, however, that even at the level of our primordial self-possession or self-constitution we must freely appropriate God's gracious gift of existence. But this appropriation is not an explicit or fully reflective act. It is rather an unthematic act. It is the exercise of our most primoridal, transcendental freedom, which recedes to the very horizon of our consciousness as we attend to the multitude of thematic, categorial acts that we undertake in each moment of our existence.[26]

But God's love also addresses us at the level of our explicit, thematic, or categorial grasp and appropriation of ourselves in relation to self, others, and God. Here, through the mediation of particular persons and events and symbolic structures we are called to make some explicit response to the divine love. The key question at this level is: how will I freely and concretely appropriate the love of God that has always already been bestowed upon me. Will I open myself to the other persons whom I actually encounter and love them in the same way that God has first loved me? Will I enact the fact that I am created and redeemed by the divine love by opening myself to others, by allowing them to qualify my own self-creation, and by acting toward others to maximize their own free self-creation or self-realization? Or, will I close myself to others, refuse to allow them to claim me decisively? Will I, in my relations to other persons, fail to participate in God's cause of facilitating the self-creation of others?

In this second sense, "grace" calls me to make an explicit decision and offers me a new possibility of existence. Even though, in the past, I have not acted in love towards others, but have sinfully preferred to advance my own self-realization at the expense of other persons, right now, in the present moment, the divine love mediated, in Christianity, through the proclamation concerning Jesus Christ, calls me to give up my self-centeredness and offers the possibility of liberation. It seems to me that this sense of grace is of paramount concern in the New Testament. The New Testament tends simply to presuppose the grace of God in the first sense, that is, the divine love as the free gift in which we always already live, move, and have our being. The New Testament is more concerned to show that, at this moment, this divine love is a gift addressed to me in my sinfulness, a gift that I have not sought and do not deserve. Here the gratuity of the divine love has less to do with the fact that God's love is God's gift to contingent creatures, than with the fact that the divine love is a gift of liberation to sinful persons who, in various ways, have refused to exist as the objects of the creative and redemptive love of God.

So, God's love is grace, a gift, because it is, on one level, the unmerited, unexacted gift of existing as an object of the divine love, and, on a second level, the gift of the new existentiell possibility of explicitly accepting and enacting the divine love for me by loving others as I am loved by God. On the transcendental level, grace is the gift of God's love that is given in each moment with existence itself and that is unthematically appropriated or, in a self-contradictory fashion, refused. On the categorial level, grace is the event of the explicit appropriation of divine love as *mine*. Here, I am called to live as one who is loved creatively and redemptively by God. I am called to appropriate and ratify concretely and explicitly the gift of the divine love that has always already been given with my existence and to which I have always already responded, in some fashion, simply by virtue of existing as a human person.

The Self-Communication of the God Who Is Essentially Love of Others

It was argued in Chapter IV of this study that the central concept Rahner employs to advance his understanding of God's love is that of divine self-communication. So far in this recasting of Rahner's view of God, the notion of divine self-communication has not been treated explicitly. I want to show, now, that the crucial issues addressed by his concept of divine self-communication need not be ignored when God is conceived to be essentially love of others.

First of all, in the alternative concept of God suggested in this chapter, there is a real sense in which the bestowal of the divine love can be called divine self-communication. God's love has been shown to be the fundamental divine activity in which God opens Godself to the creatures, allowing them to make a real difference to God, and gives or abandons Godself to the creatures by acting toward them, on the basis of the difference they make to God, so as to facilitate their free, authentic self-realization. At issue in this fundamental divine activity, as it relates to the creatures, is not the communication of some information about God, but rather the communication of God's own being, the establishment of a genuine personal relationship between God and the creatures. As Rahner says, "it is decisive for the understanding of the self-communication of God to man to grasp that the giver is himself the gift, that the giver in himself and through himself gives himself to the creature as its very own fulfillment."[27]

This means that grace, first and foremost, is to be viewed as uncreated grace. The gift given in the bestowal of the divine love is nothing other than the giver, God Godself. Grace is the gift of the divine being, not the gift of some created entity or quality. In the redemptive aspect of the divine love, the gift is the openness of the divine being to the creatures, the wonder of being received into the divine being, in which one attains an everlasting significance. In the creative aspect of the love of God the gift given to the creatures is the divine being as the ground and source of the material of the self-creation of the creatures.

As Rahner also asserts, this "ontological" communication of God to the creatures is not to be understood in a reifying or objectifying sense. In the relationship established by the redemptive and creative love of God, both God and the creatures are self-creative individuals. In other words, the relationship that exists between God and the creatures is a genuine, personal dialogue. Both parties to this dialogue depend, in radically different ways, to be sure, upon the other and must wait upon the other. God's self-creation is a self-creation in response to the achievements of the creatures in their own projects of self-creation. Yet each of the parties creates itself freely and maintains a real autonomy over against the other. The relationship between God and the world, in the alternative view of God outlined in this chapter, is a dynamic, historical dialogue in which both God and the creatures constitute themselves freely, and yet in relationship to one another.

A most important aspect of Rahner's discussion of the self-communication of God, it seems to me, is the affirmation that the one final goal of both God and the creatures is precisely immediacy to one another in a relationship of love. He argues that the *telos* or goal of the self-transcendent development or evolution of the world is immediacy to God. Likewise, the primordial divine phenomenon, the fundamental divine act, is the establishment of a personal relationship of love between God and the creatures.

As was shown in the preceding section, if God is essentially love of others, then to be is to be an object of the redemptive and creative love of God. There is no higher purpose beyond this relationship of love between God and the creatures in which

God constitutes Godself in response to the self-constitution of
the creatures and acts so as to facilitate the full self-realization of
the creatures. To use Rahner's own terms, the love of God is the
final ground and source *(das Wovonher),* and the final goal *(das
Woraufhin),* of creaturely becoming. If God is conceived to be
essentially love of others, then this can be taken literally to mean
that it is to the divine being as redemptive love that the creatures
contribute their lives. From this perspective, the following statement by Rahner takes on a coherent and unqualified meaning:

> God does not stand over against the world and its history
> merely as its transcendent first cause that remains un-
> affected by the world, but, in the ecstasy of his love, has
> established himself within the world as its innermost
> entelechy and directs this whole world and its history
> toward that point at which God, face to face, will be the
> innermost and most immediate fulfilling of our existence
> in eternal blessedness.[28]

I have argued that statements such as this, in Rahner, may be
suggestive, but cannot be taken in an unqualified sense as long as
God in Godself is conceived to lack internal relatedness to the
creatures.

In the view of God proposed in this chapter, the creative
and redemptive love of God could be understood to be an
existential within human being. Therefore, as Rahner takes
pains to show, grace is intrinsic to human being, not an extrinsic,
unnecessary superstructure beyond human "nature." The
human person cannot exist except as the object of God's love.
But this existential, although constituted by the gift of God's
love, is not "supernatural" in Rahner's sense of the word. That is
to say, human being is not even conceivable without the creative
and redemptive love of God.

With this essential qualification, however, most of the other
characteristics of the supernatural existential in Rahner's
thought can be retained in the view of God as essentially love of
others. First of all, the divine love is the offer of *Godself,* not the
offer of some created quality, as indicated above. Second, the
divine love is the *offer* of Godself, an offer that must be freely
appropriated by human beings in the dual sense outlined in the
preceding section of this chapter. Third, this offer of the divine
love, which is given with human existence as such, can be understood to be transcendental or original revelation. It is this uni-

versal offer of God's grace that is thematized in the categorial or special revelation identified with the Jewish and Christian scriptures. This transcendental offer of divine love or grace, and its free acceptance or rejection on the part of human persons, is coextensive with the entire history of the human race. Finally, salvation can be understood to be the free acceptance, by a human person, of the creative and redemptive love of God. That is, if salvation is understood in Rahnerian terms to refer to the authentic realization of the human person in relation to self, others, and God, then salvation consists in nothing more than the faithful acceptance and enactment of the fact that the final mystery and meaning of human life is the creative and redemptive love of God.

Recasting Rahner's thought such that God is conceived to be essentially love of others not only allows one to affirm, coherently, that the divine love for others is the final fulfillment of the creatures, but also enables one to conceive love to be the fundamental act of God in an unqualified sense. If God is essentially love of others, then the fundamental divine act of self-constitution is identical to the divine love of others. The fundamental divine act is the act in which God creates Godself in free, loving response to the creatures, thus establishing the necessary conditions for the continuing self-creative activity of the creatures. Rahner asserts that love of others is God's fundamental act. But this assertion is qualified in that it applies only to this particular world order. God's fundamental act is, in fact, love. However, God could have constituted Godself as God without entering into a relationship of love with the creatures, if God had so willed. In the alternative view of God in which God is essentially love of others, God cannot be conceived to be God except as the loving creator and redeemer of some world of creatures. I have tried to show that God must be conceived in this way if the New Testament proclamation is to be faithfully interpreted and if our fundamental trust in the meaningfulness of our lives is to be reflected upon adequately.

For Rahner, the striving of the creatures for God as their fulfillment and the movement of God toward the creatures in self-communicating love, are fully realized only in the incarnation, the act in which God adopts finite reality as God's own reality. I have argued that Rahner's account of the divine activity in the event of the incarnation contradicts his general principle that God does not act in the world, as one categorial actor among others, at all. If God is conceived to be essentially love of others, then the final goal of both God and the creatures can be affirmed to be their relationship of love without appeal to a view of the divine activity that would appear to be mythological, and thus inappropriate, on Rahner's own grounds.

God need not overcome, as Rahner implies, God's essential nonrelativity to the creatures by expressing or alienating Godself in the world, by becoming the world in God's other. I argued that such a notion of the adoption of a real relatedness to the creatures through God's self-expression in God's other, at best, presents merely a verbal solution to the problem it seeks to address. If God is essentially love of others, however, then God must always already be internally or really related to the creatures *in Godself*. God in Godself is constituted by a genuine receptivity or relativity to the creatures. From this starting point, one can affirm that God accomplishes a loving immediacy of Godself to the creatures not by becoming a creature (even in God's other), but by including every moment of creaturely reality within the divine reality. If God is essentially constituted by real relations to the creatures, then the notion of a divine self-alienation, even if such a notion could be coherently expressed, becomes specious.

The view of the divine activity proposed here also represents an appropriation of Rahner's fundamental concern to reconceive the divine causality. He argues that the traditional view of the divine efficient causality portrays the God-world relationship in too external a fashion. So he proposes understanding the positing of the finite creature by God through efficient causality to be a deficient mode of the self-communication of God to the creature in quasi-formal causality. If God is essentially love of others, then divine efficient causality could be conceived to be, in a certain sense, already a self-communication of God. That is, in efficient causality, God does not totally constitute another individual, but rather offers Godself to the genuinely *self*-creative finite individual. God offers to the finite self-creator the divine actuality, which, in turn, is the synthesis of all past actual divine and nondivine states. Because effects are internally related to their causes, God, in efficient causality, is an internal (not just an external) constituent of the self-creative creature, much as is the case in Rahner's view of quasi-formal causality.

Thus, efficient causality already represents a self-giving act of the divine love, and points to an intimate relationship between the creature and God. Further, as Rahner points out in relation to the quasi-formal causality of God, there can be no question of God losing Godself in self-communication, understood, in this sense, as efficient causality, for causes are externally related to their effects. As a causal agent, God is strictly unaffected by the causal relationship to the creatures. Thus, I would argue the chief motive behind the formulation of Rahner's view of quasi-formal causality is maintained in the understanding of the (efficient) causality of God in relation to the world outlined above.[29]

A final, crucial aspect of Rahner's understanding of the self-communication of God is that this self-communication has a triune character. Without attempting to offer a full interpretation of the classical doctrine of the trinity, or even claiming that an adequate Christian concept of God must be explicitly trinitarian, I would argue that the view of God as essentially love of others, which has been outlined in this chapter, is open to a trinitarian interpretation.[30]

First, a distinction that has been made previously must be reemphasized. Several times I have distinguished between a person and that person's personality. A person is concrete and actual, while the personality of that person is nothing actual at all, but rather the set of qualities that abstractly characterizes the person in all of her or his actual states. Thus, it is God, the one God, as a person who is actual, who is internally and externally related to other individuals, who includes the reality of all others within Godself, and who co-creates all other free self-creators. The divine personality, the divinity of God, then, is an abstraction from the one actual divine person. The divine personality, as a set of qualities that characterize the divine being, is not actual, is not internally related to others, and does not include others within itself.

I would argue that one could speak, in classical trinitarian terms, of the one divine *ousia* or "substance" as the one divine being as actual. The three "persons" of the trinity, the three divine hypostases, then, would refer to the divine personality, or to different aspects of it. In this view, the one divine individual is characterized by a threefold personality.

The first person of the trinity could be understood to be the divine personality as such. The first person of the trinity is the abstract character of God as included within the process of the self-creation of all other individuals (including future states of the divine actuality) and God as including within Godself the product of the self-creation of all other individuals (including past states of the divine actuality). The first person of the trinity is God as objective or externally related to others and God as subjective, or internally related to others. The first person of the trinity, as the divine personality as such, is the fountain of the trinity as a whole. This one divine personality is revealed or expressed in two modes, that is, in the second and third persons of the trinity.

The second person of the trinity is the abstract character of God as included within the process of the self-creation of all individuals, including God Godself. The second person of the trinity is God as objective, God as externally related to others. The second person of the trinity is the objective image or expression of the divine personality. As such, the second person of the trinity is God as an efficacious causal principle influential in all moments of self-creation on the part of all individuals.

The third person of the trinity, correspondingly, could be understood to refer to the abstract character of God as including within Godself the product of the self-creation of all individuals. The third person of the trinity is God as subjective, God as internally related to others. The third person of the trinity is God as the loving companion, the comforter of all, who accepts the joys and sorrows of all individuals into Godself, who redeems existence from meaninglessness. The third person of the trinity is God as affected by all other individuals.[31]

This interpretation of the trinity, as incomplete as it is, nevertheless would seem to include what Rahner identifies as the key elements of an adequate contemporary doctrine of the trinity. First of all, it is clear that the three persons of the trinity are all equally divine. For the three persons are all aspects of the divine personality and thus are fully and equally divine. Or, in more classical language, the three persons all share the same, single divine substance. The divine personality as a whole, the divine objectivity, and the divine subjectivity are alike, one and all, in being divine. The unity of the divine being is maintained. Second, though, it is clear that the three persons of the trinity are neither "persons" in the modern sense of individual centers of consciousness and activity, nor three historical modes of the divine being. The view of the trinity sketched here avoids the errors of tritheism and modalism, for, as in Rahner's view, the three persons of the trinity are three relatively distinct ways in which God subsists. These distinctions are essential to God and characterize every moment of the divine actuality. God cannot be conceived except as an actual individual or person who has a personality, a set of defining characteristics (the first person), an objectivity (the second person), and a subjectivity (the third person). These distinctions are real, for there could be nothing more different than a person and that person's personality, being an object for oneself and others, and being a subject in relation to oneself and others. Further, these distinctions are purely formal or transcendental and do not derive from any special type of experience. So conceived, it is clear that the trinity is in fact an immanent trinity, one that characterizes the divine being in itself, not simply our experience of God. And yet these intratrinitarian distinctions are relative and not absolute. They are three aspects of the one, concrete divine being, not three gods, or three historical stages in the life of God.

Finally, this view accords with Rahner's claim that the first person of the trinity is the fountain of the trinity, the unoriginate source from which the second and third persons are "begotten" or "spirated." For the first person represents the divine personality as a whole, while the second and third persons are aspects of the divine personality (God as objective and God as subjective). Thus, it is clear that the second and third persons can be derived from the first person (who holds a position of genuine logical, though not temporal, priority), while the converse does not hold true.

The Mystery of the God Who Is Essentially Love of Others

Finally, it might appear that the view that God is essentially love of others ignores the truth of the tradition of the *via negativa* that is so central to Rahner's thought. That is, it might be objected that if God is conceived to be essentially love of others, then God is longer mysterious and beyond our comprehension but is fully transparent to human reason. The view of God presented here might seem to represent the height of arrogance in that it pretends to dissolve the mystery of the divine being. I want to show here that this alternative view is not a denial of Rahner's central claim that God can never be fully and adequately conceived by human beings.

While I have not had much occasion to stress the point, since this study has been concerned to understand and appraise Rahner's *concept* of God, I feel that one of the most helpful aspects of his thought is his understanding of the nature of the question concerning God. Primarily, the question of God is an existentiell question not a conceptual or a theoretical one. It is the question concerning the final meaning of human existence.

> The question about God, if, indeed, God is not to be missed from the outset, cannot be posed as a question concerning an individual, particular being *within* the horizon of our transcendence and our historical experience; rather, it must be posed as the question concerning the supporting ground, the origin, and the future of the question that we ourselves are.[32]

The question of God concerns my basic understanding of myself. It is the question of where I put my ultimate trust, in myself and my own abilities, or in the divine mystery that encompasses my life. The question of God, the existentiell question that we each face as human beings, is the question of whether we love more the tiny island of our knowledge, our talents, our self-wrought security, or the vast encompassing ocean of the divine being, which encounters us in our human neighbor.[33] I would understand the question of God, as the final question of human existence, in just the same way.

It seems to me, further, that the *concept* of God outlined here itself in no way denies the mysterious character of God. Being able to describe, a priori, something of the essence or divinity of God is not to place God under our control. The things that have been said about God, up to this point, do not derive from any special insight into the divine being. Rather, the description of God as a free self-creator constituted by real relatedness to others, with all that went with that description, was put forward because it seemed to be the only adequate way of understanding God given our basic experience of ourselves and the elementary categories that experience sugggests. Virtually everything that has been said about God (e.g., that God is internally and externally related to others, that God is free to constitute Godself in relation to others, that God acts upon others by modifying Godself as the object of other individuals, etc.) could also be said of any other actual individual, although in a deficient or noneminent sense. The preceding concept of God as an essentially social being is a wholly formal or transcendental concept of God. It applies to God those transcendental characteristics that must apply to anything that is actual at all. Precisely because these formal characteristics apply to anything actual as such, there is a certain emptiness to this strictly transcendental talk of God, although, as Hartshorne says, this empty, formal talk is important in that it describes the logical structure of reality, or, in this case, the being of God.[34]

Thus far, in this alternative concept of God, God has been described largely in literal, metaphysical terms, or, when symbolic terms, such as love, have been used to speak of God, it has been clear that such symbolic utterances imply certain literal truths concerning God, e.g., that God is internally and externally related to others. This literal, metaphysical language about God (and even the symbolic talk of God as love, which, nevertheless, is true necessarily not contingently) describes the divine essence, the divine personality, the divinity of God. In such literal language about God, the abstract qualities that characterize the actual, concrete being of God in any given moment have been discussed. We can speak confidently about the divinity of God. We can describe, a priori, the essence or nature of God. We can describe, on strictly metaphysical grounds, something of the divine character: e.g., that God is omnipotent, omniscient, existentially independent of the creatures and yet actually dependent on the creatures for the content of the divine experience, love, and so forth. But, to have determined the essence or divinity of God a priori is not at all to have determined how the abstract qualities or characteristics of God will be instantiated or embodied in concrete situations.

To speak abstractly or metaphysically about the divinity of God is not to deny the mysterious character of God in God's actual being. Rahner argues that abstract reflection upon an actual, lived experience, while never fully capturing the original experience, need not be viewed as an enemy of the lived experience. Reflection may help us to appropriate more fully our immediate experience. Likewise, it seems to me, metaphysical or purely formal talk about God need not lead us to forget that

God, as an actual individual, is infinitely more than we can comprehend, a person, finally, to be loved and not rationally understood.

For, as I have remarked throughout this study, formal, metaphysical talk about God is not the only way of speaking of God. Indeed, the most distinctively religious language concerning God is symbolic and not literal, metaphysical language. Symbolic utterances concerning God do not attribute to God characteristics that apply to all of reality as such, but select some particular, material aspect of our own experience as human beings, such as love, faithfulness, mercy, or patience, and apply these characteristics to God. The point of such symbolic talk of God is not just, or not primarily, to assert something to be the case relative to God, but rather to speak of our own existence in relation to God.

Far from being forced to deny that much of our talk about God is symbolic and that God is mysterious and incomprehensible to us, it seems to me that, on the basis of the concept of God proposed in this chapter, one can state clearly wherein the mysterious character of God consists. I would argue, as Rahner implies in the following passage, that the mysterious character of God lies in God's actual being and activity.

> Precisely because the God who is known from the world by the natural reason of man is a free transcendent person, . . . the concrete way in which God relates himself to man and wishes to act toward him cannot be calculated from human nature, from below. . . . This question cannot be answered by way of a metaphysical projection of the essence of God on the part of man, but can only be answered by God, in the event of his own free decision.[35]

We can speak a priori of the abstract, necessary essence of God. But God's actuality, at any given moment, is contingent upon the actuality of the creatures and upon God's own free synthesis of creaturely actuality. In each moment God's actuality is slightly different in that it includes the advances made by the creatures in their processes of self-realization and the ever new level of self-realization attained by God. God's necessary essence, the divinity of God, does not change from moment to moment, and can be described a priori in a transcendental metaphysics. But such a characterization is purely formal and abstracts from

God's actual, or accidental, being which is new in each moment. God's actual being, in that it includes all past divine and non-divine states, is so infinitely vast and rich, that we, as finite creatures, can know almost nothing about it. We cannot *know* the divine actuality in even one individual instant.[36]

It is in God's actual being that God is mysterious, indeed, mystery as such. It is in God's actual relations to us that God is unknown and unknowable. Hartshorne writes:

> Rational theology may be able to show that there is a God who cherishes all his creatures; but no rational discipline can show there is a God who cherishes "me," meaning by me, the precise individual quality, incommunicable in abstract terms, that makes me different from anyone else that ever lived or ever could have lived. That about God which reason cannot know is not the essence of God, that which he is in general terms, such as all-knowing, or loving; but the particular form that this knowing or loving takes when a particular creature is its object. Not the essence, but the most particular of the accidents of God have to be felt rather than demonstrated, if we can know them at all. Even God's relation to the human race is outside the province of metaphysics and must either be deduced from anthropological data, or from the depths of personal intuition, one's own or someone else's.[37]

It seems to me that Rahner's concept of God must be recast so as to allow that we can know a priori, on purely metaphysical grounds, that God is love. We can say, abstractly, that however God acts toward me, it will be in an appropriately loving manner. But we cannot know a priori how God's love will be embodied or expressed in particular situations. As Rahner rightly says, God's personal activity toward the creatures is radically free and cannot be deduced ahead of time.

It is precisely the superabundance of God's relations to finite individuals that constitutes the mystery of God. God is mysterious not because God is unrelated to the world, a distant, aloof principle of which we can have no experience. Rather, God is unknowable and mysterious in God's actuality precisely because God is intimately internally related to every instance of creaturely actuality. God is permanently mysterious because we can never comprehend the vast richness of God's actual being, which is a being-related-to all past and present divine and non-divine states.

We can speak clearly and literally of the divinity of God, of God's abstract defining characteristics. But as an actual individual, God is incomparably rich and complex. (In the same way, we can know something of another person's personality, that she or he is trustworthy or indolent or whatever, but not know how, concretely, that person will feel and act in a particular situation.) We cannot know God as a person, in the way that we know the divinity of God. As Rahner says, finally, we must love God, not know God. We must entrust our lives to the vast, encompassing mystery that surrounds and supports us. We must give ourselves to God, risk ourselves, without knowing exactly how God acts in particular situations, although we can trust that God's activity will be characterized, somehow, by goodness and love.

God as a concrete, actual individual vastly transcends our powers of comprehension and expression. We cannot speak metaphysically or literally of God's actuality. At this point, we must adopt the *via negativa*. We must speak symbolically of God, using concepts we know to apply literally only to our own limited range of experience. We must speak of God as love, for instance, even though we know that God, literally, is not a person. But we must use such language to be able to appropriate our own being in the world, in order to express our fundamental trust in the meaning and worth of our lives grounded in the primordial experience that the final horizon of reality, called God, is receptive and affirming of us and acts to maximize our own self-realization.

At this point, the approach adopted in this alternative concept of God is not different from Rahner's own approach to theology. The problem faced is the same: the necessity of somehow speaking of the final ground and goal of our existence while, at the same time, realizing that that final ground and goal is fundamentally mysterious and incomprehensible. The necessity of using symbolic language to speak of this mysterious God is clear. Further, such symbolic talk about God's free, concrete dealings with the world implies certain literal, metaphysical truths about God. The difference is that in the recasting of Rahner's thought proposed here, the literal statement that God is constituted essentially by real relatedness to other individuals is held to be a necessary implication of the symbolic statement "God is love."

In summary, it seems to me that the recasting of Rahner's

concept of God proposed in this chapter not only provides a more coherent presentation of his basic theological insights, but also offers a relatively adequate solution to the contemporary problem of the concept of God. A consistent view of God that is genuinely based on our most fundamental experience of ourselves has been outlined. The formulation of this view of God represents an explicit acknowledgement of the two points of general consensus in contemporary theology identified in Chapter I. The concept of God as essentially love of others illustrates a thorough application of the methodological turn to the subject to reflection on the divine reality. It also seems to interpret most adequately both the apostolic witness of faith found in scripture and our common human experience.

NOTES

[1] I will not attempt to give an exhaustive list of the works of the representatives of the process or neoclassical philosophy that is associated with Alfred North Whitehead and Charles Hartshorne. Such bibliographical material is readily available in anthologies such as, Ewert Cousins, ed., *Process Theology: Basic Writings* (New York: Newman Press, 1971), and Delwin Brown, Ralph E. James, Jr., Gene Reeves, *Process Philosophy and Christian Thought* (Indianapolis: Bobbs-Merrill, 1971). Bibliographies of secondary literature concerning Whitehead and Hartshorne in particular can be found in *Process Studies* 1 (1971):2–81, and *Process Studies* 3 (1973):179–227, respectively. I wish to refer only to those works that have been most directly of use to me in the formulation of an alternative to Rahner's concept of God, which avoids the incoherence of his thought while retaining its significant contributions: Charles Hartshorne, *The Divine Relativity: A Social Conception of God* (New Haven: Yale University Press, 1948); *The Logic of Perfection and Other Essays in Neoclassical Metaphysics* (LaSalle, Ill.: Open Court, 1962); *Man's Vision of God and the Logic of Theism* (Hamden, Conn.: Archon Books, 1964); *Reality as Social Process: Studies in Metaphysics and Religion* (Glencoe, Ill.: Free Press, 1953); Schubert Ogden, *The Reality of God and Other Essays,* second edition (New York: Harper & Row, 1977); Alfred North Whitehead, *Process and Reality: An Essay in Cosmology,* corrected edition by David Griffin and Donald Sherburne (New York: Macmillan, 1978).

[2] *Wirklichkeit und Glaube,* vol. II; *Der persönliche Gott,* p. 82, my emphasis.

3 See "Die Christologie innerhalb einer evolutiven Weltanschauung," *ST,* 5:189–190 (ET: *TI,* 5:163).

4 This process of self-constitution by including the others to whom I am related within myself is, for Rahner, a temporal process. I recover, in *anamnesis,* past existentiell possibilities, possibilities that have been actualized by myself and by others. But I recover these "past" possibilities precisely as futural possibilities of existence. I grasp these possibilities in *prognosis,* as possibilities that I might actualize if I so choose.

5 *The Reality of God and Other Essays,* p. 58. Later I will show that the existential independence of God is not denied by this affirmation that God is essentially related to others.

6 Hartshorne, *The Divine Relativity,* p. 33.

7 "Über die Möglichkeit des Glaubens heute," *ST,* 5:30 (ET: *TI,* 5:21).

8 *"Theos* im Neuen Testament," *ST,* 1:127 (ET: *TI,* 1:111).

9 This description, of course, is highly abstract. In actuality, there is only one self that is passive and active in relation to others. But one can distinguish within this one actual self two abstract aspects: the self as subject and the self as object.

10 As the passage cited from Ogden above indicated, and as Rahner himself implies, the nature of reality, as disclosed in our basic existentiell experience of ourselves, is not only essentially social but also essentially temporal. In the view of most process thinkers, subjects, in the present, are internally related to the data of the past, while past actuality is externally related to the present synthesis of actuality by existing selves. Thus, objects as externally related to subjects, lie in the past. For example, the life of Julius Caesar may have been influential in the life of Napoleon Bonaparte. That is to say, Caesar's life may have been a determinative aspect in Napoleon's free self-constitution. But the inclusion of Caesar's life (object) within Napoleon's life (subject) had no influence upon Caesar. Napoleon is the internally related, or affected, term in the Caesar-Napoleon relationship, while Caesar is the externally related, or nonaffected, term. Qua object, a datum is related to a subject as past is to present. In any given moment in the ongoing process of my self-constitution, I am open to, influenced or affected by, what others, including myself in the previous moment, have been. In the present, I synthesize data from the past into my own self-constitution. The product of this present act of self-constitution becomes a datum for the future self-constitutive acts of other subjects, including my own.

11 Thus far, I have done little more than to assert that God acts with respect to the creatures by offering the divine being as, in some sense, inclusive of certain possibilities for the self-creation of the creatures. Exactly what this means will be discussed more fully below.

12 In the following discussion, I have intentionally spoken of the

redemptive and creative love of God, rather than, in more traditional terms, God's creation and redemption of the creatures. My purpose in doing this is not to suggest that there are not the best of theological reasons for speaking of the priority of the divine activity of creation. I wish simply to emphasize, as I did in Chapter IX, the importance of the passive aspect of the divine love in which God is genuinely relative to the creatures. It is this aspect of the divine love that is not accounted for in Rahner's thought.

[13] *Confessions* 1 1. 20, in *Confessions and Enchiridion*, trans. and ed. Albert Outler, The Library of Christian Classics, vol. 7 (Philadelphia: Westminster Press, 1955), p. 259.

[14] *The Logic of Perfection*, pp. 273–274.

[15] See Hartshorne, *The Divine Relativity*, p. 131.

[16] "Zur Theologie der Menschwerdung," *ST*, 4:145–146 (ET: *TI*, 4:112). Compare this statement with the objection Tillich raises against Hartshorne's neoclassical theism: "In spite of my agreement with Hartshorne in these important points, I cannot accept his assertion that these elements which characterize finite being can be applied to God 'literally,' because that would make God finite; and a 'finite God' is a contradiction in terms. . . . [God] is not subject to finitude; he is the infinite who comprises his infinity and his finitude. If this is denied, he becomes another name for the process of life, seen as a whole, and is subject to the tragic possibility which threatens every finite process. Then not only is the world a risk taken by God, but God himself is a risk to himself, a risk which may fail" (*Philosophical Interrogations*, ed. Sidney Rome and Beatrice Rome (New York: Holt, Rinehart and Winston, 1964), p. 376).

[17] "Divine Absoluteness and Divine Relativity," in *Transcendence*, ed. Herbert Richardson and Donald Cutler (Boston: Beacon Press, 1969), p. 165.

[18] P. 348.

[19] This in no way denies that the divine actuality would have been different at moment *a* if God and the nondivine individuals had acted differently previous to moment *a*. If the creatures, prior to moment *a*, had acted so as to facilitate the authentic self-realization of their fellows more fully, then God's actuality at moment *a* would have been of a higher quality in that the creatures would have more perfectly cooperated with God's own project of optimizing the free self-creation of all of the creatures. This is to say that the content of God's actual experience can vary at any given moment depending (partially) on what the creatures actually have accomplished in free projects of self-creation. But what cannot vary, what is literally imperfectible, is God's nature as the universal individual who includes within Godself all past divine and nondivine actuality.

[20] See Hartshorne, *The Divine Relativity*, p. 22.

21 *Man's Vision of God*, pp. 37–38.

22 *GG*, p. 94 (ET: *FCF*, p. 86).

23 *HW*, pp. 111–112.

24 Delwin Brown, in "Freedom and Faithfulness in Whitehead's God," *Process Studies* 2 (1972):137–148, presents a view of the divine freedom similar to the one I will outline below. However, he does argue that, "baldly put, God is faithful because he could, but does not 'sin' against his own primordial ideals. That God continues to relate himself to the world in a given way is a matter of grace, not of necessity" (p. 148). If this means that God could relate to the world in a nonloving way, then Brown's position concerning the gratuity of the divine love is not essentially different from that of Rahner. That God is love is not a matter of grace, if that means that God might not relate lovingly to the creatures, but is "necessitated" by the divine nature itself.

25 "*Theos* im Neuen Testament," *ST*, 1:131 (ET: *TI*, 1:115).

26 See Rahner, *GG*, pp. 28–30, 37–50 (ET: *FCF*, pp. 17–19, 26–39).

27 Ibid., p. 126 (ET: ibid., p. 120).

28 "Kirchliche Christologie zwischen Exegese und Dogmatik," *ST*, 9:212–213 (ET: *TI*, 11:200).

29 Of course, in the alternative concept of God in which God is essentially love of others, efficient causality does not exhaustively explicate the divine activity in relation to the world. The divine activity of including the reality of the nondivine individuals within the divine reality is not an instance of *divine* efficient causality.

30 In addition to the problems that Rahner raises with respect to the formulation of an adequate contemporary doctrine of the trinity (see "Der dreifaltige Gott als transzendenter Urgrund der Heilsgeschichte," pp. 319–328 (ET: *The Trinity*, pp. 10–22)), I would add the problem of expressing the doctrine of the trinity in nonsexist language. While this is a problem of Christian theology as a whole, the traditional language concerning God the Father, God the Son, and God the Holy Spirit makes this a particularly difficult problem in relation to the doctrine of the trinity.

31 A number of thinkers have reflected on the doctrine of the trinity from the perspective of process or neoclassical metaphysics. Charles Hartshorne writes: "Reflexive Transcendence throws some light, too, upon the idea of the Trinity. For T/T [God as the self-surpassing surpasser of all other beings] is in a manner the Father, and A [God as absolute] and R [God as relative] are the Logos and the Holy Spirit. This is not utterly fanciful. Part of what was said about the persons agrees with the logic of T/T, A, and R. The three are in a sense equal, since all are necessary to God, yet T/T is the one from which the necessity of the other two can best be understood, and in this sense it begets the other two in a logical not a temporal sense" (*Man's Vision of God*, p. 351). Norman Pittenger, although critical of the attempt to make

Whiteheadian categories such as the primordial and consequent nature of God fit neatly into a trinitarian scheme, argues: "We wish to speak of God as the everlasting creative agency who works anywhere and everywhere, yet without denying the reality of creaturely freedom—hence we point toward God as Parent. We wish also to speak of God as so working that he acts with and beside his creation, by luring it and attracting it toward realizing its possibilities and thereby achieving the fulfillment or satisfaction which is its aim—hence we point toward God as Self-Expressive Word. And we wish finally to speak of God as active in and through his creation in its accepting or 'prehending' the lure or attraction which is offered to it, and thereby perfecting and heightening the intensity of its life and achieving fulfillment or satisfaction through a response which is richer and more adequate than the possibilities available through creaturely action alone—hence we point to God as the Responsive Agency who is the Holy Spirit" (*The Divine Triunity* (Philadelphia: United Church Press, 1977), p. 116). Schubert Ogden offers the following interpretation of the immanent trinity: "The *one divine substance* is God *himself*, or the eminent *individual*, who both loves and is loved by himself and all others, and thus is the primal source and final end of reality as such. The *three divine persons* . . . are respectively: *Father*, or the essence of the eminent individual as both loving and loved by himself and all others, i.e., the divine *individuality* as such; *Son*, or the essence of the eminent individual as loved by himself and all others, i.e., the divine *objectivity* as such; and *Holy Spirit*, or the essence of the eminent individual as loving himself and all others, i.e., the divine *subjectivity* as such" ("On the Trinity," *Theology* 83 (1980): 98).

[32] "Bemerkungen zur Gotteslehre in der katholischen Dogmatik," *ST*, 8:179–180 (ET: *TI*, 9:139).

[33] "Über den Begriff des Geheimnisses in der katholischen Theologie," *ST*, 4:79 (ET: *TI*, 4:57).

[34] See *The Logic of Perfection*, pp. 280–297.

[35] "*Theos* im Neuen Testament," *ST*, 1:99 (ET: *TI*, 1:86–87).

[36] Hartshorne, *The Divine Relativity*, pp. 40–41.

[37] *Reality as Social Process*, pp. 171–172.

CHAPTER XII
THE LOVE OF GOD, THEOLOGY, AND HUMAN LIBERATION

The goal of the final chapter of this study is to consider some of the consequences of the alternative concept of God that I have just outlined in relation to the task of Christian theology in the contemporary situation. There are three specific issues with which I want to deal: the relation of the concept of God as essentially love of others to the other themes of Christian systematic theology; the meaning of this understanding of God in relation to the contemporary theological problem of the liberation of human persons from oppressive social structures; and, finally, the sense in which Christian theology itself can serve the cause of human liberation. This final chapter represents an explicit return to some of the issues raised in the Introduction to this study. I hope to show that if Rahner's concept of God can be recast in the manner indicated in Chapter XI, his thought can address, more adequately than it does at present, one of the most crucial problems facing contemporary Christian theology, namely, the problem of the meaning of Christian faith in the God who is love in a situation of global oppression and injustice.

The One Love of God and Its Many Theological Expressions

One result of the previous discussion of the Christian concept of God is the realization that there is one primordial, yet ever renewed relationship between God and the world: the mutual participation of God and the creatures in each other's act of self-creation. The individuals of the world play a role in the divine self-creation in that they are included within the divine actuality. God, in turn, plays a role in the self-creation of the creatures in that God provides the conditions and the material for creaturely self-creation. This relationship is most appropriately symbolized as love. The relationship has no goal or purpose other than the facilitation of the full, authentic self-realization of both God and the creatures. God opens Godself to the creatures, allows the creatures to make a real difference to God and to influence the self-creation of God. Then, God gives Godself to the creatures, partially determining their free self-creation. Likewise, the creatures open themselves to God and let the product of the divine self-creation influence their own self-creation. Then, the creatures bestow themselves upon God; they literally live unto God and for God's greater glory, in that the product of their acts of self-creation becomes a part of the divine actuality.

I would argue that this loving fellowship of God and the creatures, which is the final meaning and mystery of existence as such, is the one all-encompassing theme of Christian theology. All particular discussions within theology, the various doctrines, that is, are expressions or applications of this one overarching theme of the love of God for the creatures. The love of God for others is both the protological and eschatological nature of things. In Christian thought, the love of God is that which creates and redeems us. This love of God is decisively represented in Jesus Christ, and embodied in the church, the community that serves as a sign, as Rahner says, of the love of God.

This means that it is inappropriate to contrast the individual doctrines of Christian theology in such a way as to imply that one establishes most fully what the nature of God is in relation to the world. The doctrines of creation, redemption, incarnation, grace, and last things all express the one truth that God is essentially love of others. No one doctrine establishes, for the first time, that God is love. All portray the one love of God for the creatures in various ways in relation to different aspects of our experience of ourselves, other creatures, and God.

Rahner's theology represents a very important formulation of this principle. As I have shown, the love or self-communication of God is at the heart of Rahner's thought. He claims that the love of God is the basic reality of Christian faith and the central theme of Christian theology. He argues, for instance, that since, in grace, God-in-Godself and God-of-salvation-for-us are strictly identical, "*each* dogmatic treatise must speak of this God of gracious self-communication and nothing more."[1] The fact that there is a separate treatise on God in Christian theology, and that it comes first in traditional dogmatics, does not mean that the teaching concerning the God who is love is "a particular, regional treatise. [It is] rather a formal anticipation of that with which all theological treatises are concerned."[2] Elsewhere, Rahner says eloquently:

> The task of theology must be to appeal to this primordial experience of grace in all of its conceptually differenti-ated objectifications; to show man, ever anew, that this whole, immensely differentiated sum of Christian state-ments of faith expresses, in essence, . . . nothing but the one immense truth that the absolute mystery, which is, which holds sway over, and supports, everything, and which always remains, has communicated itself as itself to man in forgiving love.[3]

This principle that there is one all-encompassing theme of Christian theology is exemplified materially in several ways in Rahner's thought. As I have shown, he argues that creation has factually occurred for the sake of divine self-communication.

> Creation, in the concrete world, no longer means merely the positing of something finite out of an infinite ground, from which ground, as that which is unavailable, this creature is always kept at a distance. Rather, creation is the positing of the finite as that upon which the infinite has bestowed itself as love.[4]

The self-communication of God in love is, for Rahner, the primordial possibility of God, God's one final goal in all divine activity. It is this self-bestowal of God upon the creatures that is thematized or objectified in Christian talk concerning Jesus Christ. Rahner argues,

> . . . the express revelation of the Word in Christ is not something that comes to us from outside as something totally alien, but is only the explication of what we always already are by grace and what we experience, at least unthematically, in the limitlessness of our transcendence. The explicit Christian revelation is the reflective ex-pression of the gracious revelation that man has always already unreflectively experienced in the depth of his being.[5]

And yet, at times, Rahner's thought seems to deny this principle that all of the particular doctrines of Christian the-ology are expressions of the one love of God for the creatures. For instance, he contrasts creation and self-communication not just as different expressions of the one love of God for the creatures, but also as the love of God in a full sense, which establishes the primordial relationship of God to the world, and a deficient mode of that relationship of love. In creation, God posits, through efficient causality, the finite world as other than God. In self-communication, God bestows Godself, through quasi-formal causality, upon the creatures. Rahner argues that the creation of the world does not represent the fully personal love of God, for the act of creation does not involve genuine self-giving on the part of God. Such an ecstatic act of love, in which God steps out from Godself and gives Godself to the creature, occurs only in the self-communication of God, that is, in grace and incarnation. Creation is a deficient form of the God-world relationship that is founded upon the self-communication of God.

Similarly, Rahner argues that the real, proper *topos* for an understanding of God's presence in, or relationship to, the world in Christian theology is to be found in the doctrine of grace.[6] Further, he writes, at times, that the incarnation of the Logos in Jesus Christ not only thematically represents the love of God for the creatures, but is the act in which that love is definitively bestowed upon, or presented to, the creatures. "In him [Jesus Christ], God is irrevocably the one who has accepted us in love, who has made his infinite fullness of truth, life, and eternity our own possession."[7] I think it would be a misrepresentation of Rahner's thought to assert that he means, in a passage such as this, simply that Jesus Christ is a representation or revelation, even if *the* decisive representation or revelation, of the one love of God for the creatures given in every moment of existence, and not also that, on God's part as well as on the part of human being, the divine love is incomparably and fully offered as well as received in the life of Jesus of Nazareth.

In each of these instances there is a denial, on Rahner's part, that all of the doctrines of Christian theology are variations on one essential theme: the love of God for other individuals. It seems to me that such a juxtaposition of creation and self-communication, which is essential to Rahner's understanding of the gratuity of the divine love, is possible only if one believes that there is more than one possible fundamental relationship between God and the world. Rahner argues that, in this concrete world order, the divine act of creation was undertaken for the sake of the act of loving self-communication. But God could just as well have created the world without bestowing Godself upon the creatures in love. In such a view, love of the creatures is just one of God's possibilities, not the only conceivable divine possibility. Creation does not just express the one theme of the divine love, but constitutes, in fact, a distinct theme, one in which God is not love of creatures, but merely the aloof, impersonal ground and goal of creaturely self-transcendence. In such a view, the theme of the fully personal divine love is introduced only with the self-communication of God in grace and incarnation.

But if God is conceived to be essentially love of others, then no one particular doctrine establishes God to be love of others. Rather, all of the particular doctrines, creation, incarnation, grace, etc., express the fact that God in every act, in every moment, is love. Rahner's view that it is in the doctrine of grace, or, speaking more broadly, in reflection on the self-communication of God, that the God-world relationship is shown to be one of love is understandable, even justifiable, when one realizes that he is reacting to an inappropriate view of this relationship. He argues that traditional scholastic thought understands the God-world relation primarily in terms of the creation of the world by God. Creation is understood solely as the divine positing of the nondivine, that which is radically other than God. It is this wholly extrinsic God-world relationship that Rahner holds is inadequate in Christian theology. He proposes, in its place, the God-world relationship established by divine self-communication, conceived using the model of quasi-formal causality. In grace, God communicates Godself as an intrinsic principle of the spiritual creature; in the incarnation, God adopts the reality of the world as God's own reality. In contrasting creation and self-communication in this fashion, Rahner seeks to show that the appropriate image for the God-world relationship is not that of the watchmaker and the watch, but rather that of two free persons who love each other. But, in the view of God suggested in the previous chapter, creation is already a genuine expression, not a deficient mode, of the divine love for others. The only God-world relationship that is conceivable is one of love, for God is essentially love of others.

So, on the one hand, no one doctrine alone expresses the divine love. All of the particular doctrines of Christian theology are expressions of the divine love. They are variations on the one all-encompassing theme of Christian theology. It would be inappropriate, in Christian theology, to focus exclusively upon one doctrinal locus, as if it alone established the character of God's relation to the world. In this sense, the one theme of the divine love for the creatures relativizes all of the particular doctrines. And yet, on the other hand, since all of the doctrines of Christian theology are expressions of the one love of God, each doctrine has an important role to play as a variation on this one theme. No doctrine should be ignored, since, in its own way, it expresses the love of God.

But there is an even more serious problem in the theology of Rahner and others with respect to the use of the particular doctrines of Christian theology. The problem is that of attempting to show, by contrasting the view of God given in different doctrines, that while God in God's essential being is unrelated to others, God has freely chosen to relate Godself to the world. It seems to me, finally, that Rahner can contrast creation and self-communication in the way that he does only because divine creation and divine self-communication do not represent two necessary aspects of the one divine act of love, but rather two genuinely distinct divine possibilities: one in which God is strictly nonrelative to the creatures, and one in which God has chosen to become relative to the creatures. As I have shown, Rahner's claim that the creation of the world was oriented from the outset toward the act of divine self-communication must be qualified with the phrase, "in this actual or concrete world order." It could have been otherwise. God could have remained simply the creator of the world, the aloof, asymptotic horizon of the world process. God could have chosen not to love the world in a fully personal sense. Thus, there is a sense in which God's love for others, for Rahner, is not God's primordial possibility, but one of God's possibilities, the one, in fact, that has been actualized in relation to this world. God need not have been really related to the world. God could have remained merely externally related to the world as the creator-God. It is in the divine self-communication that God, for the first time, can be seen to be really related to the world.

As I argued in Chapter VII, the only way Rahner has of conjoining God as related to others and God as strictly independent and non related to others is by viewing the relativity of God as a free self-expression or self-limitation of the primordial mode of the divine being, namely, God as strictly nonrelative to the creatures. Rahner realizes that the Christian affirmation that God is love, that God was incarnate in Jesus Christ, entails that God must in some sense be really, not just nominally, related to the creatures. But it seems to me that what he does is to use the doctrine of the incarnation, and the God-world relationship it entails, in contrast to the doctrine of creation, or a metaphysical (i.e., natural) doctrine of God, and the God-world relationship entailed therein, to add, contingently, relatedness to others to a God who, in God's essential nature, is strictly unrelated to others. That is to say, in essence, God is not really related to others. This can be established by our natural knowledge of God as expressed in a metaphysical doctrine of God, and even in the doctrine of God as the creator of the world. It is, for Rahner, in talk of the divine self-communication, and, particularly, in the doctrine of the incarnation, that God is affirmed to have chosen freely to become really related to the creatures. As I have pointed out several times, the very way Rahner formulates his understanding of the incarnation, that is, as the self-expression, the self-externalization, the self-alienation of God, conveys the image of a God who is essentially self-possessed and independent *(bei sich selbst)*, but who freely chooses to relate Godself to the creatures.

There are other examples of this same procedure of focusing on one particular doctrine in order to establish that God is not only the absolute, independent, supreme being, but also a reality that is relevant to our concrete existence, that is affected by us and related to our actual situation. I wish to cite several instances in which the doctrine of the trinity, in contrast to a natural or metaphysical doctrine of God, is claimed to provide the means of understanding a genuine relativity of God. Jürgen Moltmann argues that the triune God, in the process of God's self-differentiation and self-identification in which God is lover (Father), beloved (Son), and love itself (Holy Spirit), wills to communicate Godself to others, and thus creates the world.[8] The love of God for the creatures is the same love that God the Father has for God the Son.

> The creation is a part of the eternal history of love between the Father and the Son. It was created by the love of the Father for the Son and was redeemed

> through the reciprocating love of the Son for the Father.
> The creation is there because the eternal love creatively
> communicates itself to others.[9]

Through the extension of intratrinitarian love to the creatures,
the divine being becomes subject to passion, to *pathos*, to suffering. Here, the doctrine of the trinity provides the grounds for
the affirmation that God, in that God is love, is really related to
the creatures.

Thomas D. Parker also employs the doctrine of the trinity to
speak of God as related to others in contrast to traditional views
of God as strictly unrelated to the world.[10]

> The unity of God, seen from this trinitarian vantage
> point, is more organic than mechanical, dynamically in-
> cluding what is static, dialectically including what is an-
> tithetic, and reconciling what is merely alienated. It is the
> unity of overcoming what hurts and divides by taking it
> into life rather than by cutting it off by radical surgery.
> Trinitarian mutuality means that the unity of God is an
> aliveness which is the foundation and fulfillment of crea-
> tures, rather than an absolute principle of undivided
> being over against beings (monad). . . . [I]nsofar as one
> of the hypostases of the trinity has assumed crea-
> tureliness into it, within the life of God itself creatures
> are present in actuality as well as in decree and pos-
> sibility.[11]

Similarly, John M. Quinn proposes to make use of the doctrine of the trinity to answer the question: "how can an all-loving
God remain unaffected by the suffering of the men he has
created?"[12] Quinn argues that although, strictly speaking, God
does not suffer, the radical intratrinitarian self-giving of Father,
Son, and Holy Spirit finds a perfect analogy in the sacrificial
death of Jesus, in which Jesus is wholly surrendered to God the
Father. "Though wholly other, the God of Christians does not
stand off at an infinite distance from and cold as a polar night to
the suffering of man."[13] In the self-giving, triune love of God
for Godself, God mirrors, and is sympathetic to, our human
suffering.

While these views raise a whole host of issues, the key
problem at this point is that the understandings of the trinity
proposed by Moltmann, Parker, and Quinn all represent what
Cyril Richardson calls a trinity of mediation, that is, an attempt

to relate an essentially unrelated God (the Father) to the world through the Son or Holy Spirit.[14] It seems to me that these trinitarian reflections, as well as Rahner's view of the incarnation, constitute denials of the position that there is one primordial God-world relationship, one in which God is essentially love of others. Implicit in these positions is the view that God exists originally and essentially as unrelated to the world. It is through the self-expression of the triune God in Jesus Christ that God freely (and contingently) adopts a real relatedness to the creatures. The function of the doctrines of the trinity and the incarnation, in contrast to the metaphysical doctrine of God, is to show that God is in fact genuinely related to the world.

I argued that God as related to others cannot be derived from God as unrelated to others in this fashion. Either the relatedness of God affirmed in the doctrine of the trinity or the incarnation is a relatedness of God in *Godself*, or else these doctrines represent merely verbal affirmations of God's relatedness, when, in fact, God is and remains strictly or essentially unrelated to the creatures. But if God is essentially love of others, then the use of the doctrine of the trinity or the incarnation to establish a relativity of God becomes specious. For God in Godself in all divine states already is constituted by real relatedness to the creatures. All trinitarian or incarnational talk, in so far as this language functions to make assertions concerning the divine being, is an expression of the one truth that God is really (as well as nominally) related to others.

There is no need, in my opinion, to "add" relatedness to an essentially unrelated God, even if this could be done coherently. The relatedness of God to other individuals is essential to God. God is not constituted as a relational being for the first time in the act of the incarnation. Rather, God as actual is really related to others and cannot, either protologically or eschatologically, be conceived in any other way. Language concerning the trinity or the incarnation is an expression of this essential relatedness of God, not a demonstration that God is related to others. The love of God for others, along with the real relatedness of God to others that is necessarily implied by the symbolic talk of God's love, is not a particular theme within Christian theology, even if the most important theme. It is rather the only theme there is, one that all of the particular doctrines express.

The Love of God and Human Liberation

As I argued in the Introduction to this study, the central problem facing Christian theology in the contemporary situation is that of the relation of Christian faith in God to the concrete oppression of human persons and their struggle for liberation. As a result of the preceding discussion of the Christian concept of God, this general problem can be specified and it can be asked what the view that God is essentially redemptive and creative love of others means in relation to the theological problem of human liberation. In other words, how does the one all-encompassing theme of Christian theology, that of the love of God, relate to the particular theological problem of human liberation?

At this point, as at so many others, the thought of Karl Rahner points in the direction of an answer. He holds that hope is the act in which the human person accepts her or his orientation to the uncontrollable mystery of God who communicates Godself to us in love.

> Hope appears, therefore, as *the* act in which the one who is not at our disposal comes to actuality [*zur Gegebenheit kommt*] as the one who sanctifies, the one who blesses, the one who is salvation, without taking from this one the character of not being at our disposal precisely because this future of salvation is hoped for, but not controlled.[15]

This hope is realized or actualized only in a person's concrete activity in society, not in an individualistic form of piety. According to Rahner:

> [Hope] is fulfilled in reality in the continuous transformation of the structures of profane life. If one prescinds from the fact that "revolution" is a very inexact and ambiguous concept, then one could say that Christian hope, here, is to be portrayed as the basis of a permanently revolutionary stance of Christians in the world. . . . Hope in the absolute future of God, in the eschatological salvation that God himself is, is not the legitimation of a conservatism that—petrifying everything—anxiously gives preference to the certain present over an unknown future. Hope is not the "opium of the people" that takes its ease in the present, even when it is painful. Rather, hope is that which empowers and demands a trusting exodus out of the present into the future (including the inner-worldly future), an exodus that must constantly be undertaken anew.[16]

As Rahner implies in this passage, the reality of God as the absolute future functions in two ways in relation to the exodus out of the present into a more just and humane future, that is, the human struggle for justice and liberation. The absolute future *demands* that a more just world be constructed and also *empowers* persons to accomplish this task. God's relationship to the world must be a dialectic of identity and difference in order both to demand and to empower the struggle for human liberation. The task of human liberation must be seen as a task that human beings themselves must take up, for, as Rahner argues, human persons retain their full autonomy and responsibility for the world even as intimately related to God in love. At the same time, human persons are empowered by the reality of God as the absolute future to undertake the task of liberation, for the human person, precisely as autonomous, depends on God as the creative ground and final validity of all her or his acts.

Rahner's understanding of this dialectic deserves closer attention. On the one hand, for Christian faith, the reality of God as the absolute future constitutes a demand that social structures be continually criticized and altered for the sake of greater justice. He writes that Christian faith in the God who is the absolute future is not to be identified with any particular inner-worldly ideology. That is, the Christian faith itself is not a concrete program for changing society. But, Christian faith does view

> . . . the progressive socialization of man, which is aimed at the achievement of the greatest possible range of freedom for everyone, as a task that is given with the divinely willed essence of man, a task to which man is obligated and in which he realizes his true religious task.[17]

The absolute future cannot be identified with any inner-worldly future or with any future social arrangement. The absolute future is God's own being and, therefore, is not constructed by human effort. But one can, according to Rahner, relate oneself appropriately to the absolute future, to God, only by actively working to modify the innerworldly future so as to create a more just world. He says, in this connection:

> Whoever, as a Christian, would simply and uncritically identify himself with his existing social situation must ask

himself, consequently, whether he really believes in the
absolute future; not just theoretically and in a private
interiority, but in the actual realization of his life. He
must ask himself how, then, he realizes, in earnest, that
the present is merely provisional, since he does not jux-
tapose to the present another innerworldly future, although one that still is always provisional. Therefore,
precisely the hope in the absolute future, which we do
not create, demands of us a historical utopia, one that
critically unsettles history, spurs it onward, and also
beings it into the social dimension.[18]

The absolute future, which is the God of self-communicating love, radically relativizes all human projects, including projects of social change. No particular social structure can be
identified with the "kingdom of God." All are finite human
constructions. And yet, although all social arrangements are
relativized in relation to the absolute future, this does not justify
a political conservatism that is satisfied with the status quo.
Rather, Rahner argues, the qualitative difference between the
absolute future and our present unjust world order demands
that action be taken to create a more just and humane innerworldly future. This is a human task, one that God Godself will
not accomplish since, for Rahner, God does not intervene in the
world process in such a fashion. Our transcendental hope in the
absolute future is made real only in our penultimate hope for a
more just innerworldly or categorial future.[19] This is the ultimate religious task of the human person since we truly love God
only by loving our neighbor concretely, even politically.

On the other hand, even though the task of creating a more
just innerworldly future is a wholly human task and responsibility, nevertheless, it is God as the absolute future, as self-
communicating love, that empowers us to create this new innerworldly future. It is the reality of God that enables human
persons to risk attempting to create a more just world order. It is
God, for Rahner, that gives us the courage to struggle for justice.
He argues that "in the power of the greater hope [hope in the
absolute future] man also has the lesser hope, the courage, that
is, to alter the 'structures of worldly life,' as the [Second Vatican]
Council says."[20] For the attitude and act of hope, according to
Rahner, represents the surrender of a person to that which is
absolutely uncontrollable and incalculable, that is, God. It is the
reality of God, he claims, that guarantees that the free acts of the

genuinely autonomous creatures have a final validity and are not rendered meaningless by perishing and being superseded as the historical process rolls on relentlessly.

While all of these claims advanced by Rahner seem to be precisely correct, it is unclear to me, as I tried to show in Chapter IX, how his concept of God, and, in particular, his view that God is the absolute future, can really demand and empower the human struggle for liberation. As I have argued, even as the absolute future, God, for Rahner, is not coherently conceived to be really related to the creatures. God as the absolute future is still conceived to be a causal agent in relation to the world, although, admittedly, an agent who acts by way of quasi-formal causality in communicating Godself in love to the creatures. Finally, the world does not make a real difference to God, for God is not essentially open and receptive to the world, or affected by the reality of the creatures. All receptivity and relativity is on the part of the creatures, while God remains wholly active with respect to the world and strictly unrelated to the creatures.

As I argued earlier, if God is not affected by or really related to the world, then God cannot provide the final ground of the significance of human activity, including the activity aimed at creating a more just social order. Once again, Rahner formally affirms this to be the case, but does not have the requisite conceptual resources to explicate the essential relativity of God.

But if God is conceived to be essentially love of others, then one can affirm unequivocally that God is the absolute future of the human struggle for liberation. The reality of God, as Rahner says, both demands and empowers this struggle. On the one hand, because human beings are genuinely self-creative and because God cannot be conceived as an innerworldly, categorial agent, it is clear that the task of creating a more just world in which all persons are optimally free to realize themselves is a task that humans themselves must accomplish. The social arrangements that shape our lives are human creations and not divinely ordained systems. Human persons, and only human persons, are responsible for these social arrangements, whether they are just or unjust. God establishes the conditions under which human beings can constitute themselves, but the nature of that self-constitution, whether for good or ill, depends on the free decisions of human beings. God acts by modifying Godself as the object of free human beings. God can seek to persuade us to act so as to facilitate the full self-realization of others. But God cannot force human beings to act justly. As the creator, God has provided the conditions that make it possible for human beings to create themselves freely, but we must take responsibility for the liberation of our fellow human beings, for the divine activity does not accomplish what the creatures ought, but fail to accomplish.

Further, in the view of God outlined above, one can make the absolute distinction between the product of human creativity and the product of the divine self-creation, which, in each moment, is the absolute future of creaturely reality. Although human acts, including acts of structural social change, contribute to the self-creation of God, no particular social arrangement can be identified with the divine being. The act of divine self-creation, the act in which worldly reality is redeemed, is a divine act, and not a creaturely one, although the reality of the creatures is a moment within the divine self-creation. Thus, no particular social arrangement has anything other than finite, human status. Christian faith is not an ideology, but constitutes a critical demand for justice within societies of all ideological types.

On the other hand, since all creaturely activity affects and is included within the divine reality, human acts of both oppression and liberation become a part of the divine actuality. As I argued in the previous chapter, God's cause is the cause of the optimal free self-creation of others. By facilitating the free self-creation of the creatures, God, as the all-inclusive individual, also facilitates God's own maximal free self-creation. Human liberation is a genuine contribution to God's self-realization, while the oppression of human persons constitutes a real opposition to the full self-realization of God. So, to act to liberate other human beings, although a fully human task, one that will be realized only by human effort, is to cooperate with God's own creative purpose. It is to act in cooperation with the creative aspect of the divine love in order to optimize the free self-creation of others.

Because this is the nature of the creative love of God, it has been suggested that God as the creator is most appropriately understood in the contemporary situation to be God the emancipator.[21] That is to say, the creative love of God is emancipative or liberating. The creative love of God sets the creatures free to create themselves. It establishes the conditions under which the creatures can create themselves freely. Thus, to participate in the innerworldly task of liberating oppressed persons is, at the same time, to participate in the emancipative or liberative activity of God.

Here, as in Rahner's thought, there is a real identity of the love of God and the love of one's human neighbor (objective genitives). One can truly love God, that is, allow God to make a difference in one's life and act toward God so as to facilitate God's full self-realization, only by loving our fellow creatures, for our activity towards other creatures contributes directly and without fail to the God whose cause is the cause of the self-realization of all individuals. To act in liberating love toward our fellow human beings is literally, not just figuratively, to act in liberating love toward God. All of our deeds, finally, are done unto God. We serve God by serving the other creatures whose reality is included within the divine reality. This is the meaning of the faith in God that works in love for other human persons, as Paul describes it in the New Testament.

It is not clear to me how, in Rahner's thought, the reality of God can constitute the demand that humans act to liberate their fellows. Since God is essentially unrelated to others, for him, it is not clear in what sense God's cause is precisely the cause of the maximal liberation of the creatures for their own self-creation. Nor is it apparent how participating in the innerworldly project of human liberation can be said, in more than a merely verbal sense, to be a contribution to God's own project of self-creation.

Further, it is clear in the view of God that I have tried to outline, in a way that it is not in Rahner's thought, how God provides the ground of the confidence that our acts on behalf of the liberation of our fellow human beings are not finally meaningless. Our acts of liberation really affect God and become part of the divine being, as do our acts of oppression. Our acts, although they are *our* free acts and not God's acts, have a permanence and a lasting value in the divine reality. The reality of God is the absolute future in the literal sense of being the final depository of all of our activities and decisions. The divine actuality itself is the final cause to which we contribute our lives. It is this fact that reassures us that our concrete acts for justice and liberation are finally valuable and not in vain even if we seem to fail in our struggle for human liberation. For we contribute not just to our particular, transitory situation in the world, but to the reality of God itself. In God's being, in the being of the supreme liberator, our acts are of lasting value and significance.

It seems to me, therefore, that the concept of God as essentially love of others provides a more adequate theoretical explication of the demand made by the Christian faith that we act for the sake of justice for all human persons than does Rahner's concept of God. In this alternative view of God, it is clear that the God-world relationship is a dialectic of identity and difference. God is infinitely qualitatively distinct from the world and yet intimately related to the world in redemptive and creative love. The reality of God constitutes a demand that we act for justice. We must *act* because it is evident that the social structures of this world do not yet embody the liberating love of God. Yet, *we* must act, for the divine activity cannot be supposed to intervene in the world to make up for the shortcomings of the creatures. Further, God empowers liberative action in that the liberation of all creatures for their full, free self-realization is God's own task, and in that the redemptive love of God provides the reassurance that our acts on behalf of the liberation of human persons are not vain and futile, but contribute to the very actuality of God itself. Only if God is essentially love of others can God be the absolute future that challenges us to take up the task of human liberation as *our* task, and that also reassures us that our acts in the struggle for human liberation are not merely perishable, but have a permanent significance in that they are literally done unto God.

How Can Theology Serve the Cause of Human Liberation?

If the struggle for human liberation is a task that is demanded and empowered by the Christian faith in the God who is essentially love of others, then how can Christian theology itself serve the cause of human liberation?

I argued in Chapter I of this study that Christian theology is the second order activity of critical reflection upon the Christian faith. Because this is the case, it seems to me that theology can serve the cause of human liberation only indirectly, as a critical, reflective science. This means that the contribution of theology, or, rather, of the theologian understood solely as theologian, to the cause of human liberation is a wholly conceptual contribution. Theology in and of itself cannot directly affect social structures. Theology, like any other science, can contribute to social change only by criticizing patterns of thought that lend support to oppressive and unjust social arrangements and by projecting a vision of more just forms of human society. This means, in principle, that as a theologian, although not as a Christian, the theologian's own social praxis is irrelevent to the contribution her or his theological reflection can make to the struggle for human liberation. Of course, in fact, it is probably more likely that a liberative social praxis and a theology that, through conceptual means, contributes to human liberation, will accompany one another in the life of the theologian.

The task of theology is to reflect on the Christian faith, in all of its practical, political, cultic, imaginative, and theoretical expressions, in the light of both the normative expression of that faith, found in scripture, and the understanding of self, world, and God of contemporary persons. The task of theology is to interpret the historic Christian faith in a way that is credible to contemporary persons. In the contemporary situation, this means that the Christian faith must be expressed in such a way as to respond to the demand for justice that is raised so forcefully by our fellow human beings who live in oppressive situations.

Since, as I have argued, the doctrine of the love of God for others is the one all-encompassing theme of Christian theology, particular attention must be paid to the adequacy with which the various concepts of God in theology respond to the demand for justice and liberation. Concepts of God that tend to lessen the value of our actual experience and action in the world, by viewing God as essentially unrelated, therefore indifferent, to the creatures, must be criticized. My chief criticism of Rahner's concept of God was that it does not adequately conceptualize the God who is essentially love of others, constituted by real relations to other individuals, testified to in scripture, and necessarily implied by our basic confidence in the meaning and worth of existence. Likewise, understandings of God that portray the divine activity in the world as that of one categorial actor among others must be criticized. In both cases, the result of such inadequate understandings of God is that the demand for human liberation is blunted, in that the divine reality does not function both to empower the struggle for liberation and to place the responsibility for such action squarely on our own shoulders, not God's.

Although theology is a second order activity of critical reflection and not social praxis, this does not mean that the Christian faith upon which theology reflects is not essentially practical. Adequate reflection on the normative expressions of the Christian faith, it seems to me, reveals that if the Christian message is not portrayed as being liberative in a concrete sociopolitical sense, then it is not being properly interpreted. The Christian faith calls us to understand ourselves as created and redeemed by the divine love. We are called to accept the gift of God's creative and redemptive love by loving our fellow human beings (and nonhuman creatures as well) as God has loved us. To love others as God has loved us means, however, to act towards other persons in such a way as to maximize their full, free self-realization as persons. In our contemporary world, the first step in such a facilitation of the self-realization of others often must be to modify social structures that do not allow the most basic human rights and the freedom of self-determination that are necessary prerequisites for personal self-realization. To exist as a Christian is to participate in the liberative love of God, in God's project of maximizing the free self-creation of all the creatures.

But this means that one cannot defend a theology that opposes or ignores the struggle for human liberation on the grounds that theology is critical reflection and not social *praxis*. For the position that I have developed here entails that a theology that does not serve the cause of liberation and justice, in its distinctively indirect, conceptual fashion to be sure, is bad theory, not just bad praxis. If theology is fully critical reflection on the Christian faith, then the theologian must be critical not only of her or his conceptual or methodological bias (for instance, a mythological world view), but also must be critical of her or his sexual, racial, economic, and political bias. A theologian whose interpretation of the meaning of the Christian faith shows an insensitivity toward the concerns of the oppressed or marginal persons of the world (whether the poor, ethnic minorities, or women) is guilty not just of having an oppressive social praxis, but, precisely as a theologian, of reflecting inadequately upon the Christian faith in light of the experience of contemporary persons. For, again, the Christian faith calls us to participate in the liberating activity of the God who is love.

I have sought, in this study, to contribute to the struggle for human liberation in the only way that is appropriate for theology as critical reflection upon the Christian faith. I have tried to show, on the basis of both scripture and our common experience as human beings, that God is to be conceived as essentially love of others. This love of God for others has socio-political implications for the Christian. The creative and redemptive love of God is liberative. God, in the process of the divine self-creation in relation to the creatures, has no goal other than the full self-realization of the creatures, which, at the same time, constitutes God's own full self-realization. We are called to participate in God's project of the liberation of all the creatures by acting to facilitate the free self-realization of those who are around us. Although God establishes the conditions under which free creaturely activity is possible, God Godself does not act directly to overcome particular oppressive structures. That is our task, and it is a task demanded by the creative love of God. And yet, at the same time, the redemptive love of God provides us with confidence to undertake the struggle for justice and human liberation. It is in the redemptive love of God that our feeble, halting human actions attain a lasting significance and finally affect not just our fellow creatures but the very God who *is* love.

NOTES

[1] "Bemerkungen zur Gotteslehre in der katholischen Dogmatik," *ST*, 8:168 (ET: *TI*, 9:130).

[2] Ibid., pp. 168–169 (ET: ibid.).

[3] "Überlegungen zur Methode der Theologie," *ST*, 9:123 (ET: *TI*, 11:110).

[4] "Das Christentum und der 'neue Mensch,'" *ST*, 5:172 (ET: *TI*, 5:147).

[5] "Die anonymen Christen," *ST*, 6:549 (ET: *TI*, 6:394).

[6] "Christologie im Rahmen des modernen Selbst- und Weltverständnisses," *ST*, 9:237 (ET: *TI*, 11:225).

[7] "Die Forderung nach einer 'Kurzformel' des christlichen Glaubens," *ST*, 8:162 (ET: *TI*, 9:124).

[8] See *Trinität und Reich Gottes: Zur Gotteslehre* (München: Christian Kaiser Verlag, 1980), especially pp. 36–76.

[9] Ibid., pp. 74–75.

[10] "The Political Meaning of the Trinity," *Journal of Religion* 60 (1980):165–184.

[11] Ibid., pp. 175, 177.

[12] "Triune Self-Giving: One Key to the Problem of Suffering," *Thomist* 44 (1980):173–218.

[13] Ibid., p. 200.

[14] *The Doctrine of the Trinity*, pp. 55–71.

[15] "Zur Theologie der Hoffnung," *ST*, 8:574 (ET: *TI*, 10:254–255).

[16] Ibid., p. 576 (ET: ibid., pp. 256–257).

[17] "Marxistische Utopie und christliche Zukunft des Menschen," *ST*, 6:83 (ET: *TI*, 6:64).

[18] "Die Frage nach der Zukunft," *ST*, 9:537–538 (ET: *TI*, 12:199–200).

[19] "Zur Theologie der Hoffnung," *ST*, 8:578 (ET: *TI*, 10:259).

[20] Ibid. (ET: ibid.).

[21] See Schubert Ogden, *Faith and Freedom: Toward a Theology of Liberation*, pp. 88–95.

SELECTED BIBLIOGRAPHY

I. Works by Karl Rahner

A. Books

Geist in Welt: Zur Metaphysik der endlichen Erkenntnis bei Thomas von Aquin. Innsbruck: Verlag Felizian Rauch, 1939.

Grundkurs des Glaubens: Einführung in den Begriff des Christentums. Freiburg: Verlag Herder, 1976.

Hörer des Wortes: Zur Grundlegung einer Religionsphilosophie. München: Verlag Kösel-Pustet, 1941.

Schriften zur Theologie. 14 volumes. Einsiedeln: Benziger Verlag, 1954–1980.

Et. al., eds. *Sacramentum Mundi: Theologisches Lexikon für die Praxis.* 4 volumes. Freiburg: Verlag Herder, 1967–1969.

With Johannes Höfer, eds. *Lexikon für Theologie und Kirche.* Second Edition. 10 volumes. Freiburg: Verlag Herder, 1957–1965.

With Herbert Vorgrimler. *Kleines theologisches Wörterbuch.* Freiburg: Verlag Herder, 1961.

B. Articles

"Bemerkungen zum Begriff der Offenbarung." In *Offenbarung und Überlieferung,* pp. 11–24. By Karl Rahner and Joseph Ratzinger. Quaestiones Disputatae, no. 25. Freiburg: Verlag Herder, 1965.

"Der dreifaltige Gott als transzendenter Urgrund der Heilsgeschichte." In *Mysterium Salutis,* 5 volumes. 2:317–401. Edited by Johannes Feiner and Magnus Löhrer. Einsiedeln: Benziger Verlag, 1967.

"Die Hominisation als theologische Frage." In *Das Problem der Hominisation,* pp. 13–90. By Karl Rahner and Paul Overhage. Quaestiones Disputatae, no. 12/13. Freiburg: Verlag Herder, 1961.

"Grundlinien einer systematischen Christologie." In *Christologie—systematisch und exegetisch: Arbeitsgrundlagen für eine interdisziplinäre Vorlesung,* pp. 17–78. By Karl Rahner and Wilhelm Thüsing. Quaestiones Disputatae, no. 55. Freiburg: Verlag Herder, 1972.

II. Works Concerning Karl Rahner

A. Books

Bacik, James J. *Apologetics and the Eclipse of Mystery: Mystagogy According to Karl Rahner.* Notre Dame: University of Notre Dame Press, 1980.

Baker, Kenneth. *A Synopsis of the Transcendental Philosophy of Emerich Coreth and Karl Rahner.* Spokane: Gonzaga University Press, 1966.

Browarzik, Ulrich. *Glauben und Denken: Dogmatische Forschung zwischen der Transzendenztheologie Karl Rahners und der Offenbarungstheologie Karl Barths.* Berlin: Walter de Gruyter, 1970.

Carr, Anne. *The Theological Method of Karl Rahner.* AAR Dissertation Series, no. 19. Missoula, Mont.: Scholars Press, 1977.

Donceel, Joseph. *The Philosophy of Karl Rahner.* Albany, N.Y.: Magi Books, 1969.

Eicher, Peter. *Die anthropologische Wende: Karl Rahners philosophischen Weg vom Wesen des Menschen zur personalen Existenz.* Freiburg: Universitätsverlag Freiburg Schweiz, 1970.

Fischer, Klaus. *Der Mensch als Geheimnis: Die Anthropologie Karl Rahners.* Freiburg: Verlag Herder, 1974.

Gelpi, Donald. *Light and Life: A Guide to the Theology of Karl Rahner.* New York: Sheed and Ward, 1966.

Gerken, Alexander. *Offenbarung und Transzendenzerfahrung: Kritische Thesen zu einer künftigen dialogischen Theologie.* Dusseldorf: Patmos-Verlag, 1969.

Grün, Anselm. *Erlösung durch das Kreuz: Karl Rahners Beitrag zu einem heutigen Erlösungsverständnis.* Münsterschwarzach: Vier-Türme Verlag, 1975.

Hoeres, Walter. *Kritik der transzendentalphilosophischen Erkenntnistheorie.* Stuttgart: W. Kohlhammer Verlag, 1969.

McCool, Gerald. *The Theology of Karl Rahner.* Albany, N.Y.: Magi Books, 1969.

Metz, Johann Baptist; Kern, Walter; Darlapp, Adolf; Vorgrimler, Herbert; eds. *Gott in Welt: Festgabe für Karl Rahner.* 2 volumes. Freiburg: Verlag Herder, 1964.

O'Donovan, Leo J., ed. *A World of Grace: An Introduction to the Themes and Foundations of Karl Rahner's Theology.* New York: Seabury Press, 1980.

Roberts, Louis. *The Achievement of Karl Rahner.* New York: Herder & Herder, 1967.

Shepherd, William C. *Man's Condition: God and the World Process.* New York: Herder & Herder, 1969.

Simons, Eberhard. *Philosophie der Offenbarung: Auseinandersetzung mit Karl Rahner.* Stuttgart: W. Kohlhammer Verlag, 1966.

Speck, Josef. *Karl Rahners theologische Anthropologie: Eine Einführung.* München: Kösel-Verlag, 1967.

van der Heijden, Bert. *Karl Rahner: Darstellung und Kritik seiner Grundpositionen.* Einsiedeln: Johannes Verlag, 1973.

Weger, Karl-Heinz. *Karl Rahner: Eine Einführung in sein theologisches Denken.* Freiburg: Verlag Herder, 1978.

Wess, Paul. *Wie von Gott sprechen? Eine Auseinandersetzung mit Karl Rahner.* Graz: Verlag Styria, 1970.

B. Articles

Bechtle, Regina. "Karl Rahner's Supernatural Existential: A Personalist Approach." *Thought* 48 (1973): 61–77.

Bradley, Denis J. M. "Rahner's Spirit in the World: Aquinas or Hegel." *Thomist* 41 (1977):167–199.

Buckley, James J. "On Being a Symbol: An Appraisal of Rahner." *Theological Studies* 40 (1979):453–473.

Burke, Ronald. "Rahner and Dunne: A New Vision of God." *Iliff Review* 34 (1977):37–49.

Corduan, Winfried. "Hegel in Rahner: A Study in Philosophical Hermeneutics." *Harvard Theological Review* 71 (1978):285–298.

Dewart, Leslie. "On Transcendental Thomism." *Continuum* 6 (1968):389–401.

Doud, Robert E. "Rahner's Christology: A Whiteheadian Critique." *Journal of Religion* 57 (1977):144–155.

Eberhard, Kenneth D. "Karl Rahner and the Supernatural Existential." *Thought* 46 (1971):537–561.

Ernst, Cornelius. "Some Themes in the Theology of Karl Rahner." *Irish Theological Quarterly* 32 (1965):251–257.

Geisser, Hans. "Die Interpretation der kirchlichen Lehre vom Gottmenschen bei Karl Rahner." *Kerygma und Dogma* 14 (1968):307–330.

Heinrichs, Johannes. "Sinn und Intersubjektivität: Zur Vermittlung von transzendentalphilosophischem und dialogischem Denken in einer 'transzendentalen Dialogik.'" *Theologie und Philosophie* 2 (1970):161–191.

Hill, William. "Uncreated Grace: A Critique of Karl Rahner." *Thomist* 27 (1963):333–356.

Hinners, Richard. "Teleology and 'Archaeology.'" *Continuum* 6 (1968):221–224.

Jüngel, Eberhard. "Das Verhältnis von ökonomischer und immanenter Trinität." *Zeitschrift für Theologie und Kirche* 72 (1975):353–364.

―――. "*Extra Christus Nulla Sallus*―als Grundsatz natürlicher Theologie?" *Zeitschrift für Theologie und Kirche* 72 (1975): 337–352.

McCool, Gerald. "The Philosophical Theology of Rahner and Lonergan." In *God Knowable and Unknowable*. Edited by Robert J. Roth. New York: Fordham University Press, 1973.

―――. "The Philosophy of the Human Person in Karl Rahner's Theology." *Theological Studies* 22 (1961):700–715.

MacKinnon, Edward. "The Transcendental Turn: Necessary But Not Sufficient." *Continuum* 6 (1968):225–231.

Mann, Peter. "The Later Theology of Karl Rahner." *The Clergy Review* 54 (1969):936–948.

Masson, Robert. "Beyond Nygren and Rahner: An Alternative to Tracy." *Heythrop Journal* 21 (1980):260–287.

―――. "Rahner and Heidegger: Being, Hearing, and God." *Thomist* 37 (1973):455–488.

Mawhinney, J. J. "The Concept of Mystery in Karl Rahner's Philosophical Theology." *Union Seminary Quarterly Review* 24 (1968):17–30.

Moloney, Robert. "Seeing and Knowing: Some Reflections on Karl Rahner's Theory of Knowledge." *Heythrop Journal* 18 (1978):399–419.

Motherway, Thomas J. "Supernatural Existential." *Chicago Studies* 4 (1965):79–103.

Nachbar, Bernard A. M. "Is it Thomism?" *Continuum* 6 (1968):232–235.

Niel, Henri. "The Old and the New in Theology: Rahner and Lonergan." *Cross Currents* 16 (1966):463–480.

Ogden, Schubert. "The Challenge to Protestant Thought." *Continuum* 6 (1968):236–240.

―――. "'The Reformation We Want.'" *Anglican Theological Review* 54 (1972):260–273.

Pearl, Thomas. "Dialectical Panentheism: On the Hegelian Character of Rahner's Key Christological Writings." *Irish Theological Quarterly* 42 (1975):119–137.

Peter, Carl J. "The Position of Karl Rahner Regarding the Supernatural: A Comparative Study of Nature and Grace." *Proceedings of the Catholic Theological Society of America* 20 (1965):81–94.

Prendergast, R. "The Supernatural Existential, Human Generation and Original Sin." *Downside Review* 82 (1964):1–24.

Robertson, John. "Rahner and Ogden: Man's Knowledge of God." *Harvard Theological Review* 63 (1970):377–407.

Shine, Daniel J. "The Being-Present-to-Itself of Being." *Continuum* 6 (1968):240–245.

Tallon, Andrew. "Personal Becoming." *Thomist* 43 (1979):7–177.

Tappenheimer, David. "Sacramental Causality in Aquinas and Rahner: Some Critical Thoughts." *Scottish Journal of Theology* 28 (1975):243–257.

TeSelle, Eugene. "The Problem of Nature and Grace." *Journal of Religion* 40 (1965):238–250.

Trethowan, Illtyd. "A Changing God." *Downside Review* 84 (1966):247–261.

Wilson, Barrie A. "The Possibility of Theology after Kant: Karl Rahner's *Geist in Welt.*" *Canadian Journal of Theology* 12 (1966):245–258.

Wood, Charles. "Karl Rahner on Theological Discourse." *Journal of Ecumenical Studies* 12 (1975):55–67.

Yearley, L. H. "Karl Rahner on the Relation of Nature and Grace." *Canadian Journal of Theology* 16 (1970):219–231.

III. Other Works

A. Books

Coreth, Emerich. *Metaphysik: Eine methodische systematische Grundlegung.* Second edition. Innsbruck: Tyrolia Verlag, 1964.

D'Arcy, M. C. *The Mind and Heart of Love.* New York: Henry Holt & Co., 1947.

Farrer, Austin. *Finite and Infinite: A Philosophical Essay.* New York: The Seabury Press, 1979.

Farley, Margaret. *A Study in the Ethics of Commitment within the Context of Theories of Human Love and Temporality.* Ph.D. Dissertation, Yale University. Ann Arbor: University Microfilms, 1978.

Hartshorne, Charles. *The Divine Relativity: A Social Conception of God.* New Haven: Yale University Press, 1948.

————. *The Logic of Perfection and Other Essays in Neoclassical Metaphysics.* LaSalle, Ill.: Open Court Publishing Co., 1962.

————. *Man's Vision of God and the Logic of Theism.* Hamden, Conn.: Archon Books, 1964.

————. *Reality as Social Process: Studies in Metaphysics and Religion.* Glencoe, Ill.: The Free Press, 1953.

Hazo, Robert G. *The Idea of Love.* New York: Frederick A. Praeger, 1967.

Heidegger, Martin. *Phänomenologie und Theologie*. Frankfurt am Main: Vittorio Klostermann, 1970.

——. *Sein und Zeit*. 15th edition. Tübingen: Max Niemeyer Verlag, 1979.

——. *Was ist Metaphysik?* 11th edition. Frankfurt am Main: Vittorio Klostermann, 1975.

John, Helen James. *The Thomist Spectrum*. New York: Fordham University Press, 1966.

Lee, Jung Young. *God Suffers for Us: A Systematic Inquiry into a Concept of Divine Passibility*. The Hague: Martinus Nijhoff, 1974.

Lonergan, Bernard. *Insight: A Study of Human Understanding*. London: The Philosophical Library, 1958.

——. *Method in Theology*. New York: Herder & Herder, 1972.

Lucas, George Ramsdell, Jr. *Two Views of Freedom in Process Thought: A Study of Hegel and Whitehead*. AAR Dissertation Series, no. 28. Missoula, Mont.: Scholars Press, 1979.

McIntyre, John. *On the Love of God*. New York: Harper & Brothers, 1962.

Macmurray, John. *The Form of the Personal*. 2 volumes. London: Faber and Faber, 1957, 1961.

Maloney, George A. *A Theology of Uncreated Energies*. Milwaukee: Marquette University Press, 1978.

Maréchal, Joseph. *Le point de départ de la metaphysique*. Vol. 5: *Le thomisme devant la philosophie critique*. Second edition. Brussels: L'Edition Universelle; Paris: Desclée de Brouwer, 1949.

Moltmann, Jürgen. *Trinität und Reich Gottes: Zur Gotteslehre*. München: Chr. Kaiser Verlag, 1980.

Mozley, J. K. *The Impassibility of God: A Survey of Christian Thought*. Cambridge: Cambridge University Press, 1926.

Muck, Otto. *Die transzendentale Methode*. Innsbruck: Verlag Felizian Rauch, 1964.

Mühlen, Heribert. *Die Veränderlichkeit Gottes als Horizont einer zukünftigen Christologie*. Münster: Verlag Aschendorff, 1969.

Nédoncelle, Maurice. *Love and the Person*. Trans. by Ruth Adelaide. New York: Sheed and Ward, 1966.

Neville, Robert C. *God the Creator: On the Transcendence and Presence of God*. Chicago: University of Chicago Press, 1968.

Newlands, George M. *Theology of the Love of God*. Atlanta: John Knox Press, 1980.

Selected Bibliography   415

Nygren, Anders. *Agape and Eros*. Trans. by Philip S. Watson, revised edition. London: S.P.C.K., 1953.

Ogden, Schubert. *Faith and Freedom: Toward a Theology of Liberation*. Nashville: Abingdon, 1979.

———. *The Reality of God and Other Essays*. Second edition. New York: Harper & Row, 1977.

Ott, Heinrich. *Wirklichkeit und Glaube*. Vol. 2: *Der persönliche Gott*. Göttingen: Vandenhoeck & Ruprecht, 1969.

Outka, Gene. *Agape: An Ethical Analysis*. New Haven: Yale University Press, 1972.

Sadler, William A., Jr. *Existence and Love: A New Approach in Existential Phenomenology*. New York: Charles Scribner's Sons, 1969.

Tavard, George H. *A Way of Love*. Maryknoll, N.Y.: Orbis Books, 1977.

Tillich, Paul. *Love, Power and Justice*. London: Oxford University Press, 1954.

———. *Systematic Theology*. Three volumes in one. Chicago: The University of Chicago Press, 1967.

Toner, Jules. *The Experience of Love*. Washington: Corpus Books, 1968.

Tracy, David. *Blessed Rage for Order: The New Pluralism in Theology*. New York: Seabury, 1975.

Whitehead, Alfred North. *Process and Reality: An Essay in Cosmology*. Corrected Edition by David Griffin and Donald Sherburne. New York: Macmillan, 1978.

Williams, Daniel Day. *The Spirit and the Forms of Love*. New York: Harper & Row, 1968.

B. Articles

Andolsen, Barbara Hilkert. "Agape in Feminist Ethics." *The Journal of Religious Ethics* 9 (1981):69–83.

Brown, Delwin. "Freedom and Faithfulness in Whitehead's God." *Process Studies* 2 (1972):137–148.

Bultmann, Rudolf. "Neues Testament und Mythologie: Das Problem der Entmythologisierung der neutestamentlichen Verkündigung." In *Kerygma und Mythos: Ein theologisches Gespräch*, 6 volumes, 1:15–48. Edited by Hans Werner Bartsch. Second edition. Hamburg: Herbert Reich Evangelischer Verlag, 1951.

Clarke, W. Norris. "A New Look at the Immutability of God." In *God Knowable and Unknowable*, pp. 43–72. Edited by Robert Roth. New York: Fordham University Press, 1973.

D'Arcy, Martin C. "The Immutability of God." *Proceedings of the American Catholic Philosophical Association* 41 (1967):19–26.

Donceel, Joseph. "Second Thoughts on the Nature of God." *Thought* 46 (1971):346–370.

Farley, Margaret. "New Patterns of Relationship: Beginnings of a Moral Revolution." *Theological Studies* 36 (1975):627–646.

Felt, James W. "Invitation to a Philosophic Revolution." *The New Scholasticism* 45 (1971):87–109.

Hill, William J. "Does the World Make a Difference to God?" *Thomist* 38 (1974):146–164.

Kaufman, Gordon. "A Problem for Theology: The Concept of Nature." *Harvard Theological Review* 65 (1972):337–366.

Kelly, Anthony J. "God: How Near a Relation?" *Thomist* 34 (1970):191–229.

McCool, Gerald. "Recent Trends in German Scholasticism: Brunner and Lotz." *International Philosophical Quarterly* 1 (1961):668–682.

Ogden, Schubert. "Lonergan and the Subjectivist Principle." *Journal of Religion* 51 (1971):155–173.

Parker, Thomas D. "The Political Meaning of the Trinity." *Journal of Religion* 60 (1980):165–184.

Quinn, John M. "Triune Self-Giving: One Key to the Problem of Suffering." *Thomist* 44 (1980):173–218.

Stokes, Walter E. "Freedom as Perfection: Whitehead, Thomas and Augustine." *Proceedings of the American Catholic Philosophical Association* 36 (1962):134–142.

———. "Is God Really Related to the World?" *Proceedings of the American Catholic Philosophical Association* 39 (1965):145–151.

———. "Whitehead's Challenge to Theistic Realism." *The New Scholasticism* 38 (1964):1–21.

Whitney, Barry. "Divine Immutability in Process Philosophy and Contemporary Thomism." *Horizons* 7 (1980):49–68.

Wright, John H. "Divine Knowledge and Human Freedom: The God Who Dialogues." *Theological Studies* 38 (1977):450–477.